The PHOTO SHOP 3 WOW! BOOK

Tips, Tricks, & Techniques for Adobe Photoshop 3

Linnea Dayton & Jack Davis

Peachpit Press

The Photoshop 3 Wow! Book, Windows Edition

Linnea Dayton and Jack Davis

Peachpit Press
2414 Sixth St.
Berkeley, CA 94710
(510) 548-4393
(510) 548-5991 (fax)

Find us on the World Wide Web at:
http://www.peachpit.com

Peachpit Press is a division of Addison-Wesley Publishing Company.

ISBN 0-201-88370-8

0 9 8 7 6 5 4 3 2

Printed and bound in the United States of America.

To: Vahé Guzel and Suzi Nawabi, for providing all kinds of inspiration

— Linnea Dayton

To our son Ryan, the ultimate expression of the creative process

— Jack and Jill Davis

ACKNOWLEDGMENTS

This book would not have been possible without a great deal of support. First, we would like to thank the Photoshop artists who have allowed us to include their work and describe their techniques in this book; their names are listed in the Appendix. We are also grateful to many Photoshop artists whose work does not appear in the book but who have passed along some of their Photoshop knowledge and experience; among them are Russell Brown, Daniel Clark, and Robert Schwarzbach. We appreciate the support of Adobe Systems, Inc., particularly Rita Amladi, Eric Thomas, LaVon Peck, Patricia Pane, and the technical support group, who kept us up to date on the development of the program, supplied us with software, and answered our technical questions. We also thank Bruce Wasserman, who advised us on making the Windows edition "platform-correct."

We are grateful to Jill Davis, whose book design made the writing and illustrating much easier; to Jonathan Parker, the most organized and thorough production man we know, who produced this edition; to Lisa King, who once again helped us with research; to Joni Faulkner, who helped with research and production; to Paul Goethel and Norbert Schulz, who offered editorial support; and to John Odam, who made the resources of his studio available when our work expanded beyond the capabilities of our equipment. Our thanks also to Tommy Yune, who provided the multilayered Liz and Elaine for the layers exercise on the Wow! CD ROM, and to Victor Gavenda at Peachpit Press, who did a lion's share of the CD ROM production. Special thanks also to Doug Isaacs at Adage Graphics in Los Angeles, who separated our PageMaker 5.0 files through Adobe TrapWise 2.1 from an Agfa AccuSet 1000 imagesetter, providing the most trouble-free film output it's ever been our good fortune to experience. We highly recommend Doug and Adage.

And finally, we'd like to thank the friends, family, colleagues, and co-workers, including those at Peachpit Press, who have so far supported us through four editions of this endeavor.

CONTENTS

WELCOME TO *THE PHOTOSHOP 3 WOW! BOOK*

ADOBE PHOTOSHOP IS ONE OF THE MOST POWERFUL visual communication tools ever to appear on the desktop. The program has expanded the visual vocabulary of designers and illustrators to include color photo imagery, making photos the "raw material" for creative expression. It also lets photographers do their magic in the light, without chemicals! And it makes it much easier to do the resizing, cropping, and basic color correction of production work. Beyond that, it provides a laboratory for synthesizing textures, patterns, and special effects that can be applied to photos, graphics, or video.

As our time spent using the program began to exceed 90% of the work day, as we watched others experiment, and as we saw the nearly miraculous transformations that appeared on-screen, the tools the program provided, the shortcuts for carrying out complicated changes, and the ways people combined the things Photoshop could do, the response we continuously heard was "Wow!" So when we needed a title for this book we were planning, it just sort of came naturally — *The Photoshop Wow! Book*. Photoshop 3 has only increased the "Wow!" factor, with the addition of numerous new features like transparent layers and Lighting Effects, to name just two.

HOW TO USE THIS BOOK

For those who have enjoyed the earlier editions of this book, this one works the same way. You'll find five kinds of information in the body of this book: (1) basic information about how Photoshop's tools and functions work, (2) short tips for making your work quicker and easier, (3) step-by-step techniques for particular kinds of projects, (4) galleries of work done by experienced Photoshop artists, and (5) illustrated lists of resources — images and other products that can make Photoshop even more valuable and easy to use.

1 You'll find the **Basics** sections at the beginnings of the nine chapters of this book. They tell how Photoshop's functions work. *The Photoshop 3 Wow! Book* wasn't designed to be a substitute for the *Adobe Photoshop User Guide*, which has always been an excellent reference manual and has even improved with version 3 of the program. Instead we've gathered and condensed some of the most important of the basics, and in some cases explained a little further,

PINPOINT PRECISION

It's hard to see exactly where the "hot spot" is on some of Photoshop's tool icons. To pinpoint the active point, press the Caps Lock key to turn the pointer into crosshairs with a single dot marking the exact center.

3

with the idea that understanding how something works can make it easier to remember and to apply in new ways. Our goal is to provide an "under-the-hood" look at Photoshop that will help you maximize the program's performance and your own productivity with it.

Most of the chapter introductions are short, with most of the meat of the chapter in the techniques sections that follow. The exceptions are Chapters 1 and 2. Since these two introductions cover the fundamentals of using Photoshop 3 — setting up your system for efficiency, understanding how Photoshop deals with color, getting the hang of scanning and resolution, and choosing the best ways to make and apply selections — it's a good idea to read these two sections before you start in on the techniques. They aren't "required reading," mind you, but if you don't read them to begin with, you may want to turn back to them later to pick up some basic underpinnings to anchor the techniques presented in the rest of the book.

2 To collect the kind of hands-on information that can make you instantly more efficient, flip through the book and scan the **Tips**. You can easily identify them by the title bar on top. The tips are a kind of hypertext — linked bits of information that we've positioned alongside the basics and techniques wherever we thought they'd be most helpful. But you can pick up a lot of useful information quickly by reading the tips on their own.

3 Each **Technique**, presented in 1 to 4 pages, is designed to give you enough step-by-step information so you can carry it out in Photoshop. Our goal was to provide enough written and pictorial instructions so you wouldn't have to hunt through the *Adobe Photoshop User Guide* to follow the steps. But to spare you a lot of repetition, we've assumed you know the basic Windows 3.1 or Windows 95 interface — how to open and save files, for instance — and we've focused on specific techniques in some cases, rather than explaining every detail of every method used in a particular project. Some of the techniques are simple and introductory; others are more advanced and challenging. If something isn't clear to you, go back to review the basics in Chapters 1 and 2.

Some techniques are presented using artwork created specifically for the demonstration. Other techniques are descriptions of the methods artists used to create particular illustrations or parts of illustrations. Some of the examples shown in the book were done with earlier versions than 3.0. However, we've updated the techniques for the current version.

The step-by-step techniques consist of numbered, illustrated instructions. The first step of each technique tells, briefly, how to get to the starting point. If you need to know more about some process described in step 1, check the index at the back of the book for references to other sections.

4

5

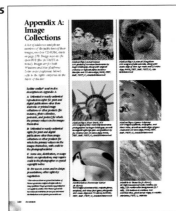

As you work with Photoshop 3, you'll notice that there seem to be at least three ways to do everything — you can choose from a menu, use a keyboard shortcut, or click on a button in the new customizable Commands palette; you can use cut and paste, or drag and drop; you can montage images with layer masks or load selections from alpha channels and then cut and paste. Because of the variety of possibilities, you'll find varied approaches used in the techniques sections. So you'll get a broad exposure to the way Photoshop works. But, in general, the methods presented are the ones that seem to be the most efficient and effective — approaches that will save you time and produce high-quality results.

4 The **Galleries** are there primarily for inspiration, though the Gallery captions include a lot of useful information about how the artwork was produced. Many of the techniques mentioned in the Galleries are described more fully elsewhere in the book. Again, check the index if you need help finding a particular technique.

5 Throughout the book, and especially in Chapter 5, "Using Filters," and in the Appendix at the back, is information you can use to locate the kinds of **Resources** Photoshop users need to know about, such as stock photo images, plug-in filters, and "how-to" references in addition to this book.

Experiment! The techniques and examples presented in this book are there to get you started using the tools if you're new at it, and to give you some new insight and ideas if you're an old hand. As you read the book and try out the tips and techniques presented here, we hope you'll use them as a jumping off place for your own fearless experimentation.

And don't miss the CD ROM — it's filled with images and plug-ins, from leading filter and photo stock resources, as well as demo versions of programs that complement Photoshop.

Linnea Dayton
Jack Davis

September, 1995

PHOTOSHOP BASICS

Blending mode

Opacity control

Layer mask

Layers, new to Photoshop 3, make it easier to combine images using the blending modes and opacity controls. Thumbnail images in the Layers palette show you what's on each layer.

IF YOU'RE NEW TO PHOTOSHOP, this chapter is designed to give you some general pointers on using the program more easily and efficiently. But it won't replace the *Adobe Photoshop User Guide* or the *Tutorial* as a comprehensive source of basic information. If you're experienced with earlier versions of the program, this chapter will help bring you up to date on some of the changes in Photoshop 3.

WHAT'S NEW?

Here's a quick look at some of the things that are new or different in Photoshop 3 and where in this book you can find out more about them:

The new feature that's likely to most change the way you use the program is **Layers**. Instead of being a single layer of *pixels* (the square dots, or picture elements, that make up a Photoshop picture), images can now be built of layers of image elements that act as if they were painted on transparent sheets of acetate, so they can be slid around from side to side or shuffled up and down in the stack of layers.

Each layer can also have its own mask to affect how it interacts with the other layers. And every layer has its own composite controls (available in a Layer Options dialog box, chosen from the pop-out menu in the Layers palette) to control how colors in the layer interact with the colors in layers underneath. The Calculation functions (which are still also available through the Image menu) have been built into each layer as a *blending mode,* or *transfer mode.* Since, in essence, layers provide a way of preserving selected elements in a file, the way they work is covered mostly in Chapter 2, "Selections, Masks, Layers, and Channels."

A **drag-and-drop** feature makes it easier to move active selections, layers, or whole images from one file into another. The rules of operation for drag and drop are also discussed in Chapter 2.

The **toolbox** has changed. First of all, single-key shortcuts have been added. In Photoshop 3 the toolbox can be operated by pressing single keys to select the tools, reverse the Foreground and Background colors, or change the way the working window is displayed. In many cases the key used for the shortcut is the first letter of the tool's name. Where this isn't possible, the keyboard shortcut usually represents another predominant sound in the word. Among the shortcuts is also one to open the separate palette for the path tools (pen/pointer).

Second, **two new tools** have been added. These are the move tool (the four-headed arrow under the lasso) and the sponge tool,

continued on page 6

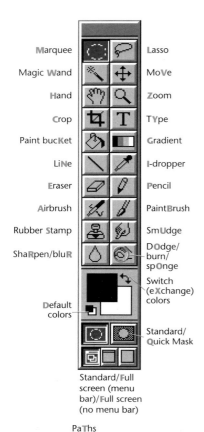

Marquee · Lasso
Magic Wand · MoVe
Hand · Zoom
Crop · TYpe
Paint bucKet · Gradient
LiNe · I-dropper
Eraser · Pencil
Airbrush · PaintBrush
Rubber Stamp · SmUdge
ShaRpen/bluR · DOdge/burn/spOnge

Default colors · Switch (eXchange) colors

Standard/Quick Mask

Standard/Full screen (menu bar)/Full screen (no menu bar)

PaThs

Single-key commands (shown in red) activate tools and toggle between tools that occupy the same space in the palette

The sponge tool controls are located in the Toning Tools Options palette. The mode can be changed from Saturate to Desaturate, and the Pressure can be varied.

which shares a spot with the dodge and burn tools at the bottom of the toolbox. Like the other tools that share toolbox spots, the sponge tool, if it doesn't show up in the toolbox, can be brought forward by Alt-clicking the tool that currently occupies that spot, by double-clicking the current tool to open the Toning Tool Options palette and choosing it there, or by typing the keyboard shortcut for the tool (see the illustration at the left.)

- The **move tool** is important for using layers and for dragging and dropping. It lets you move the contents of layers around without surrounding them with a selection border. Also, you can use it to move active selections without having to get the cursor positioned inside the selection; this can be especially helpful for moving small type, for instance. The Layers section of Chapter 2 tells more about using the move tool. (To make room for the move tool, the elliptical marquee selection tool now shares a spot with the rectangular marquee.)

- The **sponge tool** allows you to saturate or desaturate part of an image, applying the change in saturation by hand with pin-point control.

Palettes have changed in Photoshop 3. First of all, more palettes have been added.

- Photoshop 3 comes equipped with a default **Commands palette** that has "distilled" several of the most commonly used menu selections into a stack of buttons you can click rather than pulling down menus and submenus. Each command button may also list a function key (an F key, from the top row of the keyboard) that can be used instead of clicking the Command button. You can replace the default palette by choosing Load Commands and selecting from the sets that come with the program (stored with the suffix .acm in the **cmdsets** subdirectory in the **photoshp** directory). Or add one of these sets to the existing set by choosing Append Commands. You can also add a New Command, or Edit Commands to change the function assigned to a particular button or F key. And you can name and save your entire Commands palette so you can load it again later. A customized Commands palette can provide a quick way of making choices that are buried several menu choices or dialog boxes deep.

- Each tool now has its own version of a **Tool Options palette** instead of a dialog box. The Tool Options palette changes to match the tool that's selected, and each Tool Options palette can be opened at any time by double-clicking the tool in the toolbox.

Palette arrangement has changed also:

- Palettes can now be **nested** (grouped with and hidden behind other palettes). A palette hidden in a "nest" can be brought

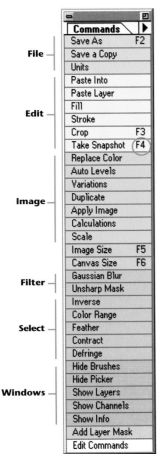

File

Edit

Image

Filter

Select

Windows

This custom, multipurpose Commands palette provides one-click access to often-used commands from Photoshop 3's menus and palettes. Commands are organized in groups by menu (and related functions), and F keys have been assigned to the ones used most often, to make them stand out at a glance. The palette is provided on the Wow! CD ROM and can be loaded by opening the default Commands palette (Window, Palettes, Show Commands) and choosing Load Commands from the palette's pop-out menu. If this palette won't fit on your monitor, you can make it shorter: Delete buttons (by Ctrl-clicking each one), or move the ones you'll use least to the bottom (by dragging the button names up or down the list in the Edit Commands dialog box) and let them hang below the window, or split the palette into two or more columns (by entering a number in the Display, Columns section of the Edit Commands dialog box).

forward by clicking on its name tab, which stays visible even when the palette itself is buried in the stack. The advantages of nesting are compactness (the nested palettes don't take up much space) and availability (you can always open the palette quickly by clicking on its tab).

Photoshop comes with certain default "nests" — the Layers, Channels, and Paths palettes are nested together, the Tool Options and Brushes palettes are paired up, and the colors palettes (Picker, Scratch, and Swatches) are together. You can separate a palette out of its nest at any time by dragging its tab, so you can have more than one of the "nestmates" open at the same time. To "renest," simply drag the palette by its tab back into the nest (or to a nest of other palettes); a heavy black border on the nest will appear when you've dragged far enough to add the palette to the nest.

Once you learn the ins and outs of using layers and channels, you'll probably want to have the Layers and Channels palettes accessible at the same time, so it makes sense to separate them.

- Palettes attract each other, so if you move one close to another it will snap into **alignment** and make a stack or a row.

Several changes in the File menu are worth knowing about:

- A new saving function — **Save A Copy** — has been added. (See "Recovering" later in this chapter for more about Save A Copy.)

- **Quick Edit,** under the Acquire submenu, lets you open part of an image file that was stored in Scitex CT (.**sct**) or TIFF (.**tif**) format (without LZW compression) and then put it back in exactly the same position after you work on it. This can be really helpful if you need to make changes to part of an image that's too big for your RAM and scratch disk to handle.

- **File Info** has been included in Photoshop 3 specifically to support information standards established by press associations for transmitting images and supporting text for newspapers. But it also provides a great "notepad" for recording any kind of information you might want to keep with an image. The File Info is retained, no matter what file format you use to save. If you open the file in Photoshop again, the info is still there, although it may not show up if you open the file in another program, depending on whether that program supports the press standards. Unlike File, Get Info at the Finder level of Macintosh operations, File Info is not erased if you rebuild the desktop.

There are changes in other menus as well. The addition of **CMYK Preview** and **Gamut Warning** to the Mode menu is discussed in the "Color in Photoshop" section later in this chapter. Changes to the Image and Select menus are described in Chapter 2. And changes to Filters are presented in Chapter 5.

Choosing File, File Info opens a dialog box where you can permanently store information in the form of text. The scrollable Caption field can hold a large text block. When you save the file, Photoshop will warn you if the File Info can't be preserved in the format you've chosen.

SCRATCH DISK CONTROLS RAM

Besides RAM, Photoshop 3 needs a certain amount of free hard disk space (called *scratch disk*) to be used as virtual memory. The program needs at least 20 MB of scratch disk space to run properly. But if you have enough RAM to assign more than 20 MB to Photoshop, you'll need at least as much disk space as assigned RAM. For instance, with 64 MB of RAM assigned, you'll need 64 MB of free hard disk space. Because of the way Photoshop uses RAM and scratch disk, it can only use as much RAM as there is scratch disk available. For example, if you have 64 MB of RAM but only 30 MB of scratch disk, Photoshop can use only 30 MB of RAM.

TRANSFER RATE

For large graphics files stored on a relatively unfragmented hard disk, the disk's *access time* (how fast it can find and begin to read a file) is generally less important than its *transfer rate* (how fast it reads a file once it's found). To double the speed of data transfer, some hard disks are composed of two drives linked in a "dual array" — it's kind of like using two fire hoses instead of one to put out a fire.

CPU, RAM, AND ACCELERATION

Photoshop files tend to be large — a lot of information has to be stored to record the color of each of the thousands or millions of pixels that make up an image. So it can take quite a bit of computer processing just to open a file (which brings that information into the computer's memory, or RAM) or to apply a special effect (which can involve complicated calculations that change the color of every pixel in the image). Photoshop needs a lot of RAM to hold an image while it works on it. Although you can do good Photoshop work on a smaller, slower, less powerful computer system, the program works best if you have a fast computer, a great deal of RAM, a monitor displaying full 24-bit photorealistic color, and a very large, fast hard disk with plenty of free space.

The minimum system **required** for running Photoshop 3 is an 80386- or 80486-based or faster PC running DOS 5.0 or higher and Microsoft Windows 3.1, Windows for Workgroups 3.11, Windows NT 35, or Windows 95. The computer must have at least 10 MB of RAM, or 16 MB if you're running Windows NT, with 8 MB reserved for Photoshop in each case.

The minimum system **recommended** for decent Photoshop performance, though, is a Pentium-based machine, DOS 6.0 or higher, and at least 16 MB of RAM available for Photoshop (32 MB for Windows NT). Adobe recommends a 24-bit color monitor set-up (millions of colors), although 16-bit color (thousands of colors) may be adequate for much color work. Adobe also recommends a CD ROM drive. You'll need to have it to load the Deluxe version of the program, and it's useful for working with stock photo collections (such as those shown in the appendix) and with your own photos processed in Kodak Photo CD format. Accelerator products designed specifically to support some of Photoshop's calculation-intensive functions, such as running filters or resizing images, are available; look for the Adobe-Charged logo to be sure they will significantly improve Photoshop's performance.

VIRTUAL MEMORY

If Photoshop doesn't have enough room to handle a file entirely in RAM, it can use hard disk space for memory — that's *virtual memory*, or in Photoshop parlance *scratch disk*. In that case, two factors become important: first, the amount of empty hard disk space (you'll want at least as much space as you have RAM and at least three to five times the size of any file you work on) and second, the transfer rate of the disk drive (the speed at which data can be read off a disk).

WHERE'S PASTE BEHIND?

Paste Behind now shares space in the Edit menu with Paste Inside. To Paste Behind, hold down the Alt key as you choose Edit, Paste Into.

Use a defragmenting program such as Windows' Defragmenter to optimize space on your hard disks. It collects all the small pieces of storage space that result when a disk is used and reused over time. The goal is to join all the free disk space into a single large block. That way, when you store a file, it can stay together instead of being broken into smaller parts that have to be sought out separately when Photoshop works on the file.

WORKING SMART

Once your system is set up with lots of RAM and a fast hard disk drive, here are some other things you can do to reduce the time you spend in "hourglass land" as you work on high-resolution full-color images:

- **Starting out in low resolution.** For some images you can do your planning and "sketching" in a lower-resolution file than you will ultimately need for output. (See "Resolution" later in the chapter for a discussion of how to determine the resolution you need.) Working at low resolution will reduce processing time for changes you make to the image. Although you'll have to make the changes again on the higher-res file, some of the changes you make at the lower resolution can be saved as dialog box settings and then loaded and applied to the bigger file with a click of the mouse. For instance, settings for the four most useful functions of the Image, Adjust submenu — Levels, Curves, Hue/Saturation, and Variations — can be saved.

- **Building a file in stages.** If you're planning to modify and combine images, do the modifications on the separate, smaller parts first, and then combine them into a larger file. With Photoshop 3's layers (described in Chapter 2), instead of having a separate layer for every piece of the image, consider building an illustration in "modules": Build one component of several layers, then flatten the file, collapsing the layers into a single layer; create other components the same way; then layer the flattened components to make the final image.

- **Saving selections as you work.** If you're making a complex selection, save it periodically to an alpha channel or to a layer mask. (Making selections and using alpha channels and layer masks are discussed in Chapter 2.) With a backup version of the selection saved, if you accidentally drop the selection, you won't have to start over completely. And be sure to save the selection as an alpha channel when it's finished, so you can reselect exactly the same area if you need to later.

  If you're using the pen tool to create a selection outline, save the selection as a path rather than as an alpha channel. It takes much less disk space this way.

The Take Snapshot and Define Pattern commands use RAM for storage, just as the clipboard does. To "empty" these caches of material you no longer need, you can use basically the same technique as for emptying the clipboard: Select an area of a few pixels and choose Take Snapshot or Define Pattern from the Edit menu, twice — once to empty the cache itself and the second time to empty the "Undo" cache.

- **"Emptying" the clipboard.** If you cut or copy something to the clipboard, it's retained in RAM even after you paste a copy in place. Since some of Photoshop's commands can be carried out only in RAM (not in virtual memory), the best strategy for releasing the RAM from a large clipboard selection you no longer need is to replace the clipboard contents with something really small. Select a small area (just a few pixels) and press Ctrl-C (the shortcut for Edit, Copy). *Then press Ctrl-C again.* (The first Ctrl-C replaces the clipboard contents with your very small selection,

Working at low resolution saves time and disk space. Several designs for the Healthy Traveler book cover were worked out at 72 dpi before one was chosen for development at high resolution, as described in Chapter 9.

but Photoshop still has to keep the old clipboard contents in RAM so it will be available in case you press Ctrl-Z; after the second Ctrl-C both the clipboard and the backup RAM contain only the small selection, so less RAM is tied up.)

- **Cleaning up virtual memory.** If Photoshop tells you it can't complete an operation because there isn't enough space in virtual memory, simply closing another file that's open on-screen may not release the space you need. After you close the files, save a document in Photoshop 3.0 format to get the hard disk to clean up its virtual memory allocation. If that doesn't do the trick, you can quit the program (File, Exit) and start up again.

KEEPING PALETTES HANDY

The control palettes for Layers (new with version 3.0), Channels, Info, Tool Options/Brushes, and colors can be stored on-screen, ready to use, without taking up much space. Click the small box in the upper right corner of each palette to toggle between its collapsed version with only its tab showing and its expanded, functional version. (Some palettes have a two-stage collapse/expand function, and you have to Alt-click to collapse the palette all the way down to its tab alone.) When you click to expand a palette, it pops *into* the window. So even if you store the collapsed palettes at the very bottom of the screen, they'll be fully visible when they expand.

PHOTOS: RETRO AMERICANA SERIES, PHOTODISC

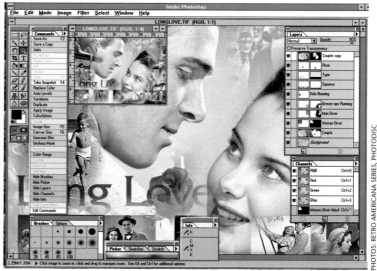

Here's one way to set up a 1024 x 768-pixel screen for working efficiently in Photoshop, with all of the palettes available. The Commands palette is stretched along the edge of the screen so that its buttons are always available. The Channels and Layers palettes are separated so both can be open at once; the Brushes palette is nested with the Tool Options palette so it's available for use with any tool; the colors palettes are nested, collapsed until needed; and the Info palette is present. The Paths palette is closed, since it can be opened instantly by pressing the "T" key. A second window is open in CMYK Preview mode (Window, New Window; then Mode, CMYK Preview) to show how the color will look if the RGB file is converted to CMYK mode. Rulers in the small window show image dimensions. The Document Size/Scratch Size window can show information about memory, file size, and image resolution.

TIDYING UP — WINDOWS 3.1

Windows 3.1 allows you to collapse any window down to an icon by clicking on the down-facing arrow in the upper right-hand corner of the active screen. To reopen a collapsed window, double-click the icon. (Another way to reopen the collapsed window of a Photoshop file is to choose the name of the file from Photoshop's Window menu.)

Fractal Design

Corel5   Main

You can use collapsed windows to keep other open applications or other Photoshop files handy but hidden so their windows won't have to be redrawn if you resize or move the currently active window.

If you're using a version of Photoshop earlier than 3.0.4 and you scan your system with the utility that Microsoft provides so you can find out if your computer is equipped to run Windows 95, you're likely to see this message:

And when you press the Details button, you'll see this:

What this means is that although you may be able to run version 3.0, you're very likely to have problems with it. To run under Windows 95, upgrade to version 3.0.4, which is Windows 95–compatible, or to the next Photoshop upgrade that Adobe brings out, which will be optimized to take advantage of Windows 95's new features.

A word of warning: Even if you have a Windows 95–compatible version of Photoshop, you may have trouble switching to the new operating system if some of the third-party plug-ins that you use with Photoshop — scanner drivers, for instance — have not yet been updated for Windows 95.

• **Closing other applications.** When you want to work in Photoshop, open Photoshop first, before opening any additional applications. This gives Photoshop first claim on RAM. As you work, if you find that you need even more RAM, close any other programs that you've opened. Even if you aren't doing anything with them, open applications reserve their assigned RAM, which may cut down on the amount available for Photoshop to use.

CHANGING YOUR VIEW

As you work with Photoshop, you'll want to change your view:

• From close-up views (so you can work in fine detail),

• To 1:1 view, which shows the image at your monitor's resolution and shows editing most accurately,

The small box in the lower left corner of the Photoshop window holds a lot of information:

• In Document Sizes mode it shows the current open size of the file with all its layers and channels (right) and the size it would be if it was flattened to one layer with all alpha channels removed (left) — that is, the amount of data that will be sent to the printer or other output device.

• In Scratch Sizes mode it shows how much RAM is available for Photoshop to use (right) and how much memory is currently tied up by all open Photoshop files, the clipboard, Snapshot, and so on (left). If the lefthand figure exceeds the righthand figure, it means Photoshop is using virtual memory to carry out its functions.

• In Efficiency mode (new with version 3.0.4) it tells how much Photoshop is using RAM alone, rather than swapping data with the scratch disk. A value near 100% means the scratch disk isn't being used much, so adding more RAM probably wouldn't improve performance. A value less than about 75% means that assigning more RAM would probably help.

• Pressing on the numbers themselves opens a box that shows the size of the image relative to the page size currently selected in File, Page Setup.

• Holding down the Alt key while pressing the numbers shows the dimensions (in pixels and in the current unit of measure), the resolution (in pixels per inch), the color mode, and the number of channels in the file.

• Holding down the Ctrl key while pressing the numbers shows the number and size of the rectangular "tiles" that make up the image. The tiles are the blocks of information Photoshop uses to store the image. (You can see them appear one by one as the screen is redrawn when you work on a file.) The amount of additional memory required by each layer depends how many of these tiles its pixels occupy. For instance, in a nine-tile file, a layer with a small circle of pixels at the center of each tile would require much more memory than a layer with all the small circles aggregated in one tile.

If RAM is limited, there are several ways you can copy and paste a selection, a layer, a channel, or an entire image without using the clipboard, which requires RAM.

To copy and paste a selection in the same file and layer:

- Hold down the Alt key and drag the selection.
- Or float a copy (Ctrl-J).

To duplicate the contents of a layer:

- Drag its name or thumbnail to the New Layer icon at the bottom of the Layers palette.
- Or hold down the Alt key and choose Image, Apply Image. In the Source section of the dialog box, choose the layer you want to copy and the composite channel (RGB or CMYK, for example). In the Result section of the dialog box, choose New Layer.

To copy and paste a selection or a layer from one file to another:

- Drag and drop from one document to the other.

To copy a channel from one image to another:

- Hold down the Alt key and choose Image, Apply Image. In the Result section of the Apply Image dialog box, choose New Channel.

To copy and paste an entire image:

- Choose Image, Duplicate
- Or hold down the Alt key and choose Image, Apply Image. In the Result section of the Apply Image dialog box, choose New Document.

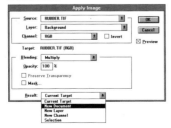

- To zoomed-out views (for making an image small, so you can get it out of the way, for example, or so you can get an overview of a large image).

Zooming in. There are several ways to get a close-up view:

- **For an enlarged view centered on the click point,** click with the zoom tool (the magnifying glass in the toolbox). The window size stays the same, but the view doubles or halves with each click. For instance, if you start with a 1:1 view, you get 2:1, starting with 2:1 gives you 4:1, and starting with 3:1 gives you 6:1.

- **To enlarge a particular area,** drag the zoom tool across the area you want to view. The area will enlarge to fill the window.

- **To increase image size in steps** from 1:1 to 2:1 to 3:1 to 4:1, press Ctrl-+ (really Ctrl-= because you don't need the Shift key, but Ctrl-+ is an easier way to remember it), or choose Window, Zoom In. Unless Never Resize Windows is chosen in the Zoom Tool Options palette, the window gets bigger as the image view enlarges. The window stops getting bigger when you run out of room, but the image continues to enlarge up to 16:1.

- **To enlarge the entire image and window to the largest size that will fit on the screen,** double-click the hand tool or click the Zoom To Screen button in the Zoom Tool Options palette or the Hand Tool Options palette.

- **To zoom to the maximum enlargement (16:1),** press Ctrl-Alt-+.

- **To get a close-up view while working with another tool,** press and hold Ctrl-spacebar and click or drag across the part of the image you want to enlarge; then release the keys to go right on using the original tool.

Zooming out. There are also several ways to "back away" from an image to get a broader view:

- **To reduce the view,** Alt-click with the zoom tool; the reduction is half the size you start with. For instance, 6:1 becomes 3:1. Odd numbers go to the next whole number above half; for instance, 5:1 also becomes 3:1.

- **To reduce the magnification** in steps from 1:1 to 1:2 to 1:3 and so on, press Ctrl-minus (that's Ctrl-hyphen) or choose Window, Zoom Out. This is a good way to have several windows open and available on-screen without stacking them on top of each other. Unless the "Never Resize Windows" option is chosen in the Zoom Tool Options palette, the window gets smaller as the image view shrinks.

- **To reduce the magnification as much as possible (1:16),** press Ctrl-Alt-hyphen.

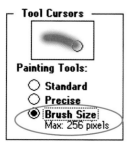
- **To zoom out while working with another tool,** press Alt-spacebar and click.

Here are some other view-changing shortcuts:

- **To return to the 1:1 view,** double-click the zoom tool or press the Zoom 1:1 button in the Zoom Tool Options or Hand Tool Options palette.
- **To enlarge or reduce an image to a particular magnification,** choose Window, Zoom Factor and specify the Magnification multiple.
- **To make the entire image fit in the window,** double-click the hand tool or choose Zoom To Screen in the Zoom Tool Options or Hand Tool Options palette. The image (and the window if necessary) will be enlarged until the image fills the window at 1:1 magnification.
- **To center an image at its current size on a black screen,** click the right-hand window control at the bottom of the tool palette. This automatically closes the menu bar. To close the palettes as well, press Tab. You can reopen the palettes by pressing Tab again.

RECOVERING

Photoshop 3 provides only one level of Undo — the familiar Windows Ctrl-Z affects only your last instruction to Photoshop. However, the program provides several other ways to work backwards if you need to. Here are some suggestions:

Saving intermediate versions. By using the **Duplicate** function, you can save several intermediate versions of a file under different file names. Choose Image, Duplicate to make a copy of the file in its current condition; the copy will become the active file, leaving the original file open on-screen as well, easily accessible (but also tying up RAM, of course). You can reduce the file size of the duplicate by choosing to merge the visible layers and discard the nonvisible ones. (Merging is covered in Chapter 2.)

In contrast to the Duplicate method, if you use File, **Save A Copy,** the duplicate file is stored (closed, not using any RAM). And you have several storage options: You can merge all the layers into one, save the file without its alpha channels, or save in a different file format.

Using the File, **Save As** command and giving the file a new name is another way to save an intermediate version. With this method the original file is closed and stored in the form that it was before you last saved, and the Saved As (current) version remains open and active.

Save As before you start to work on a scanned image, and then use Save As or Save A Copy often during the editing process. Then if you decide to change something that you did halfway through the development of the image, you can open one of the saved versions.

When you choose Image, Duplicate, the Duplicate dialog box offers
to name the file the same as the
original but with a number added
at the end. The numbers start at 1
and increase with each additional
copy you make, either from the
original or a duplicate. Choosing
Image, Duplicate is quick, but
there's an even quicker way: Holding down the Alt key as you choose
Image, Duplicate bypasses the dialog
box. (Note that the files are named
differently — "copy" is added to
the name instead of a number.)

*Holding down the Alt key makes the eraser
operate in Revert mode (right), restoring the
last saved version of the image.*

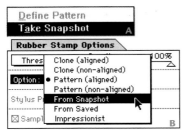

*To focus attention on a particular feature
of an image, the file can be blurred (left)
and then Edit, Fill, Saved can be used to
restore the original sharp version to an
area selected with a feathered lasso. (See
Chapter 5 for more about using the Blur
filters.)*

*Storing a current image or selection in a
Snapshot buffer by choosing Edit, Take
Snapshot (A) makes it possible to restore it
later with the rubber stamp tool (B).*

Reverting to the last saved version. Choose File, **Revert** to
keep the file open but eliminate all the changes you've made since
you last saved it.

Restoring part of the last saved version. Use the **magic
eraser,** which is the eraser tool either with the Alt key held down
or with Erase To Saved checked in the Eraser Options dialog box. Or
use the **rubber stamp tool in From Saved mode.** The rubber
stamp method gives hand-held control of the restoration process, as
does the magic eraser, but with the added advantage of being able to
control the painting mode (Normal, Dissolve, Multiply, and so on).
(Blending and painting modes are discussed in Chapter 2 and at the beginning of Chapter 6.) Or make a selection of the area you want to restore; choose **Edit, Fill,** and choose **Saved** from the Contents list in
the Fill dialog box. With any of these methods, the changes are made
to the active layer only; you can control which channels of the active layer are affected — turn them ON or OFF in the Channels palette (see Chapter 2 for more about activating layers and channels).

Saving intermediate steps. The Snapshot is a buffer, or storage
space, in which you can store one intermediate stage of an image
— either the entire image or a selected part of it. Choose **Edit,
Take Snapshot** to store the current image or selection in the
buffer. (You can make the Snapshot selection with any selection
tool; the buffer will save a rectangular area that includes your entire
selection.) Then you can restore the selected area later by using the
rubber stamp tool in From Snapshot mode or the Edit, Fill command with Snapshot selected from the Contents list. Keep in mind
that, like the clipboard, the Snapshot ties up RAM. But unlike the
clipboard, the Snapshot is file-specific — you can't use it with another image. And it won't work for restoration if you change the
image size or canvas size

Duplicating a layer. If you want to make changes to a particular
layer but you want an "escape hatch" to get back to the previous
version, copy the layer and work on the copy. You can do this by
dragging the layer name in the Layers palette to the New Layer icon
at the bottom of the palette. Once you've made changes to the
copy, you can vary the Opacity or the mode to get just the right
combination of the changed layer and the unchanged one below it.
(See Chapter 2 for more about how layers interact.)

Making a "repair" layer. If you're using the sharpen/blur,
smudge, or rubber stamp to make repairs to an image, you can
"paint" the repairs to a separate, transparent top layer. That way the
repairs don't actually get mixed into the image. So if you want to
undo part of your repair work, you can select that part (with the lasso,
for instance) and remove it from the repair layer, leaving intact the rest

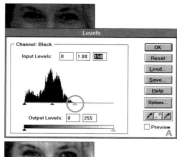

Increasing contrast in the highlights with the Levels dialog box by moving the Input white point inward: A, before; B, after

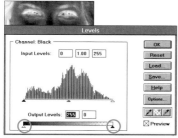

Inverting the image map (making a negative) with the Levels dialog box by moving the Output sliders to opposite ends of the bar

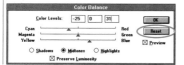
of the repairs and the layers beneath. Putting repairs on a separate layer or layers also means you can change the Opacity to vary the repair effect. (For an example of using a repair layer, see page 114.)

Making several changes at once with Levels. One way to get the most out of a single level of Undo is to use the dialog boxes available through the Image, Adjust submenu — especially the Levels box. With their Preview boxes selected, these dialogs allow you to make and view several changes to an image without leaving the dialog box, so that if you decide you don't want to keep the changes you've made, you can undo all of them at once. And you can save the dialog box settings at any point by clicking the Save button, so it's possible to save several intermediate settings before clicking OK to finalize changes. Then, if you need to press Ctrl-Z, you can restore an intermediate version of the changes by loading one of your sets of saved settings, and go on from there.

Here are some of the changes you can make without leaving the Levels dialog box, and then you can undo them all with Ctrl-Z if you need to:

- If you press the **Auto button,** Photoshop will make its best automated effort to spread the color values in the image to produce a **full tonal range.** Unless the image's tonal distribution is perfect already, the effect is to increase the contrast in the image and, if the colors are really unbalanced, to remove (or at least reduce) a color cast. Beware, though: If your photo has an inherent color cast — like the gold of a sunset scene or the blue of an underwater shot — using the Auto button can "correct" it away.

- By moving the Input Levels sliders, you can **increase the contrast** in the highlights, midtones, or shadows independently, for the entire image or for an individual color channel or alpha channel. (For a channel's name to appear in the pop-out menu at the top of the Levels dialog box, the channel must be active for writing — that is, its name must be on a white background in the Channels palette, opened by choosing Window, Show Channels.)

- By using the Output sliders to lighten or darken a selected area or an entire image, you can **decrease the contrast.**

- You can use the black (or white) eyedropper to **set the black (or white) point,** pushing to black (or white) all colors darker (or lighter) than the color you select.

- You can **get rid of a color cast** by clicking the gray eyedropper to sample an area that you think should be neutral — that is, an area that should be a shade of gray, without color.

- You can even **make a negative** (accomplishing an Image, Map, Invert) by switching the positions of the black and white sliders on the Output Levels bar.

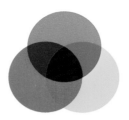

In a subtractive color model (represented by the top illustration), cyan, magenta, and yellow inks combine to make a dark, nearly black color. In additive color (bottom), red, green, and blue light combine on-screen to make white light.

COLOR IN PHOTOSHOP

Photoshop's interface for choosing and mixing color includes the Mode menu, the Foreground/Background color squares, the Color Picker, the color palettes (Picker, Swatches, and Scratch), and the eyedropper tool.

Color Modes

Photoshop employs several different systems of color representation. These systems — Bitmap, Grayscale, Duotone, Indexed Color, RGB Color, CYK Color, and Lab Color — can be selected through the Mode menu. Each color mode has a different *gamut,* or range of colors that can be produced in that color system.

CMYK Color. In any color system the *primary colors* are the basics from which all other colors can be mixed. In *four-color process printing,* which is the type of printing most often used for reproducing the photos, illustrations, and other works produced in Photoshop, the primaries (called *subtractive primaries*) are cyan, magenta, and yellow, with the potential for adding black to intensify the dark colors. Adding black makes dark colors look crisper than darkening with a heavier mix of cyan, magenta, and yellow. Darkening with black also requires less ink; this can be important because a press had an upper limit to the amount of ink it can apply to the printed page before the ink will no longer adhere to the paper.

RGB Color. The CRT computer monitor generates primary colors of light (called *additive primaries*) by bombarding the phosphor coating of the screen with electrons. The mix of red, green, and blue light that results is perceived by the eye as color. When all three colors are on at full intensity, the result is white light; when all are off, black results. Different intensities of energy excite the phosphors to different degrees, and the various brightnesses of the three colors mix visually to form all the colors of the RGB spectrum.

Because of the architecture of computer hardware and software, there are theoretically 256 different levels of energy that can be applied to each of the three primary colors of the computer's RGB system; this means that there are 256 x 256 x 256 (or more than 16 million) colors that can be mixed. This gamut provides enough colors to very realistically represent the world we see.

It takes 8 bits of computer data (a bit is a 1 or a 0, an on or off signal) to represent 256 different energy settings ($2^8 = 256$); to represent the combinations that can be generated by three sets of energy settings takes 24 bits ($2^{8 \times 3} = 2^{24} = 16.7$ million). So full color as displayed on the computer screen is called 24-bit color.

Indexed Color. Many computers aren't equipped to display 24-bit color. Instead, they can display only 256 colors at once, or 8-bit color. In such a system, 256 colors are stored in a color lookup table (or CLUT) whose storage addresses are identified by numbers between 0 and 255. The process of assigning 256 colors to represent

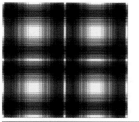

In Indexed Color mode, you can change colors quickly by clicking on the cells of the Color Table. Peter Kaye uses this method to try different colorways in fabric design, as shown here.

Photoshop's Duotone mode provides curves that store information for printing a grayscale image in one to four ink colors. The program comes with several sets of preset duotone, tritone, and quadtone curves. Or you can shape the curves yourself. By drastically reshaping curves as in this tritone, you can make individual colors predominate in highlights, midtones, and shadows.

the millions of colors potentially in a full-color image is called *indexing.* When you choose Mode, Indexed Color in Photoshop, you can choose to index the colors to:

- An **Exact** palette (if the image includes 256 or fewer colors)
- The **System** palette (this is the standard Windows palette, a set of 256 colors chosen to provide a good color representation of a wide variety of images)
- An **Adaptive** palette (a set of the 256 most representative, or most common) colors in an image. Adaptive palettes also automatically include black and white.
- A **Custom** palette (a set of colors selected for some particular purpose). Choosing Mode, Indexed Color, Custom opens the Color Table dialog box, where you can choose one of several Custom palettes that are supplied with the program or make your own color table by clicking the individual squares of the table and choosing new colors to fill them. As long as your file is in Indexed Color mode, you can choose Mode, Color Table and change the table.
- The **Previous** palette (the set of colors that was used the last time, within the current Photoshop session, that a file was indexed with a Custom, System, or Adaptive palette)

Lab Color. Instead of being separated into three colors (plus black in the case of CMYK color), color can be expressed in terms of a brightness component and two hue/saturation components. Photoshop's Lab Color mode uses such a system. So does Kodak Photo CD (its Photo YCC color system) and so does color television. Because its gamut is large enough to include the CMYK, RGB, and Photo YCC gamuts, Photoshop's Lab Color mode serves as an intermediate step when Photoshop converts from RGB to CMYK or from Photo YCC to RGB.

Grayscale. A Grayscale mode image, like a black-and-white photo, includes only *brightness* values, no data for *hue* or *saturation,* the other two components of color. Only 8 bits of data are required for storing the 256 shades (black, white, and grays) in the Grayscale gamut.

Duotone. Even though a Grayscale image can include 256 levels of gray, most printing processes can't actually produce that many different tones with a single ink color. But with two inks (or even one color of ink applied in two passes through the press) it's possible to extend the tonal range. By adding a second color in the highlights, for example, you increase the number of tones available for representing the lightest grays in an image. Besides extending tonal range, the second color can "warm" or "cool" an image, tinting it slightly toward red or blue. Or the second color may be used for dramatic effect or to visually tie a photo to other design elements.

In Photoshop's Duotone mode, a set of *gamma curves* determines how the grayscale information will be represented in each of the ink colors. Will the second color be emphasized in the shadows but omitted from the highlights? Will it be used to color the midtones? The Duotone image is stored as a grayscale file and a set of curves that will act on that grayscale information to produce two or more separate plates for printing. Duotone mode also includes tritone and quadtone options, for producing three or four color plates.

Bitmap. The least "bulky" mode in Photoshop is Bitmap, which uses only 1 bit of "color" data to represent each pixel. A pixel is either OFF or ON, producing a gamut of two colors — black and white. Photoshop's several methods for converting Grayscale images to Bitmap mode provide useful options for printing photos with low-resolution, one-color printing methods, as well as some interesting graphic treatments (see Chapter 3, "Enhancing Photos").

Other Color Tools in the Mode Menu

In addition to the color modes themselves, the Mode menu includes four more choices: Multichannel, CMYK Preview, Gamut Warning, and Color Table (the function of Color Table is described under "Indexed Color" on page 17).

Multichannel mode can be useful for viewing the plates of a Duotone image, as shown at the left.

CMYK Preview, new in Photoshop 3, lets you see how an RGB image will look if you convert it to CMYK mode with the current Separation Setup parameters. (Separation Setup is discussed in "Getting Consistent Color," which starts on page 21.) Opening a second view of your RGB file (Window, New Window) and choosing CMYK Preview lets you see the file in both the RGB and the CMYK gamuts at the same time. Unlike choosing Mode, CMYK Color, the CMYK Preview option doesn't actually make the color conversion to the file, so you don't lose the RGB color information and therefore you still have the full RGB color gamut to work with.

Gamut Warning identifies the colors in your RGB image that will be have to be adjusted to bring them inside the printable color range if you change to CMYK mode with the current Separation Setup settings.

Getting into Gamut

Once you choose Mode, Gamut Warning to identify the colors that will change when an RGB file is converted to CMYK mode, the CMYK Preview and the sponge tool can help bring the out-of-gamut colors into gamut. Most RGB colors can be brought into the smaller CMYK gamut by reducing their saturation. So you can proceed this way: Open another window in CMYK Preview mode (choose Window, New Window; then choose Mode, CMYK Preview for this window). Looking at the new window, you may decide that the colors look fine and that Photoshop's Separation Setup will do an acceptable job of bringing the color into CMYK gamut. But If

Duotone mode doesn't let you see or edit the individual color plates that will be used for printing. Photoshop provides no way to edit the plates, but to see them, you can convert the file to Multichannel mode, open a second window, and view a different channel in each window. Follow these steps exactly: First, open the Channels palette (Window, Palettes, Show Channels) and open a second view of the image (Window, New Window). Then choose Mode, Multichannel. In the Channels palette, activate a different Channel (by clicking on its name in the Channels palette) for each of the windows. View, but don't try to edit, both plates — if you make changes, you won't be able to convert back to Duotone mode. Here the black and yellow plates are shown. (To make a "painted duotone" image in which you can edit the individual plates, see page 102.)

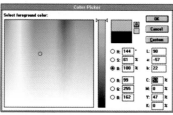

PHOTO: DON COCHRAN

The Gamut Warning (from the Mode menu) uses a medium gray (top) to indicate colors that will change when the file is converted to CMYK mode, as shown here (bottom). The gray disappears on-screen as you bring colors into gamut. If gray doesn't work well for a particular image, you can change the indicator color by choosing File, Preferences, Gamut Warning, clicking the color square, and choosing a new color.

Photoshop's Color Picker lets you enter numeric values to mix colors. Or you can pick from the color models presented in the large square. Clicking on Custom lets you choose from several color matching systems (bottom). To get the Photoshop Color Picker when you click on the Foreground or Background color square in the toolbox, first choose File, Preferences, General and choose Photoshop instead of Windows for the Color Picker.

you see a few areas of out-of-gamut colors that won't look good when converted, you may want to do some desaturation by hand: "Paint" the out-of-gamut areas with the sponge tool set to Desaturate at a fairly low Pressure. Use a soft-edged brush to prevent sharp color breaks, brushing over the out-of-gamut areas to desaturate them just until the indicator color is removed. Be careful that you don't desaturate some areas more than necessary or cause streaking where your brush strokes overlap.

Using the Color Picker and Color Palettes

The **Foreground and Background color squares** in the toolbox show what color you'll get when you paint or erase. You can choose Foreground and Background colors simply by clicking on one of the squares to open the **Color Picker** and then choosing or specifying a color. Beyond the Color Picker, the three **color palettes** (Picker, Swatches, and Scratch) can be left open on-screen and are ideally suited for certain ways of choosing colors:

The **Picker palette**, with its different modes and sliders, lets you mix colors scientifically (by reading the numbers as you move the sliders) or "by feel," or by sampling from the Color Bar at the bottom of the palette.

By default the **Swatches palette** shows a set of 122 color samples. You can click a swatch to select the Foreground color or Alt-click to select the Background color. The palette can be expanded to hold a scrolling preset palette of colors, such as the Pantone colors found in the **photoshp\palettes** directory.

The **Scratch palette** is ideal for mixing colors "by hand." You can sample colors from any open window by Alt-clicking with a painting tool (paintbrush or airbrush, for example). Then use the painting tool to mix colors in the Scratch; you'll want to have the tool's Options palette open so you can control the opacity as you apply and mix colors. Or you can select a part of your image and then drag and drop it into the Scratch palette.

Sampling Colors with the Eyedropper

The eyedropper tool can sample color by clicking on any open file or palette; the sampled color becomes the Foreground color. Alt-clicking sets the Background color. The Sample Size, set in the Eyedropper Options palette, lets you pick up the color of a single pixel or average the color from a 3 x 3- or 5 x 5-pixel area around the cursor's "hot point."

Using Color Gradients

Double-clicking Photoshop's gradient tool opens a tool options palette that lets you accomplish some amazing color effects:

• The Clockwise Spectrum and Counterclockwise Spectrum gradient Style choices in the Gradient Tool Options palette create

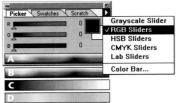

The Picker palette has a color bar from which colors can be sampled. The gamut shown in the bar can be changed by Shift-clicking on the bar to toggle through the four color bar choices: RGB Spectrum (A), CMYK Spectrum (B), Grayscale Ramp (C), and Foreground To Background (D). Or choose Color Bar from the palette's pop-out menu or Ctrl-click on the bar to open the Color Bar dialog box. The Foreground To Background bar can be locked so the color ramp will stay the same even if you change the current Foreground or Background color.

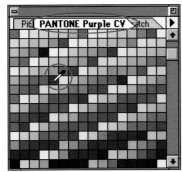

Choose Load Swatches from the Swatches palette's pop-out menu to open a custom "swatch book" like this Pantone Colors (Pro Sim), the process equivalents of Pantone ink colors. Swatch sets are found in **palettes**, in the **photoshp** directory. Custom color names appear in the palette's tab as the cursor rolls over the swatches.

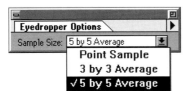

The sample size of the eyedroppers in the Levels and Curves dialog boxes is also controlled by the setting in the Eyedropper Options palette.

gradients by going around the color wheel rather than by making the most direct blend between the Foreground and Background colors.

- A Transparent To Foreground gradient can be useful for special effects, like making an image disappear into the mist.

- Applied at different angles in individual color channels, black-to-white gradients can produce quite spectacular multicolor backgrounds.

- Radial color gradients can help to create the illusion of three-dimensionality.

A Clockwise Spectrum is equivalent to moving down in Photoshop's Color Picker or moving left on the HSB slider in the Picker palette. Conversely, Counterclockwise Spectrum is equivalent to moving up or right.

ORIGINAL PHOTO: TREES, DIGITAL STOCK CORP.

Starting with a dawn image (top), we applied a transparent-to-white gradient, dragging the gradient tool from the middle of the picture to a point beyond the top edge.

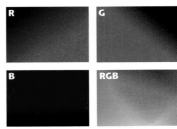

An amorphous multicolor background can be created by using the gradient tool in individual color channels.

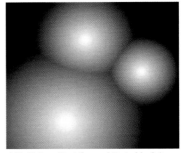

A Radial gradient from white to black in Normal mode made the large "atom." The smaller ones were made in Lighten mode. Then the color of the midtones was changed with Variations.

Offset the center of a Radial fill by using the gradient tool inside an elliptical selection.

GETTING CONSISTENT COLOR

If you've done color artwork on the computer and then printed it out, you've probably noticed some fundamental differences in the way color is represented on-screen and on the printed page. There are several contributing factors.

- First of all, **transmitted** (additive) color from a monitor looks different than the color produced by light **reflected** from ink on paper (subtractive color).

- Second, because the RGB gamut (the range of available colors) is bigger than the CMYK gamut, **not all the colors that can be displayed on-screen can be printed,** so it's possible to mix colors in RGB files that can't be reproduced on the printed page.

- Third, because you're moving from a three-color (RGB) to a four-color (CMYK) system in which black can partially substitute for mixes of the other three colors, **there are many different ways to represent a particular RGB color in the CMYK system,** and because of the way ink pigments interact, the results of all these ways can look slightly different from each other.

- And finally, **variations** in film output, paper, ink, presses, and press operators also affect the color in the final printed product.

When To Make the RGB-to-CMYK Conversion

If you're preparing an image for print, unless your final print will be made on one of a few desktop color printers that can't handle CMYK files, the image will eventually need to be turned into CMYK separations. This can be done at any of several different stages in the development of the image. For instance:

- You can choose CMYK Color mode when you first create a new Photoshop file (File, New).

- Some scanning services (and even some desktop scanning software) can make the CMYK conversion for you. The quality of the result depends on the sophistication of the software and the suitability of its settings for the kind of printing you want to do, or on the skill of the professional scan operator. (For more about scanning, see "Image Input" on page 24 and "Setting Up a Scan" on page 33.)

- You can choose Photoshop's Mode, CMYK Color at any point in the development of an image. But **once you make the conversion you can't regain the original RGB color** by choosing Mode, RGB Color. The out-of-gamut colors will have been permanently "dulled down" to CMYK-printable versions.

- Finally, you can keep the file in RGB Color mode, place it in a page layout, and allow the page layout program or color-separation utility to make the separation.

How do you decide when to convert? Here are some tips to help you choose:

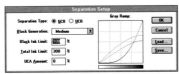

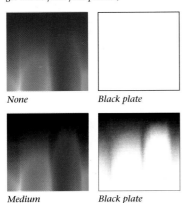

Setting the parameters for converting RGB to CMYK color (Unless you understand the technical aspects of working with color separation curves, use the default setting or get advice from your printer.)

None   *Black plate*

Medium   *Black plate*

Maximum   *Black plate*

Part of the full-spectrum palette (provided on the CD ROM that comes with this book) converted to CMYK with three different Black Generation settings

- The single advantage of working in CMYK from the beginning is that it prevents last-minute color shifts, since it keeps the image within the printing gamut during the entire development process.

- But if you're working in CMYK mode and your printing specifications change (a different paper may be chosen for the job, for instance), the CMYK specifications you chose may no longer apply. In that case, you'll have to start over from an RGB version or compensate manually (see "There's No Going Back" on page 21.)

- Working in RGB and putting off the CMYK conversion to the last possible moment allows more freedom, so you can get just the color you want on-screen and then work with Photoshop's Hue/Saturation, Levels, or Curves adjustments to tweak out-of-gamut colors to get CMYK alternatives that are as close as possible to your original colors.

- Another, very significant advantage of working in RGB is that some of Photoshop's finest functions (for example, the Lighting Effects filter described in Chapter 5) don't work in CMYK mode.

- With CMYK Preview and Gamut Warning now available in Photoshop 3, **it makes sense to work in RGB, preview CMYK in a second window, and do the actual RGB-to-CMYK conversion at the end of the process.**

- You may be able to bow out of the conversion process altogether for many jobs. **Your page layout program or** the **separation utility** used by your imagesetting service bureau **may do an excellent job of converting most of your RGB images to CMYK.** If that's the case, you can save yourself some time and angst by using this method. It's often worth the money to run a test file through film separation to laminate proof to check the result (see "Getting Consistent Color" later in this chapter).

- **In some cases doing the conversion to CMYK yourself may be the only way to control color** — for example, when you won't have the opportunity to review laminate proofs of the film separations and you don't have a printed sample to send along as a color-match target (or you don't trust the production team to use the target appropriately even if you do send one). This may be the case if you're providing a photo-illustration to a publication produced by someone else. But you'll need to know quite a bit about how the piece will be printed (the dot gain and maximum ink coverage, for instance) in order to make the right settings in the Printing Inks Setup and Separation Setup dialog boxes.

The default settings for the Printing Inks Setup dialog box covers the most common paper, ink, and press conditions used for printing color images. If you're going to do your own RGB-to-CMYK conversions, get advice about the Dot Gain setting from your printer, or from your imagesetting service bureau, since technicians there may be more familiar with Photoshop than the printer is; better yet, have the printer and service bureau technician talk to each other and then let you know how to set the Dot Gain. Specify that the dot gain compensation needs to be from the film stage to the final press sheet, not from proof to press sheet. The Dot Gain value is for the 50% point.

WARM IT UP!

Since the color characteristics of monitors change as they warm up, turn your monitor on half an hour or more before calibrating or making critical color decisions.

OVERPRINT COLORS

The Overprint Colors button in the Duotone dialog box lets you make the on-screen display of your duotone look more like it will when it's printed. Clicking any of the color squares in the Overprint Colors dialog box opens the Color Picker so you can change the display of that color mix. To use this function accurately, you need to have a calibrated monitor in a controlled viewing environment (see "Calibration and Color Matching" later in the chapter) and a printed sample or color proof that shows your ink colors overprinted solid. Hold the sample up next to the screen and match the color with the Color Picker.

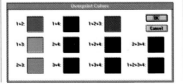

Making the Conversion

At whatever point you make the conversion, the Monitor Setup, Separation Setup, and Printing Inks Setup functions (under File, Preferences) all affect the final result. Chapter 14 of the *Adobe Photoshop 3.0 User Guide* that comes with the program walks you through the process of producing a CMYK separation in Photoshop.

To make the appropriate settings in the Separation Setup and Printing Inks Setup dialog boxes, you need certain information about the printing process that will be used to put the image on paper. For instance, you need to know the maximum ink coverage and the expected dot gain. If you make an RGB-to-CMYK conversion without knowing the maximum allowable ink coverage and the expected dot gain, you're just guessing about the outcome. (*Dot gain* is a change in the size of the tiny dots of ink that are applied to the paper. There can be a gain or loss as you go through the process of making printing plates from film or the process of transferring ink from the printing plate to the paper, depending on the paper's absorbency, and these gains or losses can cause changes in color. Photoshop's dot gain settings seem to be on the high side. So when you get advice about settings, it's good to ask someone who not only knows how your job will be printed, but also understands how Photoshop works.)

Calibration and Color Matching

In order for your computer monitor to be as accurate as possible in showing how an image will look when it's printed, each part of the display and print production system must be *calibrated,* adjusted so it produces color consistently over time. And then all the parts of the system have to be coordinated with each other.

The Gamma control panel utility that comes with Photoshop helps with monitor calibration. Chapter 2 of the *Adobe Photoshop 3.0 User Guide* tells how to use Gamma and the Monitor Setup dialog box to calibrate your monitor. Once the monitor is adjusted, it's a good idea to lock its brightness and contrast knobs in place with tape to keep them from being changed accidentally.

To get consistent color, the viewing environment has to be maintained constant also, because changes in lighting conditions can change your perception of colors on the screen. Position the room's light source above and behind the monitor, and keep it dimmed and constant. Also, wear neutral colors when you sit in front of the monitor, to minimize color reflections on the screen.

Calibrating the monitor doesn't finish the job of getting your system ready to show you predictable color. Assuming that your output process is also kept consistent over time (you don't let the inkjets get clogged up in your desktop printer and you can count on the service bureau to keep its imagesetting equipment tuned up and its processing chemicals fresh), you can do a sort of "backwards

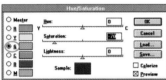
calibration" to make sure your screen display is an accurate predictor of the color you'll get in a print or proof. Here's a way to do it:

1 Print or proof a color file; this could be an image of your own, but you may also want to include the **testpict** image from the **photoshp\calibrat** directory on the Adobe Photoshop Deluxe CD ROM. "Olé! No Moiré" provides fine-tuned color and good shadow detail so you can be confident the image is right, as well as standard color swatches that your imagesetting service can check with a densitometer. Either:

- Print the file on the same system you'll use for final printing,

- Print the file on a proofing printer that your press operator assures you will be a good predictor of final printed color,

- Or produce film and a laminate proof that your printing press operators can check and assure you they can match on press. Going all the way to press, rather than stopping at a proof, is even better, but it usually isn't possible.

2 In your controlled light environment, open the file on-screen. Hold the print or proof up to the screen to compare color.

3 Readjust your monitor with the Gamma control panel until the on-screen image looks like the printed piece, and use the Save Settings button in the Gamma panel to save the settings for future use in projects that will use the same printing process. The back-to-front system calibration process depends on changing the display characteristics of the monitor, but not changing the file itself. So don't do any work in Photoshop during the process — that is, *don't change the file.*

Once your monitor has been readjusted to match the print or proof, you can assume that for files you produce in the future, when the image looks the way you want it on-screen, the print or proof will look the same.

Note: Chapter 2 in the *Adobe Photoshop 3.0 User Guide* recommends that you adjust Monitor Setup and Printing Inks Setup rather than Gamma to do back-to-front calibration. However, that assumes that you will be doing the RGB-to-CMYK conversion for all your images in Photoshop, since both Monitor Setup and Printing Inks Setup affect *the file itself,* not just the on-screen display. Using Gamma instead works for both Photoshop-separated images and those handled by a different separation utility, such as one designed to work with a page layout program.

IMAGE INPUT

Scanners — desktop, mid-range and high-end — turn photos into image files that can be manipulated in Photoshop. An inexpensive desktop flatbed scanner can capture photographic prints, other hard

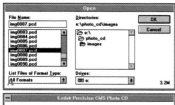

To open a Photo CD file in Photoshop 3:

*1 Choose File, Open, and then choose the CD-ROM drive that holds the Photo CD disc; within the CD-ROM drive directory, choose the **photo_cd** directory, and within that directory choose **images**. Choose the number of the image you want — you can find the number by looking at the index print that comes in the Photo CD case with the disc — and double-click that name (A).*

2 When the image dialog box opens (B), you can choose the Resolution (which of the five or six files sizes you want). Also, click the Image Info button to find out what kind of film was scanned to make the file.

3 Note the Medium Of Original and Product Type Of Original (C), and click OK to close the box.

*4 Back in the image dialog box (B), click on the Source button. Choose Kodak Photo CD for the Device (unless a special device profile is supplied for the disc), and select the appropriate film Description from the list (D). If the Medium Of Origin (in step 3) was Color Negative, choose **Photo CD Color Negative V2.0** for slide film (called "Color Reversal" in the Image Info box), choose **Universal Kodachrome V2.0** if the Product Type starts with "116/"; for all other Color Reversal film, use **Universal Ektachrome V2.0.***

copy, and even some three-dimensional objects to make files you can use for photo-illustration. Desktop slide scanners and some transparency adapters for flatbed scanners (though the quality of transparency adapters varies greatly) make it possible to capture images from transparencies in sizes from 35 mm to 8 x 10 inches.

Another input option is to **have your images scanned by a service bureau** or a color separation house using scanners with optical-mechanical systems that are more precise than those of desktop scanners. Keep in mind that the quality of a service bureau scan depends not only on the quality of the scanning equipment, but also on the operator's willingness to calibrate and maintain it, and on his or her understanding of color, and skill in operating the machine.

Besides inputting images by scanning, you can also buy collections of photos and other artwork already scanned and provided on **CD ROM**. Many stock images, patterns, and textures are now available on CD ROM, with a variety of licensing arrangements for use and payment (see Appendix A).

Kodak Photo CD technology is making it easy and inexpensive to have images from film (35 mm negatives or slides) stored on a compact disc. The easiest and least expensive way to get your images into Photo CD format is to take your film to a photofinisher who offers the Photo CD service and get the disc back along with the finished prints or slides. The images on the disc are relatively high-quality scans, very efficiently compressed, and stored in Kodak's Image Pac format, which provides each image in five different resolutions, or file sizes. Pro Photo CD discs include the five file sizes used for Photo CD plus a bigger size that can accommodate larger film formats (up to 4 x 5 inches).

Photo CD images are scanned in RGB color and then translated to Kodak's Photo YCC color system because it's compatible with tele-

PHOTO CD FILE SIZES

The five file sizes in the Photo CD Image Pac (six sizes in Pro Photo CD) are as shown below. Print sizes are for high quality at halftone line screens of 150 lines per inch. Many Photo CD files can be printed bigger than the sizes listed if the photo doesn't include hard edges and if the halftone line screen used for printing is lower than 150 lpi; the lower the line screen, the more the image can be enlarged.

Base/16	128 x 192 pixels	For thumbnail sketches
Base/4	256 x 384 pixels	For position only in layouts
Base	512 x 768 pixels	For TV, for on-screen computer presentation, or for high-quality print up to about 2 x 3 inches
4•Base	1024 x 1536 pixels	For HDTV (high-definition television) or for print up to about 3½ x 5 inches
16•Base	2048 x 3072 pixels	For print up to about 7 x 10 inches
64•Base*	4096 x 6144 pixels	For print up to about 14 x 20 inches

* Available with Pro Photo CD only

vision (Photo CD was originally designed to "play" to a TV screen), and it allows efficient compression of data so the images can be stored in less space without losing image quality. To use Photo CD, you need a CD ROM-XA (eXtended Architecture) drive and software that can retrieve the Photo CD images and convert them to a form that Photoshop can use. For this purpose Photoshop 3 includes an automatically installed plug-in module that lets you open Photo CD files with the File, Open or Open As command. Although you can get other modules that let you open Photo CD files through the File, Acquire command, the Open command does the best job.

Digital cameras, which bypass film altogether and record images as digital files on disk, are another potential source of images for manipulation in Photoshop. **Video** — from video camera, videocassette, or videodisc — can be brought into Photoshop through the File, Acquire command, using a plug-in module provided with a *video frame grabber,* a hardware-software combination designed to acquire and enhance the video images. The image quality that can be achieved with relatively inexpensive digital cameras or with video is not nearly as good as with film. But if an image is to be extensively manipulated for a photo-illustration, the convenience of having the "photo" instantly available may outweigh the quality difference.

For imitating traditional art media such as the paintbrush, pencil, airbrush, or charcoal, a **pressure-sensitive tablet** with stylus has a more familiar feel than a mouse and also provides much better control. Photoshop's painting tools (see Chapter 6) are "wired" to take advantage of pressure sensitivity.

STORAGE AND TRANSPORT OF FILES

With Photoshop, of course, you can never have enough RAM; as soon as you get more, you need *even more.* But even if you have enough RAM so you rarely need to use virtual memory, a large-capacity hard disk will be important. First of all, Photoshop requires that you have scratch disk space available, as described in "Virtual Memory" earlier in this chapter. And second, you'll need space to store the files you work with. For archiving (long-term storage of files you don't expect to need to work on often), digital audio tape (DAT) backup provides a solution that's relatively compact and inexpensive. But tape usually can't be used as a working storage medium; files have to be copied from tape to disk to be loaded into Photoshop.

Bernoulli systems and SyQuest removable-cartridge disks in several sizes have become standards for transporting files that are too large — as many Photoshop files are — to fit on a floppy disk. As magneto-optical (MO) read-write drives and desktop CD-ROM writers become less expensive, they're likely to become even more popular than tape or removable hard disks for transport and storage.

The Photoshop 3.0 file format is the only one that can save more than one layer. All other formats require that the file be flattened to a single layer. Photoshop 3.0 format can save up to 24 channels altogether, not including channel 0 (the main composite channel in a color file), but including all the individual color channels, and the alpha channels. A TIFF file can also retain all the alpha channels. (Channels and layers are covered in more detail in Chapter 2.)

You may want to save a very large file in a format you can use later with the File, Quick Edit command. Quick Edit lets you choose a part of the file to open for editing, which requires less RAM than opening the whole image. Quick Edit can open files saved in Photoshop 2.0, Scitex CT, and uncompressed TIFF formats, and the files can include alpha channels.

File, Acquire, Quick Edit lets you open part of any file saved in uncompressed TIFF or Scitex CT format. After you've worked on the part, choose File, Export, Quick Edit Save to return it to exactly the same place in the larger file. The modifiable Grid makes it possible to open and replace non-overlapping sections of an illustration, one by one, so you can modify a large image with much less RAM than you would need to work with the whole image at once.

FILE FORMATS

Photoshop 3 can save images in a broad range of file formats. Here are some tips for saving files, depending on what you want to do with them:

For the most flexibility in what you can do with the file in the future, save in Photoshop 3.0 format. Files saved in this format retain all the layers (the number of layers you can create is limited only by your computer's RAM) and alpha channels (you can have up to 25 channels, including both color channels and alpha channels).

For images that will be opened in Photoshop 2.5 or that will be used in Adobe Premiere or other programs that can accept Photoshop 2.5 files but not Photoshop 3 files, save in Photoshop 3.0 format. By default the Photoshop 3.0 format includes a flattened copy that can be opened in Photoshop 2.5, with all of the layers merged into one and with only the first 16 channels available to the image (see "Slimming 3.0 Files" on page 28).

For files you can use with Adobe Illustrator, save in EPS format if you want to be able to print the Photoshop artwork as part of the Illustrator file, or save in PICT File format if you want to use the art as a nonprinting template (see Chapter 8 for more about using Photoshop with Illustrator).

For files you can use with FreeHand, save in TIFF format.

To place images on pages in PageMaker or QuarkXPress for color separation to make film for printing, it's a good idea to check with your imagesetting service bureau to see how they suggest saving and placing the Photoshop files. But here are some general tips:

- **Both PageMaker and QuarkXPress can accept images in Bitmap, Grayscale, Duotone, RGB Color and CMYK Color modes,** although not all modes can be handled in all file formats, as described below. (Color modes, specified in the Mode menu, are described in "Color in Photoshop" later in this chapter.)

- **If you want to produce color separations directly from PageMaker** without using a separation utility program, save color Photoshop files in CMYK mode (see "Converting Color" later in this chapter) before you save in TIFF format.

- **If your PageMaker files will be separated with a utility such as Adobe PrePrint or Adobe TrapWise,** you can save color images as TIFFs in RGB mode and rely on the separation software to do the conversion to CMYK (the Photoshop files are smaller this way, and you don't have to figure out the appropriate Separation Setup settings). That's the way this book was done, because we found that the TrapWise separation algorithms worked very well, the process entailed less work for us, and the

files took up less disk space than if we had converted them to CMYK.

- PageMaker will accept TIFF files stored with LZW compression, but the compression can sometimes cause problems in color separation, as do files that have alpha channels, so **save TIFFs without LZW compression and without alpha channels before putting them into PageMaker pages.**

- **If you need to silhouette an image when you place it in PageMaker,** you'll have to use an EPS format because that's the only way the clipping path that makes the silhouette can be incorporated in the file.

- **For images to be placed in QuarkXPress,** save files in Bitmap, Grayscale, Duotone, or CMYK mode in EPS format. TIFFs will often print faster on a laser printer, and they work with QuarkXPress sometimes, but there can be some buggy interactions when TIFF is used with XPress.

- **To control the color separation of the image from within Photoshop** (File, Preferences, Separation Setup) before placing it in QuarkXPress, choose the DCS option for an EPS save. The DCS format is bulkier but it gives you direct control of the color separation.

To save a Bitmap image whose white parts will be clear instead of opaque white when you place it in an application such as Illustrator, PageMaker, or QuarkXPress, save in EPS format, choosing the Transparent Whites option.

To save a Duotone file for placement in an application such as Illustrator, PageMaker, or QuarkXPress, save in EPS format.

For images to be used for on-screen presentations, save in PICT File format, remembering to set Resolution (in the Image Size dialog box) to 72 dpi to match the screen. PICT can accommodate one alpha channel, which many programs can interpret as a mask. PICT files are quite compact. ("To compress a finished image" on page 29 tells about JPEG, a way of compressing files to a much greater degree than PICT.)

Adobe Premiere can save QuickTime movies in Filmstrip format, which can be opened in Photoshop. **To resave Premiere files** after you've opened and worked on them in Photoshop, use the Filmstrip format so they can be brought back into Premiere.

To save files to be opened in paint programs on DOS- or Windows-based computers, the BMP, PCX, Amiga IFF, TIFF, and TGA (Targa) formats work in many instances. Before choosing a file format, check to see what format(s) will work with a particular hardware-software-operating system combination.

In scans and screen displays, images are made up of pixels. The pixels are all the same size but vary in color, with over 16 million color possibilities.

Many printed images are composed of overlaid screen patterns of halftone dots. These dots vary in size, but the number of lines of halftone dots per inch remains constant and the number of ink colors is often limited to four: cyan, magenta, yellow, and black. The spectrum of printed colors results from the visual "mix" of the dots of color.

Stochastic screening is another way of using a visual mix to print color. The "cells" of the stochastic screen pattern, instead of containing halftone dots that vary in size, contain very tiny dots, all the same size, that are in randomized patterns. The number of tiny dots in a region is what makes the color more intense (many dots) or less intense (few dots). Because the tiny dots within a "cell" are not clumped together to make larger dots, no halftone pattern is generated. Since there is no visual interference from a screen pattern, more image detail can usually be seen than in an image printed with halftone screening.

To pass files to other computer systems such as Scitex, Amiga, or Pixar, use the special format provided for that system. Pixar files can include an alpha channel, which can be used as a mask.

To upload an image to CompuServe, use Indexed Color (use the System palette for consistency; see page 17), Grayscale, or Bitmap mode, and save in CompuServe GIF (graphic interface format).

To compress a finished image — in order to send it by modem or fit in on a floppy disk for transport, for instance — you can use the JPEG format (Save As, JPEG). Photoshop's own JPEG plug-in provides four different levels of compression, with the most compressed (smallest file size, called Low Image Quality) also showing the most image degradation. In compressing a file, the JPEG routines start by eliminating detail data that's likely to be lost in the printing process anyway. So compression at the Maximum Image Quality level (least compressed) usually produces acceptable results for emergency archiving or transmitting of CMYK images that will eventually go to print. The degree of compression that JPEG provides depends on the compression level and the content of the image; a typical compressed size for a 900K image might be 59K for the Low setting and 169K for the Maximum setting.

It's now possible in some cases to place images in JPEG format into page layouts for separation and printing. But the standard procedure is still to open JPEGged files in Photoshop and resave them in an appropriate format, such as TIFF or EPS, before you place them in a page. Don't recompress an image that has been stored in JPEG format and then opened; repeated compression degrades the image.

OUTPUT: PROOFING AND PRINTING

Like other desktop color files, Photoshop images can be printed on inkjet, thermal transfer, or dye sublimation printers, color photocopiers that can accept digital input, or film recorders (as negatives or positive transparencies). Typically, inkjet, thermal transfer, or dye sublimation printing is used to show generally how the image and the color will look, or to achieve a particular kind of art print quality. Photoshop files can also be produced as color-separated film for making plates for offset printing, using imagesetters or high-end color-separation systems such as Linotype-Hell or Scitex systems. And they can be output direct-to-plate (which bypasses film), or even direct-to-press, which bypasses both film and plates. Film recorders offer the options traditionally available for color transparencies.

When color separations for offset printing are made by the traditional halftone screening method, the *contract proof,* which a printer and client agree is the color standard to be matched on the printing press, is usually a laminate made from the film that will be used to make the printing plates. However, as stochastic screening

With stochastic screening it's possible to get good prints from smaller file sizes than with halftone screening. Because there's no halftone dot pattern with stochastic to interfere with the edges and detail in the image, these smaller files can produce sharper images.

But there are also some things to watch out for:

- Without extra dot gain compensation, images printed with stochastic screens tend to be darker overall and show higher contrast. This is because the dots used for stochastic screening are extremely tiny — very much smaller than halftone dots — so dot gain can be much more significant. The "spread" of the dot can be a much bigger fraction of the original dot size than it is for the larger halftone dots, and so the change in color due to dot gain is more drastic than for halftone printing.

- The tiny size of the dots in stochastic screening also means that it's much harder for press operators to make the kinds of adjustments they typically use to correct color during a print run.

- Since dot gain can be so important, and since an ordinary laminate proof doesn't accurately show dot gain, a special, alternative proofing method may be needed.

If you plan to use stochastic screening, be sure to get advice from both your printer and your service bureau. The service bureau should have an imagesetter equipped with a *RIP* (raster image processor) that uses stochastic screens, such as Adobe Brilliant Screens, Agfa's Crystal Raster technology, or Linotype-Hell's Diamond Screening. Have the service bureau run a test to separated film, and then ask the printer to check the film to make sure it will work for printing.

(see "Using Stochastic Screening" at the left), direct-to-plate, and direct-to-press printing technologies replace halftone film for some printing jobs, the "soft" proof (one that isn't made from the printing film) becomes more important.

RESOLUTION, PIXEL DEPTH, AND FILE SIZE

Resolution is the term used to describe the amount of data, or color information, in a scan, a stored image file, a screen display, or a printed image. Typically, the more data, the more you can enlarge the image before it starts to look pixelated and loses detail.

Resolution is sometimes expressed as the number of dots, pixels, or ink spots per unit of measure (inch, centimeter, or pica, for example). Or resolution may be stated as pixel dimensions — 640 x 480 pixels, for instance — giving a more direct report of how much data is present, independent of the measured size of the image.

The terminology used to discuss resolution is a hodgepodge of words from printing, computer graphics, and prepress services. Sometimes a single term is used for two or more different concepts. And a single concept may have several different names. So when you hear someone use the term "print resolution," "image resolution," "output resolution," or "printer resolution," for instance, you'll need to make sure you understand how the term is being used.

For consistency and to reduce confusion, this book uses resolution terminology the same way it's used in the *Adobe Photoshop 3.0 User Guide*. Our discussion of resolution starts with *screen frequency* because that's the piece of information you need to know first, in order to figure out how much information to collect in a scan or to build into an image file in order to get the best printed image at the size you want. If you can help it, you don't want to find yourself in the opposite position: faced with a finished file and wondering how big you'll be able to print it without losing image detail and quality.

Screen frequency refers to the resolution of halftone screens, which are the patterns of ink dots used for printing most of the pages that come off the presses today. Screen frequency is expressed in terms of how many rows of halftone dots there are per linear inch, called *lines per inch* (lpi). The higher the lpi the less obvious the halftone dot pattern and therefore the more image detail you can see in the print.

In a printed piece, the screen frequency (lpi) is the same for all the colors in the image, whether they're intense or pale. The main characteristic that changes the intensity of the color is the *halftone dot size*. A pale yellow, for example, is printed with small dots of yellow ink and perhaps no dots of cyan, magenta, or black, the other three process printing colors. The bare paper shows through between the dots. An intense red, on the other hand, might be printed with magenta and yellow dots as large as the screen density allows. Screen frequency, along with height and width of the printed image, deter-

Resolution measurement is often given "per inch" or "per centimeter." This is a *linear* measure. For instance, "72 dpi" means that the length spanned by 72 dots is 1 inch; stated another way, if you measure a 1-inch length, there would be 72 dots along it. Likewise "150 lpi" means that the length spanned by 150 halftone dots is 1 inch, or that if you measured an inch, there would be 150 halftone cells along it.

SIZING FOR COLUMNS

If you're sizing images for a publication whose column width you know, choose File, Preferences, Units and enter the column and gutter widths. Then when you size an image in the Image Size dialog box, you can choose "columns" as the unit of Width and set the number of columns wide that you want the image to be. If you specify more than one column, the calculation takes the gutter measure into account.

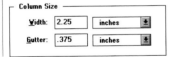

mines how much information is *needed* to print the image without its showing pixels.

Image resolution — set in the Resolution field of the New Size section of Photoshop's Image Size dialog box — is expressed as dots per inch (dpi). Image resolution, along with image height and width (which should be the same as the final printed dimensions you want), determines how much information is stored in the file. The more stored information, the more detail the print can show.

- **The image resolution you need for an image that will be printed** depends on the screen frequency (see "Getting Enough Information" on page 32).

- **The image resolution you need for an image that will be displayed on-screen** (in a multimedia presentation, for example) is typically 72 dpi, which is the standard monitor resolution. Or it may be expressed as pixel dimensions — 640 x 480 for instance.

Instead of being expressed as dpi or pixel dimensions, image resolution is sometimes expressed as file size (in K or MB). Both pixel dimensions and file size indicate how much information (or, potentially, how much image detail) is stored in the file.

Scan resolution is usually expressed as the number of *samples per inch, pixels per inch* (ppi), or sometimes *dots per inch* (dpi) recorded by the scanner. Scan resolution, along with the height of the scanned area and its width, determines how much information is *collected* for the image file. The more information the scan collects, the more image detail is recorded. With more image detail, the image that you develop from the scan can be printed at a higher screen frequency or at a larger size. Like image resolution, scan resolution is sometimes expressed as file size or as pixel dimensions.

Display resolution — or monitor resolution — is determined only by the monitor itself and the software that runs it. Some monitors have more than one setting and can display at a higher resolution than the standard 72 dpi. In general, **the size that an image appears on-screen shouldn't be used as a predictor of the size it will be when it's printed.** When you view a Photoshop image at 1:1 magnification (shown in the title bar of the image), every pixel in the image is represented by a pixel on-screen. So you're seeing it *not at the final printed size,* but at the monitor's display resolution.

Pixel depth is the other factor — besides the dimensions (length and width) and the resolution (number of pixels per inch) — that affects the amount of information stored in an image. Pixel depth is the amount of computer data required to store the color information for each pixel in the image.

There may be some instances when you *want* the individual square pixels to be obvious in your final printed image, providing a kind of computer-age electronic grain. If you want the square pixels to show, you need only decide how big you want them to be — 72 to the inch or 50 to the inch, for instance — set your scan or file resolution at that number, and set its dimensions (height and width) at the final size you want the image to be.

You may also want to set your Interpolation method to Nearest Neighbor (choose File, Preferences, General). That way, Photoshop won't try to hide the "jaggies" when you scale or rotate an image. Just be sure to remember to set Interpolation back to Bicubic when you've finished your "computer look" project.

The terms 4K and 8K are often used to describe scans made from 35 mm and larger transparencies. These terms mean that about 4000 or about 8000 samples are taken by the scanner across the long dimension of the image. For a 35 mm slide, a 4K scan takes about 4000 samples across the 35 mm width of the slide. So the scanned image is about 4000 pixels wide, enough to support enlargement to about 10 inches if you're printing at a screen frequency of 200 lpi. (See "Getting Enough Information on page 32 for more about the relationship of image resolution to screen frequency.) The calculation works this way:

At a 2:1 ratio of image resolution to screen frequency, you need 400 pixels per inch to print at 200 lpi.

approx. 4000 pixels ÷ 400 pixels per inch = approx. 10 inches

- A **grayscale** image includes only brightness data; each pixel requires 8 *bits* (also called 1 *byte*) to store this brightness information.
- A typical **color scanner** picks up 8 bits of brightness information for each of the three colors of light in the additive color model — red, green, and blue. So **a color scan** requires 8 x 3 = 24 bits of information per pixel.

Getting Enough Information

When you're trying to decide on a resolution for scanning or creating an image, the goal is to gather (or create) enough image information to print the image successfully — keeping the color transitions smooth and the details sharp. But there's also a pressure to keep the file size as small as possible: The bigger the file, the longer it takes to open, work on, save, and print; and the more RAM, scratch disk, and storage space it needs. So **to determine the appropriate resolution, the first thing you need to know is how much information will be required for printing,** and that depends on the printed size of the image and the screen frequency.

For printing with halftone screens, the output device (printer or imagesetter, for instance) needs at least 1 pixel of color information to figure out what size to make each halftone dot. (Usually 1.5 to 2 pixels are used, as described below.) The output device can't leave a blank spot if it runs short of information. Instead, it invents the information it needs to fill the blanks. Even if the device is pretty sophisticated in the way it goes about making up the information — averaging it from surrounding dots, for example — this *interpolated* color won't be as sharp and smooth as if the color information had been stored in the image file.

If your scan doesn't collect enough image information (or you create your artwork file too small), Photoshop's Image Size command can interpolate to increase the file size to the amount needed for printing. This may produce a better image than having the output device do the interpolation. But still, **an interpolated image won't look as good as if you had collected (or painted) the right amount of information in the first place.** So it's important to know before you scan (or set up a new file) how much information your printing process will need from your image file.

To get consistently good results for printing with halftone screens, an image file should provide the output device with *more than one dot* of information for each printed dot. For halftone printing, **a good ratio of image resolution (pixels per inch) to screen frequency (lines per inch) typically falls within the range of 1.5:1 to 2:1.** If the ratio is under 1.5:1, image quality may go down noticeably. Over 2:1, the extra data is essentially wasted — it takes up space in the file but doesn't add significantly to the quality of the print.

Some typical screen frequencies for printing color images are 85 lines per inch (lpi) for newspapers, 133 or 150 lpi for magazines and books, and 175 or 200 or more lpi for fine art reproduction. So, for instance, if your halftone screen frequency for printing will be 150 lpi, you'll need about 225 to 300 dots per inch in your image; the higher end of this range is needed for images with straight lines or abrupt color transitions.

SETTING UP A SCAN

A scan is a data collection, and the goal in scanning is to collect enough data to print a great-looking image. The scan resolution (in dpi) and the dimensions of the scanned file (in inches or cm, for example) can vary, as long as enough information is collected.

To figure out the scan resolution you need to specify, ideally you'll start with the size and resolution you want for the printed piece. You can then get to the scan resolution by a series of calculations, or you can let Photoshop automate the calculations for you:

1 Setting pixel depth. One of the things that will affect the amount of information collected is pixel depth, determined by the color mode used for the scan. Open a new file (File, New). This file will not be used to make an image, only to calculate scan resolution. The first step is to set the mode (see figure A at the left):

- For both color and grayscale images, the mode used for scanning should be RGB Color; grayscale images typically turn out better if you collect the color information in the scan and then convert to Grayscale in Photoshop.

- Use Grayscale mode for scanning black-and-white line art; line art usually turns out better (with smoother, more consistent lines) if it's scanned in grayscale mode and then perfected with Image, Adjust, Levels. ("Coloring Line Art" on page 185 demonstrates this method.)

2 Setting the dimensions. In the New dialog box you can also set the dimensions (Height and Width in inches, cm, or some other unit of measure) of the final printed image (refer to figure A).

3 Factoring in the screen frequency. The amount of scan data you need ultimately depends on the screen frequency to be used for printing. So now you'll account for the halftone screen. Choose Image, Image Size. In the Image Size dialog box, make sure the File Size box is *not checked*, so you can freely adjust the Resolution. The Height and Width have been set by your entry in the New dialog box in step 1. *Make sure the dimensions are set to some unit other than pixels.* To get the Resolution setting, click the Auto button. In the Auto Resolution dialog box set the Screen (halftone screen frequency) you and your printer agree on. Then choose

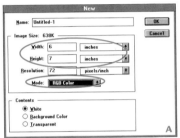

Steps 1 and 2 *To figure out how big to make a scan file, start by opening a dummy file in Photoshop, setting the dimensions and color mode. You don't have to worry about setting the Resolution at this point.*

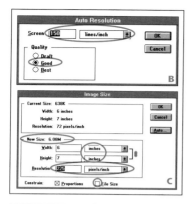

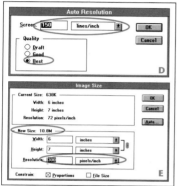

Steps 3 and 4 *Open the Image Size dialog box, set the dimensions to units other than pixels, and click Auto. In the Auto Resolution box enter the halftone screen frequency that will be used to print, and choose either Good (which uses a 1.5:1 ratio) or Best (which uses 2:1) (B). Then click OK to return to the Image Size box (C). The Resolution value is set automatically, based on your entries in Auto Resolution. The New Size value tells how large (in K or MB) the scan file will have to be. Either a larger Screen value or a higher Quality setting (D) will increase the Resolution, which increases the New Size (E).*

Good (1.5 times the screen value, for natural, organic images) or Best (2 times the screen, for images with hard-edged elements). Click OK.

4 Reading the file size. Back in the Image Size dialog box, note the New Size number (write it down). This is the file size (in K or MB), in other words, the amount of data the scanner will need to gather to support the size and halftone screen you've chosen.

You now know the dimensions, resolution, and resulting file size that you need. The relationship between the image resolution you've just calculated and the input resolution you'll need to set in the scanner software depends on the relationship between the size of the original you're scanning and the size of the final printed piece.

5 Sizing the scan. Put your original in the scanner. If your scanner has a plug-in module for Photoshop, activate the scanner by choosing it from the File, Acquire submenu. Use the scanner's Preview function to show you the image you'll be scanning, and use its cropping tool to select the area to scan. Be sure you *crop to an area with the same proportions*, if not exactly the same dimensions, *as the Width and Height you set in the Image Size* dialog box. That is, if the final printed size will be 6 x 7 inches, the scan crop should have the same proportions: for instance, 3 x 3.5 inches, or 12 x 14 cm.

Now find the place in the scanner interface that tells what the file size will be (in K or MB) for the scan you've set up. If this value is different than the New Size value you wrote down from the Image Size dialog box, and if the scanner allows you to enter a file size value, enter that New Size number. But if the scanner won't let you enter a file size value (most won't), adjust the scanner's Scale setting until the file size is close to that New Size value: If the scan file size is too small, increase the Scale factor above 100% until the file size is right. On the other hand, if the scan file size is larger than you need, you can reduce the Scale below 100% to save on the file size. (If your scanner doesn't have a scale option, change the Resolution of the scan until the file size matches the New Size.)

Other circumstances. You may not always know in advance exactly how big to make your scan. Here are some approaches you can take if you don't have all the info you need for steps 1 through 5:

- **If you don't know the screen frequency for printing,** guess high. Enter the Screen value in step 3 as 150 lpi or higher.

- **If you don't know the final printed dimensions of the image,** go for the "optimal scan": Scan the image at its full original size either at the Resolution in the Image Size box or the scanner's default, whichever is larger. If this would make the file

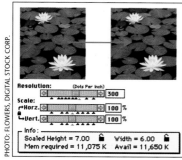

Resolution: (Dots Per Inch) 300
Scale: Horz. 100 % Vert. 100 %
Info: Scaled Height = 7.00 Width = 6.00
Mem required = 11,075 K Avail = 11,650 K

Step 5A *If the original is the same size as the printed image will be, then setting the scan resolution the same as the Resolution in the Image Size dialog box and setting the Scale factor at 100% should produce a file the same size (in MB or K) as that shown as New Size in the Image Size dialog box.*

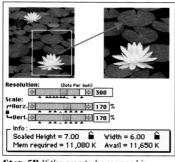

Resolution: (Dots Per Inch) 300
Scale: Horz. 170 % Vert. 170 %
Info: Scaled Height = 7.00 Width = 6.00
Mem required = 11,080 K Avail = 11,650 K

Step 5B *If the area to be scanned is smaller than the printed image will be (either because the original itself is smaller or because only part of the original will be used) and the scan resolution is the same as the Resolution in the Image Size dialog box, increase the Scale factor until the file size goes up to about the same as that shown as New Size in the Image Size dialog box.*

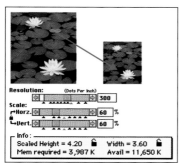

Resolution: (Dots Per Inch) 300
Scale: Horz. 60 % Vert. 60 %
Info: Scaled Height = 4.20 Width = 3.60
Mem required = 3,987 K Avail = 11,650 K

Step 5C *If your original is larger than your printed image will be, set the scan resolution the same as the Resolution in the Image Size dialog box and decrease the Scale factor until the file size comes down to the New Size value from the Image Size box.*

too big to work with, scale it down to the biggest file size you can manage.

- **If the image you're scanning will be only a small part of a composite,** you can either: Estimate the final printed size of that element and use those dimensions in the New dialog box in step 1. Or, if you really don't know how big you want to use the element, scan it at its full original size at the Resolution in the Image Size box or the scanner's default (as above). Place the scanned element on its own layer in your composite file. If you need to size it up or down, use Image, Effects, Scale. (If you need to scale down a large element, do it before you paint or otherwise change the layer or merge it, because these processes trim off whatever extends beyond the Height and Width of the image.)

RESAMPLING IN PHOTOSHOP

Regardless of how well you plan there are likely to be times when you need to *resample* — either resample down or resample up — in Photoshop. *Resampling down* means decreasing the file size. You might do it because you have more information than you need for printing and you want to reduce the bulk of the file. *Resampling up* is increasing the file size. You might do this in order to have enough information to reproduce the image at the size and screen frequency or display resolution you want. To resample, use the Image Size dialog box. But before you do, make sure the Interpolation method is set to give you the best results: Choose File, Preferences, General and ensure the Interpolation method is set to Bicubic. In the Image Size box, make sure the Width and Height are set to units other than pixels. Make sure the Proportions box is checked and the File Size box is unchecked. Then:

- **To change the image dimensions,** enter a new value in the Height or Width field. The other dimension will change automatically and so will the file size. The Resolution will stay the same.

- **To change the image resolution,** set Height and Width units to anything but pixels. Then enter a new value in the Resolution field. The dimensions will stay the same but file size will grow. *Wow!*

THE SHARPER IMAGE

Increasing the file size (*resampling up*) "invents" the new pixels that make the file bigger; the colors of these pixels are computed from the old ones, which is likely to make the larger image look a little fuzzy. The Image, Effects commands (Scale, Skew, Distort, and Perspective) and Image, Rotate also cause resampling. After any of these operations, run Unsharp Mask (see Chapter 5) to sharpen up the image.

To put together the opening scene for the movie *The Mask*, **Eric Chauvin** of Industrial Light & Magic started with a shot of the Pacific coastline above Malibu (shown at the right) and concept art by Doug Chang. The photo dictated the lighting; taken on a gray, overcast day, it had no strong shadows. Chauvin shot photos of Individual buildings in San Francisco, in one case crawling out a window onto a fire escape and from there onto the roof to get the angle he wanted for a photo. He composited the building photos with the beach scene, and then built and rendered the other buildings he needed in a 3D program, adding them to the composite. "It was difficult to figure out the vanishing points," says Chauvin. "There was a lot of guesswork involved in making things look correct." Chauvin's approach to Photoshop composites is to use a big, fast system; bring the individual elements into separate layers in one file; do all the color correction and other editing in place; and "save a billion copies" as the image develops so he can go back to previous stages if the client requests a change. When he had finished painting the dismal scene, the only thing moving in the sequence was the water. To help establish scale and add a bit more life, Chauvin animated 3D cars on the overpass (itself a 3D model), added smoke coming out of the smokestacks, and put small birds in the sky (squiggly lines moved along a "flight path").

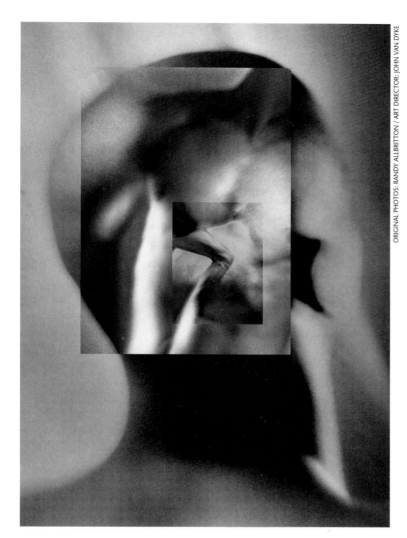

ORIGINAL PHOTOS: RANDY ALLBRITTON / ART DIRECTOR: JOHN VAN DYKE

In developing the *cover image* for the annual report of ICOS, a biotech company, **Jeff McCord** faced the challenge of combining photos from the inside of the report so that they would read as one image. Noting the beautiful dark-to-light shadow areas in the images, he layered three grayscale photos — knee, chest, and head. Lowering the opacity of the upper photos, he allowed shadow areas from the images underneath to start showing through; he split the arrowheads in the composite controls (choose Layer Options from the pop-out menu in the Layers palette and hold down the Alt key as you move the sliders) to make the images float in and out of each other.

To make *Glasses*, **Katrin Eismann** started by placing two glasses at one end of the bed of a desktop flatbed scanner and then moved them as the scan was in progress. The original scan is shown below (small). Then she used Image, Adjust, Levels, moving the Input black point slider inward to intensify the colors. She selected the white background (choose Select, Color Range), adding the greenish areas at the bottom of the image (use the "+" eyedropper to add to the selected colors). She softened the edge of the selection (adjust the Fuzziness slider in the Color Range dialog box) and then filled the selected area with black (Alt-Backspace, with black as the foreground color).

Eric Reinfeld created *Debutante Wilding*, a three-color tinted photo, as one of a series of fashion illustrations for New York's *Paper* magazine. He began with a CMYK scan of a black-and-white photo. Working in the main channel (#0), he selected all and copied. Then he activated the Black channel (#4) and pasted the copied image into the channel. Next he activated each of the other three channels — Cyan, Magenta, and Yellow — in turn and filled them with white. Reinfeld viewed all the channels together as he modified one at a time. He left the Cyan channel white, since no cyan ink would be used to print the image. In the Magenta channel he applied black paint with soft brush strokes at a low Opacity setting (about 10 to 15%) to some parts of the skirt. He filled the Yellow channel with black at a low opacity and then used the paintbrush and white paint to erase the tint in the area of the leather jacket; he painted with black, again at a low Opacity, onto the skirt and other areas of the image. In the Black channel, he used the dodge and burn tools to lighten and darken folds in the skirt and other parts of the image. In all channels Reinfeld kept his painting light in order to accommodate the dot gain that would occur when the images were printed on *Paper's* relatively soft stock.

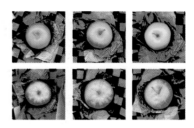

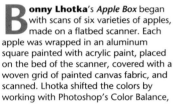

Bonny **Lhotka**'s *Apple Box* began with scans of six varieties of apples, made on a flatbed scanner. Each apple was wrapped in an aluminum square painted with acrylic paint, placed on the bed of the scanner, covered with a woven grid of painted canvas fabric, and scanned. Lhotka shifted the colors by working with Photoshop's Color Balance, Brightness, and Contrast controls. Dark areas were selected with the magic wand and replaced with a true black. Brushes and the smudge tool were used to add finishing touches. The six files were printed on a Hewlett Packard XL300 desktop color printer on Rives Heavyweight printmaking paper that had been "antiqued" for that purpose: The paper was wetted, crumpled, ironed, flattened in an etching press and coated with iridescent gold mica powder. The images were cut and glued to the sides of nine wooden blocks so the blocks could be turned to reveal all six images, with the center being a core on all sides. Shown here are photos of the piece assembled as 2 x 2-inch blocks. The final full-scale version is 90 x 90 x 30 inches.

To create *Sunbathers*, **Bonny Lhotka** began by scanning cut flowers on a flatbed scanner. To block out extraneous light without squashing the flowers, she covered them with a black cloth instead of closing the scanner lid. In Photoshop she selected part of the black background with the magic wand tool and replaced it with a yellow-to-blue Clockwise Radial gradient fill. She added Noise to give the image a grainy texture.

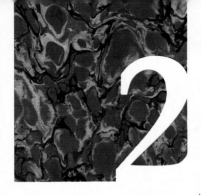

SELECTIONS, MASKS, LAYERS, AND CHANNELS

PHOTOSHOP PERFORMS MUCH OF ITS MAGIC by working on *selections*. A selection is an area of an image that you isolate so you can copy it, paint it, move it, or make any changes that you want to apply only there. To work effectively with Photoshop, you need to know about selections: how to make them, how to store them, how to load them into an image, and how to combine them. But with all the ways you can make and store selections, *the most important selection tool of all is your brain.* You can save a lot of time and effort by knowing how the selection tools and operations work, as well as Photoshop's other functions, and by thinking about what part of your image you want to change and exactly what it is you want to accomplish.

Selections are ephemeral. When you make a selection, a flashing boundary (sometimes referred to as "marching ants"), lets you see what part of the image is selected. But the selection border disappears if you click outside it with a selection tool or press Ctrl-D or choose Select, None. Unless you first turn it into a Quick Mask, an alpha channel, a pen path, or a layer of its own, the selection is gone when you deselect it.

MAKING SELECTIONS

Selections can be made with choices from the Select menu, with selection tools, or with the pen tool from the Paths palette. In general, selections that are made *procedurally* — that is, by using information like color or brightness that's intrinsic to the image — rather than by drawing a selection border by hand, can be faster and more effective.

The tool or command that works best for making a selection depends on what you want to select. Each of the tools and selection commands has its own advantages and disadvantages. To decide which to use, you need to analyze the area you want to select — Is it organic or geometric? Is it fairly uniform in color? — and choose the tool, command, or combination of techniques that will do the job.

SELECTING BY SHAPE

The marquee tools, the lasso, and the pen are the tools to use if you need to select something by shape.

To "frame" a selection, use one of the marquee tools: the rectangular marquee or the ellipse. The marquee tools offer a variety of options for selecting.

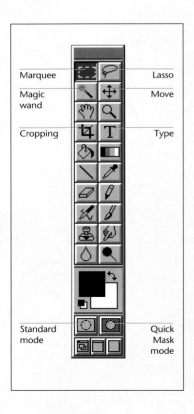

Marquee | Lasso
Magic wand | Move
Cropping | Type
Standard mode | Quick Mask mode

continued on page 42

For a vignette effect with a hard or soft (feathered) border, use the rectangular or elliptical marquee.

To select an area that has a complex outline, especially if it shares colors with its surroundings so that it's hard to select by color, use the lasso tool. Turn on antialiasing and hold down the Alt key so you can either click from point to point to operate the tool in "rubber band" mode or drag it freehand-style. The Alt key also prevents losing the selection border if you accidentally let go of the mouse button.

ANTIALIASING A SELECTION

Antialiasing smooths a selection's edge by adding partially transparent pixels to fill in "stairsteps" in the selection border. When the antialiased selection is pasted into its new surroundings, these partly clear pixels pick up color from the ones they're pasted on top of, so they end up being a blend of the colors on the two sides of the selection border. Of the selection tools in the toolbox, the elliptical marquee is antialiased automatically; the rectangular marquee, with its straight-sided selections, doesn't need antialiasing; and the lasso and magic wand can be antialiased by choosing this feature in the tool's Options palette.

Antialiasing (right) smooths the appearance of edges.

• The default mode for the marquee tools is to start the selection from the edge. But many times you have better control of exactly what you select if you draw the selection from the center out. **To start a selection at its center,** press and hold the Alt key at any time during the selection process. If the selection frame turns out to be the right size but it still doesn't encompass exactly what you want, you can hold down the Ctrl and Alt keys and drag to move the selection border itself into place, without moving any of the pixels inside it.

• **To select a square or circular area,** constrain the rectangular or elliptical marquee by holding down the Shift key as you drag.

• **To make a selection of a particular height-to-width ratio,** double-click on either of the marquee tools to open the Marquee Options palette, choose Constrained Aspect Ratio for the Style, and set a particular height-to-width ratio. Now the marquee will make selections of those proportions.

• **To make a selection of a specific size,** choose Fixed Size for Style in the Marquee Options palette and specify the Width and Height in pixels. If you want to make a selection of a specific measurement in inches or centimeters, multiply the dimension you want by the resolution of your image in pixels per inch or pixels per centimeter: for instance, 4 inches x 225 pixels per inch = 900 pixels. (You can find the resolution quickly by holding down the Alt key and pressing on the numbers in the lower left corner of the image window.)

To select a multicolored area with a complex boundary, use the lasso tool with the Alt key held down. Using the Alt key, you can either click from point to point to draw the selection border in straight-line segments or drag the lasso freeform to draw a complex, irregular border.

FEATHERING A SELECTION

Feathering is a way of softening the edges of a selection so it blends into the surrounding image. This kind of edge can be useful for making a "seamless" montage when part of an image is selected, modified, and then released back into its original unmodified surroundings. Feathering extends the selection outward but at less than full opacity so that some of the surrounding image is included. At the same time the opacity of the image is also reduced for a distance inside the selection border. The Feather Radius determines how far into and outside the selection border this transition extends.

• **To feather a lasso or marquee selection as you make it,** double-click the tool in the toolbox to open its Options palette so you can enter a Feather setting. Then make the selection.

• If you forget to set the Feather ahead of time, or if the selection method you used didn't have a Feather option, **you can feather the selection after you've made it** (but before you lift it out of its surroundings): With the selection active choose Select, Feather and set the Feather Radius.

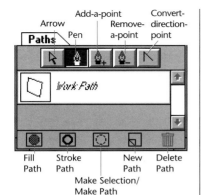

Arrow — Pen — Add-a-point, Remove-a-point — Convert-direction-point

Mark Path

Fill Path — Stroke Path — New Path — Delete Path

Make Selection/Make Path

Clicking to make corner points

Dragging to make smooth points

Closing a path

Adding a point

Deleting a point

Changing the type of point

THE PEN OR THE LASSO?

One of the advantages the pen tool has over using the lasso is that you can move the anchor points and manipulate their handles to adjust the shape of a selection border. This can be quite a bit easier than making lots of little additions to or subtractions from a lasso selection.

- **Using the Alt key safeguards against accidentally dropping or closing a selection** if you inadvertently release the mouse button before you've finished selecting.
- **Clicking a series of short line segments to define a smooth curve** is often easier and more accurate than trying to trace the edge by dragging the lasso.

USING THE PEN TOOL

Unlike Photoshop's other tools that work well for selecting by shape, the pen tool has a palette of its own, opened simply by pressing the "T" key or by choosing Window, Palettes, Show Paths. The Paths palette includes everything necessary to draw and edit a smoothly curving path (called a Bezier curve), to name it and save it so it can be recalled later, to fill it, stroke it, turn it into a selection, combine it with an existing selection, or turn a selection into a path. The filling, stroking, and selecting functions of the pen tool are found in the icons at the bottom of the palette, along with icons for creating a new path and removing a path. Everything you can do on the palette itself you can also do by choosing from its pop-out menu; in addition, the menu lets you designate a clipping path for silhouetting an image to be exported for use in a page layout, for example.

The shape of the Bezier curve drawn by the pen tool is controlled by the positions of anchor points and direction lines, or "handles," which direct the curve as it comes out of the anchor points. The *Adobe Photoshop User Guide* explains how to work the pen tool, but here are some quick tips for using it:

Drawing a path (either a line or a closed shape) with the pen tool is done by placing a series of points:

- **To place a corner point** (without handles), click with the pen. The tool creates a "corner," a point where the line can change direction abruptly, without a curve. Placing two corner points one after another draws a straight line.
- **To create a smooth (curve) point and position its control handles,** click and drag with the pen tool.
- **To constrain the position of the next corner or smooth point** to any 45- or 90-degree angle, hold down the Shift key as you place the point.
- **To close a path,** move the pen icon close to the starting point; when you see a little circle to the right of the pen icon, click.

To reshape a path after it's drawn, you can:

- **Move a point:** Drag it with the arrow tool (the closed arrow).
- **Select a control point or a curve segment so you can move it:** Click with the arrow tool. Shift-click to select more.

To be able to see the next segment of the pen path as you're drawing it, you can put the pen tool into "rubber band" mode: Double-click the pen in the Paths palette (A) to open the Pen Tool Options palette; click the Rubber Band checkbox (B). Now when you draw you'll be able to see how the curve is shaping up before you click to place the next point (C). If you're just learning how Bezier curves work, this can be a big help.

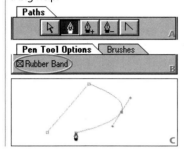

SETTING PATH TOLERANCE

With a selection active, choosing Make Path from the Paths palette's pop-out menu brings up a dialog box that lets you set Tolerance, to specify how closely the Bezier curve will trace the selection boundary when the selection is converted to a path. A tolerance of "0" means the path must trace every little nook and cranny in the selection; this can make for a very complex and calculation-intensive path. The higher the Tolerance value, the looser the path, but the less likely it is that the path will create a limitcheck error on output if it's exported to another program.

- **Add a point:** Click on the curve with the pen+ tool.
- **Remove a point:** Click on that point with the pen– tool.
- **Turn a corner into a smooth point or vice versa:** Click it with the convert direction point tool (the open arrowhead).
- **Reshape a curve by moving one handle independently of its mate:** Drag on the handle with the convert-direction-point tool.
- **Copy** (Ctrl-C) or **cut** (Ctrl-X) a path to the clipboard and then **paste** it (Ctrl-V).

To duplicate a path, hold down the Alt key, and drag with the arrow tool to position the copy where you want it.

To move a path, with the path active (on a white band in the Paths palette), hold down the Alt key and just click — don't drag — with the arrow tool to select the path. Then release the Alt key and drag the path to move it without duplicating it or changing its shape.

To save a path, double-click its name in the palette.

To convert a selection to a path, click the Make Selection/ Make Path icon in the center at the bottom of the palette.

To activate a path, click its name in the Paths palette.

To convert a path to a selection (or add it to or subtract it from an existing selection), activate the path and click (or Shift-click or Ctrl-click) the Make Selection/Make Path icon in the center at the bottom of the palette. Or, with any tool but a painting tool active, press the Enter key (or Shift-Enter or Ctrl-Enter).

SELECTING BY COLOR

Selecting by color is a *procedural* method. It uses the image's hue, saturation, or brightness information (or some combination of these) to define the selection. To make a selection of all the pixels of a similar color, you can use the magic wand tool or the Select, Color Range command. One advantage of the **magic wand** tool is that it's quick and easy.

- Turn any path tool into the arrow pointer by holding down the Ctrl key.
- Hold down the Alt key and drag with the arrow to copy a selected path. Then hold down the Shift key as well to constrain movement of the copy.

- **To make a selection with the magic wand,** just click it on a pixel of the color you want to select. It selects that pixel and all similar neighboring pixels for as far as that color continues.
- **To specify how broad a range of color the magic wand should include in a selection,** double-click the wand in the toolbox to open the Magic Wand Options palette and set the Tolerance value to a number between 0 and 255. The lower the number, the smaller the range of colors.

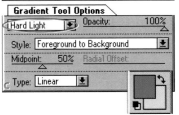

Use the Select, Color Range command in Sampled Colors mode to select a broad expanse of closely related colors. Here the challenge was to add drama to the sky without having to make a manual selection in a photo (A) with a subtle gradation at the hazy horizon and complex shapes (the palms) that had to be excluded. The Color Range eyedropper was dragged across the sky to select a range of blues. Then the Ctrl key was held down and the eyedropper was clicked on the colors we wanted to exclude. Fuzziness was adjusted between 15 and 30 — a good range for Fuzziness in general — to antialias the selection around the palms and "feather" the horizon area (B). The selection was stored as an alpha channel for safekeeping (Select, Save Selection). With the selection active, the gradient tool was used in Hard Light mode (C) to add a color ramp while retaining some of the subtle cloud structure in the original (D).

- **To control whether the selection is based on the color of only a single layer or from all visible layers combined,** turn Sample Merged OFF or ON in the Magic Wand Options palette.

Selecting by Color Range

The **Select, Color Range** command is complex, but it's well worth learning to use. It offers so much more control of what's selected than the wand does — you can select pixels from many parts of an image at once, for example — and it shows the extent of the selection much more clearly.

The little **preview window** in the Color Range dialog box shows a grayscale image of the selection. White areas are selected; gray areas are partially selected, with the degree of selection decreasing as you go toward black, which is completely deselected. This picture is much more informative than the marching ants, which is the indicator you see when you use the selection tools from the toolbox.

The **Fuzziness** is like the magic wand's Tolerance setting, but it's easier to work with, since the entire range is spread out on a slider scale and the preview window instantly shows the effect of changing it.

The **"Select" field** at the top of the box lets you choose the color selection criteria:

- **To select based on colors sampled from all visible layers of the image as if they were merged,** choose Sampled Colors, then choose the dialog box's leftmost eyedropper tool and click on the image, just as you would with the magic wand. One difference between using the magic wand and using the Color Range eyedropper is that the selection extends throughout the image (or the existing selection, if there is one), as if you had made a magic wand selection and then chosen Select, Similar.

- **To select based on color sampled from a single layer,** first make all other layers invisible by clicking OFF their "eye" icons in the layers palette (see "Layers" later in this chapter for more about the Layers palette). Then choose Select, Color Range and click with the eyedropper.

- **To extend or reduce the range of colors in the current selection,** click with the + or – eyedropper to add new colors or to subtract colors. Or click with the plain eyedropper, with Shift (to add) or Ctrl (to subtract). You can also expand or contract the selection by adjusting the Fuzziness.

- **To select a family of colors,** choose from the color blocks in the "Select" list. The color families are predefined — you can't change the Fuzziness or use the eyedroppers to expand or shrink the range.

The Color Range command makes it easy to "subselect" by color criteria, sort of like searching a database using several key words: "Select everything *magenta* that's *in this one area of the image* so I can push the color more toward red." The key to subselecting is that Color Range makes its selections *within the current selection.*

To make this kind of selection, use a selection tool to surround the general area you want to change (A). Then choose Select, Color Range; choose Magentas from the "Select" list; and click OK (B). The dialog box closes, and "marching ants" show the selection. Press Ctrl-H to hide the selection border so you can see what you're doing. Then use Image, Adjust, Variations or Hue/Saturation to adjust the color (C).

PHOTO: CLIPPIX, PHOTODISC

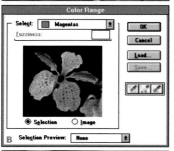

- **To Select only the light, medium, or dark colors,** choose Highlights, Midtones, or Shadows. Again, there's no opportunity to make adjustments to these ranges.

- **To bring *small areas* of RGB color that can't be reproduced with CMYK inks into the printable range,** use the Out-Of-Gamut selection criterion. See the "Getting Into Gamut" tip in Chapter 1 for information about selecting and correcting out-of-gamut colors.

For complex selections, selecting by Color Range offers a good place to start. A step-by-step example of using Select, Color Range is provided in "Retouching a Photo" in Chapter 3.

MAKING SPECIALIZED SELECTIONS

Photoshop's toolbox and Select and Edit menus provide what you need for specific selecting tasks:

To select a border area around some part of an image, select that part of the image and then choose Select, Modify, Border and specify the width you want the border to be. Once you make a border around a selection, you can modify it or fill it to create a frame. But be careful — angled or curved edges of border selections tend to look somewhat rough and pixelated.

To select an object with a very complex boundary (such as a person's hair) **or with many parts** (such as the leaves of a tree), it's often easier to select the background and then invert the selection by choosing Select, Inverse.

Unless you make a selection in an image, many of Photoshop's functions act as if the entire image were selected; for instance, if there's no active selection, paint can be applied anywhere on an image. But for some commands — such as Edit, Copy or any of the Image, Effects commands (Scale, Skew, Distort, or Perspective) — there has to be an active selection for it to work. **You can select the entire image,** including parts that extend beyond the current window, by choosing Select, All (or press Ctrl-A).

To select nothing — that is, to drop any active selection, even if it's hidden or is outside the current window — choose Select, None or use the keyboard shortcut, Ctrl-D (for "drop"). Try this if painting, filtering, or some other function doesn't seem to work. There may be a selected area off-screen or a selection hidden with Ctrl-H, and dropping it will allow the function to work on the entire image.

ADDING AND SUBTRACTING

Photoshop provides several ways to extend a selection or to remove parts of it. (The Color Range dialog box has its own enlarging and reducing features; see "Selecting by Color" earlier in the chapter.)

When a floating selection (dragged and dropped, pasted, or moved) extends outside the canvas, most operations will cause the "overflow" pixels to be clipped off. But some that don't cause clipping are: moving with the arrow or move tool; Image, Effects operations (except Perspective); Image, Flip; and Image, Rotate, Free.

The Tolerance for the magic wand also controls the range of Select, Similar and Select, Grow. If there is a lot of color variation and contrast in the original selection, you may not get exactly the results you expect when you choose Grow or Similar.

To add (or subtract) a straight-line lasso selection that starts inside an existing selection, press the Shift (or Ctrl) key and drag the pointer a very short distance; then, still holding that key down, press the Alt key and begin clicking to make the straight-line segments.

To make a selection that's partly sharp-edged and partly feathered, set the Feather in the Options palette and make the feathered selection first; then set the Feather to 0 and add the unfeathered selection by holding down the Shift key as you select. (If, instead, you make the sharp-edged selection first and then the feathered, the feather softens the junction of the two selections.)

Feathered selection made first; sharp-edged selection added

Expanding a Selection

You can enlarge a selection in any of the following ways:

- **To add more area to the current selection,** hold down the Shift key and use any selection tool to surround the area you want to add. The addition doesn't have to be adjacent to the first selection area.

- **To add the contents of an alpha channel, a layer mask, or a layer's transparency mask to an existing selection,** choose Select, Load Selection; choose Add To Selection in the Operation section of the Load Selection dialog box; and choose the Document and Channel in the Source section. (Alpha channels and layers are discussed later in the chapter.)

- **To expand a selection outward,** picking up more pixels at the edge, choose Select, Modify, Expand, and enter a pixel value.

- **To add pixels that are similar in color and adjacent to the current selection,** you can choose Select, Grow (Ctrl-G). The selection will continue to grow as you repeat the command. Each time you use the command, the range of colors selected gets larger; the amount the range grows is controlled by the Tolerance setting in the Magic Wand Options palette.

- **To add all pixels in the image that are similar in color** to the pixels in the current selection, choose Select, Similar.

Subtracting from a Selection

- **To remove part of the current selection,** hold down the Ctrl key and use any selection tool to surround the area you want to remove. Or choose Select, Load Selection, choose the Source (an alpha channel, layer mask, or layer transparency mask), and choose Subtract From Selection. (Alpha channels and layers are discussed later in the chapter.)

- **To select the intersection of the current selection and a new selection**, hold down the Ctrl and Shift keys together as you drag to make the new selection. The rest of the original selection will be removed, and only the intersection will remain selected. Or choose Select, Load Selection, choose the Source (an alpha channel, layer mask, or layer transparency mask), and choose Intersect With Selection. (Alpha channels and layers are discussed later in the chapter.)

- **To contract a selection inward,** dropping the edge pixels, choose Select, Modify, Contract and enter a pixel value.

- **To deselect some parts of a multipart selection but keep others selected,** hold down the Ctrl and Shift keys and use the lasso or marquee to surround the parts you want to keep.

To remove a "fringe" of pixels surrounding an element that you're adding to a composite image, choose Select, Matting, Defringe before you drop the floating selection or before you merge the layer with the composite. The Defringe command pushes color from the inside of the selection outward to replace the edge pixels, thus eliminating the fringe.

CLEANING UP A SELECTION

Sometimes, despite the most careful selecting, a selection retains some background color, visible around the edge. To get rid of this unwanted "fringe," you can use the commands of the Select, Matting submenu. Note that these commands work only after a selection is separated from its surrounding pixels, either by being copied and pasted, floated, or moved.

- **To eliminate an "edging" picked up by an image selected from a black (or white) background,** choose Select, Matting, Remove Black Matte (or Remove White Matte). Photoshop lightens dark pixels (or darkens light pixels) that it finds at the edges of the selection.

- **To remove edging in a color other than black or white,** try the Select, Matting, Defringe command on the floating selection.

CROPPING

Cropping is trimming an image to the size and proportions you want. In Photoshop, cropping is done by selecting the part of the image you want to preserve, and then removing everything outside the selected part. You can use either the rectangular marquee or the crop tool.

If you have an **active, unfeathered rectangular selection** and you choose **Edit, Crop,** the image will be cropped to that shape, and its window will automatically shrink to fit the new dimensions.

For some situations the **cropping tool** provides an advantage over using the rectangular marquee because you can move the cropping borders in, out, up, or down by dragging on the corner handles; you can rotate the cropping frame by Alt-dragging a corner; and you can trim and resample an image in one step. Click inside the crop with the scissors icon to accept the crop, or click outside with the "Not!" icon to release it so you can start over.

The crop tool can cause an image to be resampled (averaging pixels to shrink the image or manufacturing new pixels to enlarge it; see "Resampling" in Chapter 1), and this resampling can make the cropped image appear fuzzy. You need to understand how the cropping tool works so you don't unknowingly resample.

Double-clicking the cropping tool in the toolbox opens the Cropping Tool Options palette. If you click on "Fixed Target Size" and then on "Front Image," the dimensions and resolution of the image appear in the Width, Height, and Resolution fields.

- If you set the Width and Height values but delete the number in the Resolution field so the field is blank, the resolution will "float." When you drag the crop tool, the cropping frame will hold the proportions you set in Width and Height. When you click inside the selected area to accept the crop, the Resolution will be set at a value that won't cause resampling (adding or averaging pixels).

- If you leave the Height and Width fields empty but set the Resolution, you can drag the cropping frame to any proportions you want. And when you click to accept the crop, the dimensions will float, and no resampling will occur.

- But if instead you set the Width and Height *and* enter a value in the Resolution box, the image will be resampled as it's cropped, so it will come out to the dimensions and resolution you specify. Then you'll probably need to apply Unsharp Mask to repair the fuzziness that resampling will have introduced.

A one-step crop and rotation of a selection

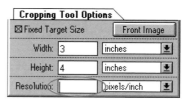

Two ways to crop without resampling

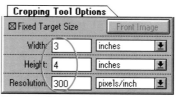

Cropping with resampling

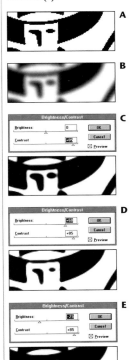
This will "push" color from inside the selection into the edge pixels. Be careful, though. Using a Defringe setting of more than 1 or 2 pixels can create "spokes" or "rays" of color at the edge.

- Besides the Select, Matting command, **another way to remove color edging is to "choke" the selection,** to shrink the selection border just slightly before copying, moving, or floating, so what's causing the edging is excluded. You can do that if you've saved the selection as an alpha channel or as a layer of its own in its original file. Load the selection border from the alpha channel or load the layer's transparency mask as a selection. Then choose the Select, Modify, Contract command to shrink the selection. Activate the layer you want to select from and use the smaller mask to reselect and move, or copy and paste, the now slightly smaller selection. (Alpha channels and layers are described later in this chapter.)

MOVING SELECTIONS

In Photoshop 3 there are several ways to move a selection:

- **To move a selection that you've made with a selection tool,** put the tool's icon inside the selection, where it turns into an arrow pointer, and drag to move the selection.

- **If you're not working with a selection tool or if the selection is in small parts that are hard to hit with the pointer,** press the "V" key to choose the move tool (the four-headed arrow) and drag. The move tool works whether you put the tool icon inside the selection or not. Dragging anywhere in the window will move the selection.

- **To constrain the movement of the selection to horizontal, vertical, or a 45-degree diagonal,** use the Shift key. This technique works with either the marquee pointer or the move tool. But if you use it with the marquee pointer, you have to press the Shift key *after* you start the dragging process.

- **To move a selection 1 screen pixel at time,** choose the move or selection tool and use the arrow keys on the keyboard. Hold down the Shift key with the arrows to move a selection **10 screen pixels at a time**.

FIXED AND FLOATING SELECTIONS

Earlier versions of Photoshop had two kinds of selections: *fixed* and *floating*. Photoshop 3 has these two kinds as well as a third kind: a *layer*.

A **fixed selection** is still part of the image around it. Moving, cutting, or deleting a fixed selection creates a hole. A **floating selection,** on the other hand, hovers "above" the plane of the image and can be dragged to another position, or deleted, without disturbing the image underneath.

When you make a selection with a selection tool or command, it's a fixed selection. But you can turn a fixed selection into a

Quick Mask lets you store a selection temporarily while you edit it. By making a selection and then clicking the Quick Mask icon (on the right side near the bottom of the toolbox), you can turn the selection into a clear area in a semi-transparent mask. The Quick Mask remains stable as you use the painting tools to edit it. Switching back to Standard mode by clicking the Standard mode icon (to the left of the Quick Mask icon) turns the mask into an active selection again.

Quick Mask has three features that make it better for some selecting tasks than using a layer mask or an alpha channel:

• It's quick — just click the icon to turn a selection into a mask.

• It doesn't tie up RAM.

• You can see both the image and the mask at the same time, which can be helpful if you're doing some fairly subtle mask painting.

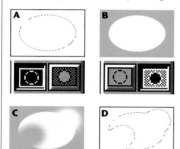

Making a selection in Standard mode (A) converting to Quick Mask mode (B), changing the selection mask by adding to the mask with black paint and removing from the mask with white paint (C), and turning the altered mask back into a selection (D)

floating selection by any of the following methods:

• Choose Select, Float (or press **Ctrl-J**) to make a copy of the selected area and float it exactly above the original.

• To float a copy of the selected area to another location in the image, **hold down the Alt key and drag**.

• Copy the selection to the clipboard and paste it wherever you want it in the image, or in another image file (**Ctrl-C, Ctrl-V**).

• **Drag and drop** the selection from its current file to another open image file (see "Drag-and-Drop Basics" later in this chapter). This leaves the fixed or floating selection active in its original file and puts a floating copy of it in the second image, just above the currently active layer.

When a selection is floating, you can apply the Opacity and blending mode controls in the Layers palette. But if you want more control of the way it will combine with the image underneath, you have to turn it into a layer so you can control it with the Layer Options dialog box (see "Layers" later in the chapter).

A floating selection can become any of three things:

• A fixed selection in the active layer (press Ctrl-J)

• A deselected part of the active layer (press Ctrl-D)

• A new layer (double-click or Alt-double-click the Floating Selection label, or drag the label to the New Layer icon at the bottom left of the palette, or choose Make Layer from the pop-out menu)

THE TYPE TOOL

First and foremost, Photoshop's type tool provides access to fonts, so you can incorporate type into images. But it also can behave as a selection tool.

When you choose the type tool and click in an image, the Type Tool dialog box opens. In the Type Tool dialog box you can specify typeface, style, and spacing, and enter the text you want to set. Clicking OK returns you to the image, where the type appears as a floating selection filled with the Foreground color from the color square in the toolbox. (So besides being a font tool and a selection tool, the type tool also has paint properties!) Because it's a floating selection, you can move the type around without disturbing the image underneath. Here are some tips for using type in Photoshop:

• If you're using PostScript fonts, make sure you have **Adobe Type Manager** (atm.ini) installed so Photoshop has access to smooth PostScript-based type outlines. If it's installed but you're

If a selection is floating, pressing Ctrl-J or choosing Select, Defloat turns it into a fixed selection that's part of the overall image but is still selected.

*Increasing the Font Cache in the **atm.ini** file from its default 256K can help with smoothing type.*

Dramatic "inline-outline" type effects can be accomplished in Photoshop by setting type, blurring it to get a full range of tones, and then putting a number of "switchbacks" into the Curves dialog box. Colorizing the type with Image, Adjust, Hue/Saturation before adjusting Curves gives even wilder results.

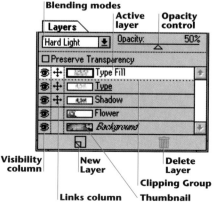

The Layers palette provides many options for controlling how the layers of an image interact.

still having problems with jagged type, open the **atm.ini** file and increase the size of the Font Cache.

- Unless you want stairstepped, jaggy type for some reason, always select the **Anti-aliased** Style option in the Type Tool dialog box to smooth the edges.

- Setting type on its own transparent layer means that you can turn on Preserve Transparency and **change the fill** (color, pattern, or image) of the type without disturbing any other part of the image.

- Putting type on its own transparent layer also lets you **hand-kern the type** (adjust spacing between letters) fairly easily, even after you've dropped the original floating selection: Turn off Preserve Transparency and double-click the magic wand tool to open the Magic Wand Options palette. Set the Tolerance at 255 (the highest possible setting). Then click the magic wand on the letter you want to move; you'll have complete freedom to drag it around. (If you want to move two or more letters at once, Shift-click with the magic wand to add characters to the selection.) To keep the type on its original baseline, press and hold the Shift key as you drag it.

- To use **type as a mask** — in a layer mask or an alpha channel, for example — set it on a transparent layer (as just described), then load the transparency mask (Ctrl-Alt-T), activate a layer mask (or alpha channel) by clicking on its icon in the Layers palette (or Channels palette), and choose Edit, Fill, Black (to hide the type area) or Select, Inverse, and then Edit, Fill, Black to make a hole so only the type area can be seen.

- Type set on its own transparent layer can also be used to **mask several layers at once** (see "Clipping Groups" later in the chapter).

LAYERS

Floating selections give you more flexibility than fixed selections do, because you can move them around and change them without permanently changing the image itself. But layers, new with Photoshop 3, add even more flexibility. As long as you have plenty of RAM and computer power, layers turn you loose to experiment — you can have all your picture elements in view, with almost unlimited Undo power.

Having layers is like having a whole stack of separate, independent floating selections at once, each one on its own transparent sheet of acetate that can accept color. A layer can have several parts:

- **Nontransparent (opaque or partly opaque) pixels,** where there is image information

- **Transparent areas,** where there's no image information

- A **transparency mask** (a mask that will select all nontransparent pixels)

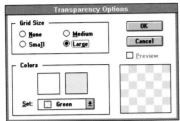

By default Photoshop 3 represents transparency on-screen with a gray checkerboard pattern so you can differentiate a transparent background from a solid white one. But you can change the color, size, and tone of the pattern by choosing File, Preferences, Transparency.

DRAG-AND-DROP BASICS

In Photoshop 3 you can drag a copy of a selection or layer across your computer's screen from one open Photoshop window to another.

- **To copy a layer from the** *active file* **into another file,** use the move (four-headed arrow) tool. Start the drag either from the active image's working window (in which case you'll be dragging the *currently active* layer) or from its Layers palette (in which case you can drag any layer you want). Drop the layer into the new file; it will appear in the layers stack above the currently active layer, and it will become the active layer.

- **To copy** *a selection* **from an active layer into another file,** use the move tool or any selection tool. Instead of appearing as a new layer, it comes in as a floating selection above the active layer.

Dragging a layer from a source file creates a new top layer in the target file.

- **A layer mask** (a mask that affects how the pixels of only that layer contribute to the composite)

To help you keep track of the layers, the Layers palette shows them in their stacked order. Here's a quick summary of what you can do with a layer.

- Paint it or filter it or otherwise **change it independently** of other layers by clicking on its name in the Layers palette to make it the active layer. Only one layer can be active at a time.

- **Make it visible or invisible** by turning ON or OFF its eye icon in the visibility column. Any or all layers can be visible at once.

- **Protect it from change** by choosing a different layer as the active layer in the Layers palette.

- **Move it independently** of the rest of the image by dragging with the move tool (the four-headed arrow).

- **Link it to other layers** so they move together, by clicking in the Links column.

- **Control its overall transparency** with the Opacity slider.

- **Control how its colors blend** with the layers below by choosing a blending mode.

- **Include or exclude pixels from the blend** based on their colors and the colors of the pixels in layers below with the composite controls in the Layer Options dialog box.

- **Hide parts of it** by creating a layer mask.

- **Turn it into a mask** for layers above it by including it as the bottom layer in a clipping group.

"Exercising Layers," starting on page 59, will give you an opportunity to apply the basics of layer operations before tackling the techniques presented later in the book.

Transparency

Transparency is the essence of layers. Except for the Background, an opaque layer at the bottom of the stack, all layers automatically start out transparent. (Even the bottom layer can start out transpar-

LAYERS SHORTCUTS

Here are some tricks for managing layer masks by using the Layers palette:

- **To add a layer,** click the New Layer icon.

- **To add a layer, bypassing the Layer Options dialog box,** Alt-click the New Layer icon.

- **To hide a layer or make it visible** (it's a toggle operation), click in the visibility (eye) column.

- **To hide all layers except one,** Alt-click in that layer's eye column.

- **To make a layer the active layer,** click on its name or thumbnail.

- **To make the next layer up (or down) the active layer,** press Ctrl-] (or Ctrl-[).

- **To change a layer's name or use composite controls on it,** double-click its name or thumbnail to open the Layer Options palette.

To be able to predict where a selection or layer will end up when you drag and drop it into another file, you need to have both files at the same on-screen magnification — 1:1 is best for looking at the image, but if you need to see more of one of the images so that you have to zoom out to 1:2, 1:3, or more, apply the same zoom to the other file. Then when you drag a selection or a layer from one file to another, it will predictably end up in one of these places:

- If the two files are the same size, pixel for pixel, the selection goes to the same position it was in its original file.

- If the two files are different sizes, it's dropped approximately where you release the mouse button.

- If you hold down the Shift key while you drag, it ends up in the center of the working window.

If you don't like where it landed, you can drag to reposition it.

When you drag-and-drop a selection (A) into another file of a different size, it lands wherever you release the mouse button (B). But if you hold down the Shift key as you drag, it lands in the center of the working window (C).

PHOTO: STOCK OPTIONS VOL. 1, DIGITAL MEDIA

LAYER OPACITY SHORTCUTS

When a selection tool is active (selected in the toolbox), pressing the number keys on the keyboard changes the opacity of the active layer (1 is 10%, 2 is 20%, and so on, with 0 being 100%).

---

ent if you set it up that way when you start the New file, or if you open an EPS file that has no background.)

Photoshop artists are used to thinking of each pixel in a Grayscale file as having a brightness level (a shade of gray) and each pixel in an RGB file as having three color values, representing its red, green and blue components. Now, in addition to these brightness and color values, each pixel in each layer of a Grayscale or RGB file also has an Opacity value.

You can see a representation of transparency if you view a layer by itself (by Alt-clicking its eye icon to turn its visibility ON while turning OFF visibility for the other layer). The transparent parts of the layer are represented by a checkerboard pattern, used to distinguish transparency from a solid white background. The transparent parts of a layer let the layer underneath show through. If there are no transparent (checkerboard) areas in a layer, it completely blocks underlying layers from view.

When you paint on a layer or you bring an element onto the layer by dropping a floating selection, the transparent pixels are replaced by ones that have color and opacity values. You can measure the opacity if you open the Info window (Windows, Palettes, Show Info), set one of the color readouts for Grayscale, RGB, HSB, or Lab, and note the "Op:" (opacity) reading at the bottom of the list of color characteristics. As you move a cursor over a layer you can watch the change in color and transparency values in the Info window. If the Opacity slider for the layer is set at less than 100, or if the edge of the element is antialiased or feathered, the Opacity value falls below 100 — antialiasing and feathering make the pixels at the edge partly transparent.

The Opacity for the layer as a whole can be controlled with the Opacity slider at the top right side of the Layers palette. The effect of the Opacity setting is cumulative with whatever opacity is already built into the pixels in the layer. For example, if you paint a stroke with the Opacity slider in the Paintbrush Options palette set at 50% and then set the layer's Opacity at 50% also, the stroke will have an effective Opacity of 25%. (See Chapter 6 for more about paintbrush controls.)

Transparency Masks

If you create a layer — by choosing New Layer from the Layers palette's pop-out menu or by clicking the New Layer icon at the bottom of the palette — the layer that's added (above the currently active layer) will consist of nothing but the transparent sheet. But as soon as you paint on it or add something (by dragging and dropping or pasting, for instance), the layer has three components — transparency, pixels, and a transparency mask.

The transparency mask is a stored selection boundary that defines the edge between a layer's opaque pixels and its transparent ones. Where there are semitransparent pixels — for instance, at the

Here are some tricks for managing layer masks by using the layer mask thumbnail in the Layers palette:

To make changes to a mask, click the mask thumbnail to make it active. A black border around the layer mask thumbnail shows that the layer is active. You'll still be viewing the image rather than the mask, but any painting, filtering, or other functions you do will affect the mask, not the layer.

To make the *mask* visible instead of the layer, Alt-click the mask thumbnail.

To turn the mask OFF temporarily so it has no effect, Ctrl-click the mask thumbnail. A red "X" on the thumbnail shows that the layer is turned OFF. Ctrl-click again to turn the mask back ON.

To load the layer mask of the active layer as a selection, press Ctrl-Alt-~.

Double-click the mask **to open the Layer Mask Options dialog box,** where you can make changes to the mask characteristics. For instance, if you want to be able to move the layer without moving the mask, click on Image in the "Position Relative To" section of the dialog box.

antialiased edge of the opaque element — the mask will be semi-transparent also. If you move an element around on its layer, its transparency mask moves with it. If you change the element by scaling it, blurring it, or painting on it, for instance, the transparency mask changes to fit.

You can make a layer's transparency mask into an active, visible selection by pressing Ctrl-Alt-T. This selection, evidenced by the typical "marching ants" border, will now operate in whatever layer you activate in the stack. That is, once a transparency mask is loaded as a selection, if you choose another layer in the Layers palette, the selection you loaded will still be active in this different layer.

Layer Masks

Besides the transparent sheet, the opaque and partially opaque pixels, and the transparency mask, you can also add a layer mask to any layer. A layer mask can mask out parts of the layer so they don't contribute to the composite image. A layer mask is a grayscale entity, like an alpha channel (described on page 57). The white part allows whatever is in the corresponding position on the layer itself to contribute to the composite. The black part masks out the pixels on the layer. And shades of gray mask to different degrees — the darker the shades of gray, the more opaque the mask. You can think of a layer mask as a mask that adheres to its own layer, with opaque parts (black) and a hole (white) that lets some of the layer's contents show. But unlike a mask in a

Loading a layer's transparency mask (Ctrl-Alt-T) can be very useful for certain tasks, such as making a mask (see examples in Chapter 8). But, as a rule of thumb, **don't load a transparency mask for use on its own layer.**

If you want to limit changes to the nontransparent areas of a layer — for instance to blur the element on the layer but not blur beyond its outline — use the **Preserve Transparency checkbox** at the top of the Layers palette instead. Here's an example that shows why:

If you turn Preserve Transparency ON and then fill the layer with color, all the current color will be removed, and the new color will take its place. Pixels that were partly transparent will have the same degree of transparency as before but will show the new color instead of the old. On the other hand, if you load the transparency mask and then fill it, the fully opaque pixels will fill with the new color, but the semitransparent pixels will be partly masked by the semitransparent mask, and some of the original color will be left behind. This typically happens at the edge of the layer element, where you find partially transparent pixels because of antialiasing.

Another job that's done better without loading the transparency mask is copying or cutting the layer's contents. If you load the transparency mask as a selection and then cut the contents of the layer, you'll see a residue of partly transparent pixels, left behind by the partly transparent edge of the transparency mask, outlining where the element used to be. Instead choose Select, All; the selection boundary (marching ants) will shrink to fit the nontransparent pixels as soon as you move the selection. (To prompt the shrinking, you can press the up arrow key once, then press the down arrow key once to put it back in place.)

Normal

Dissolve, 50% Opacity

Multiply

Screen

Overlay

Soft Light

Hard Light

Darken

Lighten

Difference

Hue

Saturation

Color

Luminosity

Photoshop's blending modes — available in the Layers palette, the Calculations and Apply Image dialog boxes, and the painting tools and Fill function — provide many ways to composite images.

physical stack of layers, the layer mask has no effect on any layer except its own; it doesn't mask the layers above, for example.

The layer mask for the active layer can be loaded as a selection that can be used in any layer by pressing Ctrl-Alt-~ (that's the tilde character). And if you have the Channels palette open, you'll see it pop up in the list of channels when its layer is active, so another way it can be loaded is by Alt-clicking its name in the Channels palette.

Clipping Groups

A clipping group is a group of layers, the bottom layer of which acts as a mask for all the layers above — it's sort of like setting up a "multiple-layer" layer mask. The layer that acts as a mask clips all the associated layers above it so only the parts that fall within the shape of its own transparency mask are allowed to contribute to the image.

You can make a clipping group by Alt-clicking on the borderline between the names of two layers. The lower of the two layers — its name is now underlined in the palette and the borderline becomes dotted — is the clipping mask, and the other layer is clipped. Working your way up the palette clicking more borderlines adds clipped layers to the group. To be members of a clipping group, layers have to be contiguous in the stack. Skipping a layer in the Alt-clicking process starts a new clipping group.

A clipping group can also be set up or added to at the time a layer is added to the stack, by checking the Group With Previous Layer box in the New Layer dialog box.

Clipping groups are "high-overhead" items. They take more computation than layer masks or alpha channels. So if you can think of another way to accomplish the "clipping" you want, you might be better off doing that instead of making a clipping group.

Blending Modes

Along with the Opacity slider and the composite controls in the Layer Options dialog box, the blending modes (also called transfer modes) are what make Photoshop 3's layers so useful for compositing.

Normal mode's name speaks for itself. The color acts normal and doesn't change in relation to the layers underneath.

At full opacity, **Dissolve** mode is just like Normal, but reducing opacity, instead of pushing all the pixels toward transparency, makes a dither (randomized) pattern, with some pixels completely transparent and others at full opacity. The lower the Opacity setting, the more pixels disappear.

The effect of **Multiply** mode is like putting two slides together in the same slide projector and projecting them. Where both of the slides have color, the projected color is darker than either. White is neutral in Multiply mode; that is, the white parts of a layer are like the clear parts of a slide — the white has no effect on the layers below. Some of the things Multiply is good for are: increasing the density

A file has to be flat — with a *Background* layer only — before it can be saved in TIFF or PICT or any other file format other than Photoshop 3.0. If a file isn't flat and you choose File, Save or Save As, all formats except Photoshop 3.0 will be unavailable.

But just because a file has only one layer doesn't necessarily mean it's flat. A *Background* layer results only if:

• You specify White or Background Color for the Contents in the New dialog box when the file is set up,

• Or you choose Flatten Image from the Layers palette's pop-out menu.

GETTING THE PICTURE

Set the size of the thumbnail sketches by choosing Palette Options from the pop-out menu.

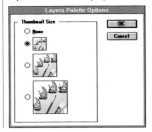

ONE LAYER AT A TIME

Although linked layers can be simultaneously moved around their own image file, the linking doesn't carry over if you drag a layer to copy it from one file to another. The linked layers have to make separate trips, which means that unless the two files are the same pixel dimensions, it may be hard to line the layers up again. To drag and drop the contents of several layers without losing their relative positions, you can choose Image, Duplicate, Merge Layers to make a new, single-layer file of the merged layers, and then drag and drop this merged copy.

of overexposed images (see page 78), applying shadows without completely eliminating the color of the shaded areas in the layers underneath, layering line work over color (see page 185), and combining an image with a simulated paper or canvas texture when you want it to appear that the paint is pooling in the recesses of the texture.

Screen mode is like projecting two slides, from separate slide projectors, onto the same spot on the wall, or overlapping colored spotlights. The result is to lighten the composite. Black is a neutral color in Screen mode, causing no effect. Screen mode is good for applying highlights to an image (see Chapter 8).

Overlay, Soft Light, and **Hard Light** provide three different complex combinations of Multiply and Screen, acting differently on dark colors than on light colors. For all three, 50% gray is neutral, which makes them good for embossing with the Emboss filter, since the flat surfaces of an embossed image are 50% gray. These modes are useful in general for applying special effects (see Chapter 8).

Lighten mode compares pixels in the overlying layer and the image underneath, channel by channel — that is, it compares the Red channels of both, the Blue channels, and the Green channels — and chooses the lighter channel component in each case.

Darken mode makes the same comparison as Lighten does, but chooses the darker channel component in each case.

Difference mode does a complex calculation to compare the overlying layer and the image underneath, generally resulting in more intense colors. Black results if there is no difference in the pixel colors, and black is also the neutral color for Difference mode, causing no change in the image underneath. Difference is good for creating psychedelic color effects. It's also good for comparing two images to see if there is any difference between the two, or to see and apply the difference between a "fat" and a "skinny" mask like those used for special effects in Chapter 8.

Hue, Saturation, and **Luminosity** modes each apply only one of the three attributes of the pixels in the overlying layer. **Hue** is good for shifting color without changing brightness or value. **Saturation** is good for desaturating selectively based on a shape. **Luminosity** is the mode to use if you want to transfer the light-and-dark information from a texture onto an image underneath.

Color mode is like a combination of Hue and Saturation modes. The layer contributes all the information except Luminosity (the brightness information). Color mode is good for applying color in painting (see Chapter 6).

Merging and Flattening

Merging and *flattening,* though different functions, both combine all visible layers into a single layer. When you've finished working on a set of layers and it produces exactly the effect you want, you may decide that you no longer need to keep all the layers separate. Reducing the number of layers reduces the amount of RAM needed

For some RGB and CMYK images, a subject may be more distinct from its background in one color channel than in the others. You can use this to your advantage: View each color channel by itself (by clicking on its name in the Channels palette) and pick the one with the most difference between subject and background. Then activate that channel by clicking its name in the Channels palette, make your selection with the selection tools, and save the selection in an alpha channel (Select, Save Selection; or click the Make Selection icon in the Paths palette if your selection is a pen path).

Any selection border that's more complex than a simple marquee and that wasn't created as a pen path should be stored as a layer or as an alpha channel in its original file in case you need the selection border again later.

- If you store the selection, unaltered, on a layer of its own, you don't need to do anything more; the selection border will automatically be stored as the transparency mask for the layer (see "Layers," earlier in the chapter).

- If you don't turn the selection into a layer, store the selection border as an alpha channel: With the selection active, choose Select, Save Selection, New. (Alpha channels are also discussed later.)

for the image and can speed up the way Photoshop works. To reduce the number of layers, you can merge the layers or flatten the file by choosing **Merge Layers** or **Flatten Image** from the Layers palette's pop-out menu. Here are some of the differences between the two processes:

- **Merging combines all visible layer**s (the ones with their eye icons turned on) **but leaves the hidden layers intact** so you can work on them further.

- **Flattening discards the hidden layers** in the process of combining the visible ones into one remaining Background layer. (A dialog box warns you about this so you can reconsider.)

- **A "merger" has to include the active layer.** If the active layer isn't one of the visible layers, nothing will happen when you choose Merge Layers. (Flattening automatically includes the active layer, since it includes all layers.)

- When you merge layers or flatten a file, any **layer masks are applied** first (their effects are made permanent) **and then discarded.**

- **Alpha channels are retained** when layers are merged or flattened.

- **When a file is flattened, the single remaining layer becomes the opaque Background.** Any transparent or partially transparent pixels are made opaque as white is substituted for transparency.

- **When layers are merged,** the resulting composite layer takes the name of the bottom layer of the merging group and also takes its place in the layers stack. If merging results in a single layer, it may or may not be the Background layer. A file that's set up as Transparent in the New dialog box, or that's made by opening an EPS file has no Background. And **if the file had no Background to begin with, it will have no Background after merging.** Even if the layer is completely filled with pixels and is therefore opaque in Normal mode, it still isn't a Background layer.

ALPHA CHANNELS

Photoshop's alpha channels provide a kind of subfile for storing selection boundaries so you can load them back into the image and use them later. A selection stored in an alpha channel becomes a mask, with white areas that can be loaded as an active selection, black areas that protect parts of the image where changes shouldn't apply, and gray areas that expose the image to changes proportionally to the lightness of the gray.

You can store any type of selection boundary in an alpha channel. When used with the program's Image, Calculations functions, alpha channels also provide some very sophisticated ways to combine selections — adding them together, subtracting one from an-

The gradient tool can produce a graduated mask that lets you apply any change in a gradual way. You can make the mask, either in Quick Mask mode, in a layer mask or in an alpha channel. Here are some things you can do with a gradient mask:

- **To make a gradual pattern fill,** define a pattern, make a gradient selection, and choose Edit, Fill, Pattern.

- **To turn a photo into a painting,** make a gradient selection and apply a painterly filter through it (A). (See Chapter 5 for more about filters.)

- **To turn a color image to black-and-white,** apply Image, Adjust, Desaturate through a gradient mask (B).

- **To combine two images,** make a gradient layer mask for the image in the upper layer, so that it gradually fades out, allowing the lower image to show (C).

PHOTOS: STOCK OPTIONS VOL. 3, DIGITAL MEDIA

- **To protect a central part of an image** from a change that you apply to the rest of the file, use a radial gradient mask.

other, and making them interact in a variety of ways far beyond what you can do with the selection tools and the Ctrl and Shift keys, or the Select, Load Selection dialog box.

A Photoshop file can have as many as 25 channels in total. So an RGB file, for example, since it has four channels tied up in the main channel and the three individual colors, can have up to 21 alphas, each providing a way to recall a particular selection independently of any other selection. A grayscale file can have up to 24 alphas, and a CMYK file can have as many as 20. Here are some tips for using alpha channels:

Making a new alpha channel. To make an alpha channel:

- Make a selection and choose Select, Save Selection.

- Or Choose Window, Show Channels and then click the New Channel icon in the center at the bottom of the Channels palette, or choose New Channel from the pop-out palette. When you make an alpha channel in this way, you have the opportunity to give it a name that will help you remember its content. To bypass the dialog box, Alt-click the icon or hold down the Alt key as you choose from the pop-out menu.

Loading an alpha channel as a selection. To turn an alpha channel into a selection:

- Choose Select, Load Selection and, if more than one alpha channel exists, choose the channel's number.

- Or click the Convert To Selection icon at the bottom left of the Channels palette.

- Or use the keyboard shortcut: Ctrl-Alt-channel number.

Combining alpha channels. The Image, Calculations command opens the very powerful Calculations dialog box. It operates like a logic puzzle, allowing you to pick any channel — alpha or color or layer mask or transparency mask or even luminosity (called Gray) — from any layer in the active document or from any other open document with the same pixel dimensions, and combine it (Add, Subtract, or use any of nine blending modes) with any other channel, through a mask of your choice. Then you can store or load the result in any qualifying open document or a new one that will be created at the same size. The Calculations command has tremendous potential for blending channels to make composite masks. Better yet, with an existing selection active you can add, subtract, or make an intersection with any other alpha channel by holding down the appropriate modifier key (Shift, Ctrl, or Shift-Ctrl) and dragging the channel's name to the Make Selection icon in the channels palette.

Exercising Layers

Overview *Duplicate the Liz and Elaine files from* **goodies\dressup** *on the Wow! CD ROM. Work with the Layers palette to learn its functions.*

TOMMY YUNE, © 1995 URSUS STUDIOS

1

Liz (left) and Elaine (holding Buster) as you find them in Dress Up!

2a

Turning off the thumbnails in the Layers palette to save screen space and RAM

2b

Layers palettes for Liz and Elaine in their original condition; refer to these if you accidentally turn off layers and need to reset visibility or stacking order.

INSPIRED BY A LAYERS DEMO featuring "Barbie/GI Joe" and presented by Russell Brown of Adobe Systems, Inc., we asked Tommy Yune, creator of the *Buster the Amazing Bear* comic books (see pages 185 through 188), to put together a file that could be used for an elementary demo of how layers work. On the Wow CD ROM open the **goodies** directory to find two Photoshop 3 files inside the **dressup** directory — Elaine (shown above on the right) and Liz, two heroines from the *Buster* series. Then follow the steps on these three pages to get the hang of turning layers ON and OFF, linking them, adjusting Opacity, trying out some of the blending modes, preserving transparency, and making a mask.

1 Making a duplicate. Before you start, copy the **liz** and **elaine** files from the Wow CD ROM to a hard disk. Then open both files and open the Layers palette (Window, Palettes, Show Layers).

2 Reducing palette size. Choosing Palette Options in the Layers palette's pop-out menu lets you choose the size of the thumbnails that appear in the palette, or choose no thumbnails at all. Large thumbnails let you see more detail. But they can also slow down your work, since redrawing them occupies RAM. To fit the entire Liz and Elaine Layers palettes on a small screen, you can turn off their preview icons: Choose Palette Options and click the None button. Yune, who often works with the Layers thumbnails turned off because it can improve Photoshop's speed, has named the layers by their content, so you don't need the icons to know what's what.

3 Hiding layers: Organizing Elaine. Elaine looks like she's prepared for anything, with sweatshirt and sunhat over her evening garb. But to get her ready to go out, click OFF the eye icons in these layers to hide them: Sunhat, Flowers, Sunglasses, Sweatshirt, and Flowers.

WATCH THOSE LAYERS!

If you click the name of a layer that isn't currently visible, it will become the active layer and visible. But all other layers will be hidden. To keep the others from turning OFF, so you can see all the layers you've been looking at *plus* the newly active layer, *first* turn ON visibility for the layer by clicking its eye icon, and *then* click the layer's name to activate it.

3a

Clicking the eye icons to toggle them OFF hides the Sunhat, Flowers, Sunglasses, and Sweatshirt layers.

4

Command-clicking on an image element can activate its layer, unless its less than 50% opaque.

5

Linking Buster and his bow tie allow them to be moved together. To link a layer to the active layer, simply click in its links column.

6

You can drag and drop layers from one file to another, but linked layers don't come along.

4 Activating a layer: Selecting Buster. You can activate a particular layer in the stack either by clicking its name in the Layers palette or by Ctrl-clicking on the visible part of the image whose layer you want to activate. The second method isn't 100% foolproof, though, because it depends on the opacity at the point where you click; if it isn't 50% opaque or more, the click acts on the next layer down, and so on. Try selecting Buster by Ctrl-clicking on him in the image window with the move tool (you can activate the move tool by pressing the "V" key).

5 Linking layers: Putting Buster on the floor. Clicking in the Links column in the Layers palette (next to the "eye" column) will *link* any layer to the *currently active layer*. A cross symbol appears in the links column of the active layer and any layers that you link to it. In the Elaine file, activate the Buster layer and then click in the links column of the BowTie layer to link it to Buster; note the link marks in the palette. Also click the BowTie eye column so you can see the tie. Now activate the Evening Gown layer and link the Heels layer to it; again note the link marks. Now link the Hose to this group also. Then activate the BowTie layer, and notice that the link marks no longer appear for the Evening Gown, Heels, and Hose layers — only for the *currently active layer* (BowTie) and the layer linked to it (Buster). When layers are linked, moving one layer with the move tool also moves the linked layers.

With Buster linked to his bow tie, use the move tool to slide him to the floor. (To give Elaine something to do with her hands now that Buster is on his own, click in the eye column of the Notebook layer to make it visible.)

6 Dragging and dropping: Cloning Buster. With more than one Photoshop 3 file open, you can use the move tool to copy a layer from one file and paste it into another. It's quick and easy, and it bypasses the clipboard. With both the Liz file and the Elaine file open, activate the Buster layer of the Elaine file and the Leather Jacket layer in the Liz file, put the move tool on the bear, and drag him into the Liz window. Since these files are different dimensions — the Liz file is wider — Buster will end up approximately where you drop him in the Liz image. Move him to Liz's shoulder.

7 Trying out blending modes: Stockings to tights. The blending mode (set by choosing from a pop-out list at the top left of the palette) controls how the pixels of a layer interact with the layers underneath. (A description of the blending modes can be found on page 55.) In this case, the result of Multiply mode is like putting sheer stockings on a bare leg. To see the effect of Multiply in the Elaine file, activate the Hose layer, switch its blending mode from Multiply to Normal and back again; you'll see the change as the muscle contours and skin color of the Background layer disappear and reappear, and the color of the clothed leg goes from a

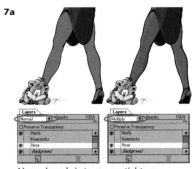

7a

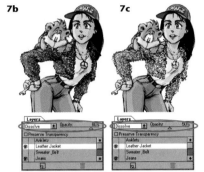

Normal mode is to opaque tights as Multiply mode is to sheer stockings.

7b   **7c**

With Dissolve mode, the degree of dissolution depends on the Opacity setting.

7d

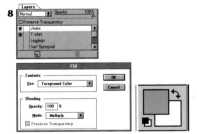

Hard Light mode can create a transparent plastic look.

8

Turning ON Preserve Transparency keeps color in nontransparent areas when you fill a layer.

9

The black area of a layer mask prevents layer contents from contributing to the composite.

blend of colors with Multiply mode (Background *darkened* by Hose) to a solid gray in Normal mode (Background *hidden* by Hose).

Going for "grunge." In the Liz file activate the Leather Jacket layer. Now change its blending mode to Dissolve. You won't notice much of an effect immediately, but if you move the Opacity slider to the left, Liz's jacket will be headed toward "threadbare" in a hurry.

Going for plastic. For a "plastic" look with exaggerated highlights, restore the Opacity of the Jacket layer to 100% and then choose Hard Light for the mode.

8 Preserving transparency: Expanding a wardrobe. The Preserve Transparency checkbox at the top of the Layers palette keeps color "inside the lines" when you fill a layer. In the Liz file, activate the Jeans layer. Click the checkbox to turn ON Preserve Transparency. Then choose a bright color (click the Foreground color square in the toolbox) and choose Edit, Fill, Foreground Color, Normal. The Jeans will change color but the folds of the cloth will be lost. Press Ctrl-Z to Undo, and try the Fill operation again; but this time choose Edit, Fill, Foreground Color, Multiply. Although the layer stays in Normal mode, the color is applied in Multiply mode, allowing the detail of the Jeans to show through.

9 Using a mask: Making patterned stockings. To add a pattern to the Hose, you could use a pattern fill with Preserve Transparency turned ON, as in step 8. But if you use a separate pattern layer and a layer mask, you'll be able to move the pattern to adjust its position within the masked area. To work with a layer mask you'll need thumbnails in the Layers palette. So choose Palette Options from the pop-out menu and choose the smallest thumbnail size.

In the Elaine file turn ON visibility for the Flowers layer and activate it. Use the rectangular marquee with the Shift key to surround a flower, copy it (Ctrl-C), and choose Edit, Define Pattern; then drop the selection (Ctrl-D) and turn OFF visibility for the Flowers layer. Activate the Hose layer and create a new layer above it by clicking the New Layer icon at the bottom left of the Layers palette. Choose Edit, Fill, Pattern, Normal to fill this new Layer 1 with flowers.

To make a mask: First activate the Hose layer and load its transparency mask by pressing Ctrl-Alt-T. Now, with this selection active, activate the flower-filled Layer 1 and choose Add Layer Mask from the palette's pop-out menu. Choose Select, Inverse to select the background area of the mask, rather than the shape of the Hose; press the "D" key to set the default Foreground and Background colors, press Alt-Backspace to fill the selection with black, and finally press Ctrl-D to drop the selection. You should now see flower-patterned Hose. To reposition the pattern, click on the image thumbnail (not the layer mask) and select all (Ctrl-A). Use the pointer to move the layer independently of its mask. Turn ON visibility for the other layers you want to complete the picture. 🐭

Putting Text over an Image

Overview *Select the area you want to lighten; copy it into a separate layer; fill with white or adjust Levels to lighten the area.*

Fortunately, of the more than one hundred species of poisonous snakes in Westoland, only about fifteen are deadly. Unfortunately, some of the deadliest are also fairly aggressive, particularly the green ones.

If you are bitten by a snake, seek medical attention straight away. Apply pressure to keep the venom from spreading. If possible, take the snake with you to the doctor's

surgery so medical personnel can identify it and administer the correct antivenin. Fortunately, you have two hands. If you are bitten on the right hand, use the left hand to grab the right wrist to create a tourniquet effect, and use the right hand to grab the snake behind

its head. Unfortunately, you may have to kill the snake in order to do this.

Once you have the situation under control, put the snake into a closed container and apply a cloth tourniquet. This can be a piece of clothing if a first-aid kit is not immediately available.

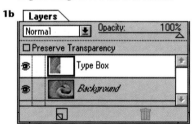

Original image with a text area selected

Floating selection turned into a layer

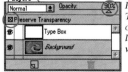

Preserve Transparency ON; Type Box layer filled with white

THERE ARE DOZENS OF WAYS to lighten a selected area of an image in Photoshop, with different amounts of detail and contrast preserved in the lightened area. The best method for a particular job will vary, depending on what the original image is and what kind of effect you want to achieve. For example, if you want to put text over an image as in this mock magazine layout, you may want to eliminate the detail so it won't "fight" with the type.

1 Making a layer for the type area. Use the rectangular marquee to select the area you want the type to overprint. Float a copy of the selection (Ctrl-J). In the Layers palette turn the floating selection into a layer by double-clicking the Floating Selection name and naming the new layer "Type Box" in the Make Layer dialog box (or Alt-double-click the Floating Selection name to turn it into a layer called "Layer 1," skipping the Make Layer dialog box).

2 Lightening the type area. Now use the Image, Adjust, Levels dialog box or fill with white to lighten the type box you've made. Here are some ways to do it:

- **Screening with white.** Make sure Preserve Transparency is turned on for the new Type Box layer. Set your Foreground/ Background colors so white is the Foreground color (by pressing "D" for default colors and then "X" to exchange Foreground with Background). Then press Alt-Backspace to fill the type area with white. In the Layers palette set Normal or Screen for the blending mode for the Type Box layer (for white, Screen and Normal do the same thing). Adjust the Opacity slider until you have the effect you want.

- **Adding a layer mask.** With the Type Box layer active choose Add Layer Mask from the pop-out menu in the Layers palette.

2b

Using a gradient-filled layer mask

2c

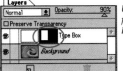

Using a feathered layer mask

2d

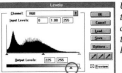

Using Levels to reduce contrast in the Type Box layer

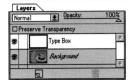

Reset the Foreground/Background colors to the default black and white, and with the mask active (it will have a dark border in the Layers palette), drag the gradient fill tool from the bottom of the image about a quarter of the way to the top to make a black-to-white graduated mask that will soften the bottom edge of the lightened area. The white area of the mask will let the type box show; as the mask turns black, the type box will fade out to show the background image. To change the way the box fades into the background image, simply redo the gradient fill.

For a mask with soft edges all around, start by adding a layer mask as just described. With the white-filled mask active, press Ctrl-Alt-T to load the transparency mask for the layer. Choose Select, Feather to soften the edge of the selection (we used a setting of 10 for this 1300-pixel-wide image). Now choose Select, Inverse and press Alt-Backspace several times to fill the selection with black and create the softened edge effect you want.

- **Using the Output Levels.** Starting with a copied portion of the image (as in step 1b), Choose Image, Adjust, Levels and move the black point slider of the Output Levels to the right. This lightens the blackest black in the image to a gray and lightens all the other tones proportionally. Because it takes all the tonal levels from 0 to 255 and compresses them into a shorter range (from 225 to 255 in this example), the contrast is reduced but variation in tone is maintained. We used this method for the image at the top of the previous page.

Adding finishing touches. Although it looked like a transparent screen, the reduced-contrast image in the type box was still at full opacity, so we could add a drop shadow on the layer below the type box without the darkness of the shadow showing through the box. We also added a layer for display type and another for the display type's drop shadow. (Pulling display type out of an image is discussed on the next two pages, and drop shadow techniques are described in Chapter 8.)

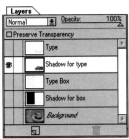

TYPE OVER AN IMAGE

Even a screened-back image will interfere somewhat with the readability of type set on top of it. Here are some tips from type consultant Kathleen Tinkel for keeping the text legible when you set type over an image or pattern:

- Avoid typefaces with unusual character forms, thin strokes, or fine serifs.
- Set the type a little looser than you would set black type on a white page so the reader won't mistake "ol" for "d," for example.
- Often the best bet is a heavy sans serif face set a little larger, looser, and perhaps with a little more leading than usual.

Making Type Stand Out

Overview *Set display type to make a new layer; adjust the spacing of the type; copy the image and paste it into the type; adjust brightness, contrast, and saturation. (Or use a layers mask method.)*

1a

Original image with edge added

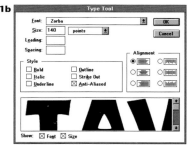

1b

Setting the type in a separate layer

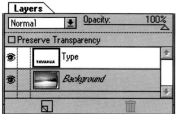

2

"Kerning" type; Preserve Transparency OFF

TO "PULL" DISPLAY TYPE OUT OF A PHOTO, you can lighten it against a dark background, or darken it on a light background (as shown here), or leave the type area unadjusted and lighten or darken the background instead. In Photoshop 3 there are several ways to pull type out of an image. An "economical" way is to set type on a layer of its own, then fill the type with a copy of the image, and set up the contrast. If you have plenty of RAM and speed, the layer mask method described at the end of this section can give you more flexibility in designing your layout.

1 Setting the type. Open a color image. Open the Layers palette (by choosing Window, Palettes, Show Layers, or by using the Commands palette or a keyboard shortcut assigned through the Commands palette).

Choose the type tool and click on the image where you want the type to start. Choose a font and size (we used Swfte International's Zorba typeface, which is somewhat like Signboard, at 140 points), make sure the Anti-aliased box is checked, and type your display heading. You don't need to worry about getting the position of the type exactly right, because you'll be able to move any or all of the letters around once the type is set.

When you click OK in the Type Tool dialog box, the type will appear on your image as a set of selection outlines. Check to see if the type is the right size in relation to the image. If not, press Ctrl-Z, click the type tool on the image again, change the size setting in the Type Tool dialog box, and click OK.

When you have the size type you want, double-click the Floating Selection name in the Layers palette, and name the new layer "Type."

2 Adjusting type spacing and placement. Now you can "kern" the type. First, make sure Preserve Transparency is turned OFF (not checked) at the top of the Layers palette. Because the type

3

Type with a copy of the image pasted in, with Preserve Transparency on

4a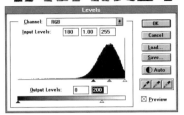

Levels adjusted to darken the type

4b

Saturation adjusted to color the type

5

Dark type on a lightened background and light type on a darkened background

is on its own transparent layer, it's easy to select individual characters or groups of characters with the selection marquee, the lasso, or the magic wand with Tolerance set to 255, and move them by pressing the arrow keys to adjust spacing. You can also use the move tool (four-headed arrow) to move the layer and thus reposition the entire block of type until you have the placement you want.

3 Filling the type with the image. When the type is set the way you want it, click on the Background label in the Layers palette to activate the Background layer. To copy the background image so you can paste it into the type, select the area behind the type and Copy (Ctrl-C). Click on the Type label in the Layers palette to activate the Type layer. Now with the selection marquee still active, make sure Preserve Transparency is checked (turned ON) at the top of the palette. That way, when you paste the image into the layer (Ctrl-V), it will go into position and into the type only; the transparent background and the antialiased edges will be preserved.

4 Setting up the contrast. Now you can use Photoshop's Image, Adjust commands to adjust the brightness, contrast, or saturation of the image within the type. We started by using Image, Adjust, Levels to increase contrast by moving the black point Input Levels slider to the right, then we darkened the image by moving the Output Levels white point slider to the left. Finally we chose Image, Adjust, Hue/Saturation and boosted the Saturation to intensify the colors. The result is shown at the top of the previous page.

5 Trying out variations. To make the contrast even more pronounced, activate the Background layer and lighten it by moving the black point Output slider in the Levels dialog box.

To use the unaltered photo inside the type against a darkened background image, start by pasting the image into the type (as in step 3). Then activate the Background layer and move the white point Output slider in the Levels dialog box to darken the Background image. *Wow!*

USING A LAYER MASK

If you have plenty of power, RAM, and scratch disk space, of if you're working on a small file, you may want to try a method that sets the type in a layer mask. An advantage of using the layer mask is that you can reposition the type anywhere on the image and the right part of the image will always show through. The disadvantage is that you'll have to carry the "overhead" not only of the type mask but also of an extra copy of the entire image. Here's how to do it:

Make a Levels-adjusted copy of the Background layer. In the Layers palette's pop-out menu choose Add Layer Mask. With the mask active, use the type tool to set type in black; then drop the type (Ctrl-D). To adjust spacing, select and move individual letters with the lasso or magic wand tool (with tolerance set at 255). To complete the mask, switch the colors (Image, Map, Invert) so the mask has white type on a black background. Now the adjusted image will show through its mask in contrast to the image on the Background layer. With the layer mask active and the Background color in the tool palette set to black, you can use the move tool to reposition the type.

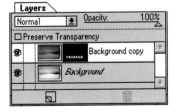

Using a Photo and Graphics as Masks

Overview *Copy a photo and graphics into two separate alpha channels of an RGB image; invert the channels to negatives; load each channel into the main RGB channel as a selection; colorize the selection.*

STEPHEN KING

Grayscale image to be used to make photo channel

Map scan

Channel 4, image map inverted

THE GRAYSCALE INFORMATION in a photo can be a very effective tool for "pulling" an image out of a background texture. For this T-shirt design, Stephen King started with an RGB scan of kraft paper and then colorized and darkened parts of this background using a photo, a scan of a map, and graphics created in Adobe Illustrator. After the colorizing had been done, he pasted in additional photos.

1 Making masks from the photo and graphics. Open an RGB file to serve as the background for the image, open its Channels (not Layers) palette, and make and name some new channels by clicking the New Channel icon once for each mask you want to make. In his scan of kraft paper, King made a channel for the photo he wanted to use and another for the map and graphics.

In the Channels palette click on the "photo" (#4) channel's name to activate that channel. Then open the photo file, select all (Ctrl-A), and drag and drop it into the background file; it will appear in the active alpha channel. Invert the colors (Ctrl-I) so the channel now contains a negative, and drop the selection.

To make a channel for other elements, such as King's map and graphics, activate the other new channel (#5) by clicking on its name in the Channels palette. Then open the scan file, select all, and drag and drop, as described for the photo. King added type and PostScript graphics by placing (File, Place) EPS files saved in Adobe Illustrator format into the channel with the scan (the process of import-

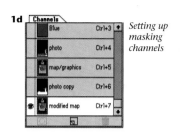

Setting up masking channels

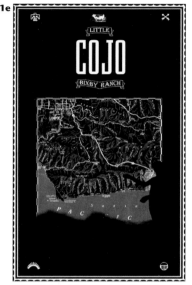

1e

"Modified map" channel, produced by subtracting "photo copy" from "map/graphics"

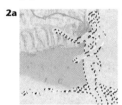

2a

Photo channel loaded in RGB channel

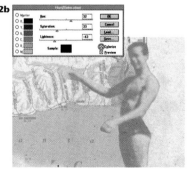

2b

Colorizing the selection

ing an EPS file is described in Chapter 7). He again inverted the color map to turn the channel into a negative, and dropped the selection.

King wanted to remove part of his map/graphics mask so the photo wouldn't overlap it. The contents of one channel can be cut away from another this way: First make a copy of the channel that contains the shape you want to use as the "cutter," by dragging its name in the Channels palette to the New Channel icon at the bottom center of the palette. In this case the new channel (#6) was named "photo copy." Then adjust Levels to turn the grays in this new channel white (Image, Adjust, Levels, moving the white point Input Levels slider). Now, working in any channel, load as a selection the contents of the channel you want to cut into. In this case King wanted to cut away part of the map/graphics channel. He Alt-clicked its name in the Channels palette to load it as a selection. (Alt-clicking a channel's name is equivalent to choosing Select, Load Selection and then choosing New Selection as the Operation option in the Load Selection dialog box.) To do the cutting, King held down the Ctrl key and Alt-clicked on the photo copy channel. This subtracted the second selection from the first. (Ctrl-Alt-clicking a name in the Channels palette is equivalent to choosing Select, Load Selection and then choosing Subtract From Selection as the Operation option.)

When you've done the subtraction, save the resulting modified selection by clicking the Save Selection icon in the bottom left corner of the Channels palette; a new alpha channel will be formed to hold the modified selection; in this case it was "modified map." At this point King had a mask for coloring the photo (#4) and a separate, nonoverlapping one for the modified map/graphics (#7).

2 Colorizing. With the RGB channel selected, load each mask (Alt-click its icon in the Channels palette) and choose Image, Adjust, Hue/Saturation to colorize it. Selecting the Colorize box applies a fully saturated, bright hue to the selection, but by moving the Brightness and Saturation sliders to the left you can tone it down to get a more subtle color. King colorized the modified map/graphics. Then he loaded the photo channel as a selection and colorized it with different settings in the Hue/Saturation dialog box.

Completing the image. After loading the two masks and colorizing with each, King loaded the "modified map" channel (#7) again several times, using the Ctrl key and selection marquee to remove parts of the selection so he could fill other parts separately.

Other photos were then added from separate files: The two color photos at the top were selected with irregular borders drawn with a slightly feathered lasso and dragged and dropped into the file. The large middle image was turned into a black and brown duotone (Mode, Duotone, and set the colors and curves) and then converted to RGB mode before dragging and dropping. *Wow!*

Distressing Type

Overview *Set type on a transparent layer in Dissolve mode and adjust opacity; merge the type layer with a white-filled layer; blur the result; adjust contrast and brightness; save the type as an alpha channel; load the alpha channel as a selection in a new layer; fill the selection with color; adjust the opacity and the Layer Options composite controls.*

THE SMOOTH TYPE OUTLINES produced by PostScript illustration programs like CorelDraw, Adobe Illustrator, and FreeHand, or even by Photoshop with Adobe Type Manager or TrueType, are just too polished for some uses. Photoshop 3's layers and Dissolve blending mode make it possible to "distress" type to simulate a photocopy, a poorly inked rubber stamp, a quickly applied stencil, or weathered paint.

1 Setting the type. Open the background photo to which you want to apply the type. We started with a photo of a brick wall, about by 2¼ inches high by 3¾ inches wide at 200 dpi, or about 450 x 750 pixels.

With black as the Foreground color, set your type: Activate the type tool (by pressing the "Y" key), and click it on your image to open the Type Tool dialog box. (We clicked where we wanted the center of the word "PARKING.") Choose a typeface, size, and alignment, and click the Show Font and Size boxes at the bottom of the dialog box so you'll be able to see how the type will look in your file. Turning ON the Anti-aliased function is usually a good idea when you set type — it makes the edges of the letters look as smooth as possible. But in this case you can skip it, since you're going to erode the edge of the type anyway.

We chose the Steamer font, set the size at 50 points, left Anti-aliased OFF, and typed the word "PARKING." **Note:** If you want to set type in more than one size, you'll have to set it in two or more separate type blocks; although it allows you to set more than one *line* of type (by pressing Enter to start a new line), Photoshop's type tool can handle only one type *size and style* at a time.

If the spacing of the type looks generally too loose (spread out) or too tight, you can enter a negative or positive number for Spacing. When the type looks about the way you want it, click OK.

The spacing on our type looked generally good; the space between the "P" and the "A" was too wide, but tightening it with a negative Spacing setting would also tighten the rest of the letters, so we left it to be done later, after all the type was set.)

1a

Original background photo

1b

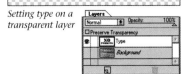

Setting type on a transparent layer

When you click OK to close the Type Tool dialog box, the type will appear in your file as a floating selection. Put the type tool pointer inside one of the floating letters and drag to move the entire block of type into position. Open the Layers palette (Window, Palettes, Show Layers) and turn the type into its own transparent layer by double-clicking the Floating Selection name.

Set any additional type you need by clicking with the type tool again to start a new type block. Press Ctrl-D to drop this new type onto the layer you made for the first block of type.

Adjusting the spaces between letters is easy when you've set type on a transparent layer. Double-click the magic wand tool to open its Options palette, and set the Tolerance at 255, which is the highest possible setting. With the tolerance set high like this, clicking the wand on a black letter will select every pixel of that black area and its antialiased edge, and you can slide the letters around by dragging. Shift-click to add more letters to the selection. To keep the type from moving off its baseline, press the Shift key after you start to drag. When the type is aligned as you like it, press Ctrl-D to drop all selections.

We clicked on the straight upright part of the "P" and then Shift-clicked on the rounded part and used the right-pointing arrow key to move the letter a little closer to the "A."

2 Eroding the type. To develop the type, you'll need both a transparent layer for the type itself and a white-filled layer to combine with the type after it's set. To make the white layer, open the Layers palette (Window, Palettes, Show Layers) and Alt-click the New Layer icon at the bottom left of the palette. Then choose Edit, Fill, White. In the Layers palette, drag the white layer's name to a position between the type and the background photo.

Activate the Type layer by clicking on its name in the palette. To begin the process of distressing the type, set the blending mode for the Type layer to Dissolve. Then adjust the Opacity slider to control the degree of deterioration. Dissolve the type to a point where it's about half black dots and half white background showing through. We used an Opacity setting of 50%.

To build the texture, you can use the Gaussian Blur filter. But for the filter to work, the type layer has to be black-and-white, not black-and-transparent. To merge the White layer with the Type layer, make sure the eye icons for these two layers are ON and the eye for the Background is OFF. Then choose Merge Layers from the Layers palette's pop-out menu. Next choose Filter, Blur, Gaussian Blur. We used a 2-pixel Radius setting for the blur.

Now boost the contrast to blacken the type and define the kind of edges you want, and then adjust the brightness to bring out "holes." We chose Image, Adjust, Brightness/Contrast, pushed the Contrast to +95, and increased the Brightness to +65.

Eroding the type in Dissolve mode

Gaussian blur applied to the merged Type layer

Adjusting Brigtness and Contrast to blacken the type

2d

Blackened type after Brightness and Contrast adjustments

3

Making an alpha channel for saving the distressed type outlines

4a

Alpha channel loaded as a selection and filled with color; White/Type layer removed

4b

Opacity and compositing controls adjusted; the result is shown at the top of page 68.

3 Coloring the paint. Now you need to put the type back onto a transparent layer so you can overlay it on the photographic background. A good way of doing this is to save the type as an alpha channel, create a new transparent layer, load the alpha channel as a selection and fill the selection with color. Start by selecting all (Ctrl-A), copying (Ctrl-C), creating a new channel (Window, Palettes, Show Channels and clicking the New Channel button), pasting the type into the new channel (Ctrl-V), and inverting the tonality of the channel to make a mask to select the type shapes (Ctrl-I).

Next create a new transparent layer (by clicking the New Layer icon at the bottom left of the Layers palette), and load the new type channel as a selection in this layer (by Alt-clicking the channel's name in the Channels palette, for instance). Now you can fill the selection with the Foreground color by pressing Alt-Backspace.

To make part of the type a different color, deselect the part you *don't* want to refill (hold down the Ctrl key as you use the rectangular marquee to surround that part of the type), choose a new Foreground color, and Alt-Backspace again. We filled all the type with black and then deselected "PARKING" and filled "NO" with red.

4 Applying the type to the image. At this point you can get rid of the black-and-white type layer so you can see your colored type on the photo background. Remove your White/Type layer by dragging its name in the Layers palette to the trash can icon at the bottom right corner of the palette. (You could simply hide the layer by turning OFF its eye icon, but you might as well get rid of it — you don't need it because you have the type preserved in the alpha channel, and removing it will cut down on the file size and thus the amount of RAM used.)

Once the intermediate layer is removed, you'll see your painted type on the photo background. Now you can use the Opacity slider for the type layer to "fade" the type. We set the opacity for the type layer at 70%.

You can also eliminate parts of the type if you want to. In our photo of the brick wall, the mortar was recessed between the bricks. So when paint was applied to the wall with a stencil, it might have colored the bricks but missed the mortar. We used Layer Options (chosen from the pop-out Layers palette menu) to partially eliminate the lettering from the mortar: We split the white point of the Underlying Layer by holding down the Alt key as we moved half of the small triangle to the left; then we could move the other half separately. Moving the Underlying Layer white point to the left kept the type from appearing on the white and near-white areas of the brick image. Splitting the white point made a gradual transition, rather than a sharp break, between the painted and the unpainted areas. *Wow*

Diane Fenster created *Things That Go BMP in the Night* for an article with that name in *Computer Life* magazine. The article took a humorous look at the BMP-format "wallpaper" pattern files that come with Windows operating system software, for use as desktop backgrounds.

Fenster began with a scan of a Polaroid transfer print (a print made from the negative part of the Polaroid print, separated after 15 to 30 seconds of processing and printed on Arches Hot Press paper). Then she scanned the image and proceeded to take it apart and put it back together with elements created from scratch or borrowed from other photos. She used the rubber stamp tool to eliminate the photo image from a copy of the

scan, replacing it with background texture cloned from the transfer print. Next she used Overlay blending mode to layer in a photo of clouds that she had solarized before inverting its colors.

One by one she made selections from the Windows BMP files, defined the selections as patterns (Edit, Define Pattern), and used them to fill the PC computer parts (selected with the Alt-lasso), the table top (drawn with the elliptical selection marquee), the walls and rug (drawn with the rectangular marquee), and the dog (chosen from a CMCD Photo CD collection). She tried various blending modes in the Fill dialog box to retain image detail where she wanted to preserve it and to get patterning effects that she liked.

Then she copied the filled elements into 12 additional layers in the main background file, positioned them with the move tool, in some cases rotated them (Image, Rotate, Free) or distorted their shapes (Image, Effects, Distort and Perspective), and experimented with the blending modes again. For instance, she used Multiply mode for the brick wall on the right, the red squares on the left, and the rug; Overlay mode for the yellow wall on the left; and Normal for the dog. She used Hard Light for the sofa and lamp, which came from the positive part of the Polaroid she had taken apart to make the transfer. The table legs were borrowed from another illustration, and a scanned photo of sky was pasted into Alt-lasso selections that defined windows in the brick wall.

For his illustration for the *Surf Industries Manufacturers Association Calendar,* **Jeff Girard** assembled images scanned from 35mm color transparencies, converted to grayscale (Mode, Grayscale) and silhouetted with the pen tool. He built one side of the montage (chicken, dead roses, surfboard feathers, and Tiki), then floated a copy (Command-J) and flipped it (Image, Flip, Horizontal) to make the other side. The wave in the background was produced by generating a gradient with the Gradient Designer from Kai's Power Tools (the KPT filters are described on pages 158 through 160) and then applying Photoshop's Twirl filter (Filter, Distort, Twirl). The mythical surfboard in the center was created as a pen path. Feathered selections inside the path were used to create shading to shape the board (Filter, Noise), and the path outlining the board was then stroked (Stroke Path from the Paths palette's pop-out menu).

Girard converted the finished grayscale file to a duotone (Mode, Duotone). Shown here in black and cyan, the image was printed as a facing page in the week-at-a-glance calendar in black and a metallic blue ink. Images contributed by 16 other artists were also designed for this black-and-metallic duotone treatment.

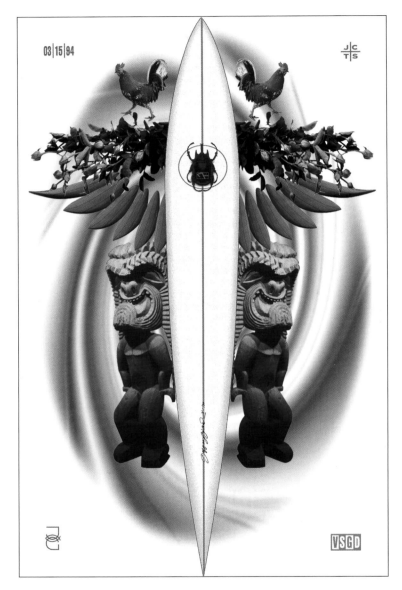

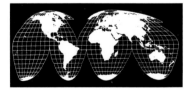

Jeff Brice has "maxxed out" his computer system to take full advantage of Photoshop's layers. With 100 MB of RAM installed in his Power Mac, a hard disk with 2 gigabytes for virtual memory, and a DAT (digital audio tape) drive for archiving, he created this ***poster for the University of Central Florida*** using 25 layers, each with a layer mask. He started by painting the background layer (shown at left, top) and built the montage with images from his collection of scanned elements, many stored with their own alpha channels that could be used to silhouette them from their own backgrounds. Elements were silhouetted and then dragged and dropped into individual layers above the painted background in the composite file. An alpha channel was used to "cut out" the map from a gradient background. The color of the cut-out and imported map was then adjusted with commands from the Image, Adjust menu. For each imported element a layer mask was added (Add Layer Mask from the Layers palette's pop-out menu) to blend the element into the composite. For many of the layers Brice started by making a black-to-white gradient in the layer mask. If the gradient mask didn't produce exactly the blend he wanted, he could redraw the gradient or paint into the mask to customize it. He also varied the Opacity settings for some layers and used Lighten and Darken modes and the composite controls (Layer Options from the pop-out menu). The Chinese logo was drawn in FreeHand, saved in EPS format, and placed in a layer.

ENHANCING PHOTOS

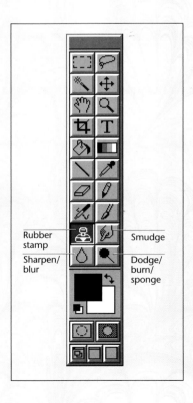

Rubber stamp

Sharpen/ blur

Smudge

Dodge/ burn/ sponge

THIS CHAPTER DESCRIBES SEVERAL TECHNIQUES for enhancing photos — from emulating traditional camera and darkroom techniques such as mezzotinting, haze, and solarization, to hand-tinting, to retouching. But much of the day-to-day production work done with Photoshop involves simply trying to get the best possible print reproduction of an unretouched photo — a crisp and clear print with a full range of gray or color tones.

The Photoshop functions most often used for improving a photo are chosen mainly from the Image, Adjust and the Filter, Sharpen submenus. The dialog boxes for two of the choices from Image, Adjust — **Levels** and **Curves** — look very "techy," and one — **Variations** — looks quite friendly. It's precisely these characteristics that make them so useful. Levels and Curves provide a lot of information about the image and a great deal of control. But Variations lets you see in advance what will happen to the image with each of your choices (pages 105 through 107 show examples).

Another choice in the Image, Adjust submenu — Brightness/ Contrast — is easy to understand and relate to, unlike Levels and Curves. But the Brightness/Contrast control has a restricted set of functions that can compromise the color or tonal range of an image if they're applied alone. If using Levels and Curves on an image is analogous to tuning up all the sections of an orchestra so it can play harmoniously, then using Brightness/Contrast is more like the brass playing loud to cover up problems in the woodwinds section.

The **sharpen/blur, dodge/burn/sponge, smudge,** and **rubber stamp** tools can play an important role in correcting local flaws in an image. Sharpen/blur applies the same functions as some of the Sharpen and Blur filters (described in Chapter 5), but with hand-held precision. Dodge/burn can be thought of as Image, Adjust, Levels in a wand, varying contrast, brightness, and detail, with independent control in the highlights, midtones, and shadows through the Brushes palette. The third phase of the tool — sponge — gives pinpoint control of the Saturation function from Image, Adjust, Hue/Saturation, again in highlights, midtones, and shadows.

IMAGE CORRECTION

Is there a standard approach to evaluating a photo and preparing it for reproduction in print? Color correction is a skill that's refined

continued on page 76

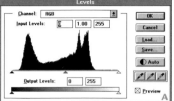

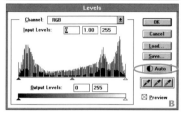

Choosing Image, Adjust, Auto Levels to adjust tonal range; before (A) and after (B)

Adjusting Curves to bring out shadow detail; before (left) and after (right)

RESETTING CURVES

To reset a Curves point to its original values, drag it out of the graph. To reset the entire curve, hold down the Alt key and press Cancel.

through long and broad experience. If you ask a color expert where to start in correcting a black-and-white or color photo, you're almost certain to hear, "It depends on the photo." That's certainly true. But here are some tips that may be generally helpful. (Remember that for your printed image to match your screen display, your monitor and output system need to be calibrated and matched. For information about color management and calibration, refer to the "Calibration" section of Chapter 1.

Extending dynamic range. In a typical image — not a close-up portrait of a black Angus bull or a photo of lace appliquéd on white satin — you'll want to get the broadest range of tones (and thus the largest amount of detail possible) by making sure the lightest area in the image is pure white and the darkest is pure black. (For printing the images, you may need to restrict the tonal range so it doesn't exceed what the printing process can produce. But an effective approach is to *first* get the image looking the way you want it, and *then* correct for the inadequacies of the printing process.)

To see whether an image uses the full brightness range, you can choose Image, Adjust, Levels and inspect the *histogram*, the graph that shows what proportion of the pixels (the vertical measure) are in each of 256 tones (spread along the horizontal axis, from black on the left to white on the right). The darkest pixels in the image are where the leftmost vertical bar of the histogram shows up; the lightest pixels are represented by the bar at the right end. If the histogram doesn't extend all the way across the horizontal axis, it means the full range of tones is not being used in the image — the blacks are not really as black as they could be and the whites are not pure white.

Working in the Levels dialog box, you can expand the tonal range (and thus increase the contrast) by clicking the Auto button or by moving the white and black sliders of the Input Levels inward to points just inside the first bars of the histogram on each end. The goal of moving the sliders like this is to tell the program to make the darkest pixels in the image black, make the lightest ones white, and spread the intermediate ones over the full range of tones in between. This is exactly the kind of adjustment that Photoshop makes for you automatically when you click the Auto button in the Levels (or Curves) dialog box — or when you shortcut the process by choosing Image, Adjust, Auto Levels. (The reason the sliders are moved *just inside* the ends of the range is to make sure the end points are defined by meaningful black and white tones. The whitest white in the image could be due to dust specks, for instance, so the sliders are moved a little inside the ends of the range.)

The Auto or manual Levels adjustment works well for images that just need a boost in contrast. Sometimes it can even correct color, because a color cast can be the result of the way brightness values in the image are distributed among the color channels (red, green, and blue, or cyan, magenta, and yellow).

Adjusting Levels and Curves overall and using the dodge/burn tool on selected local areas can restore information that seems to be lost, as shown in this image restored by Jim Belderes of Digital Design, Inc. Where damage is severe, Belderes uses the rubber stamp to paint missing features.

Correcting "exposure." One of the most common problems with photos is incorrect exposure — the image is too dark overall (underexposed) or too light (overexposed) or the shadows are too dark. If adjusting the black and white Input Levels doesn't solve a photo's color problems, it may be that they can be corrected by fixing the exposure. To increase or decrease the amount of detail you can see in the highlights, midtones, or shadows, choose Image, Adjust, Curves. To change the tonal range, click on the curve to create a point; then drag the point to change its position. The rest of the curve will change shape to make a smooth transition from the black point to the white point through the new position of the point you've moved. You can make general corrections by reshaping the curve so it bulges toward the black side to lighten an underexposed image (by default this is to the left and upward for RGB images and to the right and downward for Grayscale or CMYK images, but you can reverse this by clicking on the grayscale bar that runs across the bottom of the dialog box). Conversely, reshape the curve to bulge toward the white side to darken an overexposed photo.

Overall exposure corrections can also be made with the gamma (gray) slider in the Levels dialog box. But in the Curves dialog box you can adjust particular tones. If you move the cursor out of the Curves dialog box, it turns into an eyedropper. Click on a particular tone in the image to identify the position of that tone on the curve. Then you can move that point on the curve to lighten or darken that part of the tonal range (see pages 96 and 106 for examples).

Removing a color cast. If the image still seems to have color problems after you've expanded the dynamic range and corrected for exposure, try zooming in on some part of the image that should be neutral — that is, without color — and then select the gray eyedropper in Levels or Curves and click it on the neutral spot. Unlike the black and white eyedroppers, the gray one has nothing to do with brightness or contrast. Instead, it adjusts the color balance of the entire image based on the fact that you have told it what neutral should be. If you can't get the image color-cast-free with the Levels or Curves dialog box, try Image, Adjust, Color Balance.

Retouching. Once general corrections have been made, individual problems can be addressed. Here are some examples:

- **To correct the color of a particular area,** make a feathered selection (see Chapter 2) and use Image, Adjust, Variations or Color Balance to adjust it.

- **To correct only one particular color or family of colors throughout the image,** you can use Replace Color or Selective Color from the Image, Adjust submenu (see the "Color in Photoshop" section of Chapter 1). To constrain the color change to one area, make a selection that includes the region you want to change before you apply Replace Color or Selective Color.

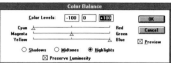

The effect of turning Preserve Luminosity on or off in the Color Balance dialog box varies with the type of color change you make and with whether the change is made to Highlights, Midtones, or Shadows. In some cases turning on Preserve Luminosity dampens changes in brightness. In other cases (like this one) the effect is exactly the opposite. The original color is shown at the top; the middle part shows changes made with Preserve Luminosity OFF; the lower part shows the same changes with Preserve Luminosity ON.

Changing the color balance of a selection can lead to harsh color breaks (top right), but feathering the selection before making the adjustment helps the new colors blend in (bottom right).

To begin to rescue a severely overexposed photo (above), copy it into two or more layers and set the mode of each to Multiply.

- **To remove dust and small scratches,** make a slightly feathered selection around the blemish and choose Filter, Noise, Dust & Scratches. The Dust & Scratches filter works by finding a distinct color break, such as you see when film has dust or scratches on it, and blurring the surrounding color into it to hide the blemish. To minimize the blurring of the rest of the selected area, start by setting the Dust & Scratches Threshold high and the Radius low. Lower the Threshold until the blemish begins to disappear, and then raise the Radius until it's gone. The feathered selection limits the area that's blurred when you run the filter, so you want to keep it small; but it also restricts the area from which the "repair" pixels can come, so you don't want to make it too small or the filter won't be able to tell what's the damage and what's the good part.

- **To remove larger blemishes,** use the rubber stamp, especially in Clone (Non-aligned) mode with a soft brush tip, Alt-clicking to pick up neighboring color and texture and clicking to deposit it.

- **To smooth the texture of a spotted area,** make a feathered selection, float it, blur it, or fill it with a single color (or a shade of gray for a grayscale image), and then use the Layers palette to set the mode (try Lighten or Darken, depending on the kinds of splotches you're trying to eliminate) and adjust the Opacity before dropping the floating selection to blend it with the original.

Sharpening. Running the Unsharp Mask filter almost always improves a scanned photo. Usually it's the last thing that should be done to an image before it's prepared for the press, because the synthetic effects of sharpening can be magnified in other image-editing processes, such as increasing saturation of the colors. Sharpening is discussed more extensively in Chapter 5, "Using Filters."

SAVE THAT PHOTO!

When you want to reproduce a photo in print, it's nice to have a good image to begin with — it may need a little tweaking of the exposure, or you may have to remove a color cast, but it's basically sound. It isn't too badly focused, it's well-framed or at least croppable, the subjects have their eyes open and aren't grimacing inappropriately, and the background doesn't include anything distracting. But there are times when a particular photo *must* be used in a publication — for example, it's the only picture of an important event, or it's free and the client's budget is limited, or the portrait is damaged but the subject is no longer available — and the photo just can't be redeemed by the normal correction processes. Here are some ideas for handling those kinds of photos:

- **To restore color to a severely overexposed (washed-out) photo,** layer two or more copies of the image, with the blending mode for the extra copies set to Multiply in the Layers palette. The result may not be perfect, but it could improve the image enough so you can proceed to rescue it.

Posterizing an image

Removing unwanted detail

Silhouetting a subject with a clipping path allows it to be exported without its background.

Blurring the background (right) can eliminate detail that competes with the subject.

- **To simplify and stylize an image,** choose Image, Map, Posterize and select a number of colors or shades of gray.
- **To show activity or setting but get rid of unwanted detail in the subject,** select the subject and fill it with black to create a silhouette against a backlit background.
- **To get rid of unwanted detail in the background,** select the background and blur it, or use the rubber stamp in a Clone mode to paint over some background objects with other background texture.
- **To get rid of a background altogether,** select it and fill it with a color. Or make a clipping path that will silhouette the subject and mask out the background when you export the photo to another program: Press the "T" key to open the Paths palette, where the pen tool resides. Outline the subject with the pen tool or make a selection by other means (refer to Chapter 2 for the specifics of operating the pen and selection tools). Save and name the path. Then choose Clipping Path from the Paths Palette's pop-out menu, and select your named path in the Clipping Path dialog box. Enter a higher Flatness value if the path is very long and complex. Now you'll be able to save the file in EPS format to be imported into another program and printed. But before you save it, convert it to CMYK mode (choose Mode, CMYK Color) in case the other program can't separate RGB EPS files.
- **To piece together a panorama,** remove and replace the original sky. Blending the part of the scene that continues from one photo to another — often this is the sky — is usually the hardest part of making a panorama sequence into a single image. One solution is to remove the sky, and then replace it with a sky from a different photo, a stretched version of the sky from one of the montaged images, or a synthetic sky.

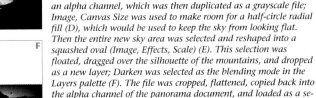

Five scanned photos (three are shown as A, B, and C) were combined using the rubber stamp to eliminate the seams. Then the sky was selected and filled with blue; the selection was also saved as an alpha channel, which was then duplicated as a grayscale file; Image, Canvas Size was used to make room for a half-circle radial fill (D), which would be used to keep the sky from looking flat. Then the entire new sky area was selected and reshaped into a squashed oval (Image, Effects, Scale) (E). This selection was floated, dragged over the silhouette of the mountains, and dropped as a new layer; Darken was selected as the blending mode in the Layers palette (F). The file was cropped, flattened, copied back into the alpha channel of the panorama document, and loaded as a selection so Levels could be used to lighten the bottom of the sky (G).

Making a Mezzotint

Overview *Experiment with the Mezzotint filter and Bitmap mode to get an effect you like.*

1

Filter, Pixelate, Mezzotint, Medium Dots

2

Mode, Bitmap, Diffusion Dither

3

Mode, Bitmap, Pattern Dither, Mezzotint-shape (from the PostScript Patterns folder)

4

Filter, Andromeda, Standard Mezzo, 85 lpi

A TRADITIONAL MEZZOTINT is produced with a halftone screen made up of custom dot shapes. (Halftone screens convert photos into patterns of tiny dots for printing.) In Photoshop you can experiment with several ways to create a mezzotint from a grayscale image:

1 Using Photoshop's Mezzotint filter. Choose Filter, Pixelate, Mezzotint; pick a dot, line, or stroke pattern in the Mezzotint dialog box's pop-out menu and click OK. (Unlike the other methods in steps 2 and 3, this treatment can also be applied to a color photo.)

2 Using a diffusion dither. Convert the image by choosing Mode, Bitmap and choosing Diffusion Dither as the Method.

3 Using a pattern dither. Choose one of the patterns supplied in the **patterns** folder inside the **photoshp** folder, and open the pattern document or paint with black on white to create your own pattern (see "Imitating Paint and Canvas" in Chapter 5 for instructions on making a seamlessly wrapping non-uniform pattern tile). If you make your own pattern, keep the balance between black and white fairly even, and then blur the file slightly (Filter, Blur, Gaussian Blur) to get a full range of grays.

When the pattern tile is ready, Select All (Ctrl-A) and choose Edit, Define Pattern. Now in your grayscale photo file choose Mode, Bitmap. Click the Pattern Dither button, enter an output resolution, and click OK. (The higher the Output resolution, the smaller the mezzotint "grain" will be and the less visible the pixels. But be careful you don't create a dot pattern too fine to print well.

4 Using Andromeda Software's Screens filter. For a variety of well-crafted mezzotint effects, you may want to buy and use this Andromeda Series 3 filter (see page 157). Install it in Photoshop's Plug-ins folder and choose Filter, Andromeda, Screens. Select one of the preset screen effects, or enter your own settings. We used Standard Mezzotint at 85 lines per inch for the 275 dpi image at the left and Mezzogram at 65 lines per inch for the 215 dpi image above.

Using an Image as a Halftone Dot

Overview *Use a grayscale image to make a custom "halftone dot" pattern; apply it to a photo.*

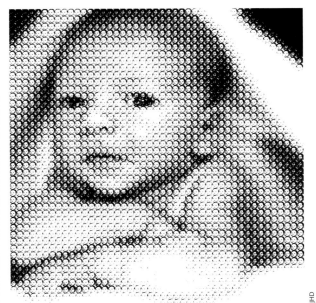

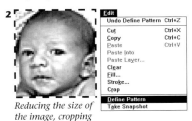

Original photo

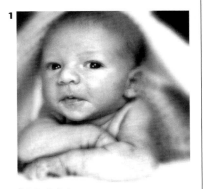

Reducing the size of the image, cropping it, and defining it as a pattern

Converting the grayscale photo to Bitmap

WORKING WITH A RECOGNIZABLE IMAGE, rather than a random, seamlessly tiling pattern, for a mezzotint effect can produce an interesting illustration. You can even use a smaller version of the image itself as the "halftone dot," as we did here.

1 Choosing an image for the "dot." Choose a grayscale image, or a selection from an image, with a broad range of tones — black, white, and a full range of grays.

2 Defining the pattern. Reduce the image or selection to the size you want it to appear when it's used as a custom halftone dot. You can do this by using Image, Effects, Scale on a selection or by choosing Image, Image Size. Then surround this small version with the rectangular selection marquee and choose Edit, Define Pattern.

3 Applying the pattern. Open the photo file that you want to "halftone" with your custom dot pattern. Convert it to Bitmap by choosing Mode, Bitmap (if the photo is in color, you'll have to convert it by choosing Mode, Grayscale first and then Mode, Bitmap). When the Mode of an image is converted from the 256 tones of grayscale to the black-and-white-only Bitmap, the intermediate gray shades are represented as dot patterns, which can be chosen in the Bitmap dialog box. Click the Custom Pattern button, enter an Output Resolution value around 300 to 600 dpi (we used 600), depending on how small you want the "halftone dots" to be relative to the image and whether you want to be able to see the pixels (lower resolutions) or not (higher resolutions), and click OK. *Wow!*

Mezzotinting with Noise

Overview *Apply a Noise filter in Monochromatic mode.*

PHOTO: CRAIG McCLAIN

1a

Original photo

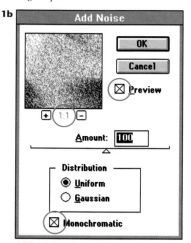

1b

Adding Monochromatic Noise

A MEZZOTINT-LIKE EFFECT for a color image can be achieved quickly and simply with the Add Noise filter, applied so that it causes a random brightness pattern on the image without introducing the color speckles of random hue variation. With Photoshop 2.5 this involved floating a copy of the image, applying a Noise filter, and then combining the filtered image in Luminosity mode with the original so that only the grayscale (brightness) information from the filtered photo was transferred to the final composite. In Photoshop 3 the Add Noise filter includes a Monochromatic option, which lets you apply hue-protected noise automatically, without having to combine two versions of the image.

1 Choosing hue-protected Noise. Open a color image in RGB mode. Choose Filter, Noise, Add Noise and choose Uniform. Click to select the Monochromatic option to produce hue-protected Noise. Within the dialog box, set the preview size (the line with the + and – boxes) at 1:1 for the most accurate view of the effect. If you want to see the effect on the image overall, not just in the preview box within the Add Noise dialog box, make sure the Preview checkbox is selected.

2 Experimenting with the amount of Noise. Use the pointer (which turns into the scrolling hand) to move the image around in the preview box until you see an area that will give you a good view of the changes.

Adjust the Amount slider until you see the effect you want in the preview window. When the preview looks good, move the Add Noise dialog box out of the way so you can see the effect on the

2a

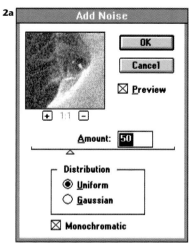

Choosing the preview area and experimenting with the amount of Noise

2b

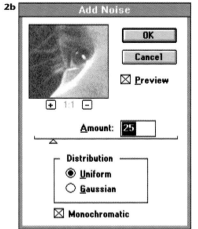

Adjusting the amount of Noise

image overall. Finally, click OK in the dialog box to accept the Noise settings and close the dialog box. We used a setting of 31 for this 590-pixel-wide image to get the effect shown on page 82.

Variations. For a larger but softer "grain," apply the Despeckle filter (Filter, Noise, Despeckle) to the image after applying the Monochromatic Noise. 📝

Applying the Despeckle filter after applying Monochromatic Noise

FILTER SETTINGS AND IMAGE SIZES

When you apply a filter or other special effect that uses "pixels" as the unit of measure — rather than "inches" or "percent," for example — the setting to use will depend on the degree of effect you want *and on the resolution* of the image you're working on. The larger the absolute size of the image — expressed either as the dimensions (in pixels) or the size of the file (in K or MB) — the higher the setting will need to be to produce the effect. In the examples shown below, note that a low setting has a much stronger effect on a smaller image than on a larger one. For the larger version, the setting has to be increased quite a bit to get a similar effect. So if you see a filtered image and want to create that particular effect on an image of your own, you need to know not only the filter settings that were used, but also the size of the image.

Image size: 250 pixels wide (157 K); Uniform Monochromatic Noise, Amount setting: 20

Image size: 500 pixels wide (625 K); Uniform Monochromatic Noise, Amount setting: 20

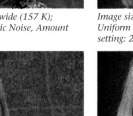

Image size: 250 pixels wide (157 K); Uniform Monochromatic Noise, Amount setting: 40

Image size: 500 pixels wide (625 K); Uniform Monochromatic Noise, Amount setting: 40

Dithering

Overview *Convert the image to Bitmap mode with a low-resolution Diffusion Dither; convert the Bitmap image to RGB color; select and copy only the black pixels to a separate transparent layer; replace black with a color gradient; make another layer for only the white pixels; replace white with another gradient.*

1a
Converting the Grayscale photo to Bitmap

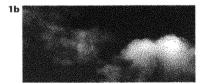

1b
The Bitmap image converted to RGB

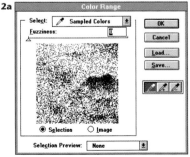

2a
Selecting the black pixels

A MEZZOTINT-LIKE EFFECT can be achieved with Photoshop's Diffusion Dither pattern for converting images to Bitmap mode. This kind of patterning can be useful for making the plates used for silkscreen printing or for adding a distinctive texture to a color illustration. If you start out by putting the black and the white elements of the dithered image on two separate layers, it's easy to experiment with color until you have exactly the result you want.

1 Converting a photo. Start with a color or grayscale image. Convert it to Bitmap through the Mode menu: If the image is in Grayscale mode to start with, choose Mode, Bitmap. If it's in color, you'll have to choose Mode, Grayscale first and then Mode, Bitmap, because you can't convert directly from a color mode to Bitmap or vice versa. When you make the conversion, specify a low resolution in the Bitmap dialog box. We used 123 dpi, but you can use any resolution low enough to show a pleasing pattern. The resolution that looks best to you may vary, depending on the content of your particular image and how large you want to print it.

2 Making a layer for the black pixels. To convert the dithered image to RGB mode so you can add color, choose Mode, Grayscale and then Mode, RGB.

Now select all the white pixels this way: Choose Select, Color Range. In the Color Range dialog box make sure the Select option is set to Sampled Colors and set the Fuzziness slider to 0 so you'll be sure to select only a single color (black). Then click on the leftmost eyedropper tool, move it onto the image, and click on a black pixel. (If you need to get a closer view in order to pinpoint a black pixel, hold down the Ctrl-spacebar key combination to turn the eyedropper into the magnifier temporarily.) Click OK to close the dialog

2b

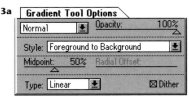

Copying the black pixels to a separate layer

3a

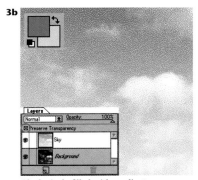

Setting the gradient options

3b

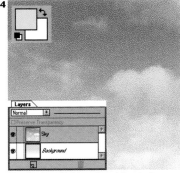

Black pixels filled with gradient

4

Gradient applied to color white pixels

5

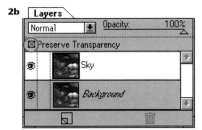

Gradients replaced with other colors (left) and with two solid colors (right)

box and make the selection. Copy the selection (Ctrl-C) and choose Edit, Paste Layer to make a layer that includes the white pixels only; we named our layer "Sky."

3 Coloring the black pixels. With this new layer active (grayed in the Layers palette), turn on Preserve Transparency by clicking in the check box at the top of the Layers palette. This will ensure that when you color the layer, only the existing pixels will be colored; the transparent areas will remain transparent.

Double-click on the gradient tool to open the its Options palette; set it for a Linear fill, for Normal mode, for Foreground To Background style, and for 100% Opacity. Then, in the toolbox, click on the Foreground and Background color icons in turn and choose colors for the extremes of the color gradient you'll use to replace the black pixels; we used a blue for the Foreground color and a lighter blue for the Background color. In the image, drag the gradient tool from where you want the gradient to begin to where you want it to end (we dragged from top to bottom). The black pixels will fill with the color gradient.

4 Adding the second color gradient. Activate the Background layer by clicking on its name in the Layers palette. You can now apply your second gradient — the one that will color the white pixels — to the entire Background layer. Set the Foreground and Background squares in the toolbox to new colors (we used a pink and white), and use the gradient tool again to apply the color (we again applied the gradient vertically, this time dragging from about a third of the way from the top to about a third of the way to the bottom). Although this operation will color both the black and the white pixels in the Background layer, the layer above (Sky in our example) will allow only the pixels that used to be white (the clouds in our example) to show through its transparent areas.

5 Experimenting with other color schemes. Now you can try new color gradients by repeating the coloring instructions in steps 3 and 4 with different colors. Or you can use a solid color rather than a gradient for either or both of the colors of the "mezzotint." Set one of the colors as the Foreground color and the second as the Background color. Instead of using the gradient tool in steps 3 and 4, use the Edit, Fill command to refill the pixels in the two layers. Whichever method you use, be sure to keep Preserve Transparency turned ON when you fill.

Combining resolutions. To use a low-resolution dither with a higher-resolution element as we did for the eye-in-the-sky image, choose a Bitmap resolution that's half or a fourth of the higher resolution. For more on combining resolutions, see page 120.

Coloring a Black & White Photo

Overview *Convert the grayscale image to RGB; add color by adjusting the color balance for highlights and shadows, by adjusting hue and saturation, or by layering color over the image.*

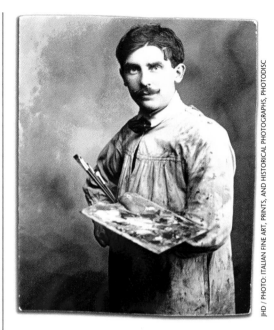

1

Original grayscale image converted to RGB

2

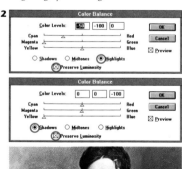

Color balance adjusted for highlights and shadows, using Preserve Luminosity

ADDING COLOR TO A GRAYSCALE IMAGE can produce from subtle to spectacular results. There are many ways to do it, and you'll see examples throughout the book. But here are three fairly quick and easy approaches, based on using Image, Adjust, Color Balance; using Image, Adjust, Hue/Saturation; and applying a new layer of color imagery in Color mode.

1 Preparing the grayscale image. Convert the grayscale image to color by choosing Mode, RGB Color. Now try step 2, 3, or 4 to get the color effect you want.

2 Changing the color balance. Choose Image, Adjust, Color Balance. Turn on Preserve Luminosity to preserve the relative brightness levels, so you can make significant changes in color without drastically changing the tonality. In turn, click and adjust the Highlights and Shadows. For a dramatic effect, use opposite settings that produce colors that are opposite on the color wheel (complementary colors). We used yellow for the shadows and pushed the highlights toward purple by increasing magenta and cyan.

3 Changing the hue. If step 2 doesn't give you exactly the color you want, modify the image further: Choose Image, Adjust, Hue/Saturation and move the Hue slider left or right to shift the colors around the color wheel until you find the option you like best.

4 Adding a layer of color. Starting again with the converted grayscale image (see step 1), this time add a layer of color over the image: Choose Window, Palettes, Show Layers (or use the Commands palette or a keyboard shortcut) to open the Layers palette.

3

Hue adjusted

4a

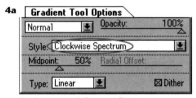

Setting up a rainbow gradient

4b

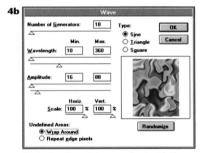

Distorting the rainbow gradient with the Wave filter

4c

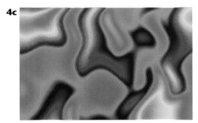

Gaussian Blur applied to distorted gradient

Add a new layer to the image by clicking the New Layer icon at the bottom left of the Layers palette. We named our new layer "Color Overlay."

To fill your color layer, you can use a color photo, a pattern, or an abstract color gradient, as we did here. To put color into our new layer, we made a color spectrum: We clicked the Foreground square at the bottom of the toolbox to open the Color Picker and chose a bright red from the purple-red end of the spectrum. After clicking OK to close the Color Picker, we opened it again by clicking the Background square. This time we chose a bright red from the orange-red end of the spectrum. We double-clicked the gradient fill tool to open the Gradient Tool Options palette and chose a Linear gradient with a Clockwise Spectrum. After dragging with the gradient tool to fill the layer with the rainbow gradient, we applied the Distort, Wave filter several times until we had the color effect we wanted. Finally, we chose Filter, Blur, Gaussian Blur and applied a 10-pixel blur to blend the colors in this 618-pixel-wide spectrum image.

When your Color Overlay layer is complete, you can experiment with its mode and Opacity settings. We changed the mode to Color, so that only the color (hue and saturation but not luminosity) was composited with the image in the Background layer, and we adjusted the Opacity to 25%.

Adding finishing touches. After you finish experimenting with color, you can combine effects if you like. We liked the overall effect we had produced inthe image we made in step 4, but we wanted to tone down the color in the upper left corner. So we used a softly feathered lasso to select an area of the color-balanced and hue-adjusted image from step 3, and dragged and dropped the selection onto the rainbow-colored image file. Both images were ex-

4d

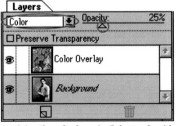

Applying the color layer in Color mode with Opacity adjusted

actly the same size, so when the selection was dragged into the rainbow-colored file, it automatically went into exactly the same position in the upper left corner of the image. The selection appeared as a Floating Selection in the Layers palette; Alt-double-clicking the Floating Selection name in the palette turned the imported piece into a layer of its own. Now the Opacity could be adjusted to achieve just the right blend with the spectrum effect, resulting in the final color blend you see at the top of page 86. *Wow*

Combining Positive & Negative

Overview *Turn the image into a negative; copy it into a new layer; turn the new layer back into a positive; adjust Layer Options settings to blend the positive and negative versions of the image.*

JEFF McCORD

Original positive image

Negative

PHOTOSHOP'S LAYER OPTIONS FUNCTION (from the pop-out menu in the Layers palette) has replaced Composite Controls, which was in the Edit menu in version 2.5. It lets you control how an image in one layer combines with the layers underneath. You can control the opacity and blending mode of the active layer, and you can choose, by brightness level, whether pixels in the combined image will come from the active top layer or the underlying image.

For an illustration for *Entertainment Weekly* magazine, Jeff McCord wanted a negative look, but he found that the facial features in a negative version of an image from the "Director's Cut" of the movie *Basic Instinct* were too ghostly. He used Composite Controls in Photoshop 2.5 to combine positive brightness values and negative color. Here's how it could be done in Photoshop 3:

1 Making a negative. Open an RGB image, and choose Image, Map, Invert to make a negative.

2 Adding a layer. Now open the Layers palette (available through Palettes, Show Layers in the Windows menu). The image appears on the Background layer. Drag the thumbnail of the image on the Background layer to the New Layer icon at the bottom of

2

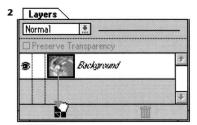

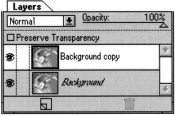

Copying the negative image into a new layer

3

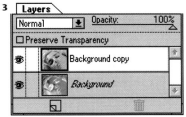

Turning the new layer positive

4

Composited in Luminosity mode

5

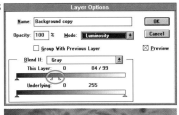

Input "trimmed" to 84 with some "fuzziness"

the Layers palette. This will create a new layer — Background Copy — above the original Background.

3 Making the new layer positive. With the Background Copy layer selected (active), choose Image, Map, Invert (Ctrl-I) to turn the negative into a positive.

4 Combining positive and negative. Now double-click the thumbnail image in the Background Copy layer to open the Layer Options dialog box, so you can control how the images in the Background Copy layer and the Background layer will be merged. (The Background Copy layer is called "This Layer" in the "Blend If" section of the Layer Options dialog box, since it's the active layer.) Use the Gray option, and select Luminosity mode so only the brightness values of the positive image (not hue or saturation) will contribute to the composite.

5 Making adjustments. Now move the slider triangles for This Layer to define exactly which part of the brightness range you want the positive to contribute. Holding down the Alt key as you drag a triangle will let you move the two halves separately so the colors will change gradually over a range of brightnesses and the transitions will be smooth. After making his composite, McCord adjusted the Levels and Color Balance of the finished image to make it a deeper blue and pasted the patchwork of frame grabs on top to make the final image. *Wow!*

"Sketching" a Portrait

Overview *Convert a grayscale image to RGB; apply a filter or special effect on the Red, Green, and Blue channels separately; experiment with removing the color from different channels.*

KATRIN EISMANN / PHOTO: DOUGLAS KIRKLAND

1

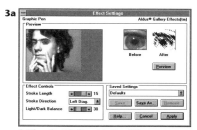

Grayscale converted to RGB and Levels adjusted

2

Setting up to work on one channel while viewing all

3a

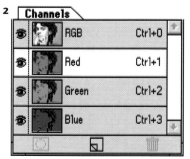

Setting the GE Graphic Pen filter

WORKING IN THE INDIVIDUAL RGB CHANNELS can produce some interesting treatments of color photos or of grayscale images converted to color. Katrin Eismann explored this technique in a portrait that began as a black-and-white photo. While there may be a number of different methods for accomplishing this effect in Photoshop, we reproduced it as shown in these steps. Looking at the steps that built the effect provides a good demonstration of how the positive and negative values in the individual channels can interact in the overall image. If you don't have the Gallery Effects filter set used here, you might want to experiment with the individual-channels technique by starting with one of the native Photoshop filters that produce random variations, such as Noise, Pointillize, or Mezzotint and then applying other effects, such as a Stylize filter, to the individual channels.

1 Converting the photo to RGB. Convert the image from Grayscale to RGB by selecting from the Mode menu. The conversion will put the same grayscale information in each of the color channels. For this photo, after the conversion to RGB, the gamma (gray) slider in the Image, Adjust, Levels dialog box was moved a little to the left to lighten the image overall.

2 Setting up to work on individual channels. Set black as the foreground color and white as the background color. (A quick way to do this is to click on the small default colors icon below the Foreground and Background color squares in the toolbox.) Select the first color channel you want to work on by clicking on that channel's icon in the Channels palette (opened by choosing Win-

3b

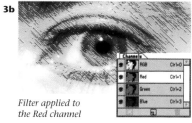

Filter applied to the Red channel

3c

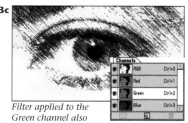

Filter applied to the Green channel also

4a

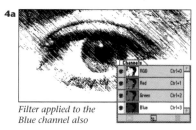

Filter applied to the Blue channel also

4b

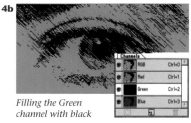

Filling the Green channel with black

4c

Working in the RGB channel: Removing the magenta

dow, Palettes, Show Channels). You can view the effect on the entire image by clicking in the eye icon column next to the RGB channel name.

COLOR CHANNELS IN COLOR

To view individual color channels in color rather than in grayscale, choose File, Preferences, General, Color Channels In Color.

3 Operating on the channels. Now make changes to the individual channels. For this image, the GE Graphic Pen filter from Gallery Effects Classic Art (Vol. 1) was applied with the maximum Length setting (15), a Stroke Direction setting of Left Diag., and a Light/Dark Balance setting of around 30. The setting was the same for all channels, but because the filter operates with a degree of random variation, a slightly different effect was produced each time it was run. The filter was run first on the Red channel, then on the Green, and then on the Blue, although the order of operations is not important. Shown here are the progressive results as seen by viewing all the channels together as each step was added.

4 Eliminating one color. Now you can eliminate the color effect contributed by one of the channels. To produce the red, blue, and black composition seen in the opening image, the Green channel was selected by clicking on it again in the Channels palette. Pressing Alt-Backspace filled the channel with black. This effectively removed the green lines from the RGB image, but it also removed the green component of the white background, leaving a strong magenta component, since magenta is the complement (opposite, or negative) of green. To remove the magenta, leaving a white background, the RGB channel (0) was activated by clicking on its icon in the Channels palette. Image, Adjust, Hue/Saturation was chosen, and the M (for magenta) button was selected; this would make the color adjustments apply only to that particular color. The Lightness slider was moved all the way to the right, to a value of +100. This turned the magenta white without affecting other colors.

ADJUSTING A SINGLE COLOR

Clicking one of the color buttons in the Image, Adjust, Hue/Saturation dialog box will let you adjust only one part of the color spectrum in an image. But be aware that this kind of adjustment in a photo can lead to artificial-looking color breaks, because one color changes but the colors that blend it into the surroundings don't change with it.

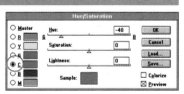

Solarizing a Portrait

Overview *Remove imperfections such as dust and scratches. Adjust the image map in the Curves dialog box to convert some of the tones to negative values.*

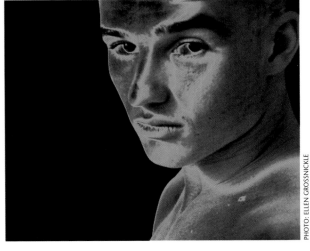

PHOTO: ELLEN GROSSNICKLE

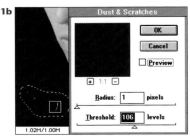

1a

Original portrait

1b

Removing dust and scratches

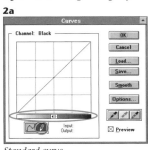

1c

Converted to grayscale

SOLARIZATION, FIRST OBSERVED BY Sabbatier in 1860 and later discovered accidentally by Lee Miller and Man Ray in 1929, is the partial reversal of negative to positive, caused by a brief exposure to light during development, often with dramatic effect. Today's photographic materials are much faster, which makes it difficult to solarize a photo in the darkroom. But you can get similar effects by manipulating Photoshop's image map.

1 Preparing the scan. Open your scan on-screen. (Both color and black-and-white images can be solarized.) The portrait shown here started out in color. To get rid of scratches on the original that had been picked up by the scan, we applied the Dust & Scratches filter (Filter, Noise, Dust & Scratches), selecting the areas around scratches, clicking the square cursor on the image to pinpoint the area to be shown in the preview window, setting the Radius at 1 and the Threshold at 128, and moving the Threshold slider down until the scratches disappeared. The file was then converted by choosing Mode, Grayscale.

2 Experimenting with solarization. To begin experimenting, open the image map by choosing Image, Adjust, Curves (Ctrl-M). Click the arrows below the curve to set the light-to-dark indicators so that white is on the left, and select the pencil icon below the curve. Also select the Preview checkbox. A lower-left-to-upper-right diagonal line is the normal image map, with every input value represented by the same value on output. Redrawing the line to make an upper-left-to-lower-right

2a

Standard curve

2b

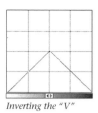

Drawing a "V"; this setting produces the same effect as the Solarize filter.

2c

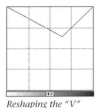

Inverting the "V"

2d

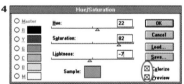

Reshaping the "V"

3

Solarizing the portrait

4

Colorizing

5

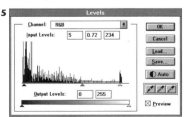

Making final adjustments

diagonal produces a negative, with each input value represented by its opposite. It follows, then, that a V- or inverted-V-shaped line will produce a partial positive, partial negative. With the pencil icon selected, experiment by redrawing the line until you get a result you like. To get straight line segments, hold down the Shift key and click at the endpoints of the segments you want to draw.

3 Solarizing the portrait. To make the solarized image shown in the opening illustration, we scanned a color photo and converted it to grayscale as described in step 1. Then we adjusted the Curves as described in step 2 and clicked OK to apply it.

4 Adding color. To get the colorized effect we were after, we converted the file back to RGB by choosing Mode, RGB Color. Before we opened the Hue/Saturation dialog box, we used the eyedropper tool to pick up a medium gray tone. Then we chose Image, Adjust, Hue/Saturation (Ctrl-U); the tone we had chosen appeared in the Sample box. We turned on the Preview and Colorize boxes, and adjusted hue, saturation, and lightness.

> **"GRAYSCALE" IN COLOR**
>
> To turn a color image into a "grayscale" but keep it in a color mode for custom coloring, use Image, Adjust, Desaturate.

5 Making final corrections. We adjusted the tonal range with Image, Adjust, Levels. Besides changing the contrast, this changed the color somewhat. We also used the lasso and the Fill command set to Lighten and with Opacity set to 40% to lighten the dark spots that had started as a too-intense highlight on the nose in the original image.

Experimenting. Solarizing can produce some dramatic effects both in grayscale and in color, and it can be particularly effective for living subjects — plant or animal. The feeling created by a solarized portrait can vary greatly, depending on what parts of the image remain positive and which appear negative. Here are some examples of color images that were solarized with image maps similar to those used in step 2. Image maps can be saved by clicking the Save button in the Curves dialog box and opened again by clicking the Load button (see step 2a).

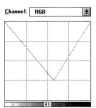

Solarizing a color image turns some tones into their complements.

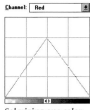

Solarizing one color channel produces a different result.

PHOTO: SUSAN HELLER

A black-and-white photo was scanned in RGB mode (above left). Altering the curves for two of the three channels colorized the photo (right).

REMAPPING COLORS

Adjusting the image map by working in the Curves dialog box can produce some wild color changes. Choose Image, Adjust, Curves and select the curve tool (rather than the pencil). Then click to establish a series of curve points, which you can drag to new positions if you want to. Shown below are the original image map and its straight diagonal Curve, along with three color variations and the Curves that produced them.

Original image

Curve adjusted in main RGB channel

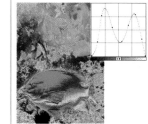

Curve adjusted in main RGB channel

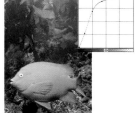

Curve adjusted in Blue channel only

Popping Color

Overview *Open a color file; copy the subject to a new layer; adjust the hue and saturation of the background layer.*

A POPULAR EFFECT IN BOTH PRINT AND VIDEO is to isolate the subject of an image by "graying out" the background. This effect can be used to emphasize the subject, to simplify the background for over-printing type, or to tie an image to others in a publication.

1 Isolating the subject. Use the pen tool (activate it by pressing the "T" key) to outline the subject. You can start with other selection methods — for instance, Select, Color Range — and then convert the resulting selection to a path by clicking the Save/Make Selection button, the center icon at the bottom of the Paths palette. Then adjust the path, if necessary, to better fit the subject. Using a path lets you fine-tune the outline without worry of accidentally dropping and losing the selection.

When the path is finished, convert it to a selection (by pressing the Enter key). Then float the selection (Ctrl-J) and save the selected area as a new layer (Alt-double-click on the Floating Selection name in the Layers palette).

2 Desaturating the background. Activate the Background layer by clicking on its name in the Layers palette. Then choose Image, Desaturate.

3 Trying another variation. For the image at the top of the page we used a variation of the desaturation process. We chose Image, Adjust, Hue/Saturation. The Colorize box was selected, the Hue slider was adjusted to the desired color, and then the color was desaturated to 25%. (When Colorize is OFF, the Saturation scale goes from –100 to +100; when it's on, the range is 0 to 100.) Finally we added type to the image.

1a

Outlining the subject with the pen tool

1b

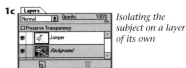

Adjusting the path

1c

Isolating the subject on a layer of its own

2

Desaturating the Background layer

3

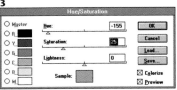

Settings for colorizing and desaturating

Retouching a Photo

Overview *Scan the image; use Curves to adjust brightness and contrast in highlights, midtones, or shadows; roughly select the background area; clean up the selection; save the selection as a mask; replace the background; make repairs.*

NOT ALL PHOTO-RETOUCHING JOBS are glamorous, but the technique can be practical and profitable. The San Diego Gas & Electric Company wanted to show the City Council of Oceanside, California how their streets would look if power lines were buried. The goal was to produce "before" and "after" photos the officials could hold in their hands for comparison.

1 Adjusting "exposure." Before retouching begins, the brightness and contrast of the original image may need correcting. We had scanned the original black-and-white photo as an RGB file to gain more information than a grayscale scan would have provided. After the scan was converted to grayscale (Mode, Grayscale), we applied Image, Adjust, Curves to bring out shadow detail.

The Curves function provides a way to isolate contrast and brightness changes to specific tonal ranges, such as quarter tones or three-quarter tones. Move the cursor out of the Curves box and onto the image (it becomes an eyedropper) and click to sample a tone you want to change. A small circle on the Curve shows the location of that tone. Note the position of the circle and click there on the Curve to establish a point; drag to adjust its position. Then move other parts of the Curve back toward their original positions.

2 Selecting the background. It can be very hard to seamlessly remove elements like power lines from a background texture like the sky, which can extend over a large area with subtle color changes. Sometimes it's easier to select the background, turn the se-

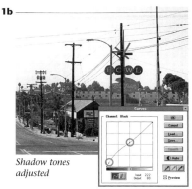

1a

Sampling shadows in the grayscale image

PHOTO: ROY ROBINSON

1b

Shadow tones adjusted

2

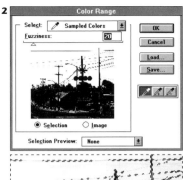

Selecting by color

3a

Selection turned into a Quick Mask

3b

Adding to the Quick Mask

3c

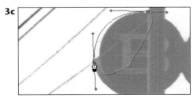

Repairing the mask

lection into a mask, edit the mask to remove the extraneous elements, and then replace the entire background with a new one. For instance, instead of trying to remove the power lines by using the rubber stamp to paint sky over them, we decided to select the sky by color, add the power lines to the sky selection, and replace the entire selected area.

To select the sky by color, we chose Select, Color Range. We wanted to make a selection that included all the grays in the sky. With Selection chosen for the display in the Color Range dialog box, we began by clicking with the Color Range eyedropper tool on a light part of the sky. To extend the range of selected tones, we held down the Shift key and clicked on what seemed to be the darkest part of the sky. We continued to Shift-click, widening the range of selected tones, until the entire sky showed up as white in the preview box. Our selection included some light spots among the buildings, and it had missed the poles and wires. But now that the selection by Color Range had done most of the work, we could correct these omissions in the mask.

CHOOSING THE RIGHT FUZZINESS SETTING

When you select by Color Range it's a good idea to set the Fuzziness somewhere around 16 to 32 to provide antialiasing. With a lower Fuzziness setting you get a very hard-edged selection and risk abrupt color breaks at the edges of the selected area. As the Fuzziness setting gets higher, you tend to get a feathered effect, making the selected area partly transparent. To select an area by color with a smooth, antialiased (but not feathered) edge, Shift-click with the Color Range eyedropper to expand the selection until it includes the area you want, and keep the Fuzziness setting around 16 to 32.

3 Using Quick Mask. When the selection is as complete as you can get it with the eyedropper and Fuzziness slider, click on the Quick Mask icon in the toolbox. Then use the selection tools, eraser, and paintbrush to edit the mask.

The goal was to create a mask to protect everything but the sky and power lines. With black and white set as the Foreground and Background colors, respectively, we started by selecting a large rectangular area at the bottom of the mask and pressing Alt-Backspace to fill it with mask material; to repair the few remaining white spots that were outside the sky, we painted with a paintbrush. We used the eraser to remove parts of the mask that covered the power lines.

We clicked and drew with the pen tool (pressing "T" to open the Paths palette and select the pen icon just to the right of the pointer arrow) to surround geometric areas that had been partially included in the selection by color, such as parts of the "BOWL" sign. We converted each path (dragging the Work Path name to the Fill Path icon at the bottom left of the Paths palette) to make it part of the protective mask.

4

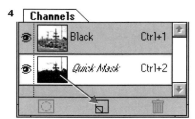

Saving the mask as an alpha channel

Replacing the sky with a gradient fill

6a

Cloning to cover the power pole

6b

Copying elements from the image

6c

Copying and flipping

6d

Trimming away hard-to-replace details

4 Saving the selection. Since the mask is a complex one, you may want to store it in an alpha channel for safekeeping: Open the Channels palette and drag the Quick Mask channel icon to the New Channel button at the bottom of the palette.

5 Replacing the background. Next make the Quick Mask selection active by clicking the Standard Selection icon (next to the Quick Mask icon in the toolbox). You can now replace the background. We used a gradient fill between two shades of the sky color from the original photo: With the main Black channel active (clicked in the Channels palette) and the sky selection loaded (in the Channels palette, drag its icon to the Convert icon at the bottom of the palette), we started by clicking the eyedropper tool on the top of the sky to set the Foreground color; then we held down the Alt key and clicked near the skyline to set the Background color. Next we double-clicked the gradient tool in the tool palette to open the Gradient Tool Options dialog box and set the tool to Normal, Foreground To Background, and Linear, with the Dither checkbox turned on. We dragged the tool from the top of the sky selection to the bottom. To simulate the grain of the original photo, we added Noise (Filter, Noise, Add Noise) at a very low Gaussian setting.

6 Completing retouching tasks. Use the rubber stamp, lasso, and other tools and functions to retouch smaller areas of the image. We used the rubber stamp in Clone (Non-aligned) mode to grab (Alt-click) textures to paint over the power pole. We also lassoed and Alt-copied parts that could be reused, such as the "e" in the "Blue Palette" sign.

For the "O" in "BOWL," we flipped a selection (Image, Effects, Flip) to mirror the intact half of the letter.

Knowing what elements *not* to restore completely can save you a lot of time. For example, rather than trying to paint the missing part of a palm frond, we shortened the frond by rubber-stamping the roof texture over it.

Printing the picture. So that city officials could compare "before" and "after," the original and retouched scans were output to negative film at a halftone screen of 200 lines per inch, and contact prints were made.

GRAYSCALE OUTPUT

Most resin-coated (RC) paper used for imagesetting was designed for high-contrast typesetting; it was not intended for printing grayscale images. To avoid overly contrasty prints, output images to negative film and then make contact prints.

Softening the Focus

Overview *Copy an image, or part of an image, to an independent layer; blur this layer; recombine it with the original.*

1a

Original image

1b

Floating a copy

SINCE THE END OF THE 19TH CENTURY, photographers have used haze and fog effects to impart a soft quality to an image, hiding the detail in the highlights, or in both the highlights and the midtones, or in the image overall. With a camera, the effect is sometimes achieved by smearing petroleum jelly very thinly on a filter placed in front of the lens, or by breathing on the filter, or even by placing fine nylon mesh over the enlarging lens in the darkroom. This technique is often used to hide small skin blemishes in portraits, to make hair look softer, or to add a romantic air. In Photoshop you can get a similar effect with Gaussian Blur and the Layers palette.

1 Making a copy of the image on a new layer. Select all or part of an image. If you select a part, feather the selection a few pixels. Press Ctrl-J to float the selection — that is, to make a copy of it that sits exactly over the original. Then open the Layers palette and turn the floating selection into a new layer of the image: Drag the Floating Selection name in the Layers palette onto the New Layer icon at the bottom of the palette to make Layer 1.

A LAYERING SHORTCUT

To make a floating selection into a layer without dragging and without bringing up the Make Layer dialog box, Alt-double-click on the Floating Selection name in the Layers palette.

2 Blurring Layer 1. Click on the Layer 1 name in the Layers palette to make it the active layer. Then choose Filter, Blur, Gaussian Blur. We used a setting of 5 pixels for this 760-pixel-wide image.

3 Adjusting mode, Opacity, and Layer Options to make haze. With the Layers palette open and Layer 1 active, make one of the following changes to the settings in the palette:

1c

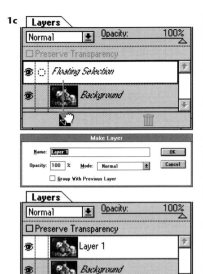

Turning the floating selection into Layer 1

2

Blurring Layer 1

- To reduce the haze effect but still apply it to all the tonal values in the selected area, choose Normal and enter an Opacity value.
- To refine the haze effect to soften the highlights only, choose Lighten and adjust the Opacity to control the strength of the haze effect. (We used this technique for the opening image.)
- To create a painted look, reducing the number of colors and softening them, choose Darken and enter an Opacity value.

Other haze effects can be achieved by using the "This Layer" and "Underlying" sliders in the Layer Options dialog box. To soften the image only within a particular tonal range, hold down the Alt key and drag the Underlying black and white sliders. Holding down the Alt key as you drag will allow you to split each slider triangle, so you can smooth the transition by defining a range of colors that are to be only partially composited. Move the two parts of each triangle apart slightly to avoid harsh color breaks. Experiment with the slider positions. The settings that work best will depend on the colors in the image and the effect you're trying to achieve.

IN THE PINK

To add a "healthy glow," particularly appropriate for a portrait or a still life of fruit or flowers, you can try a method that uses the color channels of an RGB file rather than layers: Activate only the Red channel of an RGB file but turn on the eye icons so you can view all three channels together; apply the Gaussian Blur filter. The image is softened and a small amount of the red component is blurred outward, beyond the face, flower, or fruit. The unblurred Green channel maintains the detail so that the blurring effect is not too strong.

4 Saving the file. When you have an effect you like, click OK to close the Layer Options dialog box. If you think you may want to experiment with the image some more in the future, save it in Pho-

3a

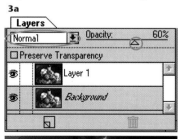

3b

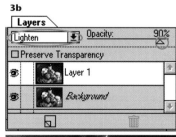

Reducing the opacity of the blurred layer

Softening the highlights with Lighten

3c

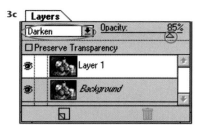

Creating a painted effect with Darken

3d

Softening only part of the tonal range

4

Palette Options...

New Layer...
Duplicate Layer...
Delete Layer

Layer Options...
Add Layer Mask

Merge Layers
Flatten Image

Two ways to flatten the image

toshop 3 format, which preserves the layers. If not, you can make the haze effect permanent by flattening the image to combine Layer 1 and Background into a single Background layer (choose Flatten Image from the Layers palette's pop-out menu). Flattening the image saves file space and also lets you save the file in a format — EPS (.eps) or TIFF (.tif), for example — that can be imported into a page layout program. Another way to flatten is to use File, Save A Copy, which automatically makes a flattened copy of the file when you choose a file format that won't support layers, but leaves the Photoshop 3 version of the file intact and open.

"FLOATING" AND "UNDERLYING" SLIDERS

The sliders in the Layer Options dialog box control how the pixels of the active layer (This Layer) and the Underlying image will contribute to the composite:

• The sliders of the Underlying bar define the range of colors in the underlying image that are made available so they can be affected by the active layer. So if you want to protect light or dark pixels, move the Underlying sliders inward to eliminate these tones from the available range.

• The sliders of the This Layer bar determine what range of colors in the active layer will be allowed to contribute pixels to the composite image by replacing the corresponding underlying pixels. So if you want to use only the dark pixels, move the This Layer white slider inward to exclude light pixels from the range of contributing colors.

Together, the two sliders set up a sort of "if . . . then" proposition for each pixel in the underlying image: "If the pixel falls within the range established in the Underlying slider bar *and* the corresponding active-layer pixel falls within the range established in the This Layer slider bar, then replace the underlying pixel with the active one; otherwise, leave the underlying pixel as it is." Of course, this can be further complicated by the Opacity setting (which determines what percentage of the final pixel colors the active layer will contribute) and the mode setting.

PRODUCTIVITY SINKHOLES

Some of Photoshop's image-editing and compositing functions are so powerful and offer so many options that it's hard to stop experimenting once you

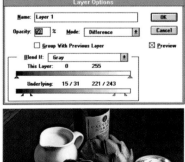

get started. Like the Filter menu, the Layer Options dialog box is one of these interfaces. A Photoshop devotee could get lost for days in the Filter menu or the Layer Options. In fact, if the artist didn't have a clear goal in mind for a particular image before opening Layer Options, the dialog box could tend to take over the aesthetic development (not to mention the schedule) of the work. Experimenting is a great way to learn about Photoshop's capabilities, but not necessarily when you have a specific design goal in mind and a job to finish.

Painting a "Duotone"

Overview _Open a CMYK file the same size as the grayscale image you want to color; in the CMYK file set up two alpha channels with custom mask colors; copy and paste the grayscale image into both; view both channels while you work in one channel at a time to alter the masks; copy and paste the contents of the two alpha channels into two of the CMYK channels for output._

Original grayscale image

Experimenting in Duotone mode

IN MOST OF THE COLOR PRINTING we see, the world is represented by the four process printing inks: cyan, magenta, yellow, and black. We tend to think this is the only way to get a wide variety of colors — a broad range of brights, neutrals, highlights, and shadows. But by using two complementary colors of ink, you can produce many more than two colors at less than half the price of a four-color piece. This comp for a wedding invitation in "retro" style is an example.

Printing a Photoshop image in two colors almost automatically suggests the Duotone mode. The program's Duotone function is ideal for taking advantage of custom color in a two-color printing job — either to add an obvious color accent to photos as part of the design of the piece, or as a subtle but effective way of extending the range of tones the printing press can produce. But Duotone mode has limitations. You can change the curves to modify the color treatment for a particular image, but no matter how you fiddle with the curves, it's virtually impossible to direct the colors to specific places in the image, independently of the highlight/midtone/ shadow information present at those spots.

The way to put the color exactly where you want it is by "hand-painting." But how can you do that, see the results interactively on-screen, and still be able to separate the file into the two spot colors so you can make the plates for printing each of two custom color inks?

One way to approach it is to take advantage of Photoshop's ability to show more than one alpha channel of a file on-screen at the same time. You can specify a custom mask color for each channel and see a close approximation of your ink colors as the channels develop. After working with the two alpha channels until you have the color combination you want, you can assign the contents of the channels to two of the CMYK channels and output only those channels to make the printing plates for the two custom ink colors.

3a

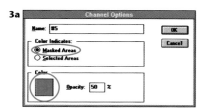

Click the color box in the Channel Options dialog box to change the mask color.

3b

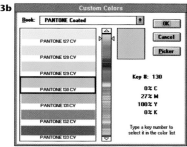

Choosing a custom color

3c

Setting the opacity of the channel "ink"

4

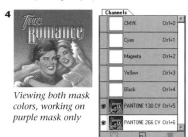

Viewing both mask colors, working on purple mask only

5a

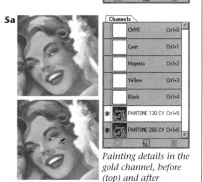

Painting details in the gold channel, before (top) and after

---

1 Setting up the file. Open the image in Grayscale mode. For this image the "True Romance" and "Jack & Jill" type outlines had been created in Adobe Illustrator, added (File, Place) to the grayscale image, and saved in separate alpha channels in the grayscale file.

2 Testing Duotone mode. Just in case a standard Duotone might produce the results you want, you can start out by experimenting with Mode, Duotone and loading and manipulating curves. You'll be "working blind," though, unable to see the result of your work until you click OK and close the color controls in the Duotone dialog box. Furthermore, although in most of Photoshop's default Duotone settings the two curves differ somewhat in shape, they both usually follow a basically lower-left-to-upper-right form. To get either of the two colors to appear alone anywhere in the image, you have to do some fairly drastic manipulation of at least one curve, as you can see in the Duotone Options dialog box shown here.

3 Making a CMYK file and alpha channels. If Duotone mode doesn't do the trick, try making a "hand-painted duotone." The first step is to copy the entire Grayscale image to the clipboard (Ctrl-A, Ctrl-C).

Now open a New file (Ctrl-N). Accept the settings in the New dialog box for Height, Width, and Resolution, but choose CMYK Color for the Mode. (Don't paste in your image just yet.)

In your new blank file create the first of the two alpha channels by choosing Window, Show Channels and then clicking the New Channel icon at the bottom of the Channels palette. When the Channel Options dialog box appears for this new channel (#5), make sure the default Masked Areas option is chosen. Click the color square to open the color picker, click the Custom button, and pick one of the two colors you will use in your custom duotone. (Check with your printer to find out the order in which the two colors of ink will be applied on the press and the approximate density of the second color when it's applied over the first. The color you use in channel 5 should be the color that will be applied second.) We chose a gold color and set the Opacity at around 85% to approximate the ink opacity.

With this new channel active in the Channels palette, paste the grayscale image from the clipboard (Ctrl-V). Repeat the new-channel and paste operations to create channel 6, to set your other custom color as its mask color, and to store another copy of the grayscale image in this new channel. This mask, representing the ink that will be applied first, should have an opacity of 100%.

4 Setting up the two-color view. Now you can view both channels (by clicking in the "eye" column of the Channels palette

5b

Loading an alpha channel from the grayscale file as a selection in the CMYK file

5c

Background removed and type filled; channels viewed together (top) and separately (below: gold, left; purple, right)

6a

Viewing the C and Y channels after pasting

6b

The gold (left) and purple printing plates

for both channels) as you work on only one of them (by clicking on the name of just one to turn its label white). With the two alpha channels set for viewing as you work, you can now see approximately how the two printed colors will interact.

5 Working in color. Use the painting and editing tools with the Foreground and Background colors set to black and white to alter each of the two channels. The background of our original image was removed from the gold channel by painting over it with white. The airbrush with black paint was used to distribute color softly but precisely for the gold highlights on the hair and cheeks.

Since the CMYK file was created to be exactly the same dimensions as the original grayscale file, the type outlines that had been saved in an alpha channel in the grayscale file could be loaded as a selection in each of the two custom color channels: With both files open and the color file active, we chose Select, Load Selection and loaded the Type channel from the grayscale file as a selection in the CMYK file.

With the selection loaded in the CMYK file, we worked in one alpha channel at a time. In the gold channel we filled the "True" lettering with black (the Foreground color, representing the mask) and filled the "Romance" lettering with a gradient from black to white (the Background color), so that it showed up in the mask as white at the top, turning to bright gold at the bottom. In the purple channel the edges of the lettering were filled with black, and "Romance" was filled with a white-to-black gradient to produce a transition from a tint of purple at the top to white at the bottom.

6 Making the printing plates. Now you'll paste the contents of the finished alpha channels into two of the four printer channels. (The C and Y channels were used in this case because they were the colors closest to the inks we were using.) Working in channel 5, select all and then copy. Click on Yellow in the Channels palette, and paste in the clipboard contents. Repeat the selecting, copying, and pasting process to put the contents of channel 6 into the Cyan channel. Save the file in CMYK mode. When the file is output, tell the imagesetting service to output only the specified plates, at the screen angles your printer recommends for your two ink colors. When you give the film to the printer, identify which plate is to be printed in each of the custom colors.

"Hand-Tinting" a Portrait

Overview *Convert the black-and-white image to RGB mode; select areas and adjust color, primarily in the midtones; desaturate light areas; add color details.*

JHD / PHOTO: RETRO AMERICANA, PHOTODISC

Original grayscale image

Converted to RGB

INCREASED CURVES PRECISION

Alt-click the grid in the Curves dialog box to get a finer scale (10% increments) so you can see more precisely where to place points when you adjust the curve.

THE COLORING OF BLACK-AND-WHITE PHOTOS with paints and pigments began very early in the history of photography, and its popularity persisted until color photography became widespread. Today the look is popular again — not a technicolor imitation of a color photo, but a subtle coloring reminiscent of the early hand-tinting process.

1 Correcting the tonality of the image. Whether you start with a color or a grayscale scan of the black-and-white image, you can use Photoshop's Levels (Ctrl-L) and Curves (Ctrl-M) adjustments to spread the tones in the image over the full range of possibilities and to bring out the shadow and highlight detail. For this image, which seemed a little dark to begin with, we used Image, Adjust, Curves to lighten the three-quarter tones, increasing the shadow detail. To find where to adjust the curve, move the cursor out of the Curves dialog box and onto the image. The cursor will turn into an eyedropper. Click and drag to pinpoint the tones that you want to adjust. As you drag the eyedropper, a small circle will move along the diagonal line in the Curves dialog box to show which part of the curve corresponds to the tone currently under the eyedropper. Then move the cursor back into the dialog box and click on the diagonal line at the point where you saw the circle.

We identified a dark area of the image with the eyedropper, clicking on the original curve at an Input value of about 15. Clicking on the diagonal established a point, and then dragging the point upward raised the entire curve. Clicking to form another point at an Input value of about 128 (halfway in the 0 to 255 range of the curve) and dragging downward closer to the center of the grid returned the midtones, quarter tones, and highlights to values close to their original settings.

1c

Shadows identified

1d

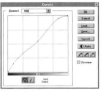

Curves adjusted

2a

Magic wand selection

2b

Selection enlarged by Shift-clicking

When making these kinds of Curves adjustments, it's important to maintain a smooth curve shape, without drastic changes in direction. Otherwise you can flatten the color or produce a sort of solarization effect with harsh tonal breaks.

LOCAL TONE ADJUSTMENTS

If you want to lighten or darken the three-quarter tones in only certain parts of an image, use the dodge and burn aspects of the dodge/burn/sponge tool

instead of Image, Adjust, Curves. In the Brushes palette choose a soft brush tip of an appropriate size. Double-click the dodge/burn/sponge tool to open the Toning Tools Options palette and choose Dodge or Burn, depending on whether you want to lighten or darken.

Hold down the mouse button and keep it down as you drag the tool back and forth over the area you want to change, watching until you've achieved the effect you want; then release the mouse button. Holding the mouse button down the entire time you're working makes it possible to undo (Ctrl-Z) the entire operation if you don't like the effect.

To reduce the intensity of the dodge/burn tool's effect, lower the Exposure setting before you start using the tool. If you want to reduce the effect even more, choose Midtones or Highlights to work in the shadow tones. At any of the three settings, these tools work on the entire range of tones (Highlights, Midtones, and Shadows) but they have a more pronounced effect on the part of the range that matches the setting you choose.

2 Making selections. Now select various parts of the image so you can make color adjustments. Select one area, change it by the method in step 3, then select another, and so on. For this image the dress was selected by clicking on it with the magic wand tool with a Tolerance setting of 32 (double-click the magic wand in the toolbox to open the Magic Wand Options palette to change the setting).

Additions to the selection were made by Shift-clicking on other parts of the dress. When the selection was complete, it was assigned a 5-pixel feather for this 1155-pixel-wide image. (To open the Feather Selection dialog box so you can set the feather radius, choose Select, Feather; or if you're using the default version of the Commands palette, either press the Feather key in the palette or press Shift-F6 on the keyboard.)

ADDING COMMANDS

You can add any of Photoshop's commands to any Commands palette by choosing New Command or Edit Commands from the palette's pop-out menu.

The skin was selected with the lasso, feathered 5 pixels (double-click the lasso to open Lasso Options to set the feather radius). This selection was drawn loosely to imitate the old hand-tinting process, which often involved soft overlapping of colors.

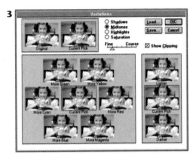

3

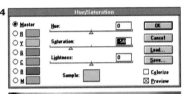

4

Adjusting color balance in the midtones

Desaturating white areas

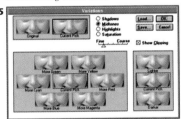

5

Adding color details

3 Coloring the selections.

Once selections have been made, open the Variations dialog box (Image, Adjust, Variations). The hue adjustment in the Variations box is especially good for skin tones — it's an electronic cosmetologist's dream that lets you see the tinting possibilities at a glance. Starting with fairly coarse adjustments (set with the slider near the top right corner of the dialog box), you can clearly see what color changes you're selecting. As you zero in on the changes you want, move the slider left to make finer adjustments.

4 Desaturating white areas. Areas that have been colored too much can be desaturated or recolored by selecting them with a very slightly feathered lasso (we used a 1-pixel feather) and choosing Image, Adjust, Hue/Saturation. For example, selecting the eyes and teeth and moving the Saturation slider to the left tends to take away most of the tint, while still maintaining the overall warm color cast that makes these features "at home" in this tinted image.

5 Adding color details. After hard-edged areas (such as the chair, butter, and bread crust and wrapper in this image) have been selected with a 1-pixel-feathered lasso and colored by using the Hue slider in the Hue/Saturation dialog box, subtle color variations can be added to the face. For instance, the cheeks in this image were selected with the lasso feathered to 5 pixels, and the Variations dialog box was used again to apply a little color by selecting the More Red version of the Midtones in the selected region. *Wow!*

Simulating Motion

Overview *Isolate the subject of an action photo on a layer of its own; copy the original photo to another layer and motion-blur the copy; adjust the blurring of the image by masking the subject or changing the opacity of the blurred layer.*

1a

Original image

SPORTS & RECREATION, PHOTODISC

1b

Subject isolated on a new layer made from a feathered selection

2a

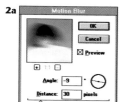

Blurring a copy of the entire photo with the Motion Blur filter

2b

Blurred copy of the original image

JHD

ADDING A SENSE OF MOTION to a photo can draw the viewer into the excitement of the scene and give a good static image the added drama to make it great. Using blurring techniques in Photoshop, you can simulate the effect of a camera panning to follow the subject (as shown above) or of a stationary camera with the subject in motion. With layers, layer masks, and the Motion Blur or Radial Blur filter, you have an amazing amount of flexibility in localizing the motion effect to a particular area of the image if you like — a waving hand, for example. And the Opacity control in the Layers palette lets you interactively reduce the blur until you see exactly the effect you want.

1. Isolating a sharp copy of the subject. You'll need a way to keep the moving subject in focus when you blur the background. First open your image file, and then open the Layers palette (Window, Palettes, Show Layers). Now select the subject: We made a rough selection, using a feathered lasso (we set a 10-pixel feather for this 900-pixel-wide image). We kept the selection border just far enough away from the subject so that the feathering didn't encroach on its outline. A rough, feathered selection can be used if the background image lacks detail, as this one does. But if the background is busy, you'll need a tighter, less feathered selection.

Next float the selection (Ctrl-J) and turn this floating selection into a layer of its own by Alt-double-clicking its name in the palette.

2 Blurring the picture. Make a duplicate copy of the full image in a new layer by dragging the Background label in the Layers palette to the New Layer icon at the bottom left of the palette. Then apply a blur to this layer. We used Blur, Motion Blur at an angle of –9° and a distance of 30 pixels.

At this point, the blurred image in the "Background Copy" layer entirely hides the original in the Background layer underneath it. But the sharp copy of the subject (in the top layer) keeps the subject in focus; and the feathered edge of the sharp subject blends seamlessly into the blurred image below it.

2c

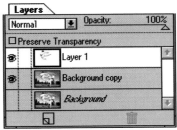

The result of layering the sharp subject and blurred Background Copy

3

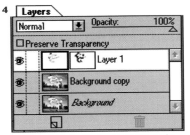

The dark parts of a painted layer mask (left) hide the corresponding parts of the subject. This will allow the blurred layer below to show through.

4

Layers palette for the image shown at the top of page 108, with the top layer and its mask offset to produce a strobe effect

5

To simulate a photo taken with a stationary camera, the subject is isolated and blurred over the sharp background image.

3 Tailoring the blur effect. If the image seems too perfect, you can add a little "blur detail" to the subject by masking out some areas of the top layer. With the top layer active, choose Add Layer Mask from the pop-out list in the Layers palette. Now the mask will be active but the subject itself — not the mask — will be visible, so you can see the blur start to show through as you use a soft paintbrush and black paint to paint the mask. Paint the areas where you want to see more of the blur; the dark areas of the mask will prevent the sharp layer from contributing to the composite image. If you "erase" too much of the sharp image, just use white paint on the mask to bring back the detail. Also, if the blur effect on the background seems too strong, you can sharpen the entire image by adjusting the Opacity slider of the blurred Background Copy layer to let the sharp original show through.

4 Simulating a strobe. To get the effect of a panning camera with a strobe (a flash that freezes part of the subject in focus while the slower shutter speed records the motion), you can offset the sharp copy of the subject. Working in the top layer, without making a selection, use the move tool to slide the subject a short distance in the direction of motion. Because nothing is selected, the mask will move along with the subject.

5 Trying a variation. To simulate a stationary camera photographing a moving subject, you can blur the subject and keep the background in focus: Select and copy the subject to its own layer as in step 1, and then apply a blur filter to this layer only.

More variations. Here are some other ways to tailor the blur to the image: You can show more motion in some parts of the subject than others by copying the subject onto two layers, blurring one more than the other, and then painting masks to allow more or less blur to show in different areas. And you can use a Radial Blur to show swinging or zooming motion.

A radial blur with a spin setting was used to show the motion of the swing. Extra height was added with the Image, Canvas Size command so the blur center could be defined outside the image — above, where the chain is fastened to a tree limb. Then the final image was cropped. For the photo of the runner, a Radial blur in Zoom mode, centered in the lower right corner of the image, brings the runner forward.

When **Julia Robertson** does *photo restoration,* she often has to repair images that are damaged by fire or water, or even torn in pieces. Photos are scanned on a desktop flatbed scanner. To restore this torn photo, she didn't attempt to put the pieces back together before scanning. Instead she worked with the pieces separately, isolating them from their torn edges by selecting each with the lasso. Then she used Select, Modify, Contract to shrink the selection inward to eliminate any remnant of the torn paper edge. With the torn paper removed, many of the pieces fitted together exactly, reducing the amount of rubber stamp work she had to do to get a seamless restoration. Robertson likes to work with layers. For torn images like this one, she builds the composite by adding pieces in higher layers. Reducing the new layer's Opacity setting to 50% lets her see how to align the layer with the composite developing underneath. Once the piece is aligned, she restores the Opacity setting to 100%. When restoration is complete, the photos are output to a film recorder as black-and-white or color negatives (from which prints are made) or as color slides.

Richard Ransier produced this image for the 1995 International Hair Show in Long Beach, California, to illustrate the theme *"What's New in the Year 2000?"* Aiming for a sci-fi look, Ransier and others designed and built an elaborate set. The set was painted, the hairdos were designed to match, and the live models were photographed in place. In Photoshop Ransier added highlights and reflections to the glass enclosures by selecting feathered triangles with the lasso in rubber band mode and airbrushing within those triangles with white paint. He found that airbrushing within feathered selections gave the glass a more convincing appearance than using a uniform fill. With the triangles of white on several layers, he could adjust the opacity of individual layers until he got just the effect he wanted.

Ransier used the burn/sponge tool to increase the color in the bottles on the table. He made a mask for the table and the man in the foreground so he could isolate this foreground area, soften it with a mild blur, and adjust its color balance to orange to shift the viewer's attention to the coiffed women in the background. The image in the computer monitor was made by selecting, copying, and scaling the face of one of the women in the enclosures.

Channel 1, Red

Channel 2, Green

Channel 3, Blue

To assemble his portrait of *Katrin Eismann*, **Russell Sparkman** started with two photographs he had taken with a digital camera. He combined negative and positive versions of these two images, using a different combination in each of the three (Red, Green, and Blue) channels of the image, in which separate gradations of light and dark had already been created. The bevel was made with pen paths that were created with the Shift key held down to make vertical, horizontal, and 45-degree diagonal paths. The paths were converted to selections so that the sides could be individually lightened or darkened with Image, Adjust, Levels to increase the feeling of depth. Noise was applied to the frame, and feathered selections were darkened to create shadows at the top and at the left.

Diane Fenster started with a still-video image to create *Rena Sketch*. She selected all and copied the image to the clipboard, and then chose from the Filter menu to run the KPT Find Edges Charcoal filter on the image in the window. Next she pasted the color version from the clipboard back onto the "charcoaled" image, selecting the Color mode (found in the Layers palette) to blend the two versions of the image.

To create *Swimmers,* **Cher Threinen-Pendarvis** started with a grayscale scan of a black-and-white photo of swimmers in a pool. She used the rubber stamp tool in Clone, Aligned mode to erase some lines that were painted on the side of the pool. She used the lasso to select the two figures, adding to and subtracting from the selection (hold down the Shift and Ctrl keys respectively) by lassoing parts of the figures. When the selection was complete, she feathered it slightly (Select, Feather, 2 pixels). She saved it in an alpha channel (Select, Save Selection). Then she duplicated the selection as a third channel and inverted it, to provide a mask that would select the water. Next, she converted this multi-channel document to RGB. To color the image, she loaded a selection from an alpha channel, chose a color from the Picker, and used Edit, Fill in the Color mode to add a tint to the selection. For the figures, she also used Lighten mode, filling the swimmers with "layers" of aqua and blue. For the water, she used the lasso, the magic wand, and the Select, Feather command on areas that were still heavy with black to fill patches with magenta and red in Lighten and Color modes. The "halos" were created by loading the alpha channel for the figures to select them, copying the figures to the clipboard, and using Paste Behind to put the copy behind the original. With the pasted figures still selected, she moved them to the left, and then feathered the edges of the selections and filled them with color in Normal mode at full Opacity. Fish were selected from another photo, colored, and copied into the image.

CHER THREINEN / PHOTO: MARY KRISTEN

Ellie Dickson had tried to paint *On Vine Street* with traditional artists' brushes but had failed to get the result she wanted. Then she tried Photoshop. She scanned the color snapshot, desaturated it (Image, Adjust, Desaturate) to retain the tones but remove the color, and then added her own tints. She began by selecting areas with a feathered lasso and applying color with the Fill command at 10 to 15% opacity in Color mode. Once the tint areas were established, she deselected everything and used the airbrush to add paint. She painted over the tints in Normal mode, varying the opacity. Finally, she added finishing touches with the paintbrush with a small brush tip setting.

Mark Siprut composed *Forgotten Bulgaria* from two photos taken with Fujichrome film and processed in Kodak Photo CD format. To make an alpha channel mask to silhouette the man, he opened the first file in RGB mode, chose the channel with the most contrast (the Red channel), duplicated it to make an alpha channel, and adjusted the contrast for the channel to isolate the figure from the background (Image, Adjust, Levels, Input Levels). He used the alpha channel mask to select the figure and dragged and dropped it into the telephone image on a layer of its own. He converted the file to Grayscale mode and adjusted its tonality with Curves and Levels; he also applied a dramatic amount of Unsharp Mask to the figure and added Noise to the image of the telephones, also darkening the shadows on the right half and using Curves to slightly solarize the left half. He converted the file to Duotone mode, chose Quadtone in the Duotone dialog box, and manipulated the curves for the four process colors, emphasizing magenta and black in the shadow tones, cyan in the midtones, and yellow and magenta in the highlights. To make the man more vivid than the background, he adjusted Levels in the telephone layer, using the Output Levels sliders to restrict the grays to between 25% and 75% of the full tonal range. This compressed the highlights and shadows so black would not be prominent in the background.

MONTAGE
AND
COLLAGE

For many montages, graduated or blurred masks do a better job of smoothing image transitions than hand tools such as the rubber stamp, smudge, or blur/sharpen tool. But if you need to use these tools to blend images, consider making a transparent "repairs" layer above your artwork. Stamp, smudge, blur, or sharpen on this new top layer in Normal mode with Preserve Transparency turned off. (Turn on Sample Merged if you want to sample all visible layers as if they were merged into one layer.) If you find you don't like some of what you've done, you can lasso the part you want to redo, delete it from the layer, and start again.

JANET ASHFORD

IN TRADITIONAL PHOTOGRAPHY and photo-illustration the distinction between montage and collage is significant. *Montage* is a method of making a single photographic print by superimposing several negatives. *Collage* is the assembly of separate photographic images mounted together, sometimes with other nonphotographic elements, to form another picture. With Photoshop, since photos and nonphoto elements can be combined, and since the "print" is likely to be output as part of a complete page layout, the distinction between montage and collage breaks down. But whatever you call it, the process becomes much easier, with no need for darkroom or glue.

Some of Photoshop's most useful compositing techniques involve feathered selections; gradient selections applied in layer masks; alpha channels; the rubber stamp tool; Paste Into (and Paste Behind) from the Edit menu; Image, Apply Image; Image, Calculations, Composite; and the composite controls provided in the Layer Options dialog box, available through the pop-out menu in the Layers palette. In addition to reading about the montage/collage projects described in this chapter, check the index for more information on these topics.

Making a successful "seamless" photo montage, when that's your goal, involves more than choosing the right kind of selection and compositing techniques — like using a feathered lasso or marquee to create a soft, blending edge for the selection, or getting rid of background pixels at the edge of a selection to get a clean silhouette, or using Gaussian Blur on the Background layer to create a realistic depth of field. For two or more images to blend seamlessly, they should match in several respects. For example, the light should be coming from the same direction, and the amount of detail and color cast of the shadows and highlights should be the same. Highlight and shadow detail can be manipulated by using Image, Adjust, Curves and Image, Adjust, Levels. And color cast can be identified with the eyedropper tool and the CMYK readings in the Info window (choose Window, Palettes, Show Info to open it); then the color cast can be adjusted — for example, with Image, Adjust, Color Balance or Image, Adjust, Variations.

However, changing the direction of the light can be much more difficult than managing shadow detail or color cast. If the elements you want to blend are fairly flat (like pictures on a wall), the

continued on page 116

Layer Options

Simply layering the images puts the moon in front of the mountains.

Leaving the layers in the same order but restricting the Underlying setting to a range of dark colors puts the moon behind the mountains, without constructing a mask.

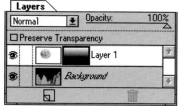

Adding a gradient-filled layer mask provides a gradual transition.

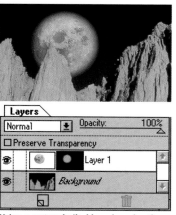

Using a custom-built, blurred mask softens the edges of a montaged element.

Lighting Effects filter may be helpful. For example, if the final effect you're looking for will tolerate it, you may be able to "overpower" the varied "native" lighting of the elements by applying the same lighting effect to all the parts. But if Lighting Effects won't work, it's generally better to continue your search for photos that match in this respect than to try to make adjustments to correct the lighting.

MAKING SEAMLESS TRANSITIONS

Photoshop 3's Layers palette makes it much easier to combine images than it was in previous versions of the program:

- To start with, elements on different layers can be **moved around** as separate objects until you're happy with the arrangement.

- The **blending,** or **transfer, mode** for each layer can be set to control how that layer blends with the image below — by color, saturation, or brightness values, independently or in combination.

- The **Opacity** of a layer can be adjusted to give an entire element an "only partly there" look.

- With the "This Layer" and "Underlying" sliders in the **Layer Options** dialog box, you can control what parts of the overlying image drop out and what parts of the image underneath can be replaced. (The control points of the sliders can be split by dragging with the Alt key held down, and the two halves can be spread apart to make the transitions look more gradual.)

- To make an element fade into the rest of the image gradually, you can create a **gradient layer mask**: Choose Add Layer Mask from the Layers palette's pop-out menu, and with the mask active, use the gradient fill tool to make a black-to-white transition, using white where you want the image on that layer to show through at full strength and black where you want it to be completely absent from the composite.

- You can also make a **custom-fitted blurred mask** for the object you want to composite: Add a layer mask, and with the layer mask active, press Ctrl-Alt-T to load the layer's transparency mask as a selection in the new layer mask. Then invert the selection (Select, Inverse) and fill this new inverse selection with black. Drop the selection and then run the Gaussian blur filter to soften the edges of the mask.

Making Montages

Overview *Open a background image file; add collage elements by selecting, dragging, dropping, and creating layer masks.*

Background image after applying Variations and inverting the color of the right half

Original Couple image

Layer Options...
Add Layer Mask
Adding a layer mask

Feathered selections filled to mask Couple

Masked Couple image over background

THERE ARE PROBABLY ALMOST AS MANY WAYS to merge photos as there are Photoshop artists. The montage shown here was put together using several different methods of blending images. It began with a number of black-and-white photos that were composited in RGB mode so both warm and cool grays could be used. The elements were layered, mostly in Normal mode and at full Opacity.

Second only to choosing the right composition to communicate your idea, the most important factor in making a successful photo montage is what happens at the edges where the parts blend. A smooth but dynamic merging of images can make the difference between a unified, effective collage and an awkward "cut and pasted" look.

1 Making a background. Open the image you want to use as a background. This collage began with two group photos — one of women and one of men. Most of this side-by-side image composite would be hidden, but it would act as a "texture" that conveyed the idea of human relationships. We reduced the contrast with Image, Adjust, Levels, moving the black point slider of the Output Levels to the right. The color change — a shift toward the cool (blue-violet) end of the spectrum — was accomplished with adjustments to the midtones via Image, Adjust, Variations, as were all the other changes used in making this collage. The right half of the composite image was selected with the rectangular marquee in its default (Normal) Style and turned into a negative (Ctrl-I) for contrast with the other images in the collage.

2 Using a feathered, freeform layer mask. The first blending method used in this montage involves making a layer mask that will mask out part of an overlaid image. Open the second image of the collage and use the move tool to drag and drop it into the background image.

Add a layer mask by choosing Add Layer Mask from the Layers palette's pop-out menu. The mask will be active (indicated by a dark

3a

Diver masked with airbrushed layer mask

3b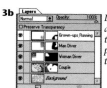

Layers palette after adding the couple, the divers, and the people running on the beach

4a

Selection made with the elliptical marquee with a Feather

4b

Selection dragged into the montage file

5a

Square images added

5b

The bottom of the layer mask for Squares

5c

Squares layer masked into the montage

border around it in the Layers palette) but you'll be looking at the image itself. Use a feathered lasso to surround the parts of the image you want to mask out. We used a feather of 75 pixels for this 1100-pixel-wide image to get a very soft blending edge. Hold down the Shift key to add new lassoed areas to the selection. To completely mask out certain areas, make sure the Foreground color is set to black and press Alt-Backspace. Once the mask is made you can reselect and lighten some areas to let the image show partially. We selected the area to the left of the couple, again with a feathered lasso, chose Image, Adjust, Levels, and moved the black Output slider to lighten this area of the mask to dark gray.

3 Softening the edge of the mask. We used a method similar to step 2 to import and mask the two diving board images and the couple running on the beach. But to further soften the edges of each layer mask, we used a fairly large, soft airbrush with white paint to paint the edge of the mask so these images would fade into the background image more gradually.

4 Making a traditional vignette. Framing an image by selecting it with a rectangular or especially a round shape is another collage technique. To create a "world of their own" effect for the boy and girl running on the beach, a feathered elliptical marquee was used to select them, along with part of their background. (To select the elliptical marquee, you can press the "M" key once or twice, or Alt-click the rectangular marquee in the tool palette, or double-click it to open the Marquee Tool Options palette and choose a Shape. Set the Feather in this palette also.)

The selection was dragged and dropped into the collage file, where it became a floating selection. Double-clicking the Floating Selection label in the Layers palette opened the Make Layer dialog box so we could turn the floating selection into a layer and name it.

5 Using a graduated mask. Another way to blend collaged images is to build a gradient layer mask, going from black to white in a vertical, horizontal, or diagonal direction. This was the method used to add the square images at the bottom of our collage and also to add the type. To make the first of the square selections, the Shift key was held down while dragging with the rectangular marquee. The selection was dragged and dropped into the collage file, and double-clicking the Floating Selection label turned it into the Squares layer. Then each of the other squares was selected, dragged into the Squares layer, and dropped by pressing Ctrl-D.

To make a black-to-white gradient, add a layer mask (see step 2), double-click the gradient tool in the tool palette to open its Op-

AVOIDING SURPRISES

If you're going to drag and drop from one image to another, display both files at the same magnification on-screen (1:1 or 2:1, for instance) so you get an accurate view of the size relationship between the parts. Then scale one of the images if needed before combining.

5e

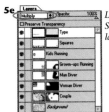

Layers palette after Squares and Type layers have been added

6a

Rose selected from its background (left) and imported into its own layer and desaturated

6b

Rose in place; all layers visible

6c

Close-up of hand-painted mask for Rose layer

6d

Rose "ghosted" through its layer mask

tions palette, and choose Foreground To Background for the Style. With the layers mask active, drag the gradient tool from where you want the image in that layer to be completely masked to where you want it to show fully. Remember — images show through the white parts of the layer mask and are blocked by the black parts. We used a gradient mask for the Squares layer and also for the Type layer; we adjusted Output Levels on the Type layer mask so that the lightest part of the mask was gray instead of white and all the type would be partially transparent. The mode for the layer was set to Multiply so the type would darken the image underneath, rather than cover it up.

6 Silhouetting with the pen tool. Open the Paths palette (by pressing the "T" key) and click with the pen to outline an element you want to add to the collage. Save the path (by double-clicking the Work Path name), then convert it to a selection (click the Make Selection icon in the center at the bottom of the palette), drag the selection into the collage, and turn it into a layer (see step 4). We selected the rose, dragged it into the collage, used Image, Adjust, Desaturate to turn it gray, and then used Variations to warm up the gray.

7 Painting a "ghosting" mask. A hand-painted mask can make it look like a collage element is partly in front of another element and partly behind it. On the Rose layer we used the airbrush with black paint and various Pressure settings in the Airbrush Options palette to paint a mask to "ghost" the rose in front of and behind the type.

We used a similar technique to bring the couple's faces to the front of the image: We copied the original Couple layer by dragging its name in the Layers palette to the New Layer icon at the bottom of the Layers palette and then dragging the new "Couple copy" name up to the top of the palette. We used Image, Adjust, Variations to give this layer a warm, brown tone. A layer mask was added and filled with black, and then the airbrush was used with white and black paint to allow parts of the brown image to be added to the collage. Opacity was adjusted to 90%.

7a

Sepia-toned Couple copy layer

7b

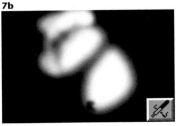

Mask for the Couple copy layer

7c

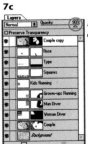

Layers palette for the completed montage

Mixing Resolutions

Overview *Create a coarse-textured, low-resolution image; change the resolution of the low-res artwork to the higher resolution without losing the coarse texture; import a high-resolution element; create a glow.*

61 dpi diffusion dither effect

Setting the interpolation method to maintain the "pixelated" look

Increasing resolution

HOW CAN YOU COMBINE TWO RESOLUTIONS in a single Photoshop image? For instance, what if you want to import a photorealistic element with a high-resolution look into a purposely coarse, textured bitmap? In his illustration for a book cover, Rob Day put what appear to be two different resolutions into a single image.

1 Starting in low resolution. Create or scan an image at the final height and width you will use to print it, and assign it a low resolution. Day scanned a leaf, applied a custom diffusion dither effect at 61 dpi, and added color (see "Dithering" in Chapter 3 for more about making a diffusion dither bitmap and coloring it).

2 Changing the interpolation method for resizing. The next step is to increase the real resolution of the image (so you'll be able to import a high-resolution element) without losing the low-resolution look. In this case, Day wanted to preserve the low-res dither pattern. To preserve the low-res look, choose File, Preferences, General and select Nearest Neighbor for the Interpolation setting. Normally, you would use the default Bicubic interpolation method (or Bilinear, which is faster than Bicubic but gives lower-quality results) for increasing the resolution of an image, so that when Photoshop added pixels, it would average the colors of the surrounding pixels and make a smooth color transition. But this

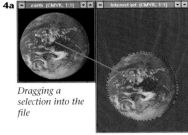

4a

Dragging a selection into the file

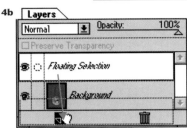

4b

Converting the floating selection to a new, named layer

5a

Making the glow

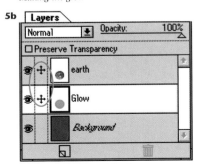

5b

Linking the object and its glow

time you want to preserve the pixellated look, so the right choice is Nearest Neighbor, which doesn't do any color averaging.

3 Increasing the resolution. Next choose Image, Image Size. In the Image Size dialog box, set the Width and Height to any units except pixels. Select the Proportion box, but deselect File Size. Leave the Width and Height as they are, but quadruple the Resolution. For Day's book cover, 244 dpi (four times the original 61 dpi) would provide plenty of data for a 150 lpi halftone printed image. (244 ÷ 150 = 1.62, which is within the suggested range of 1.5 to 2 times the halftone screen resolution for an image without precise details or angled edges, as described in "Resolution" in Chapter 1.) When you've finished increasing the resolution, don't forget to change the Interpolation setting back to Bicubic, or you won't get the smooth, high-quality results you want the next time you scale a selection or resize an image.

4 Importing the high-resolution element. Open the high-resolution file. Day used a public-domain earth image from NASA, scanned to fit the cover design at a resolution of 244 dpi.

To import a selection from one image into another in Photoshop 3, open both files at the same magnification, make the selection in one file, and drag and drop it into the other file; it becomes a floating selection. Drag the Floating Selection icon in the Layers palette to the New Layer icon at the bottom of the palette to turn the imported object into a layer of its own; in this example, the layer is named "earth."

5 Adding finishing touches. Day also created a glow behind the earth. Here's a way to do it that lets you see the glow as it develops around the object; it puts the object and its glow on separate layers, so you can change the color or intensity of the glow later, if you want to, without disturbing the object; and it links the object layer and the glow layer so you can move them together.

First you'll make a layer for the glow and copy the imported object into it: Drag the icon of the layer you just made (the "earth" layer in this example) to the New Layer symbol to make a layer for the glow; choose Layer Options and name the layer. Then drag this Glow layer down below the object (earth) layer in the palette.

Now you'll create the glow: Click on the Foreground color square in the toolbox and choose the color for the glow. Working in the Glow layer, press Ctrl-Alt-T (to load the outline of the object as a selection); choose Select, Feather, and set a Feather Radius. Then press Alt-Backspace to fill the feathered selection with color. By repeating the Alt-Backspace, you can widen and brighten the glow. Then Alt-click in the column next to the eye in the object layer (the earth layer in this case) to link it to the Glow layer.

Day added the pink veins by making a mask from the scan of the leaf, loading this selection, and filling it with pink. He saved the file in EPS format so it could be opened in Adobe Illustrator, where Virginia Evans incorporated the image into her cover design. *Wow!*

Wrapping One Image Around Another

Overview *Open part of a large image (the "first image") with Quick Edit; make a "sketchpad" file or layer; copy parts of the first image into this sketchpad and alter them to fit a "second image"; rubber-stamp from the sketchpad into the second image; copy the altered second image into the first; rubber-stamp to blend the two images.*

JACK CLIGGETT

1a

Original photo

THE MONTAGE PROCESS sometimes involves using textural "material" from one photo to modify a second image so it will blend realistically with the first. Jack Cliggett, head of the Graphic Design Program at Drexel University, did just that in creating this Absolut Vodka ad for Concept 3 Advertising to run in *Countryside* magazine. He couldn't simply composite the two images, regulating the opacity of the transparent water and glass. He had to make the water flow over the physical structure of the supersize bottle. A similar approach might also be used to drape hair around a face, or cloth around an object.

1 Opening part of an image. Open the file that will serve as the background of the image and also supply the image material you need. Cliggett began with a scan of a stock waterfall photo from Comstock. When the image was scanned at a large enough size so that the part he wanted to use could be enlarged to the final 7 x 10-

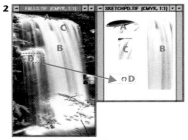

Opening part of the image

Making a sketchpad of image textures

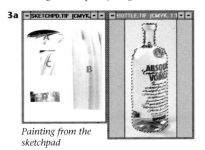

Painting from the sketchpad

inch ad, the file was 54MB, too large and slow for him to work with comfortably.

One way to deal with a large file that has been saved in uncompressed TIFF (.tif) or Scitex CT (.sct) format is to open only the part of an image that you want to work on, using Quick Edit; when you've finished your work, exporting the modified part in Quick Edit form returns it to its original place in the larger image. Here's how to do it: Choose File, Acquire, Quick Edit; when the Quick Edit dialog box opens, drag the cursor to select the area you want to open. Cliggett found that he could reduce the file size from 54 MB to about 7 MB by opening only the part he wanted to change. He saved a copy of this 7 MB file so he would have an untouched version in case he made a mistake and needed to start over.

HEDGING YOUR BETS WITH A COPY

If you open part of a file, it's a good idea to Save A Copy of the part you opened — right away, before you modify it. Save it in the same format (uncompressed TIFF or Scitex CT) as the original large file, but give it a different name. As long as you don't later change the Quick Edit selection boundaries in the large file or change the size of the partial image, the large file will accept a Quick Edit Save of either the part that you opened or the duplicate you saved. This can be very helpful for recovering from mistakes. For example, suppose you modify the original partial file and Quick Edit Save it back into its large file, but then decide you don't like the modifications you made after all. To recover, you can open and Quick Edit Save the unaltered copy you saved, and it will replace the altered part in the large file. Then you can Acquire, Quick Edit again, save a copy again for safekeeping, and start a new set of changes.

2 Making a sketchpad. Open a new empty file. Then use the selection tools to isolate textures from the first image, and copy them into the new file. Cliggett created a "sketchpad" document, where he collected the textures he wanted to use on the bottle. To copy from the image to the sketchpad, make the selection in the image and drag and drop the selection into the working window of the sketchpad.

Cliggett put an oval selection from the waterfall file (A) into his sketchpad file and flipped it horizontally (Image, Flip, Horizontal). He made an oblique rectangular selection, dragged it onto the sketchpad, and rotated it to vertical (Image, Rotate, Free) (B). Another vertical selection was flipped (C). A flat area of the falls was copied to be used for the transition from the bottle's neck to its shoulder (D).

USING A SKETCHPAD FILE

An efficient way to copy textures from a large image is to collect the material you need in a smaller "sketchpad" file. In the large file, select and copy the parts you need, pasting into a smaller file. Then close the large image and work from the smaller one. Using this smaller sketchpad file doesn't require as much RAM and you can modify the collected textures (rotating, flipping, or scaling them, for example) without changing the original image.

3b

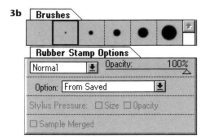

Setting up the rubber stamp to restore the logotype

3c

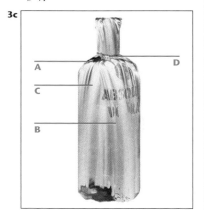

Image textures applied and logotype restored

4

Combining the two images

3 Painting the image. Select the area in the second image that you want to fill with the sketchpad image material. To select the vodka bottle, Cliggett used the lasso with the Alt key held down; that way he could draw straight selection borders by clicking from place to place, as well as curved borders by dragging. He used a feather setting of 2 pixels. (Set the Feather Radius in the Lasso Options palette.) Copy the selection (Ctrl-C), and Paste Layer to create a new layer to work on. That way, you'll have the untouched original in the background layer. If you make a mistake as you apply image texture, you can remove all or part of the altered layer and still have the original image in place underneath.

Cliggett rubber-stamped the waterfall textures in Clone, Aligned mode from the sketchpad file onto the selected area of the bottle file. (To "load" the rubber stamp with an image from any open file, hold down the Alt key and click to identify the area you want to clone.)

To partially restore the Absolut logotype on the bottle, he rubber-stamped from the original version of the bottle image, choosing the From Saved option, a small brush tip; and 40% Opacity, and using vertical strokes to blend it with the water.

4 Montaging the two images. Use the move tool to drag and drop the image you've painted with sketchpad material (in this case the bottle) into the other image (in this case the 7MB version of the waterfall).

Now use the rubber stamp tool as necessary to blend the images together. After importing the bottle into the waterfall, Cliggett inverted the selection (Select, Inverse) so his next edits would affect only the area outside the bottle. He cloned parts of the waterfall from the left to obscure the unacceptable parts of the waterfall that appeared alongside the bottle. He then held down the Shift key and used the lasso to add the bottom of the bottle to the selection so he could blend it into the mist at the bottom of the waterfall by rubber-stamping from other parts of the image.

When the edges of the bottle had been blended with the waterfall, Cliggett restored the branches in the foreground of the waterfall image by rubber-stamping from the duplicate he had made of the uncombined waterfall image.

Finishing the ad. When he had finished the montage of bottle and waterfall, Cliggett returned it to its place in the original 54MB image. (To ensure that a selection is replaced in exactly the right position in a file opened with Quick Edit, choose File, Export, Quick Edit Save, and the return is accomplished automatically.)

The finished image was cropped and saved. It was imported into a QuarkXPress file that contained the type, and was output as film separations from QuarkXPress. *wow!*

Casting Shadows & Reflections

Overview *Draw a mask for the objects; make luminance masks for reflections and shadows; open a new background image; add objects, reflections, and shadows.*

Opening the part of the product shot that includes products, reflections, and shadows

Selecting the products with the pen tool

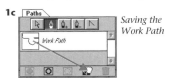

Saving the Work Path

Naming the Products path

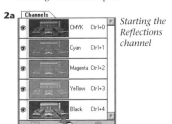

Starting the Reflections channel

SUCCESSFULLY INTEGRATING A FOREGROUND OBJECT from one photo into a new background image involves more than just cutting out the object and sticking it on top of the background. Adding a shadow cast onto the new background by the object can help to make it part of the scene, but adding a reflection does an even better job. To put together this collage illustration for promotional materials for Pioneer, Japan, we borrowed the reflections present in the original studio shot of the products and used them as alpha channels to selectively lighten and darken a new, more colorful background.

1 Making a mask for the object. From a scanned image, you'll select the object (or objects) you want to transplant by tracing its outline with the lasso or pen tool. We began with a scan made from a 4 x 5-inch transparency, a studio shot of the products, scanned and saved as a CMYK TIFF (.tif). To make the file smaller and easier to work with, we used the crop tool to eliminate parts of the image above and below the products.

To make our selections we used the pen tool rather than the lasso because the objects we wanted to select were streamlined, hard-edged, and smooth. To use the pen tool to outline the object you want to transplant, press the "T" key to open the Paths palette, choose the pen (next to the pointer arrow), click to make anchor points, and drag to adjust the curves (as described in Chapter 2). When you've completed the path and closed it by clicking on the

PATH OR ALPHA CHANNEL?

A selection border drawn with the pen tool can be stored for reuse either by saving it as a path or by converting it to an alpha channel. Use an alpha channel if you'll need to modify the selection edge, for instance by blurring it. Otherwise, just keep the path, because it takes less file space than a channel. On the other hand, a selection border drawn with the lasso is almost always better stored as an alpha channel, since the channel will preserve all the detail of the outline, whereas converting the selection to a Bezier curve path could smooth out some of the edge detail.

2b

Channel Options

Name: Reflections   [OK]

Naming the Reflections channel

2c

Black channel duplicated as Reflections channel (#5 in our CMYK file)

3

Reflections channel with Levels adjusted and Motion Blur applied

4

Products path loaded in the Reflections channel and filled with black

5a

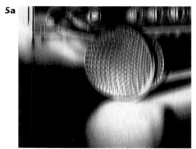

Black channel duplicated as Shadows channel (#6), with Levels adjusted, Motion Blur applied, and color inverted

original point, save the path by dragging the Work Path name in the Paths palette to the Make Path icon (next to the trash can icon) at the bottom of the Paths palette. After saving the path, we double-clicked the Path 1 name in the palette and renamed the path "Products."

(Although we've used the pen tool to draw the selection border for this example and saved the selection as a path, the shape of your object may be better suited for selection with the lasso than with the pen — for instance, if it has a very detailed edge. If so, hold down the Alt key and click and drag with the lasso to outline the object. Then store the selection in an alpha channel).

THE UNDROPPABLE LASSO

When you use the lasso tool to make a complex selection, it can be hard to hold down the mouse button continuously while you drag the tool. Holding down the Alt key while you use the lasso will preserve the open lasso path as you draw, even if you accidentally release the mouse button in mid-lasso. The Alt-lasso also lets you alternate between the tool's "rubber-band" (click) and normal (drag) operations.

2 Starting a mask for the reflections. To start a reflections mask, you'll first choose the color channel in your image that shows the reflection most distinctly. To do this, open the Channels palette, and activate the color channels one by one (in our case, CMYK, Cyan, Magenta, Yellow, and Black) so you can see which one shows the most contrast between the reflections and the rest of the image (for our image, Black was the best). In the Channels palette drag the thumbnail for this channel to the New Channel icon at the bottom of the palette to make an alpha channel. Double-click the new channel's name to open the Channel Options dialog box, enter the name "Reflections," and click OK. With the "Reflections" channel active, choose Image, Adjust, Levels and move the white point on the Input Levels slider inward to emphasize the highlight areas of the mask.

3 Creating a surface texture. If you want to "texturize" the background of your image — the surface on which the objects will rest — you can set it up at this point by adding the texture to the Reflections alpha channel. We used Filter, Blur, Motion Blur with a setting of 20 pixels to create the feeling of a "brushed" surface consistent with the high-tech nature of the products. The rubber stamp tool in Clone Aligned mode was used to touch up areas of the mask where the products had blurred into the background area.

4 Completing the Reflections channel. Now load your object path as a selection in the Reflections channel and fill it with black: With the Reflections channel active, we loaded our Products path and filled it with black by dragging its name in the Paths palette to

5a

Products path loaded into Shadows channel and filled with black

6a

Finding the dimensions of the product shot

6b

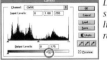

Setting the dimensions of the marquee

6c

Darkening the shadows after lightening the reflections

6d

Reflections and shadows in place

the Fill Path icon (at the left at the bottom of the palette). This isolates the reflections alone in this channel. Use the lasso and Alt-Backspace or a paintbrush and black paint to clean up the mask.

5 Making the Shadows mask. Once again, as you did in step 2 for the reflections mask, choose the best color channel: This time pick the one that shows the most contrast between the shadows and the rest of the image. Drag the icon for this channel to the New Channel icon to make another alpha channel. Name it "Shadows" and choose Image, Map, Invert to make a negative of the channel, turning the shadows into light areas that can act as selections. Again, as you did for the Reflections mask, adjust the Levels, add texture, and then fill the Products path with black, leaving behind a mask that represents the object's cast shadow.

6 Making reflections and shadows. The last step is to put the objects, reflections, and shadows into the new background. You can do this by copying part of the new background image, pasting it into your object photo behind the object, loading your Reflections and Shadows channels as selections to pull reflections and shadows out of this new background, and then pasting this altered image back into the larger new background file. Here's how we did it:

We started by using Image, Image Size on the product photo to find its exact dimensions in pixels. Then, working in the new background image file, we double-clicked the rectangular selection marquee and set its size at those dimensions. We clicked with the marquee tool on the new background image to open the marquee; then we held down the Ctrl and Alt keys and moved the marquee around until it surrounded the part of the new background image where we wanted the products to end up. We copied this selection to the clipboard, leaving the selection border active.

Working in the main CMYK channel of the product shot, we loaded the Products path as a selection (by dragging its name to the Make Selection icon at the bottom of the Paths palette). Then we held down the Alt key as we chose Edit, Paste Into to paste the clipboard contents behind the selection.

We loaded the Reflections and Shadows masks in turn (Ctrl-Alt-5 and Ctrl-Alt-6) and used Image, Adjust, Levels to lighten and darken each of the selected areas. Finally, we selected all, copied, and pasted the copy back into the larger background file.

PASTING BEHIND

Paste Behind does not appear in Photoshop 3.0's Edit menu. But holding down the Alt key and choosing Paste Into activates the Paste Behind function.

HOLDING A PLACE

If you need to select and copy or temporarily remove part of an image so you can work on it outside the original file, leave the selection border active in the original file. That way, when you paste the part back into the larger image (Ctrl-V), it will settle back into exactly the right spot.

Blending with Layer Masks

Overview *Silhouette, color-correct, and enhance the individual components of the montage; bring each element into the compositing file, position it, and create a layer mask to composite it with a softened edge; save a flattened copy of the file.*

1a

Monitor image silhouetted by removing the background

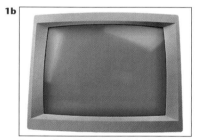

1b

Screen color adjusted with Color Balance and Levels

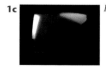

1c   *Highlights mask*

1d   *Highlights enhanced and glow added*

PHOTOSHOP 3'S LAYER MASKS provide an excellent way to fade the layered elements of a montage into one another. This cover illustration for the packaging of TurboTax and MacInTax software started with a comprehensive sketch from Harold Sweet Design. Four separate photographs were scanned on a drum scanner and saved in CMYK color. Starting with the back element (the monitor), each piece was color-corrected and enhanced in its own file to keep RAM requirements low and working speed high. Then the pieces were layered into the final composite. For all but the back element, layer masks were created, and the edges of the masks were softened to accomplish the transitions as the fingers typed, the keyboard faded into the monitor, and the finished tax form emerged. The blending of images could have been done by removing feathered selections from the elements on the individual layers. But using layer masks instead left these elements intact so that when the client wanted a minor change in the position of the keyboard, the change could be made easily.

1 Preparing the back element. It's a good idea to do as much of the color correction and enhancement of the separate pieces as you can before you begin to put them together, because once they're combined, the process of selecting parts and making changes becomes more complicated and can also be slower because of the ballooning file size.

We began with the photo of the monitor. The Paths palette was opened (press the "T" key) and a path was drawn around the monitor. The path was first saved (double-click the Work Path label in the Paths palette) and then converted to a selection as well (click the Make Selection button at the bottom center of the Paths palette to make an antialiased, unfeathered selection). Inverting the selection (Select, Inverse) and pressing the Backspace key removed the background (with the photographer's studio showing) and replaced it with white.

Another path — to isolate the monitor's screen — was drawn, saved, and turned into a selection. With this selection active,

2

Tax form/arm dragged and dropped

3a

Graduated layer mask added

3b

Monitor and tax form blended by means of the graduated layer mask

4a

Keyboard added, distorted, and scaled

4b

Layer mask with edge softened

4c

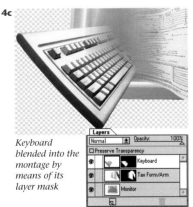

Keyboard blended into the montage by means of its layer mask

Color Balance and Levels adjustments were used to "colorize" the screen.

The still-selected screen interior was then copied (Ctrl-C) and saved in an alpha channel to make a grayscale mask that would select the highlights (open the Channels palette and click the New Channel icon at the bottom of the palette; then paste — Ctrl-V). With this highlights alpha channel (#4) active, Image, Adjust, Levels was chosen and the Input Levels sliders were adjusted to increase the contrast. This mask was then used to select the highlights on the screen so they could be brightened by adjusting Levels. A glow was added at the edge of the screen (a method for creating a glow is described on pages 218 through 220).

The original monitor outline path was loaded as a selection (by dragging its name to the selection icon at the bottom of the Paths palette). The selected monitor was then dragged into a new 1700-pixel-wide image file that had been created (File, New) with a Transparent background (chosen in the Contents section of the New dialog box), and the selection was dropped (Ctrl-D).

2 Starting to build the montage. Now start isolating the other elements from their backgrounds and assembling them into the montage. The next element we added was a hand holding a tax form. The rectangular form had been distorted using CorelDraw and printed out on paper in the stretched and skewed shape needed for the illustration. The photographer positioned this prop so that it was curving away from the hand, and the curve and distortion worked together to create the exaggerated perspective needed for the photo. The element (arm and tax form) was outlined with the path tool as had been done with the monitor in step 1. The left edge of the form was then selected by Alt-clicking with the lasso with a 50-pixel feather, and a motion blur was applied (Filter, Blur, Motion Blur). Softly feathered selections were made and Image, Adjust, Levels was used to exaggerate the shadows and highlights on the form. As was done for the monitor in step 1, the path was converted to a selection. The selected object was dragged and dropped into the compositing file, where Alt-double-clicking Floating Selection in the Layers palette made it into a new layer.

3 Making a layer mask. To make a gradual transition from one element to another, create a layer mask and apply a gradient to it: With the upper layer active (the tax form and arm in this case), open the Layers palette and choose Add Layer Mask from the pop-out menu (or use the Commands palette or a custom F key shortcut). The heavy black border around the mask thumbnail in the Layers palette signals that the mask is active, even though the layer's content, rather than the mask itself, appears in the working window.

With the layer mask active, load the transparency mask for the layer (Ctrl-Alt-T), and choose Select, Inverse. With black as the Foreground

5a

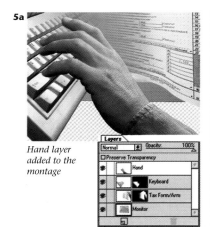

Hand layer added to the montage

5b

Fingers selected, copied to another layer, and rotated slightly

5c

Motion blur applied to the Fingers layer

5d

Layer mask for the Hand layer (left) and Fingers layer in place over masked Hand (right)

5e

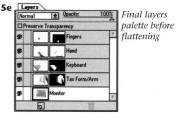

Final layers palette before flattening

color, press Alt-Backspace to create a white-on-black mask. Then, with the mask still active, use the gradient tool in Multiply mode to make a gradient from black to white. (You could get the same blending effect by making a layer mask that's a simple black-to-white gradient, without making a white shape from the transparency mask. But having the shape there helps you to see exactly how the mask is working.) The gradient mask makes the tax form seem as if it's emerging from the monitor.

4 Making a layer mask with an irregular soft edge. Isolate and adjust the other components of the image, drag and drop each one into the composite file, and create a layer mask for it.

The keyboard photo was the next piece to be added. Again, the element was selected with a path, isolated, color-corrected, and dragged into the composite file as described for the arm and tax form in step 2. Because the keyboard had been photographed in a more "straight-on" view, it had to be rotated (Image, Rotate, Free) and scaled (Image, Effects, Scale) to match its position in the original comprehensive sketch.

A layer mask was created as in step 3, except that this time the transition edge was made with a feathered lasso selection filled with black (Alt-Backspace) and then with the airbrush tool with a large soft tip and black paint applied at a low Opacity setting.

5 Creating the illusion of motion. To simulate the motion that can be caught on film with a strobe, you need more than a simple application of Photoshop's Motion Blur filter. The goal is to show both the starting and ending positions, with a blur in between.

The first step in making the fingers of the left hand appear to be typing, was to isolate the hand, correct its color, drag it into the composite file, and position it over the keyboard. An antialiased lasso was then used to select just the four fingers and copy them to a new layer.

With all the layers visible and the Fingers layer active, the Fingers layer was rotated to create a basis for the motion blur. Then Blur, Motion Blur was applied in the direction of the movement between the two positions of the fingers and with a Distance setting of 10 pixels for this 1700-pixel-wide image.

The Opacity of the separate Fingers layer was set at 50%. Then a hand-painted layer mask was added to the original Hand layer to make its fingertips partially transparent to add to the illusion of motion.

Saving a flattened copy of the file. When you've completed the layered montage, you can save a copy in a format like .TIF or .EPS that can be placed in a page layout file, and still keep the layered version in case you need to make changes or you want to use parts of it in other projects. Choose File, Save A Copy, choose a Format, and turn on the Flatten Image function. This creates a single-layer nontransparent copy of the image. In flattening the file, Photoshop retains alpha channels or not (at your option), applies and then discards all the layer masks, and fills transparent areas with white. *Wow!*

TOTAL FEES BILLED 12,654.00 TOTAL EXP. BILLED 6,228.00

CASE ACTIVITY BUDGET VS. ACTUAL

For a promotional illustration for *Caseguard* software for the legal profession, **Heidi Merscher** composited several separate grayscale images. The hand and calendar were shot as 35mm slides and scanned. The dollar bill, keyboard, and small clock face were scanned directly on a desktop flatbed scanner. And the pyramid and large clock were modeled and rendered in Strata-Vision 3d. The keyboard scan was manipulated with Photoshop's Perspective and Distort functions (under Image, Ef-

fects), and lighting effects were applied. The dollar bill was embossed (Filter, Stylize, Emboss). The shadow under the pyramid on the hand and small clock was made with a mask; to build the mask Merscher first made a selection in the shape of the shadow, then feathered the selection to soften the edges, saved the selection in an alpha channel, and used the gradient tool to darken the mask gradually, leaving the mask white at its forward edges, getting darker toward the back. When this mask was loaded as a

selection on the hand and clock, adjusting the brightness of the selected area (Image, Adjust, Levels) produced the desired fall-off in the shadow. The type was set in FreeHand and imported, and Perspective was applied. When the composite was complete, Merscher converted it to Duotone mode, assigned a blue second color, and adjusted the duotone curves. The file was then converted to CMYK mode so that it could be separated for four-color process printing.

For *Leaf Daughters* photographer **Helen Golden** combined a photo of leaves with a photograph of her three daughters, faces upturned to the sun. After scanning the photos, she selected the faces with a feathered lasso, rotated each one to the angle that would fit well on a leaf, and pasted them in place with various degrees of transparency. She used the smudge and rubber stamp to blend the faces into the leaves.

Jack Davis crafted this *Shuttle/Rainforest* illustration in Photoshop 2.5 to illustrate the concept of decibel levels and the effect of sound for an introductory psychology textbook. To combine the NASA photo of a space shuttle launch with a stock photo of a forest, Davis had to go through a fairly elaborate procedure of increasing the canvas size of one photo and resizing the other so it could be copied and pasted into the empty canvas using a customized gradient mask created with the gradient tool and QuickMask. The entire process would have been much easier in Photoshop 3: The file could have been created at the desired size and the elements dragged and dropped onto their own layers, resized as necessary, and blended with a layer mask.

JACK DAVIS / PHOTOS: NASA, GRANT HEILMAN

Russell Sparkman collected the raw material for *Dollar Signs* by photographing the dollar bill and the coins and using a 35mm slide that he had taken of painters on ladders. He determined the size of the image by how large he could scan the painters without their becoming too "soft." For this updated version Sparkman used Photoshop's layers to make "tracing paper" to sketch the dollar bill, to give it a partially painted look: He put the dollar in a layer of its own and made another layer above it, which he filled with solid white. Then he adjusted the Opacity of this top layer to 50% so that the underlying dollar appeared "ghosted" through the white "tracing paper." He used the paintbrush to sketch in the lines on the tracing layer with 100% black. After the sketch was done, he added a layer mask to the tracing layer, with white parts of the mask to protect the side portions of the sketch, but black in the middle, so the original bill showed through. To create a brush stroke effect along the edge of the mask, he applied a combination of filters: Gaussian Blur, Add Noise, and then Motion Blur. The cloud layer was then rubber-stamped at partial opacity over the sketch and other parts of the image. The faux sky was created with KPT Texture Explorer, although clouds can also be produced with Photoshop's Render, Clouds filter (see Chapter 5). The paintbrushes in the men's hands were drawn with the pencil and paintbrush tools with very small brush tips. The men on ladders were given a drop shadow (see "Dropping A Shadow" in Chapter 8) and the shadow was skewed to create the visual impression of the ladders leaning against the dollar. Sparkman added a little green paint to the sides of the buckets to fit these elements into this image.

Characteristic of **Michael Gilmore**'s *False Prophet* is that although it's composed of distinctly different elements, the components are so well-integrated that they seem to have been photographed together in a single space. Gilmore achieves this effect by combining the elements in a grayscale file, then converting the grayscale file to RGB, and selecting and coloring the parts. Working in this way allows him to compose for tonality and then to achieve consistency of color by doing all his coloring in one file. In *False Prophet*, working at 150 dpi in a 20MB file, Gilmore selected the kewpie, created a 3-pixel border (Select, Modify, Border) and applied the Noise, Median filter to that border. The effect was a kind of after-the-fact antialiasing that smoothed and blended the edge. To make the postage-stamp-like elements, he scanned one edge of a stamp, copied parts of it, and rotated them into place to create the border; he used scanned 19th-century etchings for the stamp artwork. A photo of elements from a friend's "gizmo" collection, a scan of an old map of Ireland, and objects created in Swivel 3D (now MacroModel) completed the image.

Cupid by **Michael Gilmore** started as a grayscale composition that was converted to RGB and colored with the Image, Adjust, Color Balance and Hue/Saturation commands. He also added Noise to the photo of the angel statue. The background behind the angel and 3D elements is made up of a scanned photo of the wall of an office building and a scan of a 16th-century map. The three-dimensional atoms were modelled in Swivel 3D.

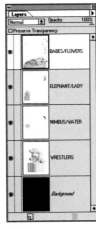

For this *Poster* for a show of his work, **Lance Hidy** assembled a variety of images. The dancing lady was scanned from a Victorian postcard. The flowers were placed directly on the scanner. The statuary (wrestlers and babies) and a detail from a sarcophagus (elephant) were scanned from black-and-white photos. All of these elements were selected with the pen tool and removed from their original backgrounds. To construct the streaked bases for the wrestlers and elephant sculptures, Hidy made a noise-filled area, chose Single Row for the Shape in the Marquee Options palette, made the selection, and stretched the single row of "noise" verti-

cally with Image, Effects, Scale to get the streaks. He pasted these rectangular base elements behind the selected statues elements, so they seemed to be part of the sculpture. The color of all scanned elements was adjusted with Image, Adjust, Hue/Saturation; for the sculpture and dancer, Hidy used the Colorize option.

The waterfall element used with the dancer and flowers on the right side of the poster was selected from a photo with the magic wand tool and Select, Similar. By scaling down a duplicate of this element (Image, Effects, Scale) and then copying, pasting, and rotating it several times, Hidy created half of the nimbus behind the figure riding the elephant; he

then copied and flipped this half to complete the circular element. With the nimbus on a transparent layer of its own, he turned on Preserve Transparency for the layer and applied a radial gradient fill to the selection; Preserve Transparency restricted the radial fill to the nimbus only.

The elements were dragged and dropped onto transparent layers above a black background. Hidy paired nonoverlapping parts to cut down on the number of layers needed. The file was flattened and saved in EPS format and brought into an Adobe Illustrator document, where type had been set in Penumbra, a font designed by Hidy as an Adobe Multiple Masters font.

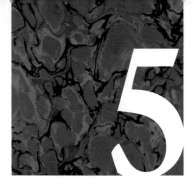

USING FILTERS

PHOTOSHOP'S FILTERS — SMALL PROGRAMS that are grouped in submenus within the Filter menu — can be run on an entire image or a selection. Along with filters for special effects and painterly treatments (described later in this chapter), Photoshop supplies three kinds of filters that can do a lot to improve the quality of scanned photographs, and can even improve painted images. You'll find these "workhorse" filters in the Sharpen, Blur, and Noise submenus.

SHARPEN

Photoshop provides four sharpening filters. Sharpen and Sharpen More accentuate the color differences between adjacent pixels of different colors. Sharpen Edges and Unsharp Mask find "edges," areas where a continuous run of pixels of one color comes up against other colors, and then they increase the contrast between that run of pixels and the pixels nearby; areas that aren't edges are left pretty much unchanged, so they still look smooth, or "soft." The use of sharpening filters comes up again and again throughout the book, but here's a quick list of sharpening tips:

Use only Unsharp Mask. In general, forget the other sharpening filters and use Unsharp Mask. Unlike Sharpen and Sharpen More, which can accentuate blemishes, film grain, and any artifacts you may have created by editing an image, Unsharp Mask accentuates the differences only at "edges," where you want the differences to be distinct. And unlike Sharpen Edges, it gives you precise control. With Unsharp Mask you can set:

- The **Amount** (the strength of the application, or how much the difference at an edge is enhanced by the filter).
- The **Radius** (how many pixels in from the color edge will have their contrast increased). Increase the Radius with increasing resolution, because at higher resolutions the individual pixels are smaller relative to the image components.
- The **Threshold** (how different the colors on the two sides of an edge have to be before the filter will sharpen it). Use higher settings for images that are "grainy" or have subtle color shifts, such as skin tones, so the filter won't sharpen the "noise."

continued on page 138

IS IT FILTERED YET?

The new dialog boxes for many filters include two ways to preview the filter effect before you apply it to an image — the small preview window and the Preview check box, which makes the effect show up in the main working window. Some filters can take a long time to run. And if you're applying a fairly subtle effect, it may be hard to tell for sure whether it's finished. Check for a flashing line first under the ± sign below the preview window and then under the Preview check box. When the line stops flashing and disappears, it means that the preview or working window now shows the effect of the filter.

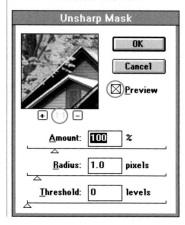

Original scan

Sharpen

Sharpen Edges

Sharpen More

Unsharp Mask default: 50, 1, 0

Unsharp Mask: 100, 1, 0

Unsharp Mask: 100, 3, 2

Unsharp Mask, 4 times: 25, 3, 2

Photo delivered at 100 dpi

Resolution increased to 200 dpi

Unsharp Mask applied: 200, 1, 0

Original scan

PHOTO: BUILDINGS & STRUCTURES, DIGITAL STOCK CORP.

Unsharp mask: 500, 50, 50; oversharpened for a special effect

Use it on scanned images. As a rule, run the Unsharp Mask filter on a scanned photo to see if it improves the image by getting rid of blurriness from a poor original or from the scanning process.

Use it on resized or reoriented images. Whenever you use Image, Image Size to make a change that affects the file size (such as increasing the dimensions or the resolution), or when you use Image, Rotate, Arbitrary or Free, or any of the Image, Effects functions (Scale, Skew, Perspective, or Distort), use Unsharp Mask afterwards. Any such change involves *interpolation* — that is, creating or recoloring pixels based on calculations — and is bound to "soften" the image (see the flag image at the left).

Use it more than once. Running Unsharp Mask more than once at a lower Amount will sharpen more smoothly than if you run it once at a setting twice as high. (Note that this is not true for Sharpen More and Sharpen, which multiply the artifacts they create if you apply them more than once.)

Use it last. Because it can create artifacts that can be magnified by other image-editing operations, Unsharp Mask should generally be applied after you've finished editing the image.

Use the sharpen tool for pinpoint precision. For handheld control of the Sharpen filter, use the sharpen (triangle) tool. If the tool isn't visible in the tool palette, select it by Alt-clicking the blur (water drop) tool. You can change the settings in the Brushes palette to control the area (brush size) and intensity of sharpening. You can set the blur tool to Sample Merged so that it blurs as if all the visible

Too much sharpening can give a photo an artificial look, so you don't want to overdo it. But if you're preparing your image for the printed page, keep in mind that sharpening tends to look much "stronger" on the screen or on a laser print than it will when the image is finally printed at much higher resolution on a press.

ADDING DEPTH

Sharpening or blurring can help add depth and form to a painting or photo. Sharpen the areas that extend toward the viewer and leave unsharpened (or even blur) the areas that are farther away.

After Francois Guérin painted a still life of fruit in Fractal Design Painter (left), he used Photoshop's sharpen tool to add dimension (right).

Blur the background to reduce the apparent depth of field and focus attention on the foreground.

BUSINESS & INDUSTRY,
DIGITAL STOCK CORP.

layers were merged, even though the blur effect is recorded only on the active layer.

BLUR

Photoshop's blurring filters can be used to soften all or part of an image. Blur and Blur More (which is three or four times as strong as Blur) smooth an image by reducing the contrast between adjacent pixels. With the Gaussian Blur filter, the transition between the contrasting colors occurs at a particular mathematical rate, so that most of the pixels in a black-to-white blur, for example, are in the middle gray range, with fairly few pixels in the very dark or light shades. And you can increase the amount of blurring that occurs by raising the Radius value.

Use Blur to make the background recede. One of the most common errors in Photoshop montage is combining a sharply focused subject with an equally sharply focused image used as background. You can fix the problem by blurring the background slightly to simulate the depth of field a real camera lens would capture. You can also apply this background-blurring technique to a single photo to reduce the perceived depth of field and focus attention on the foreground subject.

Use Gaussian Blur to smooth out flaws in a photo. Part of the repair work for damage to a photo (such as water spotting) can be done by selecting the damaged area and using Gaussian Blur on one or all of the color channels.

Use Gaussian Blur to control edge characteristics in alpha channels or layer masks. Once a selection is stored in an alpha channel or layer mask, the Gaussian Blur filter can be run to soften or smooth out the transition between black and white. Then the Image, Adjust, Levels function can be run on the channel to fatten or shrink the selection area or harden its edge, as shown on page 140.

Use the blur tool for precision. This tool (the counterpart of the sharpen tool) gives you pinpoint control of the blur.

The other Blur filters fall into the special effects category: **Motion Blur**, which lets you set a direction and an amount for the blur, produces an effect like taking a picture of a moving object. **Radial Blur** provides two options: With **Spin** you can simulate the effect of photographing an object spinning around a center that you specify in a Blur Center box; **Zoom** simulates the effect of zooming the camera toward or away from the center.

NOISE

Under Noise in the Filter menu are three filters that smooth the color in an image (Despeckle, Median, and Dust & Scratches) and one that roughens it (Add Noise). **Add Noise** creates either ran-

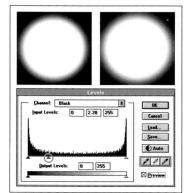

Gaussian Blur: Move the Input Levels gray point slider to enlarge (here) or shrink the mask

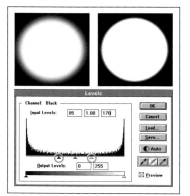

Gaussian Blur: Move the Input Levels black and white point sliders in to "harden" the edge

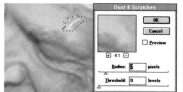

Dust & Scratches (under Noise) can be used on blemished images to eliminate the defects.

dom or Gaussian variation in pixel tone or color. **Despeckle** and **Median** detect edges and then leave these alone while smoothing out less abrupt changes in color. Median averages the brightness of pixels within an image or selection after you determine the Radius used to select the pixels to be averaged.

Dust & Scratches looks for "defects" (areas that are markedly different from their surroundings) and blurs the surrounding pixels into the defects to eliminate them. The **Threshold** setting determines how different from the surrounding pixels something has to be in order to be detected as a defect; a setting between 70 and 128 often works well. The **Radius** setting determines how far from the edge of the defect the filter goes to get the pixels used in the blur. Dust & Scratches works best if you select a fairly small feathered area around the defect and run the filter only on that area, also keeping the Radius setting as low as possible. Using a bigger selection or a higher Radius setting can noticeably blur the image.

Add Noise to improve a color gradient. Color gradients created in PostScript-based graphics programs like Illustrator, CorelDraw, or FreeHand and then imported into Photoshop can be too "slick"-looking or can show unwanted color banding. Adding Noise with an Amount setting of just 3 to 5 for a 300 dpi image and with Monochromatic checked can make the gradient look much more natural. For an especially subtle effect, you can run the filter on one or two of the RGB channels, or run it separately on the individual CMYK channels.

Add Noise as the basis for generating a texture. Adding Noise and then applying other filters can generate some interesting textures. An example appears on page 168.

Use Despeckle or Median to reduce scan artifacts. The "ridges" that can appear in desktop-scanned images can be reduced or eliminated by applying the Despeckle or Median filter. (Despeckle is a one-click operation but Median offers more control.) These filters can also help eliminate *moiré*, an interference pattern that happens when the halftone screen in the printed image you're scan-

When you apply a distortion filter, you can often get smoother results by running the filter at a lower setting several times than by running it at a higher setting once, especially if the image includes straight lines. For this example we started with a screen dump of a color palette.

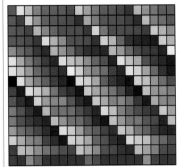
Original palette

Twirl applied 10 times at an Angle setting of 50

Twirl applied once at an Angle setting of 500

ning interacts with the scanner's sampling pattern. After these scanner artifacts are eliminated, use Unsharp Mask to sharpen the image.

RENDER FILTERS

The filters that have been added in Photoshop 3.0's new Render menu are some of the most powerful in the program.

The **Clouds** filter creates a cloudlike pattern using the Background and Foreground colors. If you use sky-blue and white, the effect looks like high, diffuse clouds. To make bulkier clouds on a more intensely blue sky, press the Shift key while you apply the filter.

Difference Clouds works the same way as Clouds, except that the cloud effect interacts with the image as if the clouds were being applied in Difference mode. In Difference mode black is the neutral color — that is, black pixels don't cause any change in the target image — so you can use Difference Clouds with the Foreground and Background colors set to black and white to apply a cloudlike pattern of color inversion. Repeated application of Difference Clouds in a grayscale image generates a veined effect like marble; in color you get the veined effect but also an "oil slick" rainbow result.

The **Lens Flare** filter simulates the photographic effect you get when a bright light shines into the lens of a camera. To apply a lens flare with maximum flexibility, create a separate top layer for the flare: Click the New Layer button at the bottom left of the Layers palette; when the New Layer dialog box opens, choose Hard Light for the Mode and use the check box to turn on "Fill with Hard-Light-neutral color (50% gray)"; apply the Lens Flare filter to this layer. The effect will be the same as if you had applied it to the image layer in Normal mode, but you'll be able to experiment by adjusting the Opacity.

The **Lighting Effects** filter's dialog box can be used to set up **ambient** lighting (diffuse, nondirectional light that's uniform throughout the image, so it casts no shadows, like daylight on an overcast day or like starlight) or any of three varieties of light sources: **omnidirectional** light sources (sending a glow in all directions, like a light bulb in a table lamp), **spotlights** (directional and focused like their namesakes in the real world), and **directional** light sources (too far away to be focused, like bright sunlight or moonlight falling on the earth).

- **To set the strength of ambient light,** use the Ambience slider in the Properties section of the Lighting Effects dialog box. The more positive the setting, the stronger the ambient light relative to the Directional, Omni, and Spotlight sources you add.

- **To add a light source,** drag the light bulb icon at the bottom of the palette into the Preview area.

- **To color a light** (either the ambient light or a light source), click on its color box to open the color picker so you can select a color.

Original photo

A Spotlight with negative Intensity can be used to shade part of an image.

Two windows were selected with the Alt-lasso, copied, and pasted into a new layer. Negative ambient light was applied to the Background layer. The windows layer was filled with White with Preserve Transparency turned on and an orange Omni light was applied to this layer. Opacity was adjusted.

- **To select one of several light sources** so that you can adjust its settings, click on the little circle that represents it in the Preview area, or use the Tab key to cycle through the lights.

- **To turn off a light source temporarily,** so you can see the effect of removing it without actually disrupting its position, click to deselect the On box in the Light Type area of the dialog box.

- **To turn off a light source permanently** (that is, to remove it), drag its circle from the Preview area to the trash can icon.

Lighting Effects works well to cast light onto an image as if it were mounted on a wall, as shown on page 162. But here are some other ways you can use it to trick the eye:

- To **unify** several fairly different images in a publication or an on-screen presentation, apply the same lighting scheme to all of them.

- To create a **shadowy area** in an image, use a Spotlight set at a negative Intensity with Ambience set to a positive value.

- To make light appear to come from **inside** something (such as a bulb in a lamp), position an Omni light at the source.

- To add a **texture** to the surface of an image, set up a light source and choose a Texture Channel to use as a bump map. A bump map is a grayscale image that interacts with the light sources for an image or layer, tricking the eye into perceiving bumpiness, or texture. The things that can be used as bump maps for applying Lighting Effects to any layer are the individual color channels (red, green, or blue, for example), any alpha channel in the file, or the transparency mask or layer mask for that layer.

The **Texture Fill** filter gives you a quick way to import grayscale files to use with the Lighting Effects filter. In your RGB file add an alpha channel to hold the texture you'll import. Then with the alpha channel active, choose Filter, Render, Texture Fill and choose a grayscale file. (The dialog box will list all files saved in Photoshop 2.5 or 3.0 file format, but it will only let you choose the grayscale ones.) The chosen texture will fill the active alpha channel. The fill is tiled, so if the grayscale image is smaller than the RGB image, the texture will repeat. If the grayscale file is larger, it will fit as much as possible into the channel at full size, starting at the upper left corner.

DON'T MISS THE TEXTURES!

The Adobe Photoshop 3.0 Deluxe CD ROM includes a "textures" subdirectory (in the "goodies" subdirectory) with about 75 seamlessly tiling grayscale files. These are designed to be loaded into alpha channels by the Texture Fill filter so they can be used as the Texture Channel with Lighting Effects, or in any other way you might use a texture-filled channel.

Filter Demos

Overview *For any plug-in filter you want to use, move it into the* **plugins** *subdirectory in the* **photoshp** *subdirectory; start the Photoshop program; open an image; select the area you want to filter (make no selection if you want to filter the entire image); choose Filter and select a filter from the pop-out submenus.*

This image was duplicated to a second layer, and then two Gallery Effects Classic Art filters were applied, one to each layer. The Background layer was treated with the Watercolor filter from Vol. 1. The upper layer was treated with the Paint Daubs filter from Vol. 3; the Opacity of this layer was adjusted to 50%, and its blending mode was set to Normal. Then the two layers were merged (Flatten Image from the Layers palette's pop-out menu) and the result was embossed with the Lighting Effects filter, using the method described in "Imitating Paint and Canvas" on page 166; a Directional light was used, with Red chosen as the Texture Channel.

This is the original image before filters were applied. The image is 405 pixels wide. Printed at the size shown in the filter demonstrations, its resolution is about 225 ppi.

IN ADDITION TO PROVIDING PLUG-IN FILTERS with Photoshop, Adobe has made available to other software developers the program code they need to write more filters. Among the many software developers now creating their own compatible filters for Photoshop are Alien Skin, Andromeda, and HSC Software. The following pages provide a catalog of many of the available filters, showing the effects of applying them to two kinds of photos — a high-contrast still life and a side-lit portrait, shown here at the left. Where numerical settings are shown in the captions, they are listed in the order they appear in a filter's dialog box, from upper left to lower right. If the default settings were used, no settings are shown.

Because filter effects require a good deal of calculation, applying a filter can be a time-consuming process. Besides showing you the results of applying the filters themselves, this gallery includes tips for using filters efficiently and effectively.

FILTER RERUNS

To reapply the last filter effect you used, press Ctrl-F. To select that filter again but open its dialog box so you can change the settings before you apply the filter, press Ctrl-Alt-F.

REPRODUCING FILTER EFFECTS

The size of an image (in pixels) is important for filters whose settings are measured in pixels. That's why image widths are given throughout the book. If you see an effect you want to reproduce, here's how to figure out a setting to try:

[Filter setting we used (in pixels) ÷ Width of our filtered image (in pixels)] x Width of your image (in pixels) = Filter setting you should try (in pixels)

(Unlilke filters whose settings are measured in pixels, those filters whose settings are in percentages or degrees will produce similar amounts of change when a setting is used with either a large or a small image.)

Adobe

Filter effects are grouped alphabetically by submenu name, with individual filters shown alphabetically within submenu. Some filters (such as Blur: Radial Blur) can be set to produce two or more very different effects.

Blur: Blur

Blur: Blur More

Blur: Gaussian Blur (2 pixels)

Blur: Motion Blur

Blur: Radial Blur (Spin)

Blur: Radial Blur (Zoom)

Distort: Displace (honeycmb.psd/stretch)

Distort: Displace (schnable.psd/stretch)

Distort: Displace (streaks.psd/stretch)

Distort: Displace (twirl.psd/stretch)

TESTING A RADIAL BLUR

The Radial Blur filter has three Quality options: Draft, Good, and Best. Use Draft (quick but rough) to experiment with the Amount and the blur center; then use Good (or on a very large image, Best) for the final effect.

SIZE RESTRICTIONS

Under Windows 3.x the Distort filters don't work on images or selections larger than 16 MB.

Distort: Pinch (100%)

Distort: Polar Coordinates (Polar to Rect.)

Distort: Polar Coordinates (Rect. to Polar)

Distort: Ripple (Medium, 100%)

Distort: Shear (Wrap Around)

Distort: Spherize (100%, Normal)

Distort: Twirl (125°)

Distort: Wave (Sine, randomize)

Distort: Wave (Square)

Distort: Wave (Triangle)

Distort: Zigzag (Around center/40/7)

DISPLACEMENT MAPS

Some of the Displacement maps Adobe supplies in the Plug-ins folder to be used with the Distort, Displace filter produce quite different effects when applied in the Tile mode than when used in the Stretch mode. If you try one of the Displacement Maps files and get an effect that seems uninteresting, try the other mode — it's likely to be more rewarding.

Distort: Zigzag (Out from center/40/7)

Distort: Zigzag (Pond ripples/40/7)

Noise: Add Noise (Gaussian)

Noise: Add Noise (Gaussian/Monochrom.)

Noise: Add Noise (Uniform)

Noise: Despeckle

Noise: Dust & Scratches (1,0)

Noise: Median (3)

Other: Custom

Other: High Pass (10)

Other: Maximum (1)

Other: Minimum (1)

Other: Offset (100/100)

Pixelate: Color Halftone (8)

Pixelate: Crystallize (10)

Pixelate: Facet

Pixelate: Fragment

Pixelate: Mezzotint (Coarse dots)

Pixelate: Mezzotint (Fine dots)

Pixelate: Mezzotint (Medium dots)

Pixelate: Mezzotint (Short strokes)

Pixelate: Mosaic (8)

Pixelate: Pointillize (5, Background black)

Pixelate: Pointillize (5, Background white)

Render: Clouds (Foreground blue)

Render: Difference Clouds

Render: Lens Flare (100%, 105mm prime)

Render: Lens Flare (100%, 35mm prime)

Render: Lens Flare (100%, 50–300mm zoom)

Render: Lighting Effects (softspot)

Render: Lighting Effects (with Texture)

Render: Texture Fill (Custom pattern)

Stylize: Diffuse (Normal)

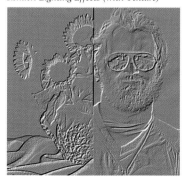
Stylize: Emboss (135˚, 3 pixels, 100%)

Stylize: Extrude (Blocks/30/30 random)

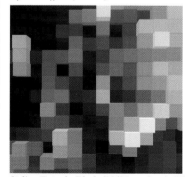
Stylize: Extrude (Blocks/30/30 random/solid)

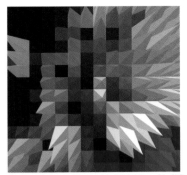

Stylize: Extrude (Pyramids/30/100 rnd/solid)

Stylize: Find Edges

Stylize: Solarize

Stylize: Tiles (10/10%/ Foreground [black])

Stylize: Trace Contour

Stylize: Wind (Blast/Left)

Stylize: Wind (Stagger/Left)

Stylize: Wind (Wind/Left)

Sharpen: Sharpen

Sharpen: Sharpen Edges

Sharpen: Sharpen More

Sharpen: Unsharp Mask (100/1/0)

Gallery Effects 1

Many of the filters in this first set of Gallery Effects can make a photo look like a painting or drawing. The filters appear in the Gallery Effects: Classic Art 1 submenu of Photoshop's Filter menu.

Chalk & Charcoal

Charcoal

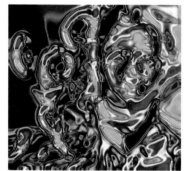

Chrome

Craquelure

Dark Strokes

Dry Brush (Texture 1)

Dry Brush (Texture 3)

Emboss

Film Grain

Fresco (Texture 1)

Fresco (Texture 3)

Graphic Pen

Mosaic

Poster Edges

Ripple

Smudge Stick

Spatter

Watercolor (Texture 1)

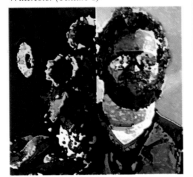
Watercolor (Texture 3)

"SOFTENING" A FILTER

If you run a painterly effects filter and the result seems too strong, one option is to Undo and run the filter again with a "milder" setting. But Gallery Effects and other special effects filters can take a long time to run. Here's a way to avoid the rerun time. Before you run the filter, duplicate the image by dragging the "Background" thumbnail in the Layers palette to the New Layer icon at the bottom of the palette. Then run the filter on this new layer. If the effect is too strong, use the Opacity slider in the Layers palette to "soften" the filter.

Original image

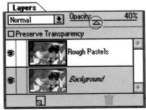
Opacity adjusted in the Layers palette

New layer, filtered with GE Rough Pastels

Final composite image

Gallery Effects 2

Along with painterly filters, Gallery Effects Classic Art 2 includes three — Rough Pastels, Texturizer, and Underpainting — that simulate textured surfaces. The filters are found in their own submenu of the Photoshop Filter menu.

Accented Edges

Angled Strokes

Bas Relief

Colored Pencil

Diffuse Glow

Glowing Edges

Grain (Clumped)

Grain (Horizontal)

Grain (Regular)

Grain (Soft)

Grain (Speckle)

Note Paper

Palette Knife

Patchwork

Photocopy

Rough Pastels (Canvas)

Sprayed Strokes

Stamp

Texturizer (Brick)

Texturizer (Burlap)

Texturizer (Canvas)

Texturizer (Custom TIFF file)

Underpainting (Canvas)

Gallery Effects 3

Gallery Effects Classic Art 3 includes filters that simulate halftone screens, graphic treatments, and other special effects. They appear in their own submenu in the Photoshop Filter menu.

Conté Crayon (Canvas)

Conté Crayon (Sandstone)

Crosshatch

Cutout

Glass (Blocks)

Glass (Frosted)

Glass (Tiny Lens)

Halftone Screen (Circle)

Halftone Screen (Dot)

Halftone screen (Line)

Ink Outlines

Neon Glow

Paint Daubs (Dark Rough)

Paint Daubs (Simple)

Paint Daubs (Wide Sharp)

Plaster

Plastic Wrap

Reticulation

Sponge

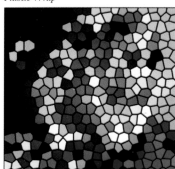

Stained Glass

Sumi-e

Torn Edges

Water Paper

Andromeda Series 1

Andromeda Software's Photography Filters provide special effects similar to those you can achieve with 35mm camera lenses. The filters are listed in the Andromeda submenu.

cMulti

Designs (Mezzo/Pattern/Basic #3)

Designs (Mezzo/Pattern/Grains)

Diffract

Halo

Prism

Rainbow

Reflection

sMulti

Star

Velocity

Andromeda Series 2

Andromeda Software's Three-D Filter allows 3D surface mapping in Photoshop. The filter appears under the Andromeda submenu in the Filter menu.

3-D (Cube)

3-D (Cylinder)

3-D (Plane)

3-D (Sphere)

Andromeda Series 3

Andromeda Software's Screens Filter provides preset Mezzotint treatments for screening images, as well as an interface that lets you choose your own settings and preview several settings at once.

Standard Mezzotint, 45 lpi

Standard Mezzotint, 65 lpi

Standard Mezzotint, 45 lpi

Standard Mezzotint, 65 lpi

Kai's Power Tools

HSC Software's Kai's Power Tools (KPT) plug-ins include Gradient Designer and Texture Explorer — either of which is like a cross between your favorite power tool and a bagful of lollipops. (Menu listings shown are for Windows; on the Macintosh, filters are spread over several Filters submenus.)

KPT 2.0 Extensions: Fractal Explorer 2.0

KPT 2.0 Extensions: Gradient Designer 2.0

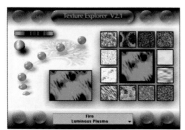
Texture Explorer 2.0 Interface

KPT 2.0 Extensions: Gradients on Paths 2.0

KPT 2.0 Extensions: Seamless Welder

KPT 2.0 Extensions: Texture Explorer 2.0

KPT 2.0 Filters: 3D Stereo Noise

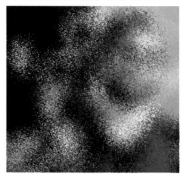
KPT 2.0 Filters: Diffuse More

KPT 2.0 Filters: Fade Contrast

KPT 2.0 Filters: Find Edges Charcoal

KPT 2.0 Filters: Find Edges & Invert

KPT 2.0 Filters: Find Edges Soft

KPT 2.0 Filters: Glass Lens Bright

KPT 2.0 Filters: Grime Layer

KPT 2.0 Filters: Hue Protected Noise Max

KPT 2.0 Filters: Hue Protected Noise Med

KPT 2.0 Filters: Hue Protected Noise Min

KPT 2.0 Filters: Page Curl

KPT 2.0 Filters: PixelBreeze

KPT 2.0 Filters: PixelStorm

KPT 2.0 Filters: PixelWind

KPT 2.0 Filters: Scatter Horizontal

KPT 2.0 Filters: Sharpen Intensity

KPT 2.0 Filters: Smudge Left - Darken

KPT 2.0 Filters: Smudge Left - Lighten

KPT2.0 Filters: Special Blue Noise

KPT 2.0 Filters: Vortex Tiling

KPT CONVOLVER

Not a part of the Kai's Power Tools filter set, KPT Convolver is a separate plug-in application from HSC Software that can be installed to appear in Photoshop's Filter menu. It has both corrective and creative aspects. It not only makes it easier and faster to do basic work like sharpening, color correcting, and increasing saturation, but also lets you try a host of special effects, subtle or blatant. The plug-in's Explore, Design, and Tweak modes provide unlimited possibilities.

GOING BY THE NUMBERS

Many of the single-step KPT filters (the ones like Smudge and Grime Layer that act as soon as you select them from the Filter menu instead of presenting a dialog box for input) can be varied by using the keypad numbers on an extended keyboard. You set the variation by holding down a number key as you select the filter. In general, the higher the number, the stronger the effect.

For the KPT Page Curl filter, however, the corner keys (1, 3, 7, and 9) determine which corner of the image will be curled. The Caps Lock key determines whether the curl will come in from the top or bottom edge of the corner (a horizontal curl, set with the Caps Lock key down) or from a side edge of the corner (a vertical curl, set with the Caps Lock key up).

Page Curl (7 and 3)

For the KPT Glass Lens filters (Bright, Normal, and Soft) the keypad numbers change the direction of the lighting, with "5" (at the center of the keypad) being direct front lighting, the surrounding keys providing lights that aim inward from their positions, and the "0" key providing back lighting.

For the KPT Vortex Tiling filter, the keypad numbers control the depth of the zoom into the vortex created by the filter. The higher the number, the deeper the zoom.

Glass Lens Bright (8)

Vortex Tiling (3)

Vortex Tiling (6)

The Black Box

Four of the filters in Alien Skin Software's The Black Box series apply their effects around (rather than upon) a selection. Here we've used type in an alpha channel to make the selection. Where you see "lightened" in the caption, the selection was reloaded after the filter was applied, and the selected area was lightened with the output slider in the Levels dialog. The Black Box filters are found in the Alien Skin submenu of Photoshop's Filter menu. Shown here are the relatively subtle default settings.

Drop Shadow (selection then filled with white)

Glass (Flat; lightened)

Glass (Mesa; lightened)

Glass (Rounded; lightened)

Glow (selection then filled with black)

HSB Noise

Swirl

The Boss (Flat; lightened)

The Boss (Mesa; lightened)

The Boss (Round; lightened)

Lighting Up a Wall

Overview *Layer the elements of your montage, adding drop shadows if you like; treat all but the shadow layers with the Lighting Effects filter.*

JHD / PHOTOS: PHOTOGEAR, IMAGE CLUB GRAPHICS

1a

Original montage of three images

THE LIGHTING EFFECTS FILTER IS IDEAL for helping the elements of a montage look at home in their surroundings. Start with the different lighting effects provided in the Style list. Then customize them by changing the Light Type and Properties settings, the direction, or even the number of lights. To add surface texture, choose a color channel or a specially prepared alpha channel to use as the Texture channel. Here we've combined drop shadows with the filter's ability to light and to "emboss."

1 Assembling the pieces. Open an RGB file to use as the "wall" in your image. Open each of the other component images, select the part you want to use, and drag and drop it into the wall file to form a new layer. We used a brick background, a frame, and a landscape photo. Then we added a drop shadow between the image layers. (The technique for making drop shadows is described on pages 215–217.)

2 Lighting the image. Now choose Filter, Render, Lighting Effects and apply the Lighting Effects filter to each layer except the shadows. Use the same Style setting in each case (we used "2AMSPOT" for the image at the top of the page). But if the image in any layer has an inherent texture, as our brick wall did, use one of the color channels of that layer (we used Green) as a Texture Channel when you apply the filter to the Background layer.

If the light parts of your texture channel represent structure that protrudes from the surface, you'll want to turn ON White Is High in the

1b

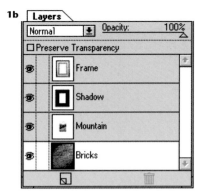

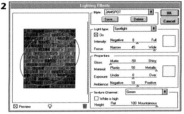

The layered, lit images and the unlit drop shadow

2

Applying Lighting Effects with a Texture Channel to the bricks layer only

Texture Channel area of the Lighting Effects dialog box. For our montage of the painting on the wall, we wanted the white mortar to look like it was recessed between the bricks, so we turned OFF White Is High.

Experimenting and saving styles. To experiment with lighting, try other settings from the Style list. Depending on what kind of lighting you set up, you may want to make the drop shadow layer invisible by clicking to turn off its eye in the Layers palette, or reposition the shadow with the move tool to match the direction of the lighting.

To experiment with texture, you can fill an alpha channel with a scanned texture, or generate a texture by choosing Filter, Noise, Add Noise. Or use Filter, Render, Texture Fill to turn one of the many grayscale files in the **goodies\textures** directory into a seamlessly repeating pattern to fill an alpha channel.

There's no reason why you can't "texturize" more than one layer. For instance, we could have used a canvas texture on the Mountains layer to help turn the photo into a painting.

When you have the Light Type, Properties, and Texture Channel settings you like, click the Save button in the Lighting Effects dialog box and name the style. Your new style will appear in the Style list whenever you use the filter. The styles shown here are included on the Wow! CD ROM in the back of this book.

WOWRGB lighting consists of three colored Spotlights and a white Omni light. Colors for the lights are set with the color square in the Light Type section of the dialog box.

The WOWSoft lighting style consists of a blue Spotlight with pink ambient light, set in the Properties section of the dialog box.

The WOW3Down lighting style consists of three white spotlights, two angled in from the 11 o'clock and 1 o'clock positions, and one pointing directly down from the top.

Combining Filter Effects

Overview *Duplicate the image into two layers; apply separate filter or color effects to each; combine the effects by adjusting the Opacity of the top layer.*

MICHAEL GILMORE

Original photo

2

Making two layers for filtering

FILTERS OFFER ENDLESS POSSIBILITIES for combining their potentially spectacular effects. For an illustration for the Japanese edition of *Step-By-Step Electronic Design,* Michael Gilmore was inspired by *Jurassic Park* to use this dinosaur as the centerpiece.

1 Choosing an image. An out-of-the-ordinary original image works well as the subject for the unusual effects that filters can apply. Gilmore started with a photo he took of a toy dinosaur from a local hobby shop. He scanned the photo and began experimenting to make it look a bit more fearsome.

DUPLICATING FOR SAFEKEEPING

In the rush of inspiration, it can be hard to remember to save a copy of your original so you can start fresh if you want to. Even with the Revert command available, it's a good idea to start a project by duplicating the original image, and then save often during image development. Choose Image, Duplicate to quickly make a copy to work on, or use Save A Copy or Edit, Take Snapshot.

2 Setting up layers. To give yourself two layers that you can filter and then blend by experimenting, open the Layers palette (Window, Palettes, Show Layers) and drag the Background icon to the New Layer icon at the bottom of the palette to copy the image to a new layer. Repeat the process to make another layer.

3 Applying the first filter. Make the top layer active in the Layers palette and rename it if you like. (Double-clicking a layer in the

3

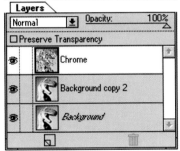

Applying the first filter.

4

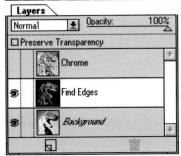

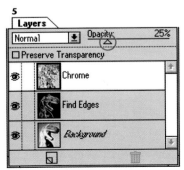

Applying the second filter

Layers palette opens the Layer Options dialog box so you can re-name the layer.) Choose an effect from the Filter menu and, if nec-essary, set its parameters. Gilmore had installed the Gallery Effects Classic Art 1 filters (see page 150 for more about these filters). He chose Filter, Gallery Effects, Chrome and tested various settings on a part of the image in the interactive dialog box. When he was happy with the result, he clicked the Apply button.

4 Applying a second filter. Click the eye icon on the already fil-tered layer to hide this layer from view so you'll be able to see the new filter effect when you apply it to the layer below. Now activate the second layer of the Layers palette and rename it if you like. Ap-ply another filter. Gilmore applied Photoshop's Find Edges and then used Image, Map, Invert to get bright lines on a dark background.

5 Blending the two effects. Now you can adjust the way the two images blend. With the top layer active and all layers visible, choose an Opacity setting. Gilmore blended the Chrome layer at 25% Opacity so the Find Edges filter would have a stronger effect than the Chrome. The result is shown at the top of the preceding page. (Try adjusting the opacity of the middle layer to let some of the original image show through, or experiment with the blending modes — Multiply, Difference, and others.)

6 Experimenting with filters. Try out other filter combinations. Shown at the right are two of Gilmore's ex-periments combining the use of Adobe Photoshop filters, a Gallery Effects filter, adjust-ments to color (through Image, Adjust, Hue/Saturation), and changes to the color map (Im-age, Map).

6a

For this effect, Photoshop's Ripple filter was applied (at its default settings) to the original; color was adjusted through Image, Adjust, Hue/Saturation; and the Gallery Effects Dry Brush filter was applied.

6b

To produce the image above, the original was solarized (Filter, Stylize, Solarize), and Image, Map, Equalize was applied to brighten the result.

Blending the filter effects

Imitating Paint and Canvas

Overview *Use filters (or painting tools) to get a brush effect; "emboss" the dark areas of the image with Lighting Effects; emboss the light areas with Lighting Effects and a custom canvas pattern stored in an alpha channel.*

1a

Original image

1b

Applying the Gallery Effects Dry Brush filter

FILTERS SUCH AS PHOTOSHOP'S FACET, CRYSTALLIZE, AND MEDIAN, or the Gallery Effects filters (see pages 150 through 155) can automatically generate some pretty amazing painterly effects. But no one filter provides control over all the attributes you might like to include in a painting: the gestural brush strokes, the built-up texture of thickly applied paints, and the texture of the white canvas, showing through in areas where paint is thin or absent. Fractal Design Painter has built-in functions to do this kind of imitation of natural media, and you can also do it with Photoshop if you use the right combination of filters. To turn this photo of flowers into a painting, we used a Gallery Effects filter and the Lighting Effects filter from Photoshop's Filter, Render submenu to get the look of the paint; then we used the Offset filter and Lighting Effects again to make and apply the custom canvas texture.

1 Painting the photo. Open a photo in RGB mode and apply a paint effect. (It has to be in RGB mode in order to use Lighting Effects later, since this filter works on RGB images only.) We used the Dry Brush filter from Gallery Effects Classic Art (Vol. 1) with Texture 1, a Brush Size of 5, and Brush Detail set at 8. But you can use any of a number of other settings or filters. Or hand-paint the photo with the rubber stamp tool in Impressionist mode. Or finger paint with the smudge tool. Or start from scratch rather than from a photo and use the painting tools (described in Chapter 6) to make your picture.

2 "Embossing" the brush strokes. Now use the Lighting Effects filter to add dramatic lighting to your painting and to create the "feel" of the paint with a texture channel. To create the texture channel, open the Channels palette (by choosing Windows, Palettes, Show Channels, for instance) and look at the Red, Green, and

2

Applying Lighting Effects with Green as the Texture Channel to "emboss" the paint

3a

Offset	
Horizontal: 120 pixels right	OK
Vertical: 120 pixels down	Reset
Undefined Areas	☒ Preview
○ Set to Background	
○ Repeat Edge Pixels	
◉ Wrap Around	

Applying the Offset filter to a scan of canvas

3b

CANVAS.TIF (1:1)

Using the rubber stamp tool to hide the "seams" revealed by the Offset filter

Blue channels one by one, to see which shows the most detail in the paint strokes. (To look at an individual color channel, click its name in the Channels palette.) In our painting, the Green channel showed the most paint detail.

Once you've picked the channel, choose Filter, Render, Lighting Effects and set up a lighting style. We used a Directional light, but you could also try a spotlight with a wide focus to add drama. In setting up the Texture Channel section of the Lighting Effects dialog box, select the channel you identified as having the most detail. Be sure to turn OFF the check box for White Is High, so the dark areas (the areas that will appear to have the most paint) will be raised when the filter is run. Use a low Height setting — you're aiming for a painted look here, not a plastered effect. (We used a setting of 10.) And turn the Material setting all the way up to Metallic. This won't make the paint look like metal; it just preserves the color in the image, which will tend to wash out if the slider is moved any closer to the Plastic end of the scale. Adjust the Ambience slider to restore something similar to the original overall light level. (We used a setting of +25.) With all settings in order and the preview looking good, click OK to run the filter.

3 Creating a canvas texture. Scan a canvas texture, or create one (see "Creating Canvas" on page 168). We scanned a small piece of canvas and selected a rectangular area from it.

To turn the canvas into a seamlessly wrapping pattern, you'll first use the Offset filter to reveal the "seams" that would appear between tiles and then use the rubber stamp tool to eliminate them: Apply the Offset filter (Filter, Other, Offset). Enter Horizontal and Vertical settings that will move the edges of the image into the center of the image. (We offset our 256-pixel-wide image 128 pixels right and 128 pixels down.) Choose Wrap Around for the Undefined Areas (so the pixels that are pushed out of the file at the right and bottom edges will reappear at the left and top to fill the empty space created there).

To eliminate the seams, double-click the rubber stamp tool in the tool palette to open its Options palette. Choose one of the Clone options — Aligned might work best for a woven texture and Non-aligned for a random grain. Choose a soft brush from the Brushes palette, about twice the size of the "grain" of your canvas. Hold down the Option key and click the rubber stamp on a part of the image away from any seam to pick up cloning texture. Paint over the seam with the rubber stamp, using short strokes if you're working in Non-aligned mode. (In Aligned mode, it doesn't matter whether strokes are long or short because the image is reproduced as a single copy, as described in the "Clone" section on page 176.)

4 Applying the canvas texture. When the seams are gone, save the image (in case you want to use it again later). Then Select All (Ctrl-A), and choose Edit, Define Pattern.

Capturing the selected area as a pattern

4b

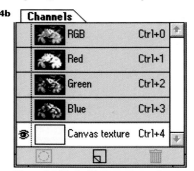

Channel 4 filled with the canvas pattern

4c

The Blue channel loaded to select the highlights

4d

Applying Lighting Effects with the canvas pattern (channel 4) used as the Texture Channel

In the Channels palette of your RGB painting, create an alpha channel by clicking on the New Channel icon in the center at the bottom of the palette. With this new channel active, choose Edit, Fill, Pattern. The alpha channel will fill with seamlessly tiled canvas pattern.

Now you'll add the canvas texture to the painting. In this case the effect you want to create is to have the texture show through in the highlight (white and very light) areas of the painting, to create the impression that little or no paint has been applied there. (The dark areas have already been textured with paint.) To isolate the light areas so the canvas texture can be applied, look at the Red, Green, and Blue channels again (as in step 2) and choose the one that shows the most contrast between the light areas and the rest of the image. In the Channels palette, Alt-click that alpha channel's name to load it as a selection in the image. (In our image the Blue channel was best for highlights.)

Now apply the Lighting Effects filter again (as in step 2). Use the same Light Type and Properties settings. But this time turn ON the White Is High check box, reduce the Height setting even more, and set the Texture Channel to #4 (the alpha channel with the canvas pattern). When you click OK to apply the effect, it will be applied to the selected areas (the white and light parts you selected by loading the channel you chose for the highlights) but not to the dark, unselected areas, which already show the paint texture.

CREATING CANVAS

You can generate a custom paper or canvas texture to "interact" with paint in Photoshop. Start a new Grayscale file with a white background. Choose Filter, Noise, Add Noise. Here, for a 225 dpi file, we used a setting of 500, Gaussian.

Then apply a blur filter. We used Blur, Gaussian Blur with a setting of 1.0. Next apply the Facet filter (Filter, Pixelate, Facet). Then experiment until you have a texture you like. We used Filter, Blur, More and then Filter Stylize, Emboss. Then use Image, Adjust, Levels to whiten the paper, moving the white Input Levels slider to the left to increase detail in the highlights and moving the black Output Levels slider to the right to reduce contrast. The painting surface should be white and the shadows caused by the texture should be medium to very light gray. The greater the tonal difference between the surface and the shadows, the coarser the grain of the "paper."

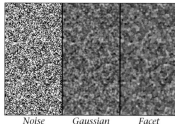

Noise Gaussian Blur Facet

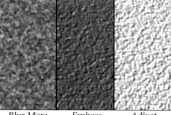

Blur More Emboss Adjust Levels

New York Lady is one of a series that **Jack Davis** submitted to client Thunder Lizard Productions as possible cover illustrations for a New York Photoshop conference brochure. First he made sketches and thumbnails, and then he located the three images he wanted to use and began working back-to-front, starting with the sky.

Davis bumped up the sky's saturation with Image, Adjust, Hue/Saturation, then moved to the statue image and used the pen tool to select the lady of liberty and cut her out from the background. He dragged and dropped the statue image to make a new layer in the sky document, used the pen tool again to select and remove the statue's face, and placed that in its own layer. To create the illusion of the statue's thickness, Davis added a bevel effect to the edges around the face cutout.

The main difficulty with the woman's face image was finding a photo taken from the right view: from below but with the eyes making contact. Davis cropped, scaled, rotated, and colored the image to fit the final collage, dragged and dropped it into a new layer in the collage file, and moved that layer behind the statue layer. The shadow cast on and below her face by the floating Statue of Liberty mask was done with the dodge/burn/sponge tool.

After roughly selecting the areas of the sky around the statue's crown spikes with a feathered lasso, Davis lightened them with Image, Adjust, Levels. Then he flattened all the layers into one. Next he duplicated the flattened image in a new layer of the same file by dragging its Background icon (now the only icon left) to the New Layer button at the bottom of the Layers palette. He ran the Reticulation filter from Gallery Effects Classic Art 3 (see page 154) on this new layer, which resulted in a grayscale mezzotintlike effect. With this layer above and the color version below, he set the blending mode for the upper layer to Multiply and adjusted the Opacity.

Louis Fishauf created *Money Swirl* with the Twirl, Spherize, and Radial Blur filters. The image was composited from two files: one for the vortex in the middle and another for the bills on the outside. For the vortex, Fishauf started with a black "+" shape on white and applied the Twirl filter. In the other file, he arranged scans of four bills in the four quadrants of a square, applied the Spherize filter to achieve the distortion, and then applied a Radial Blur (Spin) to the ends of the bills, using the center of the illustration as the center of the spin. "It took about 20 tries to get the effect I wanted," says Fishauf. "I wish I had written down exactly how I finally did it."

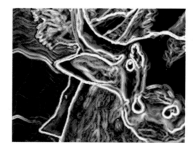

To create *Neon Cowboy,* **Ellie Dickson** started with a scanned photo of a bull and one of a cowboy. She cut and pasted the two images together and made changes to the color with painting tools and Image, Adjust functions. Then she selected the edge of bull and rider with a lasso with a 15-pixel feather (the image itself was about 1100 pixels wide altogether) and copied the selection to the clipboard. With the selection still active, she pasted the copy from the clipboard behind the selection at 50% opacity. She offset the pasted-behind edge by dragging it to the left. Then she pasted behind again, this time at 40% opacity, again offsetting the pasted edge. She repeated this at 30% and 20% opacity. Then she used the Motion Blur filter, applying it to the image in the same direction as the fade she had been creating. She applied the Wave filter and then Find Edges, and finally finished the piece by choosing Image, Map, Invert to create the neon effect.

Anna Stump painted *Ginger* in Fractal Design Painter (detail below). Then **Mark Siprut** opened the file in Photoshop, converted it from RGB to CMYK mode, and copied it to an additional layer. On the layer underneath he ran the Watercolor filter from Gallery Effects Classic Art 1 (see page 151) on the individual color channels, causing a unique interaction of the filtered colors. He adjusted the Opacity of the layer above and set its mode to Multiply, to add emphasis to the line work.

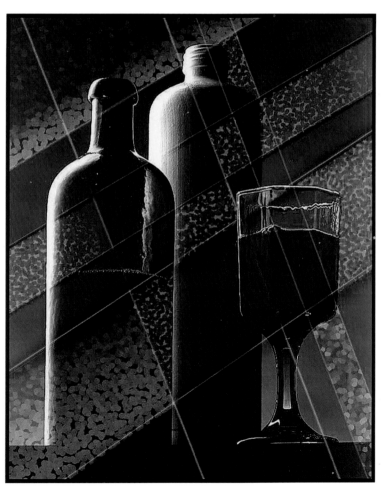

To make *Still Life* **Nino Cocchiarella** used the pen tool to draw the shapes, which he saved as paths. He used the paths in two ways: He turned them into selections (Make Selection from the Paths palette's pop-out menu) and saved them as alpha channels. Then he painted each path (click the Stroke Path icon at the bottom of the Paths palette). To round the shapes of the objects, Cocchiarella used the gradient tool in Lighten or Darken mode in the alpha channels he had made from the paths; then he loaded the graduated masks and adjusted Levels to highlight or shade the shapes. The lichen-like texture in some areas of the image was created by running the Pointillize filter and then the Noise filter in some of the channels and then loading these masks into the main image and adjusting Levels. Colors were adjusted by loading masks and applying Image, Adjust, Hue/Saturation.

To make *Neo Fragile,* **Kai Krause,** co-developer of HSC's KPT filters (see page 158), used the KPT Mandelbrot Set Explorer filter with the Copper Something setting and the Interior set to black to generate a fractal design. Then he applied the KPT Glass Lens Bright filter and adjusted the color through the Hue sliders in the Image, Adjust, Hue/Saturation dialog box. To clean up the edges, he Shift-selected the resulting highlighted sphere with the elliptical selection tool, copied this circular selection to the clipboard, and pasted it into a new black background. He made a mask from this file, adjusting Levels to increase the contrast of the mask, to which he added some black lines to match some of the spikes in his "plasma green sphere" file, which he generated with a star explosion displacement map. He used Image, Calculations with the fractal image as Source 1, the Blending mode as Normal, the Mask box checked and the altered mask as Mask, and the plasma green sphere as Source 2. Where the mask was white, Source 1 contributed to the *NeoFragile* image; where it was black, Source 2 contributed.

To generate *Marble,* **Nino Cocchiarella** started with a single scan of a piece of marble. He selected areas of the image with the ellipse and rectangle selection marquees, saved the selections as masks, and loaded them to experiment with color. He used Image, Adjust, Hue/Saturation to color selected areas and Image, Adjust, Levels to make the drop shadows. He had made some of the masks with linear or radial gradient fills, so that the coloring, lightening, or darkening effect was applied differentially through the mask. The airbrush was used to add detail to the shading. The round but slightly flattened shapes were made by selecting areas and applying the Spherize filter twice, once with a setting of 100% and then again with a setting of 50%, and then adjusting Levels to light the objects.

Jack Davis used elements from three 3D files — rocket ship and trail, letterforms, and large planets — to assemble this *Planet Studios Logo*. He set the type in Adobe Illustrator and then extruded it in a 3D program, but he couldn't get the exaggerated perspective he wanted, so he imported it into Photoshop and applied the Image, Effects, Distort command to complete the illusion. To emphasize the edges on the type and the rivets on the rocket, he used the Photocopy filter from Gallery Effects Classic Art 2: He copied the type layer, applied the filter to the copy, and used the Multiply mode and a slightly reduced Opacity in the Layers palette to composite the filtered image with the original. The large planets in the background were from a ray-traced image, which was rendered at low resolution and without antialiasing; this relatively crude rendering was acceptable because Davis planned to use Photoshop's Gaussian Blur filter on the planets to create depth of field between the lettering and rocket in the foreground and the planets in the background.

To create the spark for the *Megamorph Logo Comp*, **Kory Jones** used the KPT Julia Set 3 filter (see page 158). Working in an RGB Photoshop file, he specified black-and-white output for the filter and cut and pasted together parts of the fractal design to make the spark the shape he wanted. When the spark was complete, he cut it from the RGB channel and pasted it into

an alpha channel he created for that purpose. He created a black background in the RGB channel, loaded the selection from the alpha channel, and filled it with blue. To emphasize the spark's main trunk, he drew a path with the pen tool and stroked the path with the airbrush tool, first with a medium-size brush tip with blue in Color mode and then with a smaller brush with white in Normal mode.

He pasted the two spheres and the coils (created in a 3D program) into the RGB channel, using composite controls (now in Layer Options) to make the spheres partially transparent so the ends of the sparks would show. A copy of the spark was pasted into the lettering, and its color was adjusted by using Image, Map, Invert to turn the white part dark and then adjusting the Hue to restore the blue color.

6

PAINTING

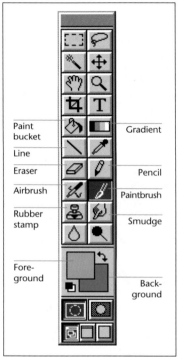

Paint bucket

Line

Eraser

Airbrush

Rubber stamp

Fore-ground

Gradient

Pencil

Paintbrush

Smudge

Back-ground

In addition to the tools in the palette, the Fill and Stroke commands from the Edit menu are part of Photoshop's painting equipment.

The pen tool can also act as a painting tool: Draw a path (as described in Chapter 2). Then choose a painting tool and choose Stroke Path from the pop-out menu in the Paths palette. This path was stroked with a paintbrush with Wet Edges and a fade from Foreground to Background color.

AS THE WORK IN THIS CHAPTER shows, Photoshop painters have extended their toolkits beyond the brushes and pencil, to use the editing tools, alpha channel "friskets," layers, and many of the program's color controls and layer options. But if we define painting tools as those that can apply Foreground color, Background color, Transparency, or pixels from an image, Photoshop's painting tools include the paint bucket, gradient fill, line, eraser, pencil, airbrush, paintbrush, rubber stamp, and smudge. All of these tools can be operated by selecting the tool and then clicking to make a single "footprint" on the canvas, or by holding down the mouse button or stylus and dragging to make a stroke. Most of these tools can also be constrained to a straight line by holding down the Shift key and clicking from point to point. (The line tool, which always paints in a straight line, is constrained to 45- and 90-degree angles when the Shift key is used.) Each of the tools has its own set of controls, found in a Tool Options palette that appears when you double-click the icon in the toolbox. The tool's footprint is chosen in the Brushes palette, which by default is nested with the Tool Options palette so you can open it by clicking on the Brushes tab.

Here's a list of the painting characteristics that can be controlled through the **Tool Options** palette:

Antialiasing: For the paint bucket only; the line, airbrush, paintbrush, rubber stamp, and smudge tools are always smooth-edged (antialiased) except in Bitmap or Indexed Color mode; the pencil tool is not; for the gradient fill tool, antialiasing depends on the selection into which the gradient is applied. For the eraser tool, Antialiasing cannot be set manually; In its Paintbrush and Airbrush modes it is antialiased; in Block and Pencil modes it isn't.

Arrowheads: For the line tool only, you can put a custom arrowhead on the beginning or end of a stroke, or at both ends.

Auto Erase: For the pencil tool, if you start a stroke on an area of the image that is currently the Foreground color, the stroke is made in the Background color; if you start the stroke on a pixel of any other color, the stroke is made in the Foreground color as usual.

Blending (or Transfer) Mode: Controls the interaction of the paint with the current colors of the pixels in the image. All the modes available in the Layers palette and in the Calculations and

continued on page 176

175

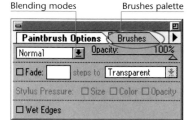

Blending modes — Brushes palette

Leaving the Tool Options and Brushes palettes nested together makes it easy to display the current set of brushes by clicking on the Brushes tab.

Custom arrowheads can be automatically applied to lines drawn with the line tool.

Painting with the paintbrush with Wet Edges, using no Fade setting (top), with Fade To Transparent in 25 steps (center), and with Fade To Background in 25 steps (bottom)

IF PAINTING DOESN'T WORK

If an image has an active selection or more than one layer, the painting tools will work only *inside the selection* and *on the active layer*. If a painting tool doesn't seem to be working, it may be because there's an invisible active selection — either outside the window, or hidden because you've pressed Command-H. Or the area you're trying to paint may be protected from paint because you're trying to paint on a layer with Preserve Transparency turned on in the Layers palette.

Apply Image dialog boxes (see Chapter 2) are also available in Tool Options. In addition, in **Behind** mode, only the transparent areas of a layer will accept color; the effect is like painting a background behind any already colored pixels in the layer. **Clear** mode (available for the paint bucket and line tool and for the Fill and Stroke commands from the Edit menu, and only in layers with transparency) is like painting with paint remover.

Clone: For the rubber stamp tool, the two Clone options (Aligned and Non-Aligned) paint with a portion of a sampled image. The source area that the image is taken from is defined by holding down the Option key and clicking. Samples can be taken from any open image, from a single layer or from all layers, as if they were merged (see "Sample Merged" on page 177). Once the sample has been collected, you drag the tool to apply the clone of the sampled image. In Non-aligned mode, each time you start a stroke, the clone starts over at the sampled point, so you end up with many copies of the sampled area. In Aligned mode, only one version of the clone can be produced, no matter how many stokes are applied; with enough painting, the entire sampled image is reproduced.

Fade: For the airbrush, paintbrush, and pencil, strokes fade from the Foreground color to the Background color or to nothing (Transparent); the Distance setting affects the total distance from the beginning of the stroke (at full-strength Foreground color) to the point where the background color is full-strength or the paint is completely transparent. In a sense, the gradient tool always operates in Fade-out mode, applying a color gradient from Foreground to Background color or to Transparency. And the eraser tool's fade-out (in Airbrush, Paintbrush, or Pencil mode) is always from the Background color (or from Transparency for a transparent layer) to the existing image on that layer.

Finger Painting: For the smudge tool only, which normally just smears existing paint, this option instead applies the Foreground color at the start of the smear.

From Saved: For the rubber stamp, this option restores the last saved version of the file in the areas you stroke. (The eraser, which normally applies the Background color or Transparency, restores the saved image when the Alt key is held down or when the Erase To Saved box is checked in the Eraser Options palette.)

From Snapshot: For the rubber stamp, as you apply strokes, this Option restores the version of the file (or a selection) that was temporarily stored by choosing Edit, Take Snapshot.

Gradient Tool Options: These are covered briefly in Chapter 1.

Impressionist: For the rubber stamp, painting produces an Impressionist (though somewhat smeared) rendition based on the last saved version of the file; Impressionist is a kind of "painterly filter in a brush."

DEFINING A PATTERN

To make a repeating pattern, you can use the rectangular marquee to select all or part of an image, and choose Edit, Define Pattern. Now you can fill all or a selected part of an image file with your pattern. You can stop there or set the pattern up so the elements in alternate rows are offset, like the prints typically used for wrapping paper or fabric: Select one column of the pattern and use the Offset filter (with Undefined Areas set to Wrap Around) to shift it vertically by half the height of your original pattern element. Use the rectangular marquee to select this column and the one next to it, and choose Edit, Define Pattern again.

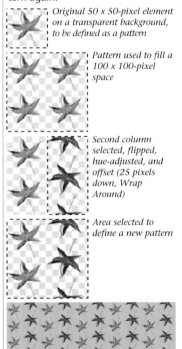

Original 50 x 50-pixel element on a transparent background, to be defined as a pattern

Pattern used to fill a 100 x 100-pixel space

Second column selected, flipped, hue-adjusted, and offset (25 pixels down, Wrap Around)

Area selected to define a new pattern

Color background filled with the new pattern

Opacity: For the paint bucket, gradient tool, line, pencil, paintbrush, and rubber stamp (as well as the eraser in Paintbrush or Pencil mode), opacity of the applied paint can be varied from 1% to 100% by means of the Opacity slider, operated by dragging with the pointer. Or press the number keys on the keyboard to change the Opacity setting in 10% increments; the "1" key sets Opacity at 10%, the "2" key at 20%, and so on, with "0" producing 100%.

Pattern: For the paint bucket, which can fill an area with the currently defined pattern; and the rubber stamp, which can paint with the currently defined pattern, either Aligned (painting as if the pattern filled the area behind the image and the rubber stamp was erasing to it) or Non-aligned (starting a new application of the pattern from the upper left corner of the pattern tile each time the mouse button is pressed to start a new stroke).

Pressure: For the smudge and airbrush tools (and the eraser in Airbrush mode), the slider in the Tool Options palette regulates the tool's pressure (how much paint the airbrush applies in a given time, or how long a smear is produced by the smudge tool) rather than controlling the opacity of entire strokes.

Sample Merged: For the paint bucket, rubber stamp, or smudge tool, the color (to be filled, cloned, or smeared, respectively) is selected as if all visible layers were merged. When Sample Merged is turned off, only the active layer is sampled, cloned, or smeared.

Stylus Pressure: For the airbrush, smudge, paintbrush, pencil, and rubber stamp (as well as the eraser in all its modes except Block), you can set the characteristic that will vary when pressure is applied to the stylus of a pressure-sensitive tablet; characteristics that can be varied, depending on the tool, are Size, Opacity, Color, and Pressure.

Wet Edges: For the paintbrush (and the eraser in Paintbrush mode), color builds up along the edges of the stroke while leaving the center semitransparent as it does with traditional watercolors.

Width: For the line tool, set in terms of the number of pixels.

Size and Shape: The pop-out menu in the Brushes palette allows you to add a brush up to 999 x 999 pixels in size to the palette (by choosing New Brush and specifying characteristics in the New Brush dialog box, or by selecting an area of an existing image and choosing Define Brush from the palette's pop-out menu). You can also **delete** brushes from the palette one by one by Ctrl-clicking on the ones you want to remove. You can **edit** an existing brush (by double-clicking it in the palette or by clicking it and choosing Brush Options from the pop-out menu). You can also name and **save** a particular palette of brushes (choose Save Brushes), **load** a palette you've previously saved (choose Load Brushes), or **append** a palette to the current one (choose Append Brushes).

Beginning with Gray

Overview _Paint an image in grayscale; select areas of the image and fill with color, varying the opacity and blending mode; add finishing touches with painting and editing tools._

1

Original grayscale painting

2

Blurred to soften the image

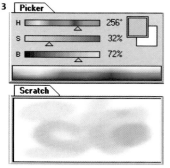

3

Mixing colors

CHER THREINEN-PENDARVIS

WHEN CAPTURING THE LIGHTING is all-important in a painting, you can sometimes get good results by starting out in grayscale and laying in the color later, taking advantage of Photoshop's Lighten, Darken, and Color modes. To paint _Tranquil Beach_, Cher Threinen-Pendarvis started out in grayscale, painting from memory and a pencil sketch. Working with a single layer, she applied color using masks and a series of floating selections.

1 Establishing lights and darks. Open a file in Grayscale mode and use the painting tools to rough in the light and dark areas. Threinen-Pendarvis used primarily the brush, airbrush, smudge, and blur tools to make her gray painting.

2 Smoothing transitions. To eliminate abrupt color changes and hard stroke edges, you can soften the image (or a selected part of it) by choosing Filter, Blur, Gaussian Blur. Threinen-Pendarvis applied a 2-pixel Gaussian blur to the entire 440-pixel-wide image.

3 Making a palette. Choose Mode, RGB Color to convert the file from grayscale to color. Open the Picker and Scratch palettes, and use them to mix the colors you'll need for your painting.

4 Selecting areas to color. Open the Channels palette so you can save selections as you make them. Use the lasso tool to select areas of the gray image where you want to apply color. As you make each selection, click the Convert icon at the bottom left of the Channels palette to save it in an alpha channel. Being able to load the selection again later will make it possible to add color in

4

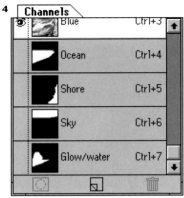

Saving selections as channels

5

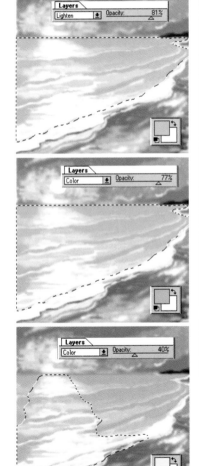

Coloring the floating selections

stages. Threinen-Pendarvis used the lasso with various feather settings to make selections for the sky, the water, the beach, the glow in the sky and in the water, and other areas, and saved the selections in alpha channels.

5 Laying in color. Now open the Layers palette along with the Channels palette. With the RGB channels targeted and visible and the alpha channels inactive and invisible, load an alpha channel as a selection by Alt-clicking on its icon in the Channels palette or dragging its icon to the Convert icon at the bottom left of the Channels palette. When you have an area selected, press Ctrl-J to float a copy of the selected area; this will make it possible to use the Layers palette to control the mode and opacity of the paint you apply. Click on the Picker or Scratch to select a Foreground color. Then press Alt-Backspace to fill the selected area. Use the Opacity slider and the pop-up blending mode list in the Layers palette to experiment with different ways of blending the floating color into the image. Use Lighten (which affects only those pixels that are darker than the foreground color), Darken (which affects only those that are lighter), or Color (which changes hue and saturation but not tonality).

Threinen-Pendarvis loaded selections from the alpha channels she had made and floated and colored the selected areas of her image. For the glow in the water, for example, she filled the floating selection with a greenish blue in Lighten mode and adjusted the opacity. Then she dropped the selection (Ctrl-D) to set the color, loaded and floated the same selection again, and filled it with the same blue, this time in Color mode, again with opacity adjusted. Next she loaded and floated the glow selection and filled it with a pale yellow in Color mode; setting the opacity at 40% blended the blue and yellow to make a light green, and the highlights took on a yellow tint. As she filled the remaining areas with color, the feathering at the edges of the selections blended colors to soften transitions between areas.

Adjusting the darks and lights. Use the painting tools and smudge and blur; vary the painting mode and the percentages of opacity to emphasize the dark and light areas of the painting. Among other final changes, Threinen darkened some of the shadow areas of the waves and altered the beach. *Wow!*

OPACITY KEYS

Even without a pressure-sensitive tablet, you can have some control over the opacity of paint or the "pressure" with which it's applied, without moving the pointer from the painting to the Layers or tool options palette. Press a number key, either in the main keyboard or in the keypad, to vary the opacity in 10% steps — "1" produces 10%, "2" is 20%, and so on, with "0" being full opacity. This works with all the painting, drawing, and editing tools, including the gradient tool. You have to stop painting, though (by releasing the mouse button), in order to make the change.

Painting with Light

Overview *Start with a sketch; rough in the color; build volume; add highlights and detail.*

FRANCOIS GUÉRIN

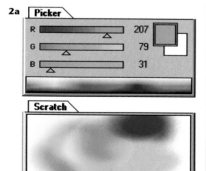

Sketching with the pencil

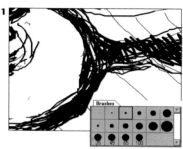

Mixing colors

ACHIEVING A PAINTERLY EFFECT with the computer involves some mental translation from traditional tools to electronic ones. Artist/ illustrator Francois Guérin, who also works with oils, pastels, gouache, and Fractal Design Painter, has found several ways to work effectively with Photoshop as a painting program. For *The Meal*, painted from memory, he used primarily the painting tools, the lasso, the Gaussian Blur, and functions from the Image, Adjust submenu. Guérin worked with a cordless pressure-sensitive tablet. He likes the brushlike feel of the stylus but doesn't vary the pressure much.

1 Making a sketch. To start out, click the pencil tool and begin drawing. Choose pencil tips of different sizes from the Brushes palette. Guérin used a larger tip to darken the shadow areas.

2 Laying down color. Choose Window, Palettes and open the color palettes you need. You can use the Picker and Scratch to mix and sample colors, and the Swatches to store and recall colors that you want to use again. You can apply the first strokes of paint with brushes from the top row of the Brushes palette, which provide smooth-edged, solid strokes. Paint in Normal mode so the strokes cover the black-and-white sketch.

3 Building volume. Use the Scratch palette to mix the color variations you need to begin painting shapes. At this point, use the paintbrush and airbrush tools, which have softer edges, to achieve color blending in the painting.

THE BEST SKETCHING TOOL

The pencil gives you hard-edged lines regardless of the size tip you use. Because Photoshop doesn't have to antialias the strokes, the pencil can draw dramatically faster than a brush, providing a very responsive stroke.

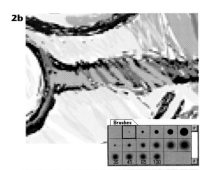

2b

Laying down color with the paintbrush

3

Blending colors with the airbrush

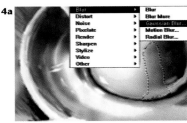

4a

Smoothing color with the Gaussian Blur filter

4 Indicating textures. Guérin used the smallest pencil point to add "grain" to the wood of the table, which he later smoothed with the smudge (finger) tool. He also used the Blur filters to add a smooth sheen to some of the surfaces in the image. For instance, he used a feathered lasso to select some areas of the cup and saucer, and applied a Gaussian Blur. (Double-click the lasso icon in the toolbox to open the Lasso Options palette for setting the Feather amount.)

5 Putting the colors in context. To modify the colors to be consistent with the light in the scene, you can use a feathered lasso and the Hue/Saturation, Levels, and Color Balance commands of the Image, Adjust submenu. Guérin used a more highly feathered lasso to surround parts of the image so he could change their tonality with the Image, Adjust functions.

6 Adding modeling and highlights. To mold elements in the painting, you can use traditional painting techniques, such as applying strokes to follow the form of an object. Guérin shaped the napkin beneath the fork in this way, for example. The blur tool (water drop) can be used to smooth areas such as the reflections on the glass. (If the water drop isn't showing in the tool palette, Alt-click the sharpen tool — the pointed icon at the lower left of the toolbox — to toggle the water drop ON.)

The smudge tool does a good job of adding texture and making color transitions in some areas where light and shadows meet — in the wood of the table, for instance. It can also be used to pull specular highlights out of white paint, as on the tine of the fork.

Developing electronic painting technique. For a painting of his cactus collection, Guérin again started with an electronic pencil

5

Modifying colors

6

Adding texture and highlights

Sketching with the pencil and filling sketched areas with paint

Smoothing color with Gaussian Blur

Differential blurring to create depth

sketch. He poured color into the pencil-drawn shapes with the paint bucket tool and added some detail with the paintbrush. Then he used a feathered lasso and the Gaussian Blur filter to blend the colors. He used the smudge tool to blend the edges where colors met, and added more color with paintbrushes. With the paintbrush and airbrush he built volume in the rounded plants, and he added spines with the paintbrush and pencil. To capture the lighting on the scene, he selected areas of the image with the lasso and played with the color balance, brightness, contrast, hue, and saturation, as he had for *The Meal*. When he selected areas to adjust color, he used alpha channels to store complex selections such as the flower in the foreground so he could make additional color adjustments without having to draw the selection border again. Another way to do this in Photoshop 3 would be to copy the selected areas and paste them into separate layers. To create the illusion of depth, he used the Blur filter, applying it three times for the round cactus on the right side of the painting, which was farthest in the background, twice for the closer, spiky one in the upper left corner, and once for a still closer one in the center. *Wow!*

SELECTING BRUSH TIPS

Press the opening or closing bracket key ([or], next to the P on the keyboard) to move from tip to tip up or down in the Brushes palette. Using the Shift key along with the bracket selects either the first ([) or the last (]) brush in the palette.

EXTRACTING A PALETTE

To pull a color palette from a painted RGB or CMYK image so you can use it as a resource for a related painting, follow this procedure (be sure you don't miss the Revert step!):

1. Convert the painting to Indexed Color mode (temporarily — you'll be changing it back to full color) by choosing Mode, Indexed Color and then selecting 8 bits, Adaptive.

2. Choose Mode, Color Table, click the Save button, and give the table a name. Now choose File, Revert to convert the painting back to its original color mode. (Use Revert, not the Mode menu, to make this change so you won't lose any of the original color from the painting.)

3. In your new painting file, choose Window, Palettes, Show Swatches. Choose Load Swatches and select the named color table. The small squares of the palette will fill with the colors you saved from the first painting.

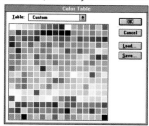

Making an Electronic "Woodcut"

Overview *Trace the contours of a photo; convert that sketch to a pattern; convert a copy of the original photo to a bitmap using the pattern; treat the original photo with the Median filter; layer the bitmap back over the filter-treated photo.*

1a

Original photo

1b

Hand-drawn sketch, scanned

2

> **Define Pattern**
> **Take Snapshot**

Turning the sketch into a pattern

3a

Applying the Median filter to the photo

ARTISTS STRIVE TO FIND WAYS to take advantage of the computer's power and automation without losing the hand-crafted look of traditional artists' methods. Here we've achieved a unique "woodcut" effect by combining the computer's muscle with the subtleties of drawing by hand.

1 Making and aligning the sketch. Open a color photo file in Photoshop. Now you'll trace over the photo to make a sketch that follows the shapes of the objects in the image. One way to trace the photo is to add a new transparent layer (open the Layers palette and click the New Layer icon at the bottom left of the Layers palette) and use a digitizing tablet (with pressure sensitivity turned off) and a paintbrush tool (it's antialiased) with a hard-edged stroke (chosen from the Brushes palette) to sketch over the image. Another way is to print out a copy of the photo at full size and hand-trace the contours with a marking pen with strokes of uniform width. In either case keep the line width about the same as the white spaces between the strokes, so that if you squint at the page, the drawn areas seem to be about 50% gray overall. If you do your artwork by hand (we used a black marker on white tracing paper), scan it into the computer in grayscale mode at 100% size and at the same resolution (pixels per inch) as the color photo file. (You can find the resolution of the photo file by holding down the Alt key and pressing the number block in the lower left corner of its working window.)

You'll need a fairly full range of gray tones to successfully use the sketch as a pattern in step 3. If the edges of the line work in your sketch file don't have a range of grays, you can experiment with blurring (we used Filter, Blur, Blur More for this 900-pixel-wide scan).

3b

Copy of the photo converted to grayscale

4a

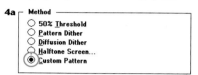

Converting the grayscale to a bitmap

4b

Converted bitmap layer

5

Setting the blending mode and Opacity

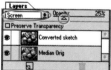

6a

Soft Light, 100% Opacity over color

If you're using a scanned sketch, it's time to line it up with the photo. Make the scan file active and use the move tool (four-headed arrow) to drag a copy of the scan from its file into the photo file to make a new layer. Set the opacity of the layer at about 50% so you can see the color image through the sketch. Use the move tool to align the sketch with the photo underneath.

2 Converting the sketch to a pattern. With the sketch layer active, Select All (Ctrl-A) and choose Edit, Define Pattern. (Unless you quit the program or use Define Pattern again, Photoshop will hold the pattern in memory until you need it at step 4.)

3 Preparing the color and grayscale images. In the color photo layer run the Median filter (Filter, Noise, Median) to soften the details of the original photo so they won't fight with the line work. Median averages the brightness of pixels within the Radius you set to generate a new brightness value for each pixel, but it leaves alone those pixels that are greatly different from their neighbors. So the overall effect is to blur the fine details of the image while leaving any edges (the outlines of the apples, stems, and leaves, for example) quite distinct.

After running the Median filter, duplicate the color photo: Activate the color layer and turn off the eye icon in the sketch layer; choose Image, Duplicate, Merged Layers Only to copy the layer to a new file. Convert this file to a grayscale image (Mode, Grayscale).

4 Converting the grayscale to a "woodcut." With the sketch defined as a pattern (at step 2), convert the copy of the photo to Bitmap mode (Mode, Bitmap), choosing the Custom Pattern option for the Method. (Keep the Output resolution the same as the Input.)

5 Layering the images. With the converted (woodcut) photo active, use the move tool to drag and drop it back into the color file as a new layer. Because you made the copy from the color file, it will be exactly the same size as the original, so it will snap into place when dropped. Turn off the eye icon for the original sketch layer so it doesn't contribute to the final image, and turn on the eyes for the newly imported bitmap layer and the original color layer. Adjust the blending mode and Opacity of the imported layer.

6 Experimenting. Try out other opacities, modes, and arrange-ments. We used Screen mode and 75% opacity to get the image at

6b

Soft Light, 100% Opacity over desaturated

the top of page 183. We also tried applying the custom bit-map layer in Soft Light mode at 100% Opacity. In another ex-periment, we desaturated the color layer (choose Image, Ad-just, Desaturate) to produce a "woodcut" image in shades of gray.

Coloring
Line Art

Overview *Scan and clean up hand-drawn line art; fill the artwork with gray tones; convert grays to color; add depth by blurring, desaturating, and reducing color.*

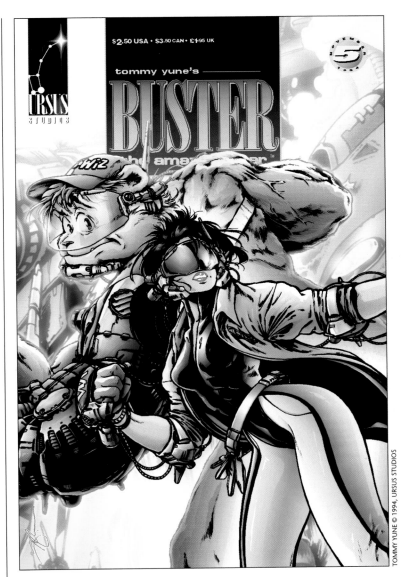

$2.50 USA • $3.50 CAN • £1.95 UK

tommy yune's

BUSTER
the amazing bear™

TOMMY YUNE © 1994, URSUS STUDIOS

1a

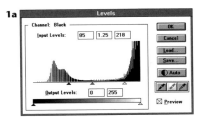

Tonal distribution of the scanned artwork before adjusting levels and Despeckling

1b

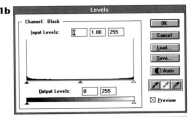

After the levels adjustment, the line work is clean and smooth.

"WITH PHOTOSHOP," SAYS TOMMY YUNE, creator of the *Buster, the Amazing Bear* series of comic books, "you can get clean, slick visual effects a lot easier than with an airbrush." He starts his cover illustrations as hand-drawn black-and-white line art, scans the art, and cleans it up in Photoshop. So that he can treat foreground, midground, and background separately to increase the depth of the illustration, he starts with separate scans — in this case for Buster, Liz, and the background picture.

1 Drawing, scanning, and cleaning up the artwork. Make a black-and-white drawing, or more than one if your artwork has

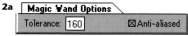

Magic Wand Options
Tolerance: 160   ☒ Anti-aliased

Settings for selecting the white background

2b
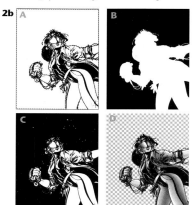

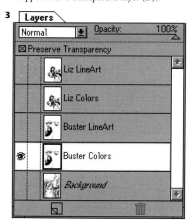

A magic wand selection (A) was inverted and saved as an alpha channel (B). The background area of the scan was filled with black (C), and the alpha channel was loaded to select the figure so it could be dragged and dropped into a transparent layer (D).

3

Layers

Normal ▼   Opacity: 100%

☒ Preserve Transparency

Liz LineArt

Liz Colors

Buster LineArt

Buster Colors

Background

Each imported layer is duplicated to provide a Line Art layer (in Multiply mode) and a Colors layer (with Preserve Transparency ON).

elements that you want to work with separately. Make sure the line work is continuous, creating enclosed shapes without breaks in the lines.

When your drawings are finished, scan them in grayscale mode at full size and at a resolution that's at least twice the line screen the piece will be printed at. Yune scanned at 300 dpi for a screen of 138 lpi.

For each scan look at the histogram in Photoshop's Levels dialog box (choose Image, Adjust, Levels) to see what kind of adjustment is needed to get clean, smooth lines with good contrast. The histograms for Yune's Buster and Liz scans showed two humps (for the black ink and white paper) with fewer pixels at the intermediate grays — noise from the scanning process. For each scan Yune moved the black and white sliders of the Input Levels inward to the middle of their respective humps. This boosted contrast, pushing the near-whites and near-blacks recorded by the scanner to clean black and white. Next he ran the Despeckle filter (Filter, Noise, Despeckle) to get rid of the noise in the scan. Then he adjusted the Levels sliders again because the Despeckle filter, while it reduces noise overall, introduces some noise at the extremes of the tonal range. When the clean-up was finished, the Levels histogram showed two sharp peaks at the ends (black and white) and a short "fur" of the intermediate gray tones required for antialiasing.

2 Isolating the hand-drawn elements. Open each of your scan files and select the artwork independently of its white background. The goal is to be able to put each piece of white-filled black line art onto its own transparent layer in a composite illustration. To select each of his characters from its scan file, Yune has devised a method for selecting the character without getting a fringe of light pixels around the black line art: Click the white background with the magic wand tool. (Yune finds that a magic wand Tolerance setting around 160 produces a smooth, accurate selection edge.) Next choose Select, Inverse to select the character rather than the background, and save this selection as an alpha channel (#2) so you can load it again later. (To save the selection, choose Select, Save Selection, New.) Then, back in the Black channel, invert the selection again (Select, Inverse) and fill the selected background area with black (Alt-Backspace with black as the Foreground color; the black fill will prevent a "halo" of gray pixels around the black line work when you load the alpha channel as a selection (Ctrl-Alt-2) and drag and drop the selected character into a composite file at step 3.

3 Setting up layers. Once the hand-drawn element is selected, use the selection arrow to drag and drop it into another file that contains the background illustration. For his background illustration Yune used an action scene from inside the comic book. Open the Layers palette so you can see how the layers stack up (Window, Palette, Show Layers).

4

Building tones with gradient fills in the Colors layer, using the gradient tool's Multiply setting

5

File converted to RGB; grays colored with Image, Adjust, Color Balance; and Levels adjusted to reduce contrast

6a

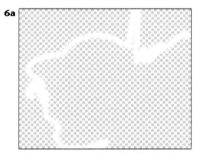

Glow added using Select, Modify, Border; Select, Feather; then Edit, Fill, White

Each drag-and-drop will result in a Floating Selection; double-click its label in the Layers palette and name the new layer. You can drag and drop the elements in any order and then arrange the layers by dragging their names up or down in the Layers palette.

Duplicate each of your line drawing layers, so you have one layer for line art and one (directly beneath it in the stack) for color. (Yune dragged in Liz and Buster and made "Line Art" and "Colors" layers for each.)

For the Line Art layers, choose Multiply from the pop-out list of blending modes. That way the black line art will appear over the color layer, but the white (neutral in Multiply mode) will be transparent, letting the color underneath show through. For the "Colors" layers, use Normal mode and turn ON Preserve Transparency (click the checkbox). The opaque white fill inside the lines will hide artwork from layers underneath, and Preserve Transparency will prevent the color you'll be adding from going outside the edges of the artwork.

4 "Coloring" with gradient fills of gray. Now you can begin the process of filling the line art in the Colors layers. Working in Grayscale mode will help you get the light and shading right; also, working in Grayscale can be faster than working in a color file.

In Yune's image file, the background illustration had already been "colored" with gray for use inside the book. So he worked on the Colors layers for Buster and Liz to get them to a similar stage. He opened the Lasso Options dialog box (by double-clicking the lasso in the tool palette) and turned ON Anti-aliasing but set the Feather value to 0. In the Gradient Tool Options palette (opened by double-clicking the tool) he set up a Foreground To Background (black to white) gradient in Multiply mode. Then he lassoed shapes and applied Linear and Radial fills.

Your lassoing doesn't have to be precise at the outer edges of the line art, because Preserve Transparency will keep the fills from going outside the outline. By using the number keys on the keyboard to vary the opacity of the fills, and by starting and ending the gradients outside the lassoed areas, you can get a wide variety of gray fill effects. Using the gradient tool in Multiply mode also allows you to build up gray tones by selecting and filling smaller and smaller overlapping areas to get an interaction of tonal values.

5 Converting grayscale to color. When you have the artwork in the Colors layers filled with gray tones, convert the file to RGB (Mode, RGB Color). Now you can select the areas you want to color and apply the Color Balance and Hue/Saturation functions. Working on the Colors layers, Yune selected areas of

MODIFYING THE TONES

To change the tonality of the gray or colored areas without affecting black lines or white highlights, choose Image, Adjust, Levels and move the Input Levels gray (gamma) slider.

6b

Lens Flare filter applied to the background layer

7

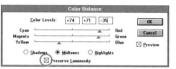

Final layers palette before duplicating and flattening

gray tones for color adjustment by clicking with the magic wand and also using the lasso tool. He used Image, Adjust, Color Balance to bring colors out of the grays in the highlights, shadows, and midtones.

6 Building depth. With the color in place, you can use blurring, desaturation, and other techniques on individual layers to create depth in the illustration. Yune applied lens flares to the Background layer (Filter Render, Lens Flare) to "blow out" the image, reducing its contrast. He moved the flares around in the preview window of the dialog box until he had the effect he wanted. He also applied a Gaussian Blur and reduced saturation (Image, Adjust, Hue/Saturation).

In the Buster (midground) layer he chose Image, Adjust, Levels and moved the Output Levels black point slider inward to a setting of 64 to reduce contrast. He also created a glow around the bear to add dimensionality: With the Buster layer active, he loaded its transparency mask as a selection (Ctrl-Alt-T); then he clicked the New Layer icon at the bottom of the Layers palette to make a Glow layer above Buster. With the Glow layer active, he chose Select, Modify, Border (he used a 12-pixel setting for this approximately 2400-pixel-wide image) and then chose Select, Feather with a setting of 8 pixels. He chose Edit, Fill, White (Preserve Transparency OFF) to finish the glow.

7 Finishing the cover illustration. Yune added his signature on another layer. He duplicated the file (Image, Duplicate), flattened the duplicate (Flatten Image from the Layers palette's pop-out menu), converted it to CMYK, and saved it as a TIFF so he could import it into FreeHand to add the logo and type.

Jack Davis created *Analog Flame* by applying paint with the paintbrush tool and then smearing it with the smudge (finger) tool. He used a Wacom tablet and stylus for a natural painterly feel, but found that he had to work with a fairly small brush tip in order to get the smudge tool to respond quickly enough to follow his strokes. So he created the painting at half the final size he wanted, with a half-size brush, and then scaled it up later with the Image Size function and with the default Bicubic Interpolation setting in the General Preferences dialog box. With a continuous-tone image like this without any hard edges, the interpolation that Photoshop does during the scaling-up process is very effective at maintaining smooth color transitions. Another technique Davis found helpful for painting the upward curls of the flame was to paint the image upside down, since it's easier to control the direction of the strokes if you "pull" the brush toward you rather than "push" it away, just as in painting or drawing with natural media.

Trici Venola painted *The Scarlet Letter* as a cover for a comic book edition of the classic Nathaniel Hawthorne story. She started the image with the pencil tool in Photoshop to produce a rough black-on-white gesture drawing, sketching the figures and keeping the strokes loose and free. (Because the pencil is not antialiased, it draws more quickly than any of Photoshop's other painting and drawing tools.) Next she used a large airbrush tip to rough in the color. At this point she saved the image and opened it in Fractal Design Painter, whose tools she prefers for painting detailed texture such as the wood grain and hair in this image. She saved the image again and went back to Photoshop to finish it. Venola uses Photoshop's smudge (finger) tool at various sizes to do much of her painting and the dodge/burn/sponge tool to deepen or lighten colors. She also uses the lasso to adjust proportions. For example, she can narrow a face by lassoing the outside part of it, feathering the selection, and then moving it inward. She often floats a selection, flips it horizontally or vertically so she can get a fresh look at the lines, paints on it, flips it back and drops it in place. She saves often (Save A Copy) so she will be able to go back to a previous stage if she "wears out" a part of the image and needs to lasso, copy, and paste an earlier version. She also copies parts of the image in order to work on them separately: Floating a selection and then turning it into a layer of its own isolates it so it can be worked on separately from the rest of the image.

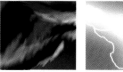

To make this cover illustration for his comic book, *Buster the Amazing Bear,* **Tommy Yune** began by scanning a faint pencil sketch. Working in Photoshop's Grayscale mode, he used the lasso tool to "block out" regions that he filled with different shades of gray. Then, with the tones of the illustration set, he used the smudge (finger) tool with a Wacom tablet and stylus to smear the grays to make the fur. He converted the image to RGB mode and added a storm scene behind the bear. (Add a layer and drag and drop the new image into the old.) Then he created an alpha channel (choose New in the pop-out menu of the Channels palette), turned it black by selecting it all (Ctrl-A) and filling it with black (Alt-Backspace), and painted a bolt of white lightning in it. He duplicated this channel (Image, Calculate, Duplicate) as a new alpha channel in the same file and ran a Gaussian blur on this new channel (Filter, Blur, Gaussian Blur) to make a mask for the glow around the lightning. After adding some finer streaks of lightning to the first alpha channel, he returned to the main RGB channel of the storm layer and used the two alpha channels (Select, Load Selection) to select the lightning and the glow separately from each other and from the other elements of the illustration; he turned them white (Edit, Fill, White). To select other areas, he set a large Feather on the lasso. Then, for each area that he selected, he used Image, Adjust, Color Balance to add color to the illustration.

To "paint" *Parker's,* **Bert Monroy** used a different technique than he had used for many earlier photorealistic paintings. As usual, he began with a photograph as visual reference but didn't scan it. This time, however, instead of starting out in Photoshop, he used Adobe Illustrator's drawing tools to construct the building as one file and the complex bridge elements as four separate Illustrator files, breaking the construction down into layers and drawing "fine detail that would have been impossible in Photoshop." In Illustrator he assigned flat color fills to the elements he had built. Then, after saving them in EPS format and placing them in Photoshop, he "texturized" them by selecting areas of the image and adding Noise, with settings between 8 and 24 for this image that was over 1500 pixels wide. To simulate street grime, he made selections with a feathered lasso so when he textured and darkened them, their edges would blend with the surroundings. The cars in the parking lot and the reflections in the windows were not begun in Illustrator, but painted entirely in Photoshop. In Monroy's current digital painting process, Photoshop stands in for paints and brushes, and Illustrator plays the role once performed by ruler and Rapidograph pen.

For the *Bow Down* Album Cover showing the rainbow around the heavenly throne of God, **Jack Davis** scanned a Doré woodcut and selected the background with the lasso. He applied a Clockwise Radial gradient fill from a white Foreground color (chosen from a blue range of the spectrum) to a red Background color. He added Noise, which contributed texture to the image. When the background was complete, he used the airbrush in Darken mode to add rainbow highlights to the robes.

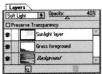

Cher Threinen-Pendarvis began *Sunrise* as a hand-drawn sketch in colored pencils. With the sketch as a reference, she painted with the paintbrush and airbrush tools, using the Brush Size cursor (File, Preferences, General) so she could see the edge of the area she was painting. For most of her painting, she set the Paintbrush Options palette at Normal mode and used the number keys to control Opacity, usually set at 20% or 30% for a glazing effect. In areas where she wanted to combine the light quality in the atmosphere with the topography, she painted in Multiply mode with a very low opacity, 10% to 20%. By putting the sunbeams on a separate layer, she was able to work on detail in the cliffs behind and also to control the interaction of light and land by setting the layer's blending mode to Soft Light and by adjusting the Opacity.

COMBINING PHOTOSHOP AND POSTSCRIPT

Now that Illustrator paths can be copied and pasted into Photoshop (see page 195), it's possible to make PostScript-smooth clipping paths for image-filled type: Set type in Illustrator, convert it to paths, select and copy the paths to the clipboard, and then paste them into a Photoshop file. Save the outlines as a clipping path (choose Save Path and then Clipping Paths from the Paths palette's pop-out menu).

Type converted to outlines in Illustrator

Paths pasted into a Photoshop file and stroked with the paintbrush with Wet Edges

Path saved as a clipping path; file placed in PageMaker

YOU CAN MOVE ARTWORK between Adobe Illustrator and Photoshop almost seamlessly, and you can import both kinds of files into page layout programs such as PageMaker and QuarkXPress. How do you decide when it makes sense to combine Illustrator (or other PostScript object-oriented) artwork with an image created in Photoshop? And when it does, how do you decide whether to import a Photoshop illustration into Illustrator, or an Illustrator drawing into Photoshop, or when to assemble the two in a third program? These pointers can help you make the decision:

- Although the pen tool in Photoshop can draw smooth Bezier curves, the program doesn't have the snap-to features and guidelines of object-oriented drawing programs such as Illustrator, FreeHand, or CorelDraw. So, if you need precise geometry, it's easier to do the work outside Photoshop.

- Photoshop's text tool, working with Adobe Type Manager (ATM), can set smooth-looking antialiased type, and the program can produce some amazing type treatments (see Chapter 2 for more about using type in Photoshop). But for really designing with type, kerning, or fitting type to a particular shape, PostScript drawing and page layout programs excel.

- When you want to maintain the PostScript nature of certain elements — for instance, for a brochure cover in which the Photoshop artwork is just one element of a page that includes logos and a lot of type — incorporate the Photoshop artwork into the PostScript file. That way, you can include the painted or photo-realistic Photoshop art and still take advantage of the highest resolution of the output device to produce crisp type and the clean edges of the PostScript elements.

- Bring both the Photoshop files and the PostScript artwork into a page layout program for a multipage document, or to assemble a number of things with precise alignment, and especially if large amounts of text will be typeset. A page layout program also provides a way to assemble Photoshop files of different resolutions.

Although PostScript elements play a role in techniques described elsewhere in the book, this chapter presents some how-to examples of using PostScript programs extensively. First, though, here are

continued on page 194

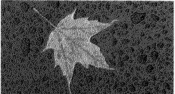

For a better-quality template (top), a Photoshop file saved in EPS format can be placed on a layer of its own in Illustrator and used as a template in Preview mode. But if you want to work in Illustrator's Artwork mode for faster screen redraw, a placed EPS file won't show up, whereas a PICT template will (bottom).

some tips that will help you move artwork from PostScript drawing programs to Photoshop and vice versa.

ILLUSTRATOR TO PHOTOSHOP

Although it's possible to import encapsulated PostScript (EPS) files from other PostScript illustration programs, Adobe Illustrator shows the greatest compatibility with Photoshop. In fact, any CorelDraw or FreeHand file more complex than black- or white-filled line work may not transfer well when opened or placed. So the best way to make illustrations available for use in Photoshop is to save them in (or convert them to) Illustrator EPS (**.ai**) format. (Even Illustrator files are not 100% compatible. Patterns, stroked type, and placed graphics are not included when an Illustrator EPS is imported.)

- **FreeHand** files can be saved in Illustrator format, and these files can then usually be opened successfully in Photoshop.

- **CorelDraw** files can be saved directly in Illustrator format by using the program's Export To command.

    (FreeHand and CorelDraw have different ways of dealing with some objects — such as patterned fills, composite paths, and masks — than Illustrator does. So the translation of a complex file from one PostScript drawing program to another may not be completely accurate, and the resulting Illustrator file should be checked in Illustrator before it's imported into Photoshop.)

Illustrator files can be imported in either of two ways:

- **Open** an Illustrator file to bring the entire file into Photoshop with a transparent background as "Layer 1."

- **Place** the file to bring all its objects in as floating selections, which can be dropped into the Background or any other layer.

    There are several ways to Place the elements of an Illustrator file into Photoshop separately, so you can control them as independent elements. For instance, while in Illustrator, select all objects except the ones you want to place together in a layer, and convert them into Illustrator's Guides (this method is covered on pages 201 through 203). By converting back and forth between objects and Guides and placing the file into Photoshop several times on several different layers, you can independently control the imported elements. Another way to separate the elements of an Illustrator file so they can be independently imported is to use Illustrator's Save As command to save several copies of the file and then selectively delete elements from each of the saved copies. To keep the various parts of the illustration in register when they are placed in Photoshop, you need to define a bounding box for the entire illustration and convert it to crop marks (Objects, Cropmarks, Create) before the file is separated into its various parts. This is true whether you separate the elements by the Guides method or by saving several copies of the file.

If you plan to use a Photoshop PICT file as a template for tracing or for setting type in Illustrator, there are some things you can do in Photoshop that will result in a better template. In the Image Size dialog box set the Height and Width at the dimensions you want the Illustrator artwork to be; or double the dimensions if you want to work large in order to see the shapes in more detail. Then choose the color channel with the best contrast and use Image, Adjust, Levels or Brightness/Contrast to improve contrast even more in critical areas. Finally, you can convert the file to Bitmap mode at 72 dpi with a Diffusion Dither; this often produces a better-looking template than letting Illustrator do the conversion.

Optimized template from the Red channel

Besides using Open or Place, you can also transfer single or multiple Illustrator **paths** by selecting them, copying them to the clipboard, and then **pasting** them into Photoshop, choosing Paste As Paths in the Paste dialog box.

PHOTOSHOP TO ILLUSTRATOR

If you want to import a Photoshop image into Illustrator in order to add type or geometric elements, or to trace or autotrace parts of it to produce PostScript artwork, there are at least three ways to do it:

- One way is to save the Photoshop file in **PICT** format and open it in Illustrator as a **template,** through Illustrator's Open command. The Photoshop image appears as a nonprinting low-resolution black-and-white bitmap.

- Another way is to save the Photoshop file in **EPS** format (include a Preview image so you can see it on the screen) and use Illustrator's **Place** command to import it onto a nonprinting layer. This method has the advantage of letting you see the image in the Illustrator file at high resolution and in color in Preview mode. But it won't be visible in the faster Artwork mode.

- If your objective is to fit type to a particular part of your Photoshop image, the simplest way may be to use Photoshop's pen tool to create a path in the shape you want to fit, then export only the path (through File, Export, **Paths To Illustrator**), and open the path file in Illustrator; it will be invisible in Preview mode, being stroked and filled with None. Use Illustrator's path type tool in Artwork mode to set the type, save the Illustrator file in EPS format, and use Photoshop's Place command to import it back into the Photoshop image. (The Photoshop path can be copied and pasted rather than exported, but exporting has the advantage of maintaining the bounding box of the entire Photoshop image. The bounding box is turned into crop marks in Illustrator, so that when the Illustrator type on a path is placed back into the Photoshop image, it comes in exactly in register with the original Photoshop path.

Rasterizing with Photoshop

Overview *Make the drawing in a PostScript program and save it in Adobe Illustrator EPS format; import it into Photoshop; apply filter effects; print to a composite color printer from Photoshop.*

MAX SEABAUGH / ADAPTED FROM BALTHUS

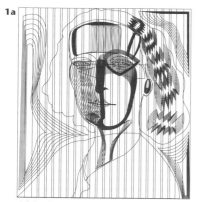

Adobe Illustrator, artwork only mode

Adobe Illustrator, preview mode

IN ORDER FOR A COMPUTER-GENERATED IMAGE to be printed, it has to be *rasterized,* or converted into the dot pattern needed by the printer (or high-resolution imagesetter) to put it on paper (or film). Typically, the printer does the rasterizing with a built-in or added-on *RIP (raster image processor).* But a PostScript drawing, such as an Adobe Illustrator or CorelDraw file, can also be rasterized through Photoshop. And once the image is rasterized, even fairly simple Photoshop modifications can produce some dramatic changes in the artwork.

Max Seabaugh of San Francisco's MAX studio drew this portrait in Adobe Illustrator. He wanted to soften its precise PostScript lines, create a pointillistic effect, and print it on his 300 dpi non-PostScript desktop inkjet printer, because he likes the color quality it produces.

1 Drawing and saving the file in Illustrator. You can use any of Illustrator's or CorelDraw's tools and functions to complete your artwork. To keep the file size low, you can save the file without a Preview or an EPS Header.

2 Opening the file in Photoshop. In Photoshop choose File, Open and select the name of the Illustrator file. In the Rasterize

2

Rasterizing into Photoshop at 72 dpi

3

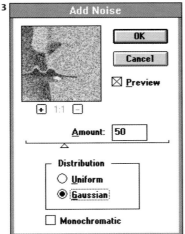

Adding Gaussian Noise

Adobe Illustrator Format dialog box, enter the size, mode, and resolution you want the image to be. Seabaugh accepted the size of the original Illustrator drawing, Photoshop's default CMYK Color mode, and 72 dpi for a coarse texture, but you can change the size if you like and raise the resolution for a smoother look.

3 Modifying and printing the file. Make any changes you like to the rasterized art. For example, you can apply the Noise filter to add texture as Seabaugh did; he chose Filter, Noise, Add Noise, Gaussian and set the Amount at 50, introducing a multicolor texture to the illustration. When changes are complete, print the file.

Experimenting with other filters. Add Noise is only one of the filters that can give a distinctive look to a PostScript illustration. Here, with the artist's permission, we've tried two more Adobe filters and two from the Gallery Effects collections on Seabaugh's rasterized artwork. *New*

GE Texturizer (from Gallery Effects Classic Art 2); Canvas setting

Lighting Effects (from the Render submenu); set for Soft Omnidirectional light

Difference Clouds (from the Render submenu)

GE Photocopy (from Gallery Effects Classic Art 2); Detail set at 8; Darkness set at 11

Making a Montage with a PostScript Mask

Overview *Make two Photoshop image files; combine them as separate layers in a single file; draw a masking shape in Illustrator or another PostScript drawing program; place it in a layer mask in Photoshop; blur the mask; position the layers and the mask until the montage effect is right; merge the layers.*

an evening with
Peter Sprague and friends:
Peter Sprague: guitar,
Fred Benedetti: guitar,
Tripp Sprague: saxophone, flute,
performing jazz, classical,
and new music.
Sunday, April 26 7:00 pm,
Theatre East,
A Division of the
East County Performing Arts Center,
210 East Main Street, El Cajon.
$8 General, $6 Students/Seniors.
Box Office 440–2277 Noon–6 pm.
No service charge
for phone or mail orders.
Visa, MasterCard
and checks accepted.
Free parking.

Blurring the Edges

JOHN ODAM

1

Two original image files

PHOTOSHOP'S PEN TOOL draws Bezier curves, but the program lacks the precision drawing features found in PostScript drawing programs. So if you need to create a mask with smooth, repeating curves, you can start in Adobe Illustrator, FreeHand, or CorelDraw. Designer John Odam wanted a simple blurred transition for this poster for an evening of classical and jazz guitar music. So he created a shape in Illustrator to use as a mask to blend the two guitar images. Photoshop 3's Layer Mask function makes it easy to combine images through a mask.

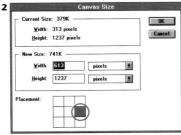

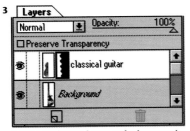

Making space for the second image

Setting up the two layers and a layer mask

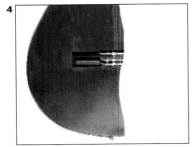

Placing the EPS mask shape, viewing only the Classical Guitar layer

1 Preparing the two Photoshop files. Create the two files, one with each part of the image. In this case, each of the guitars was placed on a flatbed scanner and scanned. It took three scans to capture the full length of each instrument. The scans were made to the final tabloid size of the poster at 300 dpi for printing on a thermal color printer. Odam decided to keep the green iridescent sheen introduced by the scanner rather than remove it. Putting the three parts of each image together was a fairly simple job of cut and paste; little repair work was needed to hide the seams.

2 Making space. With the two files open, use Image, Canvas Size to add empty space to one image so it can accommodate the other image. In this case, the canvas Width for the right half (the jazz guitar) was doubled and a right-hand Placement was chosen to make space for the classical guitar's left half.

3 Setting up layers and a layer mask. Now click on the window of the image you *didn't* widen (the classical guitar in this case) so it becomes the active window, and then use the move tool to drag and drop that image onto the one with the enlarged canvas. If you haven't yet opened the Layers palette of the larger image, open it now so you can see the relationship between the parts — you can see if either part needs to be scaled down in order to get the two parts to fit together. If so, click its name in the Layers palette, and then choose Image, Effects, Scale and drag on the corner handles to change the size; click with the gavel to accept the reduction.

With the top layer (the classical guitar in this case) activated in the Layers palette, choose Add Layer Mask from the pop-out menu to open a mask for this layer.

4 Drawing and importing the mask shape. Working in the PostScript drawing program, use the pen tool to draw a shape that will be used to select the edge where the images will blend together. Give the shape a fill, but no line. Save the file in EPS format.

Working in the Photoshop file again, click on the layer mask icon to activate the mask. Then import the EPS with the File, Place command, and adjust the size and placement of the imported shape, if necessary. When you click with the gavel to accept size and placement, the imported art becomes an active Floating Selection.

The next step is to turn the Floating Selection into a black-and-white mask. Choose Select,

SCALING A PLACED IMAGE

To proportionally resize an object imported from Adobe Illustrator as you place it, drag one of the corner handles of the bounding box. To change the proportions, hold down the Ctrl key while you drag. To move the object, drag on one of the sides or diagonals of the bounding box. Click inside the box with the gavel icon to finish the placing action.

5

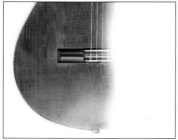

Blurring the mask, viewing only the Classical Guitar layer

6

Save Selection and in the Save Selection dialog box choose the layer mask as the destination Channel. The imported shape becomes the white part of the layer mask, so it will allow the image to show through the shape. (If instead you want the image to show through the other part of the mask, choose Image, Map, Invert at this point.)

5 Blurring the mask. When you've completed the mask, drop the selection (Ctrl-D). You can now blur the mask to soften the transition between the images in the two layers. Apply Filter, Blur, Gaussian Blur; then use Image, Adjust, Levels, if you like, moving the black, white, and midpoint Input sliders to change the nature of the black-to-white transition of the blurred edge. (To see how blurring and adjusting Levels affect the image, view both layers [eye icons showing in the Layers palette and Preview turned on in the Gaussian Blur or Levels dialog box] while you experiment with the blur. Or Alt-click the layer mask icon to get a full-size view of the mask itself; then Alt-click again to restore the image view.)

6 Making the montage. Now you can experiment with moving the image and the mask, together or independently, until you have exactly the edge transition you want.

MOVING LAYERS AND MASKS

The image in a layer and its layer mask can be moved together or separately.
• To move the image and mask together, click on the layer name in the Layers palette and then drag in the image window with the move tool.
• To move the mask independently of the image, click the mask icon to activate the mask and then drag in the image window with the move tool.
• To move the image without the mask, click the image icon to activate the image, Select All, and drag in the image window with the lasso or marquee tool.

Using the mask again. To make the blurred border underneath the type at the bottom of the poster, Odam rotated the mask shape 90 degrees in Illustrator. Then he opened a new Photoshop file in Grayscale mode, placed the shape in the Photoshop file, selected the curved edge, and applied a Gaussian Blur. The hybrid guitar and blurred edge were saved in TIFF format and assembled in PageMaker, where text type was set. Twenty copies of the 11 x 17-inch poster were output on a composite color printer.

CONVERTING RGB TO CMYK

If you've been working in RGB and want to print the file on a composite color printer, you can select Print As CMYK in Photoshop's Print dialog box to have Photoshop make a conversion from RGB to CMYK instead of letting the composite printer do it. This often gives a better result than letting the printer make the conversion, but you can try the print both ways to see which you like better.

Back and Forth Between Photoshop and Illustrator

Overview *Design the background art in Photoshop; draw PostScript elements in Adobe Illustrator, for example; save each element as a separate file; place them in the Photoshop file; return to the PostScript drawing program to add the final type.*

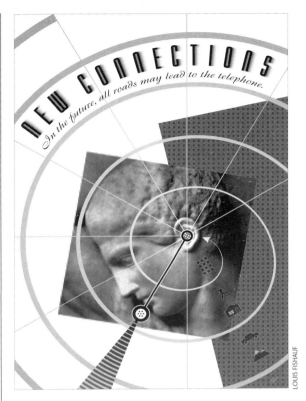

LOUIS FISHAUF

1

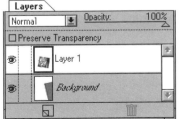

Background art in Photoshop

THERE ARE MANY WAYS to combine the "soft" effects that can be achieved in Photoshop with the precision of drawing and typesetting in a PostScript drawing program. For instance, you can do what Louis Fishauf did to make this full-page black-and-white illustration for the *Wall Street Journal*. Import your Photoshop background art into Illustrator and create type and graphic objects in precise relation to it. Then import the PostScript artwork into the original Photoshop file and add special effects. The challenge at this step is to import individual type and graphic objects separately, so you can apply different effects to them as you bring them in, but also to keep all the objects exactly in position. One solution is to set up a bounding box in Illustrator. When you've finished importing Illustrator art and adding special effects, you may want to go back into Illustrator to add the final PostScript type so it will come out as smooth as possible when the file is output.

1 Creating the background. Paint or assemble a background in Photoshop and save it in EPS format so it can be placed in Illustrator. Fishauf assembled this background by opening a new file 500 points (about 7 inches) wide and 716 points high at 200 pixels per inch. He figured that with the 85-line screen that would be used to print the newspaper, 200 dpi at this size would provide more than

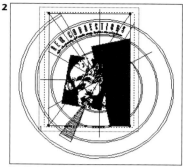

PostScript artwork added in Illustrator

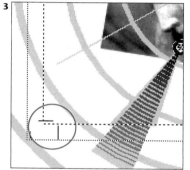

Bounding box set with Illustrator's crop marks

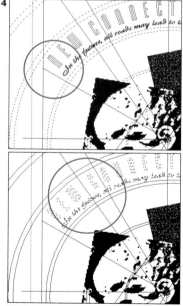

Illustrator elements — spiral (above) and type turned to outlines (below) —made invisible as guidelines

enough information for good reproduction. (For images with straight lines, resolution should be 2 times the halftone line screen: 2 x 85 = 170.) Fishauf created his background by selecting and pasting parts of two scans; one scan was a photo of a sculpture, to which he applied the Mosaic filter, and the other was a grid pattern to which he applied a Noise filter. (To work out relationships of size and orientation of the background elements, you can place them on separate layers. When the arrangement is as you like it, choose Flatten Image from the Layers palette's pull-down menu to finalize the background.)

2 Creating elements in Illustrator. Open a New file in Illustrator and use the File, Place Art command to bring in the Photoshop art. Make sure the Show Placed Art option is selected in Illustrator's Preferences dialog box, accessed by choosing Edit, Preferences. Add type and graphic objects, using the imported artwork as a guide. Fishauf used Illustrator's curve tool to draw the spiral, the line tool to draw spokes, and the blend function to create a series of equally spaced arcs of increasing line weight in the lower left corner of the image. He used the type-on-a-path tool to fit type to a curve and the Create Outlines command to turn the type into graphic objects, and he imported a series of small elements in the lower right corner by cutting and pasting from an Illustrator file of icons he had collected, drawn, or traced.

3 Defining a bounding box. In the Illustrator file add a large rectangle exactly on top of the boundaries of the imported Photoshop artwork. Choose Object, Cropmarks, Make to turn this rectangle into an invisible bounding box. Fishauf's crop marks would "trim" the Illustrator artwork when he brought it back into Photoshop.

4 Separating the Illustrator elements. This step lets you import the Illustrator artwork in pieces so you can layer them and apply different Photoshop effects as they come in. The trick is to get all the pieces to land in their original positions.

For each piece he wanted to import, Fishauf selected all the other elements of the illustration and turned them into guidelines (Object, Guides, Make). This locked these elements in place in the file but made them invisible for the purpose of importing into Photoshop. (The importation is described in step 5.) After he had imported the first non-Guide piece, he went back to the Illustrator file. He released the guides (Object, Guides, Release), turning them back into objects; then he selected a new set of elements and turned these into

MAKING GUIDES

In Illustrator type can't be converted to guidelines. To turn type into invisible guides, first make it a graphic element (Type, Create Outlines).

5

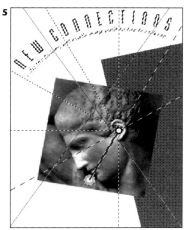

Importing the type outlines

6a

Turning off Preserve Transparency to run filters

6b

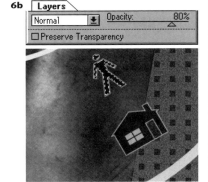

Adjusting the opacity of placed art

TO OPEN OR TO PLACE?

When you want to open an entire Illustrator file in Photoshop, there's another option worth considering: Start a new Photoshop file and then Place the illustrator art in it. Placing instead of Opening brings the Illustrator elements in as floating selections, which makes it easy to change the fill, adjust the color, and so on.

guidelines, leaving a different set of non-Guide elements available for import to Photoshop. The result was several versions of the file: one with the spiral and spokes, and others with various part of the communication imagery.

5 Importing an Illustrator element. To import an Illustrator element into Photoshop, first open the background art file in Photoshop. If you want smooth outlines on the imported objects, be sure that Anti-alias PostScript is selected under File, Preferences, General, More. Then choose File, Place and select the illustrator file that you modified by making guides. An "X" will appear in the Photoshop file to indicate the bounding box around the placed element, and the imported element will appear as a floating selection.

SOME THINGS AREN'T IMPORTED

Some kinds of elements — patterns, certain kinds of text, and imported artwork — are eliminated from an Illustrator file when it's opened or placed in Photoshop. This is actually helpful when you're moving files back and forth between Photoshop and Illustrator: You don't have to delete your Photoshop artwork from the Illustrator file before bringing the Illustrator artwork into Photoshop because it will be deleted automatically in the import process.

6 Modifying the PostScript elements. Each time you import the Illustrator file, the non-Guide element comes in as a floating selection. Before releasing the selection, you can correct its color, apply filters, or make other changes. For example, Fishauf applied a radial blend to the spiral and spokes, and applied a radial blur to the large type using Filter, Blur, Radial Blur with the Spin setting. (Turn OFF the Preserve Transparency checkbox at the top of the Layers palette to apply filters.)

Fishauf made the small icons in the lower right quadrant of the composition semi-transparent. (Use the Opacity setting in the Layers palette.)

You can make each placed element into a new layer by Option-double-clicking the Floating Selection name in the Layers palette. Or make the floating element part of the layer directly below it by pressing Ctrl-D to deselect.

Adding the final type in Illustrator. To make sure that type looks as smooth as possible, Flatten the Photoshop file, bring the art back into the Illustrator file, and add the PostScript type (or type converted to outlines) there. Fishauf opened the modified Photoshop file in Illustrator and cut and pasted the curved lettering on top of its shadow (see the opening illustration). *wow!*

Putting Things into Perspective

Overview *Draw perspective guides in Adobe Illustrator or another PostScript drawing program; draw components of the illustration within these guides; import components into separate layers in Photoshop; make masks and use them to add details; import perspective guides; distort imported images to fit the guides.*

BERT MONROY / ART DIRECTOR: KAZUMOTO YOKUOCHI

1

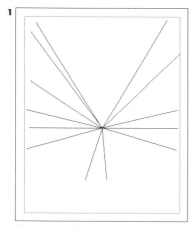

Drawing guidelines in Adobe Illustrator

2

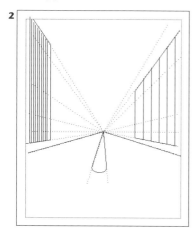

Drawing primary shapes in perspective

RENOWNED FOR HIS PHOTOREALISTIC STREET SCENES, Bert Monroy was commissioned to create the cover image for Pioneer's new merchandise catalog. The project called for a Times Square kind of setting with a home entertainment center as a building at the main intersection. The home entertainment center and other images that would serve as billboards in the scene were supplied as transparencies and scanned. Monroy began by drawing in Adobe Illustrator.

1 Drawing perspective guides. To draw a series of perspective lines, you can work in Adobe Illustrator, with its snap-to-point precision. Monroy drew lines to serve as guides for the tops of the buildings and all of the windows. The lines met at a single vanishing point that established the perspective of someone standing in the middle of a boulevard looking down it. The perspective lines were converted into locked guides by choosing Object, Guides, Make.

2 Shaping the elements of the image. Using the perspective guides, draw vertical lines to develop the shapes of the image. Monroy shaped the buildings between the guidelines.

3a 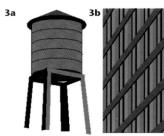 **3b**

Screen view of Illustrator artwork defined as solid-color shapes

Blue building shape drawn behind the lines that define the windows

4a

Artwork rendered in Photoshop and modified through gradient-filled masks

4b

Layer mask for selecting the window area

4c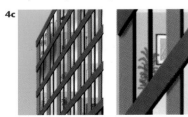

Internal building detail placed and masked with the window layer mask

3 Drawing and importing detailed elements. Still in Illustrator, draw the details of the image, filling the individual shapes with solid colors. When these drawings are imported into Photoshop, the solid-filled shapes will be easy to select for making masks.

Monroy drew detailed elements such as water towers and theater marquees. He also set up some of his Illustrator artwork so that he could use a "blue screen" technique for creating masks in Photoshop (described in step 4). For instance, after he had drawn the structure of the windows, he drew the overall shape of the building behind the windows and filled it with a bright blue (100 C, 20 M), a color that was quite different from those used in the artwork itself.

When your drawing in Illustrator is complete, bring the elements from Illustrator into a Photoshop file created at the same dimensions as the Illustrator file and at the final resolution you want the image to be, using File, Place to put them in separate layers (or to gang them in layers) so they can be modified without affecting the rest of the image. Monroy worked at a resolution of 350 dpi, two times the 175 lpi halftone screens typically used for printing in Japan. (For more about the relationship between image resolution and halftone screen resolution, see "Resolution" in Chapter 1.)

4 Making and using masks. Monroy typically uses many masks so he can select and reselect areas for making modifications like filling with gradients, textures, or images and adjusting Levels and Color Balance. There are several ways to start a mask by selecting areas filled with solid colors. For instance, you can choose Select, Color Range and click the eyedropper on the solid color. Click OK to close the Color Range dialog box and choose Select, Save Selection.

Another way to start a mask is with the blue screen technique Monroy used for the windows. Choose Image, Calculations and choose the file's Red channel as Source 1 and its Blue channel as Source 2. Choose Difference as the Blending method. Put the Result in a New Channel. For Monroy's building the result was an alpha channel mask that exposed the window openings while protecting the structure of the building.

With either of the selection methods described — Color Range or blue screen — it's likely that the mask will need adjustment. In Monroy's Difference mask, for instance, the windows were light gray and the rest of the building a darker gray. With the alpha channel active, Monroy adjusted the black point and white point Input sliders in Levels to force the mask to black-and-white.

When the windows mask was complete, Monroy created a new layer with a layer mask, copied the windows mask into the layer mask, and imported scenes drawn in Illustrator into the layer.

Details such as the light spilling onto the sidewalk from doors and windows were also made with masks. The basic lighting shapes were drawn with the path tool, the path was converted into a selection by pressing Enter, and the selection was saved (Select, Save

4d

Starting the highlights mask alpha channel

4e

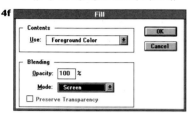

Modifying the highlights mask for fall-off

4f

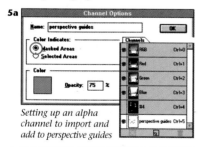

Filling the highlights in Screen mode

5a

Setting up an alpha channel to import and add to perspective guides

5b

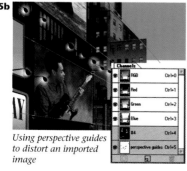

Using perspective guides to distort an imported image

Selection, New channel). Then the gradient tool was used inside the white areas of the mask to create the illusion of fall-off of the light with increasing distance from the source, and black paint was also applied with the airbrush to soften the distant edges of the mask.

Next, working in the main RGB channel, Monroy loaded the mask as a selection (Ctrl-Alt-channel number) and filled the selected area with color in the Screen mode (Edit, Fill). This created a smooth blend of the new color with the original colors and textures of the sidewalk. (For more about Monroy's techniques for adding photorealistic detail, see his "Parker's" painting in the Gallery section at the end of Chapter 6.)

5 Making nondestructive guidelines. In Monroy's illustration, the scanned images that would appear as billboards needed to be distorted to fit into the perspective of the image. So he imported his original perspective guides from Illustrator into an alpha channel, where they could be made visible without actually becoming part of the drawing. Here's one way to do it: Make a copy of the Illustrator file with the guidelines, Select All, and delete. This will remove all the artwork but will leave the guidelines intact. Then choose Object, Guides, Release to turn the guides back into lines.

In your Photoshop file open a new alpha channel by clicking the New Channel icon (in the center at the bottom of the Channels palette). In the Channel Options dialog box choose a viewing color and an opacity that will contrast with your image so you can see it easily, choose Selected Areas (rather than the default Masked Areas) as the setting for "Color Indicates," name the channel, and click OK. In the Channels palette, turn on the RGB channels and your new Perspective Guides channel for viewing (by clicking in the eye column) but activate only the Perspective Guides channel for writing (by clicking its name or thumbnail). Now choose File, Place to put the guidelines file into the Perspective Guides channel. When the imported art is lined up, click with the gavel to accept the position and press Ctrl-D to drop the selection.

Now you can use the line tool with black as the Foreground color to draw more guidelines. Monroy added guides for his billboard scans.

To use the guides, turn OFF the Perspective Guides channel for writing, turn ON the RGB channels, and leave both RGB and Perspective Guides visible. Now you can import a scan (by dragging and dropping from another file, for example) and use Image, Effects, Scale and Image, Effects, Distort to size the scan and align its corners so it lines up with the perspective guides. When you've finished the image, delete the Perspective Guides channel or make it invisible by turning OFF its eye. 🖌

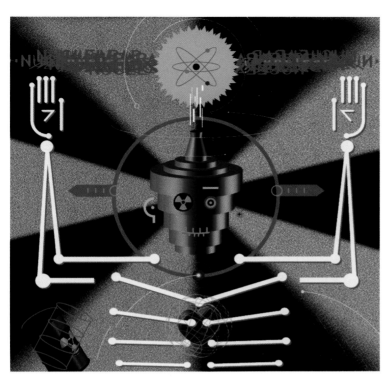

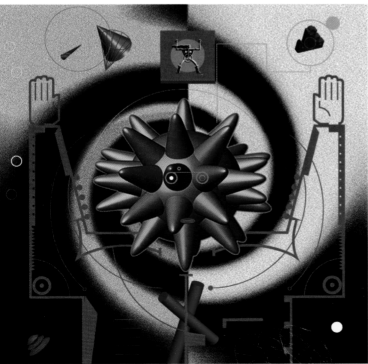

To create *nUkeMan,* illustrator **Steve Lyons** started with a pencil sketch that he scanned and opened as a template in Adobe Illustrator. He used Illustrator's pen tool to draw the black-and-white background shapes, assigning them a fill but no line. Then he saved the file in EPS format and opened it in Photoshop, where he made feathered selections, applied Noise and Blur filters to add texture, and altered the color of some of the white areas. He saved the file in the EPS format appropriate for importing into Illustrator (Save As, EPS, Binary, 8 Bits/Pixel). Next, working in Illustrator again, with the same sketch used as a template, he drew the hard-edged PostScript artwork, selected it all, and grouped it so he could move all of it together. Three-dimensional elements were created in a 3D program, saved in EPS format, and imported into Illustrator. To combine the soft and smooth layers, he imported the Photoshop art into Illustrator (File, Place Art) and sent it to the back (Edit, Send to Back). He saved the file in EPS format for separation with Adobe Separator.

Steve Lyons created *nubART* by the same process he used for *nUkeMAN,* except that the background started out as a "checkerboard" design, to which he applied the Twirl filter before adding Noise. The nubby sphere in the center of the image was created in a 3D program, saved in EPS format, and placed in the Photoshop background file. Then he completed the illustration as for *nUkeMAN.*

Jack Davis developed this *Series of Icons* starting with clip art from a picture font called "Dick and Jane," converted to outlines in Adobe Illustrator and placed in Photoshop over a white background. He added dimension to the shapes using variations on the technique described in "Creating Chrome" in Chapter 8. The icons were then colored using HSC Software's KPT Texture Explorer filter with a Procedural Blend of a rainbow pattern. Drop shadows were made by copying the logos to another layer underneath the first, filling the copies with black, blurring them (with Preserve Transparency turned off) and offsetting the layer with the move tool. He lightened the shadows by reducing the Opacity for the shadow layer, allowing the white background to show through.

Louis Fishauf created this illustration for *Macworld Expositions* in Adobe Illustrator, with the lettering on the globe built in Adobe Dimensions and brought back into Illustrator. But when he tried to output the file, he ran into PostScript errors related to the imported sphere, so he decided to rasterize the image in Photoshop. He opened the encapsulated PostScript file at a resolution of 250 pixels per inch at the dimensions at which it would be printed. When he examined the CMYK channels, he found banding of the black and one other color in some of the gradations. By selecting these areas, such as the two gradations above the eyes, he could apply the Blur filter to smooth the gradients. He found the Channels palette very helpful for this process, because he could view all four color channels while running the Blur filter in only two of them. The Photoshop trapping function (Image, Trap) allowed him to build trap into the image so that no white gaps would show if misregistration occurred during printing. Trapping usually isn't necessary in photo images because most individual pixels share one or more of the process printing colors (cyan, magenta, yellow, or black) with neighboring pixels. But Photoshop's trapping function can be helpful in images like this one, where there are smooth-edged shapes and lines of contrasting colors.

For this cover of *Design Graphics*, an international computer graphics magazine) editor/publisher **Colin Wood** began with a file from Ian McPherson's *Power Backgrounds* CD-ROM. To make the multicolor line that crosses the cover, Wood filled a selection with a gradient made with the KPT Gradient Designer at an angle slightly off horizontal to spread the colors along the line. He created a glow around the line (see page 121 for a method of making a glow) and applied a lens flare (Filter, Render, Lens Flare). He placed a star created in Adobe Illustrator in an alpha channel, blurred it (Filter, Blur, Gaussian Blur) and used it to make a selection in the image, which he then filled with white. Wood imported the finished image (in TIFF format) into QuarkXPress, where he added the type, title graphics, and bar code, as well as a scanned photo of featured artist Bill Niffenegger and details from two of Niffenegger's images. The multicolor line was repeated inside the magazine in the opening spread of an article about scanning. Rather than using a single graphic the full size of the two-page spread, which would have required many megabytes, Wood made a long and narrow high-resolution graphic to include the line and a background of Photoshop's default black; then he made a small, very low-resolution file filled with the same black, imported it into XPress behind the illustration, and stretched it to fit the spread.

Stephen King imported PostScript line work to serve as the basis for the neon profile in this *ImagiTrek Ad*. The line work was first placed in an alpha channel (#4) of the background image file, rather than in the main RGB channel. Then this alpha channel was duplicated to another alpha channel (drag the channel's name to the New Channel icon at the bottom center of the Channels palette). A Gaussian blur was applied to this mask (#5) to make a selection for the glow around the neon. This blur channel was loaded into the main RGB channel as a selection (Ctrl-Alt-5) and was filled (Alt-Backspace) with a bright blue that had been designated as the Foreground color. Then the linework channel was loaded and filled (Alt-Backspace). More color elements were added by using the paintbrush tool and a Wacom tablet with pressure-sensitive stylus. "Glow spots" were added with the airbrush tool and a fairly large brush tip. King painted highlights on the neon squiggles with a small paintbrush and lighter tints of paint. This illustration could also have been done using a different approach. The initial Bezier curves could have been drawn with the pen tool rather than imported, and then Stroke Path (the second icon from the left at bottom of the Paths palette) could have been used to add the diffuse airbrush glow first and then the neon tube with a smaller, more compact paintbrush tip.

Wayne Rankin created this *background for a poster* designed for Tower Technology, a company offering data storage on CD ROM. He began by painting a small piece of artwork in Photoshop using the paintbrush and airbrush in various sizes. When he had finished painting, he used Image, Adjust, Hue/Saturation to experiment with color changes. Rankin applied Image, Adjust, Levels, using the Input sliders to brighten the colors. He scaled the image up to its final size and applied the Unsharp Mask filter.

Artwork consisting of ellipses and dots was created in FreeHand, saved in Illustrator EPS format, and placed in several layers in Photoshop (see "Back and Forth Between Photoshop and Illustrator" earlier in this chapter for more about importing Illustrator EPS files). Rankin adjusted the Opacity of the layers and used Multiply mode to blend their colors.

To make his *Digital Light* self-promo poster, **Nino Cocchiarella** started out in CorelDraw, producing the fractal background and fractal-filled 3D type, which he exported as a TIFF and opened in Photoshop. There he added a partially transparent scan of a compact disc, as well as the 3D cone, sphere, and cube. He Saved As to make an additional low-resolution version of the image, which he imported into CorelDraw as a template for adding line work and type. The line work and type assemblage was exported as a PostScript file, and final assembly of the Photoshop and PostScript components was done in QuarkXPress.

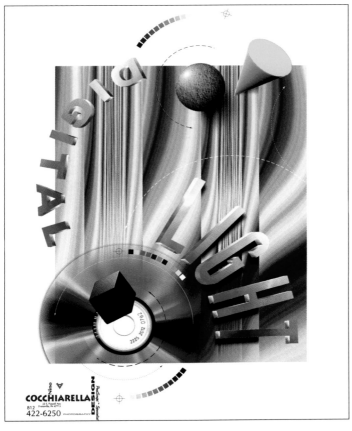

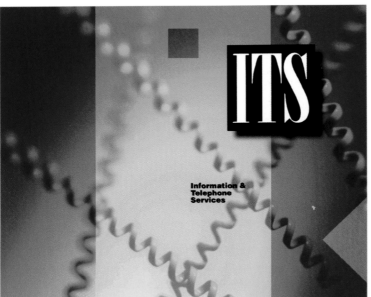

For the combined front and back covers of this *ITS Brochure* about telephone services, **Nino Cocchiarella** began with a dramatically lit photo of telephone cords, shot with a shallow depth of field and with green filters on the light. The rectangles and diamond were drawn in CorelDraw, and the Export To command was used to convert the file to Illustrator format so it could be placed in an alpha channel in the photo file. To color the background, he loaded the mask into the main image channel as a selection, adjusted Hue/Saturation to produce the yellow color, and then inverted the mask and repeated the adjustment process to

refine the green. The black rectangle and its drop shadow were added (see "Dropping a Shadow" in Chapter 8 for a method). Type was added in QuarkXPress. The printed cover was folded in half to enclose the booklet.

SPECIAL
EFFECTS

THE SPECIAL EFFECTS in this chapter are mostly simulations of the interaction between light and materials — from a simple drop shadow to the complex reflection and refraction that define chrome or crystal. Photoshop's layers, channels, and color and tonal manipulations make up a powerful toolkit for creating photo-realistic and superrealistic effects.

The layers make it easy to control objects and their shadows or highlights independently. They also make it possible to apply several special effects to the same object (one effect on each layer) and then blend the effects by changing the blending modes of the layers and adjusting opacity.

Transparency masks, layer masks, clipping groups, and alpha channels store images and selections so they can be loaded in precisely determined, exactly repeatable positions. The Gaussian Blur filter plays a big part in softening edges and creating rounded surfaces in these masks, and the Emboss and Lighting Effects filters can add a dramatic sense of dimension. Through interaction with offset copies of identical masks, blurring, embossing, and lighting effects can also play an important role in modelling the play of light on reflective, transparent, and translucent surfaces.

The ability to make "skinny" and "fat" versions of the same graphic by using the Maximum, Minimum, Expand, Contract, and Stroke functions provides the basis for "cookie cutter" masks that can be used to sharpen certain of the rounded edges produced by blurring and embossing. The blending modes, particularly Difference, can capture interactions between masks to create new masks for complex highlights and shadows.

Once the finished masks have been constructed and loaded into an image as selections, the Levels, Color Balance, and Variations functions can be applied. They provide the subtle changes in color or brightness that can differentiate the selection from the background to create an object — embossed, carved, chiseled, chrome, or crystal — where none existed before.

CHOOSING THE RIGHT METHOD
The addition of layers to Photoshop 3 has greatly increased the number of ways to create special effects such as drop shadows and rounded and beveled edges. Applying special effects using layers is

continued on page 214

often quicker and easier than using alpha channels. But there may be drawbacks. Here are some things to consider when choosing a method for implementing a special effect:

- Is the illusion convincing? Sometimes a method that makes a nice-looking embossed, highlighted edge works fine on a rounded object or letterform but looks like a "white shadow" when you apply it to something with sharp corners.

- Does it give you the control you need? Some methods that lighten or darken an edge using layers and blending modes don't let you change the color balance of a highlight or shadow, while methods using alpha channels give you more flexibility in making fine adjustments to color and tonality.

- Does it produce a clean edge? Some methods leave a residue around edges. Although you can fix some problems after the fact, it's usually cleaner and quicker if you can avoid having to clean up.

The techniques in this chapter introduce a broad range of approaches to creating special effects. For example:

- To achieve dramatic lighting, you can apply the Lighting Effects filter (as in "Dropping a Shadow") or adjust Levels in a selected area (as in "Carving, Embossing & Stamping").

- A drop shadow can be sandwiched in between the subject and the background (as in "Dropping a Shadow") or applied from the top using a mask to keep it from darkening the subject (as in "Chiseling" or "Carving, Embossing & Stamping.")

- A carved effect can be achieved by applying highlights and shadows as layers (as in "Carving, Embossing & Stamping" or "Working with Widgets") or by using channels and Image, Adjust, Levels (as in "Carving in Stone"). "Chiseling," a specialized type of carving, is achieved with the Displace filter, the KPT Gradient Designer filter, and Lighting Effects.

- A "snowy mask," made by using Difference mode to combine blurred and offset copies of the same graphic and then making more major changes to Curves, is the basis of the specular highlights seen in "Creating Chrome" and "Creating Crystal."

- A color glow can change in hue from the center outward, or it can reflect the colors of the glowing object itself; both possibilities are accomplished using layers in "Aglow at the Edges." *wow*

Dropping a Shadow

Overview *Open a background image; in a new layer create an object to float above the background; make a duplicate and blur it to create a shadow between the object and the background; use Lighting Effects to add dimension to the object and dramatize the scene.*

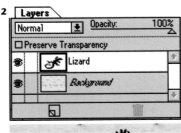

Original pine background image

EPS artwork imported as a new layer

SOONER OR LATER, almost everyone who works in Photoshop needs to produce the proverbial drop shadow, the shadow created by an object floating above the background behind it. Your shadowed object could be a selection from your background image or from another image, or a placed EPS file. And of course there's more than one way to make a drop shadow (see the Gallery at the end of this chapter for more shadow tips). Of all the methods, though, Photoshop's Layers palette provides perhaps the most flexibility for making changes later. It lets you control the shadow — its position, density, and color cast, for example — independently of the object and the background. So you can later change the shadow without disturbing the rest of the image, or even replace the background without disrupting the shadow.

1 Making the background. Open an RGB file to use for the background; we used a pine texture from ArtBeats Wood & Paper. Then open the Layers palette.

2 Bringing in the object. Now bring in the object you want to shadow. You could drag and drop a selection from another file, use the type tool to set type, or use File, Place to bring in EPS artwork, for instance; in this example we used a lizard character from Incidentals, one of Letraset's Design Fonts. Reorient or resize the placed EPS if necessary (for details on the process of placing an EPS, see page 201). When you click with the gavel to complete placement, the EPS becomes a Floating Selection, listed in the Layers palette. (If you set type or drag and drop a selection from another file, it will be a floating selection at this point also.)

Drag the Floating Selection name to the New Layer icon at the bottom left of the palette to turn the object into a new layer; to name our new layer, we typed in "Lizard" to replace the "Layer 1" entry in the Layer Options dialog box.

3a

Gaussian Blur

Radius: 5.0 pixels

Blurring the shadow

3b

Drop shadow in position

4a

Save Selection

Destination
Document: Untitled-1
Channel: Lizard Mask

Making the layer mask from the object selection

3 Making the drop shadow. To start a shadow, duplicate your object into a new layer by dragging its name to the New Layer icon or by choosing Duplicate Layer from the Layers palette's pop-out menu. (The Duplicate Layer dialog box gives you a chance to name this additional layer "Shadow.") In the Layers palette drag the Shadow layer into place below the object layer.

To proceed to make the shadow, the shape needs to be filled with black. In our case, the artwork was already solid black. But if you need to fill the shape, make black the Foreground color (press "D" for Default Colors), make sure Preserve Transparency (at the top of the Layers palette) is turned ON, and press Alt-Backspace to fill the object with black.

Then turn OFF Preserve Transparency and choose Filter, Blur, Gaussian Blur to soften the edges of the shadow. (Note: To be able to blur outward as well as inward from the edge of the shadow, the Preserve Transparency checkbox in the Layers palette must be turned OFF when you run the filter.) We used a Radius setting of 5 pixels for this 1155-pixel-wide image.

Now you can use the move tool — by hand or with the arrow keys (or Shift-arrows for 10-pixel steps) to offset the shadow; we moved our shadow up and to the left. Adjusting the Opacity slider for the Shadow layer varies the density of the shadow; we used 65% opacity. We also used Multiply mode to apply the shadow, which combined the darkness of the shadow with the color of the surface.

At this point your shadowed object is complete. But you can add dimension and sophistication to the image by using a layer mask and the Lighting Effects filter, as described in steps 4 through 7.

4 Adding a texture. Next you'll make a layer mask and use it as a "cookie cutter" to texture-fill your shape. Working in your object layer, first press Ctrl-Alt-T to load the object as a selection. Then choose Select, Save Selection and choose the name of the layer mask (in our case Lizard Mask) as the destination Channel.

Now open an RGB texture file (we used an oak image, also from ArtBeats Wood & Paper). With the object thumbnail (our Lizard) active in your project file, drag and drop all or a selected part of the texture image into the project file's working window. The object will appear to fill with the imported texture image.

5 Emphasizing the texture. To bring out the texture in your filled object (such as the wood grain in our example), you can apply the Lighting Effects filter: In the Layers palette, click on your object layer thumbnail (the texture block to the left of our Lizard) to activate it. Then choose Filter, Render, Lighting Effects, and set up the kind of lighting you want. We chose the Default, which creates the illusion of light coming from the lower right. For the Texture Channel setting choose one of the color channels; we used Red since the Red channel showed the most contrast.

4b

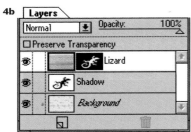

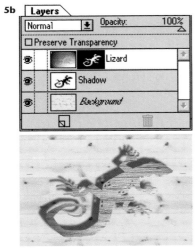

Masking a texture

5a

Setting up Lighting Effects with the Red channel as the Texture Channel

5b

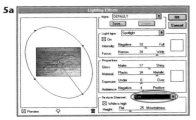

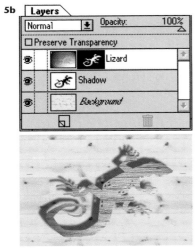

Wood grain texture emphasized inside the lizard

WORKING IN RGB

The Lighting Effects filter works only in RGB mode. So if you want to use lighting in a CMYK image, you have to start in RGB mode, render the lighting effects, and then convert to CMYK. You can see your image in CMYK as you work, however, by periodically turning on CMYK Preview (in the Mode menu) to see how the file, in its current condition, would look if converted to CMYK mode. Or open the file in another window (Window, New Window) and set it to CMYK Preview so you can see it while you work in the RGB window.

6 Adding thickness to the object. Working again in the object (Lizard) layer, press Ctrl-Alt-F to reopen the Lighting Effects dialog box. Without changing the direction, Style, Light Type, or Properties settings, apply the Lighting Effects filter again, this time selecting the layer mask as the Texture Channel setting (we chose Lizard Mask). Adjust the sliders until the lighting looks right; the Height slider controls how thick the object will appear. Click OK to close the dialog box.

7 Putting the object in context. Now click on the Background thumbnail in the Layers palette to activate the Background layer. Press Ctrl-Alt-F and apply the Lighting Effects filter once more. Once again, we used the Red layer as the Texture Channel setting.

Flattening the file. Flattening can be accomplished either by choosing Flatten Image from the Layers palette's pop-out menu or by choosing Save A Copy and picking a file type that doesn't support layers. This second method preserves the original file with its layers as well as making the flattened copy. We saved the file as a TIFF so it could be imported into PageMaker.

6

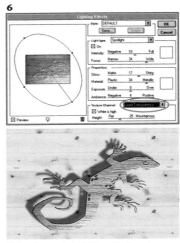

Using the mask to thicken the lizard

7

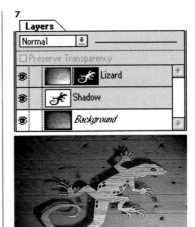

Background lit to match the lizard

Aglow at the Edges

Overview *Place type or an imported graphic on a layer above the background; make a duplicate of the graphic layer (the glow layer) in between the graphic layer and the background; load the graphic as a selection, feather and fill it to create the glow.*

1

Background layer

2

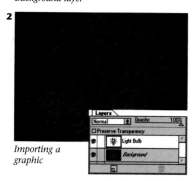

Importing a graphic

3a

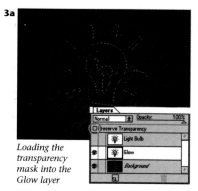

Loading the transparency mask into the Glow layer

A GLOW EFFECT applied to type or graphics can light up the page. Here are directions for adding a glow that extends both inward and outward from the edges. The technique can be applied to lettering or shapes created in Photoshop or to a graphic element imported from a PostScript drawing program, as in the example shown here.

1 Making a background. Open an image or a new file (Ctrl-N) and create a background. We modified a texture created with KPT Texture Explorer (see page 158 for more about KPT filters).

2 Placing the imported art. After making sure that Anti-alias PostScript is turned ON (choose File, Preferences, General, More and click the checkbox), place an EPS file (choose File, Place). We imported a light bulb graphic from Mark Van Bronkhorst's font "Dick and Jane"; it had been given a black fill and no stroke in Illustrator before being saved in EPS format. The placed art comes in as a floating selection; turn this into a new layer by dragging its name in the Layers palette to the New Layer icon at the bottom left of the palette; we named our new layer "Light Bulb."

3 Adding a glow. Duplicate the imported artwork (Light Bulb) layer by dragging its name in the Layers palette to the New Layer icon. Double-click this new layer's name and rename it "Glow" in the Layer Options dialog box. Then drag the Glow layer below the artwork layer in the palette.

Now you'll create the glow. First, so you'll be able to see the glow develop, make the imported artwork (Light Bulb) layer invisible by clicking its eye icon to turn it OFF. Then, with the Glow layer active (white in the Layers palette) press Ctrl-Alt-T to load the transparency

3b

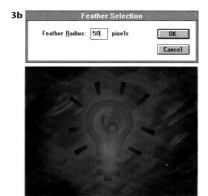

Making the red glow (viewing only the Glow layer and the Background)

3c

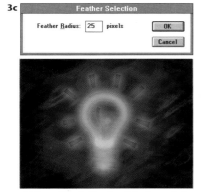

Adding yellow to the glow (viewing only the Glow layer and the Background)

3d

Adding white to finish the Glow layer (viewing only the Glow layer and the Background)

mask as a selection. Make sure Preserve Transparency is turned OFF in the Layers palette. Then choose Select, Feather and set a large Feather Radius; we used a Radius of 50 pixels for this 1155-pixel-wide image. Click the Foreground color square in the toolbox to open the Color Picker and choose a red. Then Alt-Backspace to fill the feathered selection and form the glow.

To add color depth to the glow, you can repeat the color fill operation with hotter colors, each time using a smaller feather setting. But because you modified the transparency mask of the Glow layer when you applied the large feather and filled the selection with red, it won't be a good starting point for more feathered selections. Instead, use the unchanged transparency mask of the artwork (Light Bulb) layer: Activate the artwork layer by clicking on its name in the Layers palette, use Ctrl-Alt-T to load the transparency mask, and then click on the Glow layer name to make it the active layer; the selection you loaded from the artwork layer will now be active in the Glow layer only. We feathered this second selection with a setting of 25, changed the Foreground color to yellow, and filled the selection (Alt-Backspace). Then we loaded the artwork transparency mask into the Glow layer again, feathered (this time at 10), and filled with white.

4 Turning up the heat. If you were making a single-color glow such as that shown on page 120, repeating the Alt-Backspace on a feathered selection in the Glow layer would make the glow more intense. But since this is a multicolor glow, using the Alt-Backspace multiple-fill procedure would be cumbersome — you would have to start over, using Alt-Backspace twice with the red, for instance, before going on to Alt-Backspace the yellow twice and then the white. And if you didn't like the final result, you'd have to start over. But it doesn't have to be that difficult. You can brighten your multicolor glow easily by adding a second glow layer: Drag the Glow layer name to the New Layer icon to make a "Glow copy" layer.

The interaction of the two layers of feathered colors brightens the glow effect. It also starts to build a thin dark outline of the artwork within the glow, so the visual effect is of a shape with a glow inside it, extending outward.

5 Emphasizing the edges. Making the top (Light Bulb) layer visible changes the effect. (To make the layer visible, click in the "eye" column for the layer.) With the original black artwork visible and in Normal mode, the glow seems to be behind, rather than within, the original shape. This wasn't the effect we wanted for our light bulb, so we experimented with different blending modes, settling on Overlay, which darkened up the edges of the light bulb to define them better, without taking away from the brightness of the glow both inside and outside of the edge.

4

Making the glow
brighter by
duplicating the
Glow layer
(viewing only the
Glow, Glow copy,
and Background)

5a

Finished glow
with the Light
Bulb layer visible
and in Normal
mode

5b

Finished glow
with the Light
Bulb layer visible
and in Overlay
mode

Glow layer in Dissolve mode creates sparkle

Experimenting. With the top layer in Overlay mode, try different blending mode settings for the Glow and Glow copy layers — for instance, Dissolve, Multiply, Screen, and Difference. *wow!*

UNDERSTANDING OVERLAY MODE

The Overlay blending mode works like a complex combination of Multiply and Screen. Dark colors in the Overlay layer darken the image underneath (the Multiply effect), and light colors lighten it (the Screen effect). The dark areas of the image underneath are darkened more than the light colors, and the light areas of the image underneath are lightened more than the dark areas. A black graphic in Overlay mode affects only the dark underlying pixels — not light areas, because black has no effect in Screen mode. Likewise, a white element in Overlay mode doesn't affect dark pixels, since white is neutral in Multiply mode.

MAKING A MULTICOLOR GLOW FOR A LAYERED OBJECT

How can you make a glow to match a multicolor object that was created in several layers? You do it by making a flattened copy of the layers, blurring it, and inserting the blurred copy between the object and its dark background, as we did for this "W!" from the cover of this book (A). The "W!" was built as a clipping group, shown here above a black background. To make a flattened copy of this multicolor lettering without the background, the background's eye

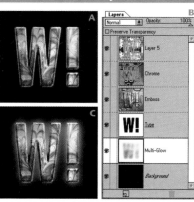

icon was turned off, Duplicate was selected from the Image menu, and Merged Layers Only was selected in the Duplicate dialog box. Then the merged copy was dragged and dropped back into the original file. In the Layers palette this new layer was dragged to a position between the clipping group and the background (B). Making sure that Preserve Transparency was turned OFF for this layer, we ran a Gaussian Blur. Adjusting Levels and increasing Saturation brightened the effect (C).

Carving, Embossing, & Stamping

Overview *Make an alpha channel from black-and-white artwork; from this mask create a "fat" mask that can be blurred, embossed, and developed into masks for bevel highlights and shadows; copy the masks to separate layers and use blending modes to apply them to a background image; make a trimmed shadow and offset the image to enhance the carved look.*

1a

Original woodgrain image

SAMPLER, ARTBEATS

1b

Illustrator EPS placed in channel #4 and inverted

WITH CHANNELS, LAYERS, LAYER MASKS, AND BLENDING MODES, there are bound to be numerous ways to create any special effect you want to try. The trick is to pick the method that best fits the job. For a logo for the Australian Olympics in the year 2000, a carved effect, with a subtle beveled edge and cast shadow, would add dimension to the typography. The best approach seemed to be one that would allow quick and easy change of any of the elements, including the beveled edges, shadow, and even the material used for the recessed and raised surfaces.

1 Importing the artwork. Open a Photoshop RGB file that contains the texture or image you want to carve into. (This logo treatment started with a woodgrain image that was about 5 x 4¾ inches at 225 dpi, or about 1100 pixels wide.) Then open the Channels palette (Window, Palettes, Show Channels), and create an alpha channel by clicking the New Channel icon at the bottom center of the palette and naming the channel (#4) something like "Original," to remind you that this is the artwork you started with.

With the alpha channel active, choose File, Place and import an EPS file containing black-on-white artwork. (Our EPS file was created in Adobe Illustrator.)

Stretch the imported graphic to fit before clicking with the gavel to accept placement in the alpha channel, and press Ctrl-D to drop any active selection. Once you see the artwork in place, you can use the rectangular selection marquee and the Edit, Crop command to trim the shape

Original artwork (channel #4; skinny mask)

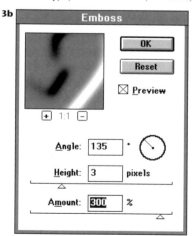

Adding a white stroke to a copy of the Original to "fatten" the white part of the mask to make the Stroked Version (channel #5)

Blurred copy of the stroked version (channel #6)

Emboss

OK

Reset

☒ **Preview**

[+] 1:1 [−]

Angle: 135 °

Height: 3 pixels

Amount: 300 %

Applying the Emboss filter to channel #6

of the document if necessary. Invert the "color scheme" of the black-on-white artwork in the alpha channel to white-on-black (Ctrl-I); the parts that are white will end up being carved away.

2 Making a "fat" mask. Besides channel #4, the original artwork mask, you'll need a "fat" (stroked) mask and an embossed mask to start the other masks that will be used for the highlight and shadow for the beveled edge. To make the fat mask, duplicate the Original mask (channel #4) by dragging its name in the Channels palette to the New Channel icon; give this channel a name like "Stroked Version." Working in this new channel (#5), load the channel itself as a selection (Ctrl-Alt-5) and stroke it with white, since it's the white part of the mask that you want to "fatten": Set white as the Foreground color (press "D" for "Default colors," then "X" to "eXchange Foreground and Background colors); choose Edit, Stroke; choose Center for the location; and enter a Width value that's twice as wide as you want the bevel to be, since only half of the white centerline stroke will expand into the black part of the artwork. (For the Oz logo, the Width setting was 10 pixels. In the "Oz" portion of the logo, the lettering was white, so it got fatter; in the "2000" portion, the numbers were black, so their strokes got narrower as the white "background" fattened.) Drop the selection (Ctrl-D).

3 Making the embossed mask. To make the embossed mask, make a copy of the Stroked Version channel (#5) by dragging its name to the New Channel icon; this will be channel #6. Blur this channel (Filter, Blur, Gaussian Blur); for the Oz logo, the setting for the blur was 5 pixels. Then choose Filter, Stylize, Emboss; choose an Angle, Height, and Amount.

4 Trimming the embossed mask. Now you'll "trim" the embossed mask to define a sharp bevel at the edge. Trim one edge of the bevel as follows: Working in the embossed channel (#6), set the Foreground color to medium gray by choosing the eyedropper tool from the toolbox and clicking it on the gray background of the channel. Then load the Stroked Version mask as a selection

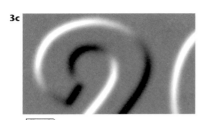

3c

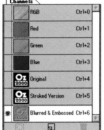

Channel #6 after embossing

4a

Trimming the embossed mask (channel #6) by loading channel #5 as a selection, inverting the selection, and filling with gray

4b

Additional trimming of the embossed mask (channel #6) by loading channel #4 as a selection and filling with gray

4c

Channel #6 embossed and trimmed; channel #7 will be identical.

(Ctrl-Alt-5), invert the selection (Select, Inverse) and press Alt-Backspace to fill it with gray.

Now trim the other edge: Still working in channel #6, load channel #4 (the Original mask) and press Alt-Backspace to fill with gray. Drop the selection, and rename the channel (#6) "Embossed & Trimmed."

5 Separating the highlights and shadows masks. For optimal control of the beveled edge, you'll need a mask for the bevel highlights and a separate one for the bevel shadows. The first step will be to duplicate the Embossed & Trimmed channel and turn the duplicate into the highlights mask. Then you'll turn the original Embossed & Trimmed channel into the shadow mask.

Start by dragging the thumbnail for channel #6 in the Channels palette to the New Channel icon to make a new channel (#7); give it a name like "Edge Highlight" to describe its contents. Choose Image, Adjust, Levels and use the black point eyedropper from the Levels dialog box to click on the medium gray background of the embossing. This will turn the medium gray, as well as everything darker, to black, leaving only the edge highlight.

Now click the original Embossed & Trimmed channel (#6) in the Channels palette to activate it (or press Ctrl-6). Again open the Levels dialog box, but this time use the white point eyedropper to click the gray background. The mask turns white except for the edge shadow area. To help you keep track of what's going on, you can rename the channel "Edge Shadow."

6 Applying the bevel highlight and shadow masks. Now it's time to copy the bevel highlight and shadow channels into the Layers palette and apply them with the palette's blending modes. Open the Layers palette (Window, Palettes, Show Layers). Activate the Edge Highlight channel (#7), select all (Ctrl-A), and copy (Ctrl-C). Activate the RGB channel (Ctrl-zero) and choose Edit, Paste Layer to create a Bevel Highlight layer. Activate channel #6 and copy it into a layer as Bevel Shadow (to do it "by the numbers" press Ctrl-6; Ctrl-A; Ctrl-C; Ctrl-zero; Edit, Paste Layer).

With the Bevel Shadow layer active (white in the Layers palette), choose Multiply from the list of blending modes. Click the Bevel Highlight layer name and set its blending mode to Screen; if the highlight looks too shiny for the texture you're using, adjust the Opacity. The Opacity setting for the Oz logo was 75%.

Make sure the eye icons for all three layers are turned on. White is neutral in Multiply mode and black is neutral in Screen mode, so only the bevel shadow and highlight will show up on the background image.

7 Making a cast shadow. Activate the top layer so that when you add another layer in this step, it will come in at the top of the stack. Using the method in step 6, copy the Original in channel #4 and paste it into a new layer called "Cast Shadow" (Ctrl-4; Ctrl-A; Ctrl-C;

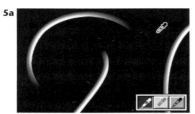

5a

Using the Levels dialog box's black point eyedropper to turn channel #7 into the Edge Highlights mask

5b

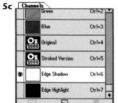

Using the Levels dialog box's white point eyedropper to turn channel #6 into the Edge Shadows mask

5c

Completed alpha channel masks

6

Edge Shadow and Edge Highlight copied and pasted into layers above the Background image; applied with Multiply and Screen modes

Ctrl-zero; Edit, Paste Layer). Then move it in the appropriate direction to serve as a cast shadow: Choose the move tool, and drag the layer to reposition it. Then apply a Gaussian Blur. (For the Oz logo, the layer was moved down and to the right, and the blur setting was 2 pixels.) Set the blending mode to Multiply and adjust the Opacity.

MOVING THE LAYER ONLY

If you use the move tool on a masked layer, the mask moves along with the image. To move the image *without* shifting the mask, select all (Ctrl-A) before dragging.

Now you'll make a mask to protect the areas that shouldn't be shadowed, to create the illusion that the shadow is on the background image, without actually modifying the image layer itself. Choose Add Layer Mask from the Layers palette's pop-out menu, and with the Original art from channel #4 still in the clipboard, paste it into the mask (Ctrl-V, Ctrl-D).

The farther you moved the Cast Shadow layer, the more likely it is that the carved elements will look detached from the background, with a drop shadow rather than a cast shadow. If you don't want that "floating" look, use a small, soft paintbrush with black paint to touch up the cast shadow layer.

8 Adding depth. To boost "legibility" of the artwork and to give separate control over the carved and noncarved parts of the logo, you can make a layer that controls only the inset areas: Duplicate the Cast Shadow layer by dragging its thumbnail to the New Layer icon at the bottom left of the Layers palette. Activate the Background layer with the texture by clicking on its name in the Layers palette, select all, and copy. Then activate the duplicate layer you just made; with the layer itself active (not the layer mask), paste the texture you copied from the Background layer (Ctrl-V, Ctrl-D). Choose Image, Adjust, Levels and move the white Output slider to darken the image. You can also select all (Ctrl-A) and offset the image a little (in the same direction as the shadow) to add to the depth illusion; we moved the inset texture 3 pixels down and right.

9 Adjusting the lighting. If you want to accentuate the lighting effect, you can sometimes do it more subtly and quickly with Quick Mask than with the Lighting Effects filter. Activate the Background layer and click the Quick Mask icon (near the bottom of the toolbox on the right side). Press "D" to set the default Foreground and Background colors. Use the gradient tool to make a black-to-white gradient across the image; the gradient should follow the angle of your lighting, with white where you want to lighten and black where you want no effect. Click the Standard mode icon to convert the Quick Mask to a selection. Choose Image, Adjust, Levels and move the Input sliders to lighten the selection (see the final Oz 2000 logo on page 221).

10 Trying variations. By replacing the Inset and Background versions of your texture with another image (or with two images), you can

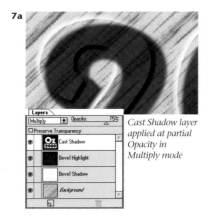

7a

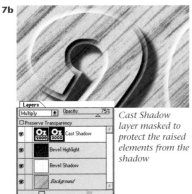

Cast Shadow layer applied at partial Opacity in Multiply mode

7b

Cast Shadow layer masked to protect the raised elements from the shadow

7c

Touching up the Cast Shadow layer with the paintbrush and black paint

7d

The beveled logo with a cast shadow

instantly get a new effect. Or if the client wants the light area to be lighter, the dark area darker, the shadow more pronounced, or a change in the color of the carved or uncarved areas, you have complete, instantaneous, and separate control over all these elements.

More variations. Three primary alpha channel masks served as the basis for the carving effect: the Original (or skinny), the Stroked Version (or fat), and a blurred, embossed version of the fat mask. You can also use the skinny mask, the fat mask, and a blurred, embossed version of the skinny mask — or its complement, made by inverting the image map — to get blind embossing, bas relief, stamping, quilting, or routing, for instance. Examples E through J on the next page are some combinations of the skinny mask, the fat mask, and the inverted embossed version of the skinny mask. Any of these examples can be substituted at the "embossed and trimmed" stage of the carving technique (at the end of step 4) to make channels that can be turned into highlight and shadow layers as described for the Oz logo. Or you can use them to make highlight and shadow channels, as described in step 4 of "Carving in Stone," which starts on page 231. *Wow!*

8

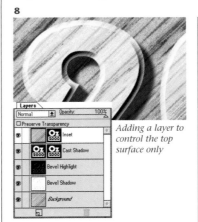

Adding a layer to control the top surface only

9

Creating a gradient selection with Quick Mask; the result of adjusting Levels using this mask as a selection is shown at the top of page 221.

10a

WRAPTURES ONE

A metal texture was copied and pasted into the layers that held the wood texture.

10b

UNDERSEA LIFE, LANDSCAPES, DIGITAL STOCK

A desert image was pasted into the Background wood layer, and an ocean image was pasted into the "Cast Shadow copy" layer.

The original "skinny" mask (channel #4 from page 221) is shown in A above. B is the stroked ("fat") version of the mask (channel #5). C is a blurred, embossed version of the "skinny" mask. If you invert the tonality of C (Image, Map, Invert), you get D. D is referred to as "channel #6" here because it corresponds to channel #6 at step 4 on page 222. But there's a difference between this channel #6 and the one on page 222 — this one was developed from the skinny mask, not from the fat, stroked version.

Channel #6 with #4 loaded and filled with medium gray produces a sharp edge for the top surface an a soft bottom edge.

Channel #6 with #4 loaded, selection inverted, and image map inverted (Ctrl-I) produces a "quilted" effect.

Channel #6 with #4 loaded and filled with gray, and #5 loaded, selection inverted (Select, Inverse), and filled with gray, to produce sharp edges at both top and bottom surfaces.

Channel #6 with #4 loaded, selection inverted (Select, Inverse) and filled with medium gray produces a rounded top edge and a sharp bottom edge.

Channel #6 with #4 loaded and image map inverted (Ctrl-I) produces the "flip side" of the quilted effect in G.

Channel#6 with #4 loaded and the image map inverted (Ctrl-I), and #5 loaded and the image map inverted again (Ctrl-I) produces a "double-carved," or routed effect.

Chiseling

Overview *Run the KPT Gradient Designer on a type selection to create a mask to be used for the Displace filter and Lighting Effects; apply both filters to create raised, chiseled type; make an adjustable shadow with blurred type and a layer mask.*

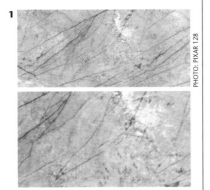

Original background (top) and close-up view

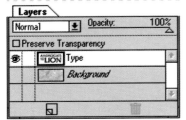

Type set on a transparent layer above the background

A KEY CHARACTERISTIC OF CHISELED TYPE — like you see on the marble entrances of banks and lawyers' offices — is the sharp, "V"-shaped cross-section of the carved strokes of the letters. Whether you raise the lettering or cut it in, the key to creating chiseled type in Photoshop is the KPT Gradient Designer filter, which is part of Kai's Power Tools (see page 158). Using this filter in Circular Shapeburst mode with a black-to-white gradation gives you the raw material needed to create the smooth, raised center ridge and corners characteristic of raised chiseled lettering or the sharp-sided channel of recessed carving. It even produces the gouge marks of the chisel; The illusion is completed using the powerful combination of Photoshop's Distort, Displace and Render, Lighting Effects filters, along with some added visual effects that help define the lettering as raised or cut in.

1 Selecting a surface to chisel. Open a background texture in RGB mode, or create a texture that's appropriate for the look you want. Here we selected a marble texture with long veins that could be displaced to enhance the carved look. The image was 5 inches wide, at a resolution of 300 pixels per inch.

2 Setting type. Open the Layers palette (Window, Palettes, Show Layers). Now you'll set type in a transparent layer above the background. We chose Adobe's Friz Quadrata for its classic look and prominent serifs.

One way to set the type is to use Photoshop's type tool: With black as the Foreground color, choose the tool and click on the image. (You may have to wait for the fonts menu to build.) In the Type Tool dialog box, specify the typeface, size, leading, and spacing, turn on antialiasing, and type your lettering. Click OK to close the dialog box.

The type will be a floating selection. If you need to move it into place, put the pointer anywhere inside the selection and drag. When the type is positioned the way you want it, double-click the Floating Selection name in the Layers palette to turn it into a layer; name the layer "Type."

Instead of setting type in Photoshop, you may want to do it in Adobe Illustrator or another object-oriented drawing program, especially if the type is complex, as ours was, with several sizes and fairly

3

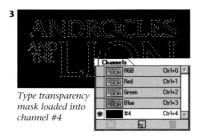

Type transparency mask loaded into channel #4

4a

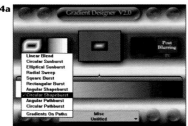

Setting up the Circular Shapeburst gradient

4b

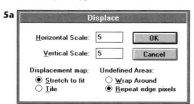

Gradient-filled type in channel #4

5a

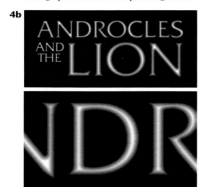

Running the Displace filter

5b

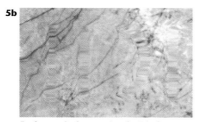

Background after running the Displace filter (close-up)

complex spacing. These drawing programs provide more automated control of size and spacing. After you set the type in black in Illustrator, convert it to outlines, save the file in EPS format, and rasterize it by placing it in Photoshop (File, Place). If necessary, scale the type to fit the image (drag a corner handle to resize and click inside the selection with the gavel cursor to accept the placement). Double-click the Floating Selection name to turn the type into a layer.

3 Starting the mask for Displace and Lighting Effects.

To carve the type, you'll need both a separate file for running the Displace filter and a mask for running Lighting Effects. Actually, the two images are identical but they have to be stored in different places in order for the two filters to find them.

To build the mask, start by adding an alpha channel to the background-and-type file: Open the Channels palette (Window, Palettes, Show Channels) and click the New Channel icon at the bottom center of the palette. This will create a new, black-filled alpha channel (#4); it will be active (its label will be white in the Channels palette) and the RGB channels will be inactive. With the Type layer active, (white in the Layers palette), press Ctrl-Alt-T to load its transparency mask as a selection.

4 Making the gradient.
Next you'll run the KPT Gradient Designer on the active type selection in channel #4. (If you haven't installed the Gradient Designer filter from Kai's Power Tools, quit Photoshop, install the KPT filters, and restart Photoshop.) With the filter installed, choose Filter, KPT extensions, Gradient Designer, and choose Circular Shapeburst from the left-hand pull-down menu. Position the cursor at the left end of the gradient band (below the curved bracket that extends across the middle of the Gradient Designer interface) and press and hold the mouse button. The cursor will turn into an eyedropper; a spectrum gradient band will appear, and above it a thinner black-to-white gradient; drag the eyedropper over to the white end of this thin gradient and release the mouse button. Then repeat this color-sampling procedure, but this time drag the eyedropper from the right end of the gradient to the left (black) end of the thin gradient band. When you finish, the interface should look pretty much like the one in figure 4a, with a shapeburst in the center box that's white in the middle and black at

6a

Running the Lighting Effects filter

6b

Raised type accentuated with Lighting Effects filter

7a

Duplicate Type layer, blurred and masked to make a shadow

the edges. (If it's black in the center instead, pop out the menu from the gradient icon — the second from the left — and switch from Sawtooth B->A to Sawtooth A->B, or vice versa, so that your Gradient Designer setup matches figure 4a.) Click OK to run the filter.

Channel #4 will now show gradient-filled lettering, selected, on a black background. Choose Image, Adjust, Auto Levels to maximize the tonal range of the gradient, to get a complete range of grays from black to white. If you have several sizes of type as we did here, you'll need to select and adjust them separately, because a uniform adjustment won't work equally well for all the type elements. To correct the type elements, surround each size type in turn with the marquee tool and run Auto Levels. When all the gradients have been adjusted, press Ctrl-D to drop the selection.

5 Displacing the background. Now it's time to "displace" the background image in the area where the type will be chiseled, to enhance the illusion of raising the type. The Distort, Displace filter needs a Photoshop file (not just an alpha channel) to serve as a displacement map. So now you'll copy channel #4 into a file of its own. With channel #4 active, select all (Ctrl-A), copy it (Ctrl-C), and make a new file (Ctrl-N). When the new Grayscale file opens, paste in the contents of the clipboard (Ctrl-V). Save the file in Photoshop 3.0 format.

Now, back in your background-and-type file, click the Background layer's name in the Layers palette to activate the background image. Choose Filter, Distort, Displace and set the Horizontal and Vertical Scale in the Displace dialog box; to shift the veins in the marble as shown in figure 5b, we used settings of 5 and 5 in our 1500-pixel-wide file. Since the displacement map and the file it's distorting are the same size, the Tile and Stretch To Fit options are irrelevant. Click OK, and then choose the Photoshop 3.0 file you just made as the displacement map.

6 "Carving" with Lighting Effects. With the now "displaced" Background layer active, it's time to make the distortion stand out. Choose Filter, Render Lighting Effects and choose "#4" as the Texture setting. Adjust the lighting characteristics to get the effect you want. To get a dramatic raised effect, we lit the image from the upper left, used Spotlight, set Wide, with settings for Shiny (rather than Matte), Metallic (rather than Plastic), and White Is High, to raise the ridge. We set the Height at Mountainous to get the maximum "embossed" effect. When the preview shows an effect you like, click OK to close the Lighting Effects box.

7 Adding a shadow. To enhance the illusion of raised carving, we added a shadow. Duplicate the original Type layer by dragging its name in the Layers palette to the New Layer icon; name the new layer "Shadow." With Preserve Transparency turned OFF, choose Filter, Blur, Gaussian Blur; we used a setting of 3. Use the move tool to offset the Shadow slightly in the direction opposite where you put

Shadow in place and Type layer removed to save on file size

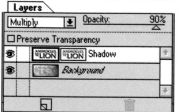

Type selected and isolated on a black background

Changing the Lighting Effects settings, desaturating and slightly blurring the carving, and sharpening and adding texture to the surface can help create a carved-in look. If the "carving" looks ambiguous — it might be raised or it might be cut in — adding an element with a shadow (not shown) clearly defines the angle of the lighting and so solidifies the carving illusion.

your light source in the Lighting Effects dialog box — for instance, if your light was at the upper left, move the blurred type down and to the right. Activate the Type layer again (not the Shadow but the original type), load its transparency mask (Ctrl-Alt-T), and then activate the Shadow layer again. Add a layer mask to the Shadow layer (choose Add Layer Mask from the Layers palette's pop-out menu), and fill the selection with black (Alt-Backspace with black as the Foreground color). The effect will be to mask out the Shadow where it would otherwise overlay the type. Set the blending mode for the Shadow layer to Multiply. The final result is shown at the top of page 227.

This shadow provides the same flexibility as one created by the method described in "Dropping a Shadow" on page 215, but without adding an entire layer to do it. If you want to change the position of the shadow, you can activate the layer — not the layer mask — in the Shadow layer, select all (Ctrl-A), and use the move tool to move the shadow without moving its mask, so the chiseled type is protected as the shadow moves. (To anchor the carved points so they don't seem to be floating, you could now use a tiny, low-opacity paintbrush on those areas of the Shadow layer. See step 7c of "Carving, Embossing, and Stamping" earlier in this chapter.)

Isolating the type. You can now delete the original Type layer to save on file size: Drag its name to the trash can at the bottom of the Layers palette. If you need the type outline as a selection again — for instance to copy the lettering separate from its background as shown here — you can re-create it by loading the transparency mask for the Shadow layer's layer mask (Ctrl-Alt-~) and inverting the selection (Select, Inverse).

Cutting type in. To make the type look carved-in is harder than making it look raised. With raised type a shadow enhances the illusion. But with cut-in type, there's nothing above the surface to cast a shadow, and the optical illusion becomes ambiguous — sometimes the type looks cut in and sometimes raised. However, there are some things you can do to help make the illusion work.

Set the type and make the alpha channel and displacement map exactly as for raised type. Run the Displace filter the same way, but when you run Lighting Effects, choose Directional instead of Spotlight, move the Gloss and Material sliders more toward the Matte and Plastic ends of the scale, and turn OFF White Is High. After you finish the lighting, don't throw away the Type layer. Load its transparency mask to select the carving from the background layer, and change it to make the carving appear to recede. For instance, reduce the Saturation or Lightness of the carving or blur it very slightly. Then invert the selection and make the flat surface pop — for instance, apply a texture that draws the eye, sharpen the image, or increase Saturation. Best of all, adding something else to the composition that casts a shadow can solidify the illusion.

Carving in Stone

Overview *Import or create graphics or type; make five alpha-channel masks: "skinny," "fat," "bevel highlights," "bevel shadow," and "interior shadow"; apply the masks to a directionally lighted background.*

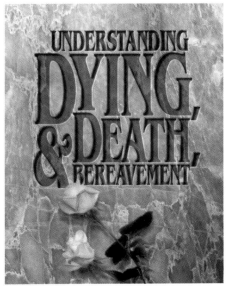

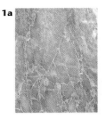

Background   *Importing lettering*

"Skinny" mask

The "fat" mask, made by thickening the white type with the Maximum filter and then inverting the tonality

Starting the "highlights" mask by blurring a copy of "skinny"

FOR THIS LOW-RESOLUTION BOOK COVER COMP, the type needed to be not only recessed but beveled. Though similar to the Oz logo in "Carving, Embossing, & Stamping" on page 221, this beveling was achieved by using alpha channels and Levels adjustments rather than layers and blending modes, so you can compare the two methods.

1 Making the "skinny" mask. Start with an RGB image of a surface to be carved, open an alpha channel (choose Window, Show Channels and click the New Channel icon at the bottom center of the palette) and name it "skinny." Place the elements to be carved (File, Place) into the new channel (#4).

2 Making the "fat" mask. Duplicate the "skinny" channel by dragging its name to the New Channel icon. Double-click the new channel's name and rename it "fat." Apply the Maximum filter (Filter, Other, Maximum); a value of 2 was used in the 750-pixel-wide image. Then choose Image, Map, Invert to save this fattened mask (channel #5) as black-on–white. The "skinny" and "fat" channels will be used to isolate the beveled edge.

3 Making an embossed mask. Now use the same process as in step 2 to make another copy of the "skinny" channel in a new channel ("highlights," #6). Apply a Gaussian Blur (Filter, Blur, Gaussian), and emboss the result (Filter, Stylize, Emboss). (We used a setting of 5 for the blur and 3 pixels for the emboss.)

4 Making masks for the highlighted and shaded parts of the bevel. At this point duplicate the "highlights" channel to make "shadows," a second embossed channel (#7). Then to increase the contrast in the "highlights" channel mask, choose Image, Adjust, Levels

3b

Blurred "highlights" mask, embossed and ready for black point setting

4a

The result of loading the "fat" mask into the darkened "highlights" channel and filling with black

4b

The result of loading the "skinny" mask into "highlights" and filling with black

5a

'Skinny" duplicated, blurred, and offset to start the "interior" channel

5b

"Skinny" loaded into "interior," selection inverted and filled with black

6a

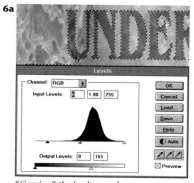

"Carving" the background

and click the black point eyedropper on the 50% gray of the embossing background. In the "shadows" channel choose Image, Map, Invert to turn the shadows white. Increase contrast as you did for "highlights."

To turn the "highlights" and "shadows" channels (#6 and #7) into masks that will isolate the highlighted and shaded parts of the bevel, work first in the "highlights" channel and then in "shadows." In each of these channels, load the "fat" mask (Ctrl-Alt-5) and press Alt-Backspace (with black as the foreground color) to make a sharp edge for the embossing. Next load the "skinny" mask and fill with black to trim away all but the bevel highlight or shadow.

5 Making a mask for the interior shadows. Duplicate the "skinny" channel in another new channel ("interior," #8) and invert the image map to produce black lettering on white. Gaussian Blur the channel (we used a setting of 5) and choose Filter, Other, Offset to move the mask down and to the right. Now load "skinny" as a selection (Ctrl-Alt-4), invert the selection (Select, Inverse) and fill with black.

6 Applying shadows and highlights. To make the bottom surface of the carving, activate the RGB channel (Ctrl-zero) and load the "skinny" channel (Ctrl-Alt-4). Choose Image, Adjust, Levels and darken the carved area. Then load "highlights" (Ctrl-Alt-6) and "shadows" (Ctrl-Alt-7) in the same way and use Levels to lighten or darken.

6b

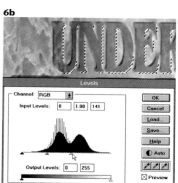

Making the bevel highlight

7a

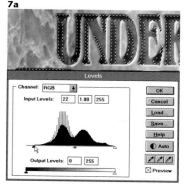

Making the interior shadow

7 Finishing the shadows. Load the interior shadows mask (Ctrl-Alt-8) and darken. To anchor the carved points so they don't seem to be floating, use the dodge/burn tool in its burn (hand) mode to connect the interior shadows with the points. (Compare the point of the "Y" [already "burned"] with the point of the "N" [not yet done].)

7b

Retouching the shadow

Creating Chrome

Overview *Starting with black-and-white artwork, make blurred copies in two separate layers and offset them; use Difference mode and merge the layers to create specular highlights; merge a blurred photo with the highlights; use a layer mask to cut out the artwork; vary the color; add a drop shadow.*

1

Adobe Illustrator artwork saved in EPS format and opened in Photoshop

2a

Blurring a copy of the logo

2b

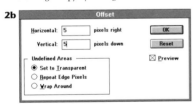

Setting up the Offset Down layer

2c

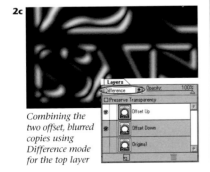

Combining the two offset, blurred copies using Difference mode for the top layer

ONE GOAL IN SIMULATING CHROME is to achieve the organic, irregular look of reflections from a mirrored surface without having to paint them by hand. The technique used for this logo for an interactive software company can also be used to add reflections to other special effects, such as crystal or water drops. The process involves stacking and merging layers with different blending modes.

1 Importing the artwork. Open an EPS graphics file by choosing File, Open, then choosing Grayscale mode and setting the dimensions and Resolution. We started with a logo designed and produced in Adobe Illustrator. Designing for print at a halftone screen of 150 lpi, we set the Resolution in the Rasterize Adobe Illustrator Format dialog box at 300 pixels per inch (see "Resolution" in Chapter 1 for more about determining the right resolution). The imported logo was 5 inches tall, making its height 1500 pixels.

WHY THE PIXEL DIMENSIONS?

Throughout the book, but especially in this chapter, the pixel dimensions and resolution of the example images are given. That's so you can evaluate the effect of the settings for filters and other functions that were used in the technique. Remember that any function whose setting is in *pixels* will have a different effect on images of different sizes or resolutions. With files of different sizes, you'll get a very different look if you treat both with the same filter or stroke settings. If your image is half the size of the example, try cutting the filter settings in half. Even if dimensions and resolution are the same, if the elements that make up your image are a lot bigger or smaller than those in the example, you may have to experiment to get the look you want.

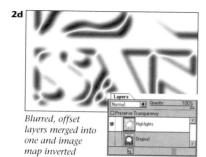

2d

Blurred, offset layers merged into one and image map inverted

3a

Photo scanned (left) and blurred

3b

Photo pasted into a new layer at 50% Opacity

3c

Reflections layer merged with the specular highlights layer

2 Making specular highlights. To make specular highlights at the edges of the graphic elements, you'll need two blurred, offset versions of the art. First open the Layers palette (Window, Palettes, Show Layers). If the graphics file you opened in step 1 is black-and-transparent rather than black-and-white, make it black-and-white by choosing Flatten Image from the Layers palette's pop-out menu; otherwise the blurring step that follows won't work right. Double-click the layer's name in the Layers palette to open the Layer Options dialog box so you can rename the layer "Original."

Duplicate the Original layer by dragging its name to the New Layer icon at the bottom left of the Layers palette. Rename the new layer "Offset Down." With the new layer active and Preserve Transparency OFF, choose Filter, Blur, Gaussian Blur; we used a setting of 5.

Now duplicate the Offset Down layer by dragging its name to the New Layer icon; rename this new layer "Offset Up." With the Offset Up layer active choose Filter, Other, Offset and enter settings that will move the image up and left.; we used −5 and −5.

Next activate the Offset Down layer by clicking its name and run the Offset filter with opposite settings — in other words, settings that will move the blurred image the same amount, but this time down and to the right; we used settings of 5 and 5.

Now change the blending mode for the top layer (Offset Up): Choose Difference from the pop-out list. Turn OFF the eye icon for the original artwork (the bottom layer) and the result you'll see is what Kai Krause (developer of the Kai's Power Tools filters) calls the "snowy mask." (Krause first created the effect with channel operations, combining alpha channels using the Calculations functions.)

With the two Offset layers visible (eye icons ON) and the Original art layer invisible, choose Merge Layers from the pop-out menu. Invert the tones of the merged layer (Ctrl-I) and rename it "Highlights."

3 Making the reflection. Now you'll add an image to make a reflection in the metal. Open an image file and copy and paste it (Ctrl-A; Ctrl-C; Edit, Paste Layer) or drag and drop it (use the move tool) into the chrome file. The image can be abstract, a random snapshot (like this one), or something specific that you want to see reflected, like a photo of a horizon line or a group of palm trees. Use Image, Effects, Scale, if necessary, to resize it. Then blur this Reflections layer by choosing Filter, Blur, Gaussian Blur; the degree of blurring will depend on whether you want the image to be recognizable or not. Adjust the Opacity of this Reflections layer to approximately 50%. Finally, with the eye icons turned ON for Reflections and Highlights, you'll now merge these two (choose Merge Layers from the Layers palette's pop-out menu), and rename the merged layer "Chrome Highlights."

4 Turning up the contrast. To get the high-contrast banding that's characteristic of a curved mirrored surface reflecting its environment, experiment with Image, Adjust, Curves in the Chrome Highlights layer. In the Curves dialog box you can redraw

4

Experimenting with the Curves dialog box

5

A layer mask in the Chrome Highlights layer cuts away the negative spaces of the artwork.

6

Fattening the white part of the layer mask with a stroke lets more of the curved highlights come through.

the curve wildly, either by dragging with the dialog box's Bezier curve tool to create and move points or by drawing freehand with the dialog box's pencil and then clicking the Smooth button. Or take a more scientific approach: Move the cursor out of the dialog box so it becomes an eyedropper, and click on an area where you want a drastic tonal shift. A small circle shows the part of the curve where this particular tone is located. Use the Bezier curve tool in the Curves dialog box to drag this point and others until you get the banding you want.

5 Cutting away the open areas. Now that the chrome effect is in place, you'll create a layer mask to trim out the negative spaces from the Chrome Highlights layer. Activate the Original artwork layer by clicking on its name in the Layers palette. Then select all (Ctrl-A) and copy (Ctrl-C). Now activate the Chrome Highlights layer, and choose Add Layer Mask from the pop-out menu. The icon for the new mask will have a heavy border around it to show that the mask is the currently active part of the layer. Paste the copy of the artwork from the clipboard into the mask (Ctrl-V) and invert the tones (Ctrl-I). This produces a sharp edge that cuts away the background, leaving the original artwork in chrome.

6 Fattening up the highlights. Now try a "Fat" variation that retains more of the light flowing along the curves of the chrome: Duplicate the masked layer by dragging the layer's name to the New Layer icon.

Rename the duplicate (Fat) layer, drag the layer's name below Chrome Highlights, and click on the mask icon to activate it. Then press Ctrl-Alt-~ (that's the tilde character to the left of the number "1" key in the top row of the keyboard). This loads the layer mask as a selection. Set the Foreground color to white (press "D", then "X"). Choose Edit, Stroke, Center, 10 pixels. This makes the white parts of the mask 5 points fatter, allowing more of the highlights to show. Press Ctrl-D to drop the selection.

7 Experimenting with color and a shadow. Convert the grayscale file to RGB (Mode, RGB Color, Don't Flatten). Then use Image, Adjust, Color Balance or Variations to change the color of highlights, midtones, and shadows in the Chrome Highlights and Fat layers. To add depth, duplicate the Original layer and turn the duplicate into a shadow, as described in "Dropping a Shadow" earlier in the chapter.

7a

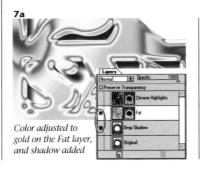

Color adjusted to gold on the Fat layer, and shadow added

7b

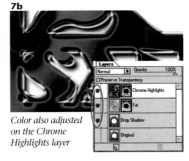

Color also adjusted on the Chrome Highlights layer

Creating Crystal

Overview *Make a displacement map and crystal highlights from a white-on-black graphic; layer the crystal highlights with two copies of an image, one of them lightened and displaced; add a drop shadow and dramatic lighting.*

1a

Type file, 2x4 inches at 300 dpi. Image map inverted, and stored in channel #2 of a Grayscale file

1b

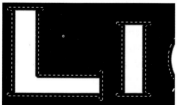

Loading channel #2 into itself as a selection and stroking the selection border with black

PHOTOSHOP 3 PROVIDES ANY NUMBER OF WAYS to distort an image. Some are controlled by hand, such as Image, Effects, Distort; others are formulaic and mechanical, such as the Ripple filter; and still others combine hand control with mechanical precision, such as Image, Effects, Perspective. But there's one tool — the Distort, Displace filter — that can be used to control precisely how an image will be reshaped. The default displacement maps that come with Photoshop produce variations on random patterns, as do those that serve as the basis for a number of painterly filters. But if you use a recognizable image as a displacement map, you can get some very interesting results, such as the look of water, crystal, or carving.

The Displace filter works by moving the pixels of an image. The distance each pixel moves depends on the luminance (or brightness) of the corresponding pixel in the displacement map. Any Photoshop 3 image except a bitmap can serve as a displacement map. White pixels move their corresponding pixels in the filtered image the maximum positive (up or right) distance, black pixels produce the maximum negative (down or left) displacement, with 50% brightness producing no displacement at all. Scale factors determine how large the maximum will be. If the displacement map file has two or more color channels, the first controls horizontal displacement and the second controls vertical. If there's only one channel, it's applied for both the horizontal and the vertical displacement. The maps can be wrapping patterns (like the Widgets on the Wow CD ROM) or graphics, like the "Liquid Assets" type used for this crystal effect.

1 Making the displacement map. The displacement map for the crystal effect needs only one channel. So it can be created in Grayscale mode — grayscale files are faster to work with than color files. Begin with a white-on-black graphic in a grayscale file. We started by opening a file of black type on a white background and inverted the tonal values (Ctrl-I). (If your graphic is black on a *transparent* background, before you invert the tonal values, make the background *white* by choosing Flatten Image from the Layers palette's pop-out menu. Then Ctrl-I will produce a white-on-black layer.)

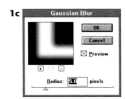
1c

Blurring inside the selection in channel #2 to produce gray tones for the displacement map

1d

Displacement map made from channel #2 and saved as a separate file

2

Crystal Highlights layer produced by merging two offset blurred layers, inverting the image map, and then merging the result with a blurred, lightened photo

3

Crystal Highlights layer with a layer mask made from the Black channel of the Original logo layer

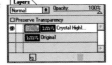

Open the Channels palette (Window, Palettes, Show Channels) and duplicate the single Black channel by dragging its name to the New Channel icon at the bottom center of the palette. This new channel (#2) will be modified to make the displacement map.

In developing the displacement map, the objective is to maintain the shape of the white-on-black type or graphic elements while adding gray tones that will make the displacement map produce a smooth transition from high areas to low areas. With the new channel active (white in the Channels palette) load it as a selection on itself by Alt-clicking its name in the palette or pressing Ctrl-Alt-2. The selection boundary will serve as a basis for adding a stroke and for containing the blur that will be applied to get the gray tones: With black as the Foreground color, choose Edit, Stroke, Center to add a black stroke along the selection border; make the Width setting twice as thick as you want the stroke to be, since only half of it will intrude into the white graphic. We used a 10-point stroke.

With the selection still active, choose Filter, Blur, Gaussian Blur to blur the black stroke into the white interior of the graphic. We used a Radius setting of 5 pixels. Then select all (Ctrl-A), copy (Ctrl-C), open a new document (Ctrl-N), and paste (Ctrl-V). Save the document in Photoshop 3.0 format.

2 Developing the crystal highlights. The next part of the crystal-making process (steps 2 and 3 here) is similar to the technique used for "Creating Chrome." If you need more detail than you find here, see steps 2 through 5 starting on page 233.

You'll need two blurred copies of the artwork, each on its own layer. Working in the crystal file (not the displacement map file), paste a copy of the Black channel (#1) into a new layer: With the Black channel active, select all (Ctrl-A), copy (Ctrl-C), and choose Edit, Paste Layer. Blur this layer at about the same setting you used for step 1. Duplicate the blurred layer by dragging its name in the Layers palette to the New Layer icon at the bottom left of the palette. Offset the two layers in opposite diagonal directions as in step 2b in "Creating Chrome." Set the blending mode for the top layer as Difference. To see the specular highlights effect, turn on the eye icons for the two blurred layers only. Then merge these two visible layers into one by choosing Merge Layers from the Layers palette's pop-out menu. Finally,

4a

Surface texture photo

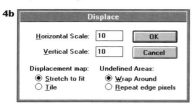

4b

Setting up the displacement

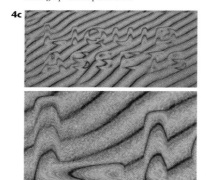

4c

Distortion created by the displacement map

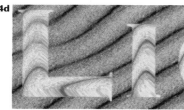

4d

Visible here are "Background Photo" and "Interior," which is the displaced, lightened version of the background photo, with a layer mask made from the Black channel of the Original logo layer.

invert the tonal values of the merged layer (Ctrl-I) to complete the Highlights layer.

Open another image to use for the reflection on the surface of the crystal, and copy (Ctrl-A, Ctrl-C) and paste it into the developing crystal file as a new layer (with the crystal file's window active, choose Edit, Paste Layer). Or use the move tool to drag and drop the new image into the crystal file. Blur this Reflections layer and adjust its Opacity. We used an image of international currency, a Gaussian Blur of 10 pixels, and an Opacity setting of 50%.

With only the Reflections and Highlights layers visible (eye icons ON), combine them by choosing Merge Layers. With this new merged layer active (we renamed it "Crystal Highlights"), choose Image, Adjust, Curves and redraw the curve to get high-contrast banding of the gray tones (as in step 4 of "Creating Chrome").

3 Cutting out the crystal graphic. The original white-on-black artwork should still be intact in the Black channel (#1) of the bottom layer of your developing crystal file. Activate this layer (click on its name in the Layers palette) and press Ctrl-Alt-1 to load the Black channel as a selection. Then activate the Crystal Highlights layer and choose Add Layer Mask from the Layers palette's pop-out menu. The black border around the mask in the Layers palette shows that the new mask is now the active part of the layer. Choose Select, Inverse and Edit, Fill, Black to complete the layer mask. If you now view only the Crystal Highlights layer, you should see crystal letters on a transparent background.

4 Applying the crystal to a surface. Now it's time to bring in the background image that will be displaced to simulate the distortion caused by the crystal. If you use a fairly colorful image with distinct lines or a grid, the effect will be easier to see. We used a photo of sand with diagonal ripples. First convert the developing crystal file to RGB (Mode, RGB Color, Don't Flatten). Then open the image you want to use for the background and either copy and paste (Ctrl-A; Ctrl-C; Edit, Paste Layer) or drag and drop (use the move tool) to make a new layer in the crystal file. Then duplicate this new layer by dragging its name to the New Layer icon in the Layers palette, so that you have two copies in the file. One of these will serve as the Background Photo and the other will be displaced and lightened to serve as the Interior of the crystal graphic.

First, displace the Interior layer by activating it and choosing Filter, Distort, Displace. Set the scale in the Displace dialog box (we used settings of 10). (The other options in the dialog box are irrelevant because the displacement map and the crystal file are exactly the same size, having been developed from the same file.) Click OK, and when the dialog box asks you to choose a displacement map, choose the displacement map file you made in step 1.

Next, to make the crystal elements "pop" from the background, lighten the surface of the crystal graphic by choosing Image, Ad-

4e

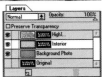

Crystal effect, with layers and layer masks

5

Crystal effect with drop shadow added in Overlay mode

6

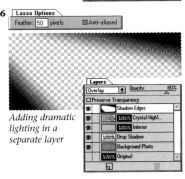

Adding dramatic lighting in a separate layer

just, Levels and moving the Input sliders to lighten the Interior layer. Then make a layer mask to isolate the "crystal," following the same steps you used for masking the crystal graphic in step 3.

The two image layers are at the top of the stack in the Layers palette. For the crystal illusion to work, you'll need to rearrange them into the right order by dragging individual layer names up or down in the palette: Crystal Highlights (with its mask) should be at the top in Overlay mode; then Interior (the lightened, displaced image with its mask) in Normal mode; then the plain image (Background Photo) in Normal mode. Make sure the eye icons for all these layers are turned ON.

5 Adding a shadow. Activate the Interior layer and press Ctrl-Alt-~ to load the layer mask as a selection. Then activate the Background Photo layer and click the New Layer icon to make a layer immediately above it. Choose Edit, Fill, Black. Then drop the selection (Ctrl-D), make sure Preserve Transparency is turned OFF, and choose Filter, Blur, Gaussian Blur to soften the edges of the shadow (we used a setting of 5 pixels). Offset the shadow. In the Layers palette, drag the Drop Shadow name between Interior and Background Photo. Change the blending mode for the Drop Shadow layer to Overlay to get the effect of light shining through the crystal. (If you need more detail to build the drop shadow, see "Dropping a Shadow" at the beginning of this chapter.)

6 Adding dramatic lighting. You can apply dramatic lighting with the Lighting Effects filter, as described in "Lighting Up a Wall" in Chapter 5 and elsewhere in the book, or with Image, Adjust, Levels applied through a Quick Mask, as described in "Carving" in this chapter. Another way — the way we used here — is easy and gives you a lot of control over the effect. Create the lighting in a layer of its own: Activate the top layer of the stack and click the New Layer icon to add still another layer above it. Double-click the lasso in the toolbox to open the Lasso Options palette, and set a fairly high feather value (we used a Feather setting of 50 pixels). Then use the lasso to draw the shape of the lighted area in the new layer. Choose Select, Inverse and use Edit, Fill, Black to fill the dark corners of the layer.

To apply the shadow, experiment with the blending modes: Try Multiply, Overlay, Soft Light, and Hard Light, and choose the effect you like best. You can also vary the Opacity. To get the image at the top of page 236, we used Overlay mode at 80% Opacity.

Working with Widgets

Overview *Copy an image and paste it into the "Picture" layer of a Widgets "**hs**" (for highlights and shadows) file; apply the Displace filter to the Picture layer, using the matching "**disp**" file.*

IHD

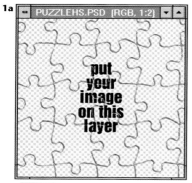

The **puzzlehs.psd** file

PEOPLE & LIFESTYLES, PHOTODISC

Original photo

THE WIDGETS ON THE WOW CD ROM are "ready-to-wear" special effects that you can apply to any grayscale or color image. To apply the special effect, you can simply insert your own photo on the bottom layer of the file. The built-in Highlights layer (in Screen mode), the Shadows layer (in Multiply mode), and in some cases other layers interact to create the effect. Then apply the matching displacement map to "mold" the effect into your picture. In addition to the Puzzle shown here, there are five more Widgets on the disc. Examples of the Widgets applied to the same photo are shown on the facing page.

1 Importing your photo. Choose a Widget from **goodies\widgets** on the Wow CD ROM. Open the "**hs**" file for that Widget — for example, the **puzzlehs.psd** file in this case. Open its Layers palette and activate the Picture (bottom) layer by clicking on its name. Then open a photo, select all (Ctrl-A) and drag it with the move tool into the Widget file; then deselect (Ctrl-D). At this point you'll be able to see your image with the special-effect highlights and shadows in place.

2 Running the Displacement filter. Now, with the Picture layer active, choose Filter, Distort, Displace and set both of the Scale factors at 5. (The Displacement Map and Undefined Areas settings are irrelevant, since the displacement map you'll be using exactly fits the file.) Click OK and then pick the matching "**disp**" file — in this case **puzzdisp.psd** — to complete the Widget effect.

Using Widgets on larger images. If your image is larger than the Widget file (as ours was), you can apply the Widget as a repeating pattern for a result like that shown above: First duplicate the **hs** document (Image, Duplicate). Then increase the dimensions of this document to the size you want by choosing Image,

1c

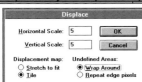

Photo dragged and dropped into the Picture layer

2

Molding the surface with the Displace filter

Canvas Size and entering new dimensions. Carry out step 1 (on page 240) using the duplicate file.

In the original **hs** file, activate the Shadows layer by clicking on its name in the Layers palette. Turn OFF the eye icons for all the other layers. Then Select All, and choose Edit, Define Pattern. Back in the duplicate (enlarged) document, activate the Shadows layer, select all, press Backspace to delete the contents of the layer, and choose Edit, Fill, Pattern. Repeat the process of defining a pattern, deleting, and refilling for all other layers of the Widget except the Picture layer. Finally, run the Displace filter on the Picture layer, choosing Tile for the Displacement Map setting in the Displace dialog box. Whether you choose Repeat Edge Pixels or Wrap Around as the setting for the Undefined Areas, you may want to use the crop tool to get rid of artifacts at the edges.

Variations. We activated the Grooves layer, and for each piece we wanted to remove from the puzzle image, we clicked the magic wand in the transparent interior of the piece, then activated the Picture layer, and pressed Backspace. We repeated the deleting process for the highlights, shadows, and grooves layers. (Some touch-up with the eraser may be required.) 🌀

Wow Drops (**drophs.psd** and **dropdisp.psd**)

Wow Rough (**roughhs.psd** and **rghdisp.psd**)

Wow Ice Cubes (**icehs.psd** and **icedisp.psd**)

Wow Tiles (**tilehs.psd** and **tiledisp.psd**)

Wow Balls (**ballhs.psd** and **balldisp.psd**)

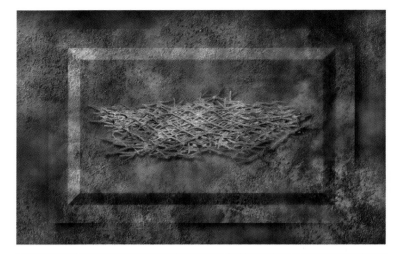

For his series *Kane, Kani, Ki,* **Russell Sparkman** created the textured backgrounds from two scanned photos of textures composited together using two different layers whose blending was controlled through the Layers palette's Opacity slider and the Layer Options dialog box.

After the combined texture was completed, the two layers were merged into one. This texture layer was then duplicated, and a masked object — metal, crab shell, or driftwood — was dragged from another file into the texture file to create a third layer. A drop shadow was created under the object (see "Dropping a Shadow" in this chapter), and then the object, shadow, and top texture layer were merged, reducing the file to two layers again.

Sparkman created a new layer (click the New Layer icon), specifying Overlay mode and Fill With Overlay-Neutral Color (50% Gray) in the New Layer dialog box. A bevel highlight and shadow were created on this layer, making a rectangular selection, filling it with black, dropping the selection, and running the Emboss filter to create the highlight and shadow. The neutral layer was then merged with the object-shadow-texture layer.

Sparkman applied a Gaussian Blur to the underlying layer and darkened it using Image, Adjust, Levels. Then he used a combination of selection tools and masks to delete parts of the upper layer to transparency, to partially reveal the underlying blurred and darkened original texture layer.

All layers were then merged and a duplicate of this layer was made. A Gaussian blur was applied to the top layer and then it was darkened with the Output slider of the Levels dialog box. Then, using Layer Options in the top layer, Sparkman split the "This Layers" white point slider (hold down the Alt key while dragging) and dragged the left-hand portion over to a setting between 20 and 25. This began to reveal the brighter, sharper underlying layer through the darker, blurred upper layer.

Using heavily feathered selections, he made small "amoeba-like" selections of the upper layer and deleted these areas to transparency, revealing more of the underlying layer. After many areas had been selected and deleted, the end result was an effect of mottled light, with areas of sharpness and softness.

Finally he merged the layers, made tonal adjustments with Image, Adjust, Curves, and went out for a beer.

For his images in the award-winning *Industrial Strength Eyewear* catalog, **Jeff McCord** constructed the transparency and reflectivity of the clear lenses, and the drop shadow beneath the glasses, in Photoshop. He started with product shots of glasses on glass against a neutral backdrop. McCord worked with prepress consultant Doug Peltonen to select the gray background (Select, Color Range works well for this kind of selection) and inverted the selection (Select Inverse) to isolate the glasses. The next step was to make the drop shadow. (Drop shadow techniques are described earlier in this chapter.)

With the shadow in place, McCord brought the glasses into his background image. He adjusted the Opacity to 60% to let the background and shadow show through.

To restore the highlight that had been lost in making the lenses transparent, McCord layered another copy of the glasses on top of the first, this time setting the blending mode to Lighten. He used Image, Adjust, Levels to increase the contrast until he achieved the specular highlights he wanted.

To create the *Lost & Found Logo* for a CD-ROM title, **Kory Jones** prepared the line work in a black-and-white Adobe Illustrator file. He saved the file under three different names and then removed different elements from each of the three files, so that he had one file with the outlines of the puzzle pieces, one with the bodies of the letters, and one with the letter borders. He placed the three files into alpha channels in a Photoshop RGB file. (Layer masks could also have been used.) In a separate Photoshop file he created a color gradient by using the KPT Gradient Designer filter (see page 158). Then he loaded the letter-body mask as a selection in his original RGB file and pasted the gradient into the selection. Next he loaded the letter-edges mask as a selection and again pasted the gradient into it. With this selection still active, he chose Image, Map, Invert to change the color in the letter borders, so that the colors in each letter were bordered by their complementary colors. Finally, he added drop shadows and shaded the edges of the puzzle pieces (creating drop shadows and edge shading are described in "Dropping a Shadow" and "Carving, Embossing, & Stamping," earlier in this chapter).

Jack Davis designed the type and graphics for this *Packaging Label* for a desktop drum scanner in Adobe Illustrator and placed them in a Photoshop background file. The background was an enlarged scan of printed halftone dots, though Photoshop's Pixelate, Color Halftone filter could have approximated the effect. The color of the halftone dot pattern was altered with Image, Adjust, Hue/Saturation. To create the metamorphosis of pixels to halftone dots, the Mosaic filter was applied through graduated masks in two stages with progressively larger cell sizes. The type was filled with clouds, using the Edit, Paste Inside command, and shaded as described for embossing and stamping in "Carving, Embossing, & Stamping," earlier in this chapter. The small type was given a glow (see page 121 for a method). The photos and collage in the lower right-hand corner were pasted into soft-edged selections made by applying the Gaussian Blur filter to the pie shapes that were imported from Illustrator into alpha channels. (Layer masks could have been used.)

To make the *San Diego Comic Convention Logo*, **Jack Davis** used displacement techniques like those applied in "Creating Crystal" earlier in this chapter. After running the KPT Texture Explorer to generate a background in an RGB file, he imported lettering from Adobe Illustrator into an alpha channel. He used the same lettering to create an alpha channel for the lettering itself and one for making specular highlights. He also used the lettering to make a displacement map file. He applied the Distort,

Displace filter, loading the map he had made from the lettering. He applied the highlights and shadows and made a drop shadow. When the displacement and lighting were complete, he removed the "ComiCon" lettering from the active selection (use the lasso with the Ctrl key) and used Color Balance to change "San Diego 1994." Shown here are the displacement map (left), an alternate version of the background after the Displace filter was applied, and the highlights mask.

For this *HiRez Audio* CD ROM Cover, **Jack Davis** began by manufacturing a background: He started in an RGB file with a random noise pattern (Filter, Noise, Add Noise) and applied the Motion Blur filter to make multicolored streaks. After adjusting Levels (Ctrl-L) to get the color and contrast he wanted, he imported the lettering from Adobe Illustrator, also saving it in an alpha channel for future use, and added the shadow (see "Dropping a Shadow" earlier in this chapter). He selected the top half of the background with the rectangular marquee and inverted the color map (Ctrl-I). The chrome texture was assigned with a beta version of the Gallery Effects Chrome filter. A bevel mask was made by loading the "skinny" mask (the original alpha channel of the imported lettering) into a "fat" one made bolder with the Maximum filter, and then filling with black (press "D" to get the default colors and then Alt-Backspace). The resulting edge mask was loaded as a selection, and the color map was inverted to make the bevel. The gradient tool was used in Quick Mask mode to make a mask for lightening the upper left corner of the letters and for recoloring this region using Image, Adjust, Color Balance.

Jack Davis began the design for The *Journeyman Project poster*, a collage of overlapping disc shapes filled with images from this interactive game, in Adobe Illustrator. He drew borders to define the discs, saved the file in EPS format, and opened it in Photoshop as a Grayscale file. Then he used the magic wand tool with Tolerance set at 250 to select one of the disc shapes. He copied the image and loaded its selection outline into an RGB background file of exactly the same dimensions. With the selection active, he used Paste Into to add the image. After all the discs had been filled in this way, he made two other alphas. The first was a fatter version of the original alpha (Select, Load Selection and then Edit, Stroke), which he loaded as a selection in the RGB file so he could adjust Levels to lighten the rims of the discs. The second was a shadow mask, created by blurring and offsetting a copy of the mask used for lightening, and then loading the first mask and filling it with black; again he loaded the mask and adjusted Levels to darken. The last step was to load the original alpha and fill the selection with black to clean up the edges left by the wand selections.

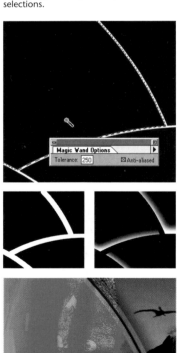

PIONEER CAR AUDIO

ART DIRECTOR: KAZUMOTO YOKOUCHI

Before Photoshop 3 was available, **Jack Davis** used Specular Collage and Fractal Design Painter to provide the layering and lighting features he needed to create this brochure cover for a *Pioneer Car Stereo promotion*. He began by scanning a toy model of a Toyota Supra with a 3D scanning system. Then he opened the resulting DXF file in Electric Image and tried out several angles of view and different reflection maps that he had created in Photoshop. Shown at the left is the car in its final orientation but with a sharper, more reflective surface than the one he finally settled on.

When the car was finished, he created a glow around it in Photoshop (see "Aglow at the Edges" for a method of making a glow) and then masked out the car so he could control the glow separately. Next he layered the parts of his image in Collage: two copies of the car (one in Add mode and another in Difference mode), its glow, the glowing lettering (also created in Photoshop), and the background (a scanned photo of burnished steel, motion-blurred in Photoshop and lighted in Painter). The interaction between the two car layers and the burnished metal background produced the somewhat surreal image that he wanted, to convey the quality and power of the Pioneer sound system but without its looking like a car advertisement.

3D/4D – ADDING DEPTH AND MOTION

IN ADDITION TO LENGTH AND WIDTH, a third dimension — depth — is implied in almost all photographs and in many illustrations. To make the image look more three-dimensional and real, the Levels command, applied to selected areas, can create shadows and highlights that add depth to a scene. In addition, three of Photoshop's Image, Effects functions (Skew, Perspective, and Distort) allow you to select part or all of an image and telescope or "bend" it to exaggerate perspective; the Spherize filter also creates depth illusions.

Filters supplied by other developers, such as the KPT Glass Lens and Andromeda's Series 2 Three-D (described in Chapter 5), can also add dimensionality. But only a stand-alone 3D program allows you to *model* — to *extrude* or *revolve* a two-dimensional element into a 3D shape, and even to move points to modify the solid object. Three-D programs also allow you to *stage* an entire scene, arranging the models you make, and then quickly change the viewpoint or lighting to produce a new perspective. Most 3D programs can also *render,* producing a photo-like view of the scene that assigns surface characteristics to the models and includes the interaction of light and shadows with these textures.

Photoshop can work with the artwork from 3D programs in two kinds of ways. It can serve as the recipient of an object or scene modeled and rendered in three dimensions, so it can then be re-touched or enhanced. Or it can serve as a generator for images to be used as surface maps to add color, texture, and detail to a 3D rendering. This chapter includes examples of both.

PHOTOSHOP TO 3D

Many 3D programs accept color PICT files that can be applied to 3D models as flat surface textures (called *texture maps*) or as tactile effects (called *bump maps*). Photoshop's Lighting Effects filter can be useful to quickly test out *bump maps* to be used in 3D images (see page 254). Some programs can also generate 3D models from gray-scale PICTs, translating the shades of gray as different distances above or below a surface, to create mountains, canyons, or other 3D models.

3D TO PHOTOSHOP

Programs like Adobe Dimensions and Ray Dream's addDepth are designed to make relatively simple 3D models from type or from

continued on page 250

CHECKING COLOR CHANGES

To quickly get an idea of what colors will change when you convert an image to NTSC colors for television, duplicate the image as a second layer in the same file, convert the new layer (Filter, Video, NTSC Color), and choose Difference for its mode in the Layers palette. The light areas of the mostly black image will show the where color has changed. Now you can change the mode to Normal and examine the color in those areas of the filtered image. Based on what you see, you may want to go back to the original image and adjust its colors so that converting to NTSC results in less color change.

REPEATING OPERATIONS

If you hold down the Alt key as you choose one of the Image, Adjust functions followed by " . . ." the dialog box opens with the last settings used. This makes it easy to apply the same changes to a series of images, such as an animation saved as a series of PICT files.

The Ray Dream Designer 3D program can produce a distance mask with background surfaces and objects in white, foreground objects in black, and intermediate objects in shades of gray. In Photoshop you can adjust the mask using Levels or Curves to get the desired range from black (near) to white (far). Then load the distance mask as a selection in the color image and apply a filter or other effect. Mitch Anthony rendered this image (top left) in Ray Dream Designer, where he saved it, choosing the **.psd** format and clicking on Distance in the Artwork Settings dialog box to save the distance mask as an alpha channel (top right). In Photoshop this channel was loaded as a selection and the Clouds filter was applied (bottom).

artwork drawn in PostScript programs such as Adobe Illustrator or FreeHand. They can extrude or revolve models around the height, width, or depth axes and they can create perspective views, but they can't provide the complex texture, lighting, and shadowing effects of more powerful 3D programs. Effects such as highlights, shadows, and embossed textures can be added to Dimensions and addDepth artwork with Photoshop's filtering and layering techniques.

Even if you use a more sophisticated 3D program with advanced modelling and rendering functions, Photoshop can save you time. Setting up your models, lighting, and camera angles in a 3D program is time-consuming, and rendering can take a long time. So if you find that you want to change the color or brightness of a 3D image once it's rendered, it may make sense to adjust Color Balance or Hue/Saturation for all or part of the image in Photoshop instead of going back to the 3D program to change the lighting and rerender the scene. In addition, some kinds of shadows and other details are more convincing if applied "by hand" with Photoshop's airbrush or masking techniques than by a 3D program's rendering algorithms.

In addition to full-color rendered images, some 3D programs can produce a mask that accompanies the file, appearing as an alpha channel when the file is opened in Photoshop. This channel can then be used in any of the ways Photoshop masks are applied — for instance, to isolate parts of an image so the color can be changed, or to apply a blur or another filter selectively.

VIDEO AND MULTIMEDIA

Photoshop includes filters and functions designed specifically for adapting both still and animated images for display on computer screens or on television. For example, Photoshop can open and save files in Filmstrip format for QuickTime animations (see page 256). And the Save, Load, and repeat functions built into Curves, Levels, and other Photoshop color adjustment dialog boxes make it quick and easy to apply the same corrections to a series of related images.

For video, the NTSC Colors filter (under Video in the Filter menu) restricts images to the standard color gamut used for television. The De-interlace filter (also under Video) smoothes video-grabbed images.

Also, creating Photoshop images to be viewed on-screen sometimes involves color restrictions. For instance, PICT files used in multimedia are often produced using a standard 8-bit palette. This reduces file size to a third and also prevents the "color flashing" that can happen when images with different 8-bit palettes follow each other in an animated sequence.

FIXING SHIFTED LINES

One use for the Single Row setting for the rectangular selection marquee (set in the Shape menu of the Marquee Options dialog box) is to select a single renegade offset row in a video grab so that it can be re-aligned by moving it right or left.

Taking a 3D View

Overview *Prepare artwork in a PostScript illustration program; import it into Photoshop and put it into perspective; incorporate other elements; create shading, shadows, and reflections to complete the 3D illusion.*

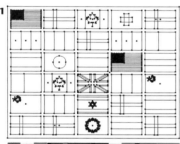

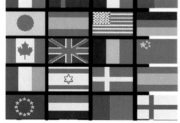

One set of flags created in Illustrator; Artwork mode (top) and Preview mode

SMOOTHING DIAGONALS

To smooth a diagonal line — created with Image, Effects, Perspective, for example — choose the blur tool (the water drop) with a small brush tip, hold down the Shift key, and click on the beginning and end of the diagonal.

THIS ILLUSTRATION FOR THE COVER of a book about health issues in foreign traveling includes a horizontal surface in perspective, made from an assemblage of flags, and a backdrop that blends the original vertical version of the flags into an image of international currency. Adobe Illustrator provided the precise, crisp shapes needed to trace the flags from a scan. Then one set of flags was "laid flat" in Adobe Dimensions on the Macintosh to make the horizontal surface. Since a Windows version of Dimensions was not available as this book went to print, an alternative method of creating the flags in perspective is presented here. The currency was scanned, and the globe was produced from line art generated by mapping software.

1 Drawing the artwork in Illustrator. Create two pieces of artwork in Adobe Illustrator, one for the vertical part of the backdrop and another for the horizontal surface, using filled shapes only — no lines. We started with two rectangular assemblages of flags and grouped each set. Save the files in EPS format.

2 Placing the artwork files. In Photoshop set up a new background file (Ctrl-N) at the size and resolution you need. In this case the file (a medium-resolution comp version) was 7½ by 9¼ inches at 200 dpi, making it 1500 pixels wide altogether. Open the Layers palette (Window, Palettes, Show Layers).

Make sure that Anti-alias PostScript is selected under File, Preferences, General. Then use File, Place to import the first Illustrator file (the flags that will make up the vertical wall in this case). The

2

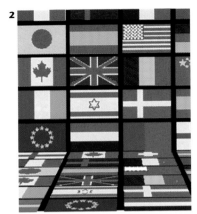

Flags files imported into Photoshop

3

Money grid image

4

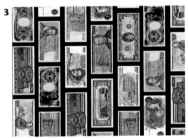

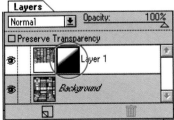

Currency dragged into flags image and montaged with a graduated layer mask

placed art will come in as a Floating Selection. Drag on the corners of the placed image to scale it to fit your file. After clicking with the gavel to accept the size, press Ctrl-D to drop the artwork into the Background layer.

Next use File, Place again, to bring in the Illustrator file for the horizontal assemblage. While it's still a Floating Selection, use the move tool to align the horizontal assemblage so its top edge meets the bottom of the vertical surface, and enlarge it to the same proportions. While this placed image is still a floating selection, choose Image, Effects, Perspective and drag one of the bottom handles up (and outward if necessary) to make the image appear to be extending toward you on a horizontal plane. You may need to do some work at high magnification with the pencil or a small paintbrush to clean up edges within your distorted image. When the horizontal-vertical combination is as you like it, merge the layers (in the Layers palette, turn on the eye icons for the layers you want to merge and then choose Merge Layers from the palette's pop-out menu).

3 Preparing the other image. In another Photoshop file paint or import the other image you want to combine into your backdrop. In this case we scanned an assemblage of bills on a desktop flatbed scanner, color-corrected and retouched it to create a "money grid," and used Image, Image Size to make it 1500 pixels wide. We used Filter, Sharpen, Unsharp Mask to get rid of any blurriness caused by scanning and resizing.

Next drag and drop this artwork into the background file (the flags in this case) with the move tool (four-headed arrow). The dragged artwork will come in as a new layer.

4 Making a mask to blend the two images. With the new layer active, choose Add Layer Mask from the Layers palette's pop-out menu. Then, with the mask active (selected in the Layers palette), use the gradient tool to draw a gradation. In this case Normal mode was chosen in the Gradient Tool Options palette; a Linear setting was used with a 50% Midpoint Skew to make a balanced gradation. The gradient tool was dragged diagonally over a short distance near the middle of the window; this made a fairly quick transition from currency to flags.

5 Adding a 3D object. Now create or import a 3D foreground object. The globe for this illustration started as a black-and-white illustration made in a mapping program, opened in Photoshop as a separate file, and given a "quilted" treatment, as in figure G on page 230.

After the quilting effect was applied, a pseudo-reflection was created by selecting a part of the original flags image with the rectangular marquee, copying it to a new layer (Ctrl-C and then Edit, Paste Layer), spherizing it (Filter, Distort, Spherize), and then reduc-

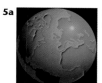

5a

Globe "quilted" and highlighted

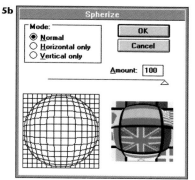

5b

Spherizing a selection

6a

Applying the graduated channel 4 mask to darken the top of the illustration

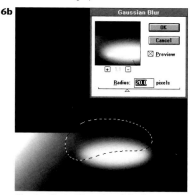

6b

Blurring the trailing edge of the drop shadow mask in channel 5

ing its Opacity in the Layers palette. The globe and reflection layers were merged. Then the merged image was dragged and dropped onto the main file, creating a floating selection. Alt-double-clicking the Floating Selection label in the Layers palette made the globe into a layer of its own, and then the move tool was used to position the globe in the composition.

6 Adding shadows. You can darken or lighten areas of the image for adding type, and you can create shadows to add to the 3D illusion you created with the perspective effect. We used two alpha channels to make selections that we could use with the Levels command to complete the shading for the Healthy Traveller illustration. To make an alpha channel, open the Channels palette and click the New Channel icon in the center at the bottom of the Channels palette.

First we needed an alpha channel that could be used to select an area at the top of the illustration so that it could be darkened with Levels to make a background for the title type. We created a new alpha channel (#4) and then made a black-to-white gradient by dragging the gradient tool upward from a point about a third of the way from the top to the top edge itself.

Since the shading at the top of the illustration would involve both the money grid and the flags, we needed to merge those two layers into one before doing the actual darkening. We merged the money grid and flags to a single layer (as described for the globe in step 5). Then we Alt-clicked channel 4 in the Channels palette to load it as a selection. We adjusted Levels (moving the Input Levels white point slider to the left) to darken the top of the merged layer.

Finally, we needed another alpha channel to make selections for creating a shadow in the corner of the scene and for making a drop shadow for the globe. We made another alpha channel, and then, working in this channel, we selected the bottom half of the merged layer with the selection rectangle. The gradient tool was used to create a black-to-white gradient at an angle in the corner of this selection. This would make possible a graduated selection that would shade the corner (as shown in the opening illustration).

Next a feathered selection was made with the elliptical selection marquee (set the feather in the Marquee Options palette). This ellipse would be used to make a drop shadow for the globe. Pressing Delete filled the feathered selection with white. To soften the transition of the shadow into the background, a lasso with a 50-pixel feather was used to select the trailing edge of the ellipse and a Gaussian blur (Filter, Blur, Gaussian, 20 pixels) was applied.

With the merged money grid/flags layer active, we Alt-clicked channel 5 in the Channels palette, which loaded the channel as a selection. Adjusting Levels created the shadows in the corner and under the globe.

Animating a Logo

Overview *Import QuickTime movies and images from Photoshop into Adobe Premiere; animate the still images with the roll filter, using Photoshop alpha channels to mask the animations in Premiere; assemble the animations in Macromedia's Director or Premiere; use Photoshop to composite still images into the animation.*

ANIMATION: GREG UHLER / LOGO: JHD

1a

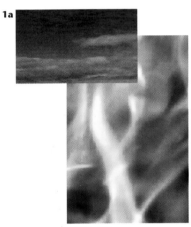

Video clips

1b

Still images

PHOTOSHOP HAS BECOME AN ESSENTIAL TOOL for developing desktop animation. It can provide frame-by-frame image editing, color conversion functions that surpass those of most desktop animation programs, and alpha channels that can be imported into Adobe Premiere and used for masking. To create an animation based on the original Presto Studios logo by Jack Davis, Greg Uhler used Adobe Premiere, Macromedia's Director, and Photoshop. To start, he divided the logo into a foreground and a background. The foreground layer, consisting of the hat and glowing pearl, would remain motionless. The background, where all of the motion would take place, was divided into four areas: Earth, Air, Fire, and Water. He decided to animate each of the background areas separately, bring them all together, and then add the foreground layer.

1 Using "clip animations" and animating still images. Use Adobe Premiere to create seamlessly looping movies. Uhler was able to find video clips for the Air and Fire animations. So he cropped them to the right size. Since he had no video for Earth or Water, he created them from still images. To animate each still image, he imported it from Photoshop into Premiere and applied the roll filter. Uhler animated the Earth to roll from left to right and the Water from top to bottom.

2 Importing alpha channels. To create two levels of animation in the background, import black-and-white alpha channels from Photoshop. These can serve as masks that allow one animation to run in the white part of the mask and another in the black. Use Premiere's Transparency function to load the alpha channel into the right track.

Photoshop alpha channels

Assembled background animation exported from Director

Elements and alpha channels for compositing in Photoshop

Uhler scaled Davis's original alpha channels used in creating the logo and imported a mask for each of the four background areas. For each of his four animations he used both the "A" video track and the "S1" (Superimpose) video track in Premiere. The "A" track held the image that would be inside the lettering in the alpha channel. The "S1" track held the part of the image outside the lettering, so he assigned the alpha channel, with its black lettering on white background, to the "S1" channel. To make the text readable, he had used a darker version of each animated image or movie in the "A" track (for inside the lettering) and a lighter version in the "S1" track (outside).

3 Combining the animations. The next step is to arrange the animations into a single background. Uhler exported them as a series of 24-bit PICT files and brought them into Director (although it could have been done in Premiere), where he positioned them together. Then he exported the combined animation as a series of PICT files that could be opened and edited in Photoshop.

4 Adding the foreground elements. Now composite the foreground elements onto each frame of the animated background. In Photoshop Uhler used an alpha channel to hold the position of the hat and pearl so that these elements could be pasted precisely in the same position in each frame of the animation. For each image he opened the image file, loaded the alpha channel, pasted the hat and pearl from the clipboard, loaded the edge alpha channel, adjusted Levels to darken the edge, closed the file, opened the next file, and so on.

Adjusting color palettes. A commercial desktop animation product needs to be designed to run on the lowest-common-denominator color Macs and Windows-based machines, so the final composited color images were converted to the 8-bit Apple System and Windows palettes. Photoshop does this conversion more successfully (with less obtrusive dithering) than many of the other programs that have this capability.

Producing the final animation. When the images had been composited and color-converted, Uhler imported them back into Director and synchronized them to music.

Rotoscoping a QuickTime Movie

Overview *Export an Adobe Premiere clip as a Filmstrip; open it in Photoshop; add a layer for rotoscoping; paint the special effects; save in Filmstrip format.*

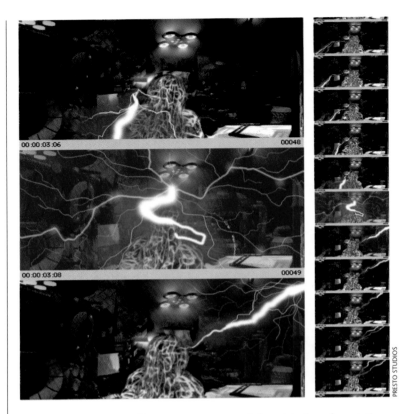

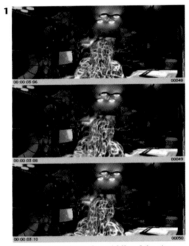

Three frames from the middle of the time-travelling clip, exported from Adobe Premiere as a Filmstrip file and opened in Photoshop

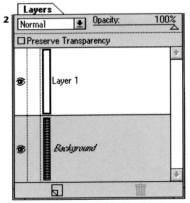

Rotoscoping layer added to Filmstrip file

ADOBE PREMIERE AND PHOTOSHOP can work hand-in-hand, so animations created in Premiere can be imported into Photoshop for *rotoscoping* — painting, drawing, or adding a special effect to the individual frames of an animation or video sequence. Victor Navone of Presto Studios used Photoshop's rotoscoping power on several animated scenes from *Buried in Time*, the sequel to the photorealistic interactive adventure game *The Journeyman Project*. The rotoscoping techniques for two of the animations are described here, and the animations themselves are included in **goodies\clips** on the Wow CD ROM, so you can play them with the Adobe Premiere demo program (also included on the CD ROM) to see how they turned out.

1 Exporting files from Premiere. Open an animation or video clip in Adobe Premiere and choose File, Export, Filmstrip File to save the file in the Filmstrip format that can be opened in Photoshop. For the animation showing time travel, in which the traveler is transported from one time and place to another, Navone started with a clip composited in Premiere from live video and a computer-generated background. He exported this animation as several 3-to-4-second Filmstrips, breaking it into these parts so it would be a smaller file and therefore easier to handle in Photoshop.

3a

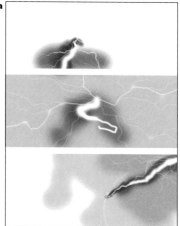

Lightning bolts painted with large, soft airbrushes with purple paint and varied Pressure settings, and a small, hard paintbrush with white paint

3b

Layer 1 after the lightning bolts have been added to each frame

The Adobe Premiere demo files on the Wow! CD ROM include **filmst8b.8bi**, a plug-in filter that Photoshop needs in order to open files that have been saved in Filmstrip format. This plug-in should install itself in your Photoshop **plugins** directory when you install the Premiere demo on the same hard disk drive. If somehow it doesn't get installed, you can copy it from the **premiere\4_pshop** directory to your plugins directory.

2 Adding a layer. In Photoshop, choose File, Open and choose the Filmstrip file by name. Open the Layers palette and create a new layer (Layer 1) by clicking on the New Layer icon at the bottom left of the palette. With both Background and Layer 1 visible (eye icons turned ON) and Layer 1 active (white in the Layers palette), you'll be able to use Layer 1 to experiment, painting and correcting mistakes without permanently changing the original frames.

3 Painting the frames. Now use any of Photoshop's tools to work on the top layer. You don't have to worry about the gray bars between frames; painting on them will have no effect on the animation. To create the bolts of electricity needed for the transmogrification, Navone used a large, soft-edged paintbrush to paint the glow and a smaller, hard-edged brush to paint the bolts themselves.

Exporting the Filmstrip. If you have an extended keyboard, you can check the effect of your painting on the animation by holding down the Shift key and the Page Up key or Page Down key

GETTING PRECISE ALIGNMENT

Photoshop's "understanding" of the Filmstrip format makes it possible to repeat a selection or selection outline from one frame to the next, situating it in exactly the same position in the next frame:

- **To cut a selected element** from one frame and move it to the same position in the next (or previous) frame, hold down the Shift key and press the up (or down) arrow key.

- **To copy a selected element** from one frame to the next (or previous) frame, use Shift-Alt-arrow.

- **To move a selection border, without its contents,** from one frame to the next (or previous) frame, use Ctrl-Shift-Alt-arrow.

Copying a selection from one frame to the next using Shift-Alt-arrow

Moving a selection border, without its contents, from frame to frame using Ctrl-Shift-Alt-arrow

Four frames from the cannon-firing sequence from Buried in Time *before the explosion and retouched cannon ball were added*

The same four frames as above, after the explosion and cannon ball were added in Photoshop. Varying the Opacity of the rotoscoping layer helped create the illusion of dissipating smoke. "Before" and "after" versions of the animation are in **goodies\clips** *on the Wow CD ROM.*

to simulate forward or reverse animation. When you have a result that looks promising, check it in Premiere: Choose Save A Copy from Photoshop's File menu and save in Filmstrip format. Then open the Filmstrip in Premiere, convert it back to a clip by choosing Project, Make, Movie, and view the clip. If you need to make additional changes, export the file in Filmstrip format again and go back into Photoshop for more editing.

Another way of working. Photoshop's ability to vary a layer's Opacity can come in handy for animating effects that dissipate over time, such as explosions. For an animation of a cannon blast, Navone created a puff of smoke and then cleared it away slowly. Again he used a top layer for painting in Photoshop, but this time he did the work on a series of PICT files rather than a Filmstrip. That way he could use the top layer's Opacity control to help dissipate the smoke; if he had used a Filmstrip, all the frames would have been included in one file, and he wouldn't have been able to vary the Opacity setting of the layer to clear the smoke.

With the individual PICT files, he could airbrush the smoke in the first frame and then copy it to the next frame by dragging the layer name from that PICT's Layers palette to the working window of the next PICT in the series. There he expanded the smoke with Image, Effects, Scale; blurred it; and then reduced the Opacity to thin it. Dragging and dropping this expanded, thinner smokeburst to the next PICT, he applied the same techniques to dissipate it more, and so on. Since the animation involved the camera panning across a stationary object — a model created on the Macintosh in Form Z and rendered in Electric Image — one of the most difficult aspects of the job was aligning the smoke from frame to frame. Navone picked elements in the model to use as reference points for alignment.

To make a Premiere movie clip into a series of PICTs, choose Make, Movie from Premiere's Project menu. In the Project Output Options dialog box, specify how much of the project to Output (Entire Project or Work Area) and choose Numbered PICT Files from the "as" pop-out menu. Each file will be saved with a number indicating its order in the sequence. After you've finished the work in Photoshop, the PICTs can be saved together in a folder and then opened and automatically reassembled into an animation in Premiere by choosing File, Import (or File, Open), selecting the image with the lowest number in the series, and clicking the Open button. 🔊

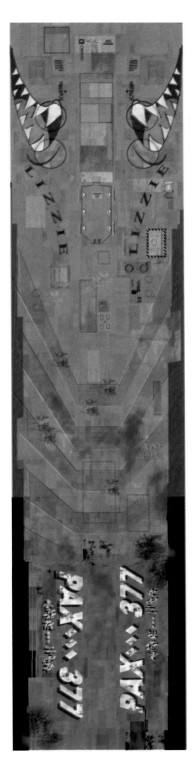

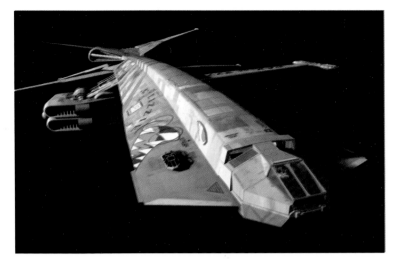

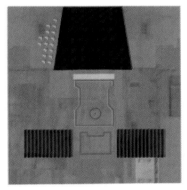

To design the *Sling Ship* for the science-fiction television series *Space Rangers*, **John Knoll** of Industrial Light & Magic, and a co-developer of Photoshop, used a 3D program to translate ILM art director Ty Ellingson's sketches into a 3D model. Then he used Photoshop to create texture maps (the flat artwork to be applied to the surfaces of the model to make it look like it's made of real materials) to turn the vehicle into a beat-up spaceship for chasing criminals for this futuristic show about an understaffed, underfunded police outpost. Knoll scanned several photos of the side panels of military aircraft and cut and pasted these elements, turning them into the "paint" he needed to assemble a patchwork image of dull gray metal with rivets, small doors, and scuff marks from which to build the more than 2000-pixel-long texture map for the fuselage. Because he knew that the front end of the ship would be used in several close-up shots, Knoll created the fuselage at a higher resolution than the wings and back of the plane. The shark's teeth that "personalized" the ship were scanned directly from sketches by Ellingson. Knoll rendered the ship (that is, applied the texture maps to the model) and animated its motion in Electric Image.

To build this *Blast Wall* element for the game *Buried in Time: The Journeyman Project 2,* **Frank Vitale** used a 3D model constructed by **José Albañil** in the Form Z program. Vitale wanted to apply a texture map (made in Photoshop; A) to color its surface and a matching grayscale bump map (also made in Photoshop; B) to give the masonry surface a realistic, 3D look. Because rendering the wall would be a very time-consuming process, Vitale followed his usual procedure of using Photoshop's Lighting Effects filter to test out the effectiveness of the bump map. He applied light to the wall, using an alpha channel containing the bump map as the selected Texture setting. After the initial test he adjusted Levels on the alpha channel and applied Lighting Effects again, repeating the process until he achieved the effect he wanted (C). Then he did the final rendering in Electric Image (top).

To make the layered lettering in the *Hybrid Logo* for an interactive television application, **Steve Lomas** layered the "HYBRID" type in two parts, and then created two separate drop shadows (see "Dropping a Shadow" in Chapter 8 for a technique for making a shadow); a larger offset and softer blur were used for the "H," "B," and "I," so that these letters seem to float higher above the gray paper texture of the background.

The bar at the top of the logo was imported from a 3D program, where it had been created by Kory Jones as part of the Hybrid interface.

Lomas used the logo in making a series of "luggage tag" cards like the one shown here for members of the Hybrid Applications Team.

For these two cover illustrations for Japanese editions of *Step-By-Step Electronic Design* newsletter, **Jack Davis** created 3D environments with elements generated from grayscale images. *Sky Pool* began with a scan of a hand placed flat on a desktop scanner. The grayscale file was touched up in Photoshop, saved in PICT format, and opened in HSC Software's KPT Bryce, a 3D environment explorer, where it was extruded into a 3D form. A ball (one of Bryce's 3D primitive objects) was added. Textures were applied, lighting was set up, and the scene was rendered. Bryce currently can't import 3D models (only grayscale images), and it doesn't have the capacity to cut up its primitives into complex 3D shapes. So the "well" was modelled and rendered separately in Bryce from another grayscale image, with the same lighting and relative placement as the ball, and then montaged with the ball in Photoshop.

For *Ocean Seed* **Davis** used the Texture Explorer filter from HSC Software's Kai's Power Tools to generate four grayscale patterns in Photoshop, one for each column. Then he extruded them using CyberMesh, an export plug-in designed for Photoshop by John Knoll, which produced DXF files. (One of the grayscale patterns and the CyberMesh interface are shown below.) The DXF files were imported into Electric Image (a 3D animation and rendering program) along with color surface textures created in Photoshop, which were applied before the scene was rendered. The seed itself was created in the same way, except that spherical rather than cylindrical mapping was used in the CyberMesh conversion. The final rendering was then opened in Photoshop, where Davis added the glows to the seed and the water, created depth of field by applying a Gaussian Blur through a graduated mask, and adjusted color in selected areas.

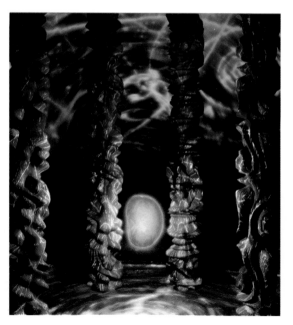

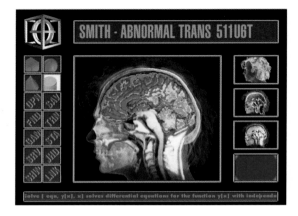

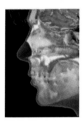

D esigning interfaces for interactive multimedia and simulating the tactile space of their navigational systems makes use of virtually all the pieces of Photoshop's building set. For the interfaces on these two pages, **Jack Davis** used everything but the kitchen sink. For example, to make the computer read-out of the boosted brain activity of the "innocent villain" Jobe for the computer interface in the movie *Lawnmower Man,* he used a half-dozen photographs, from monkey brains to Polaroid prints of the actor. The skull and brain were made to follow the contour of the actor's profile by using feathered lasso selections, the Image, Effects, Scale function, and the rubber stamp tool.

T he interface for *A Radius Rocket Home Companion,* a corporate informational CD ROM, involves a background of textured stucco wall (imported PostScript art that was treated with Noise and embossed), lighted with a spotlight. (Photoshop 3's Lighting Effects filter provides a wide variety of spotlight and other options.) The embossed color-coded buttons provide the navigational interface. The buttons for "chapters" of the CD ROM publication are displayed along the top of the screen, and the subsections of the current chapter are stacked along the right edge.

T he interface for Linnea Dayton's *"Look & Feel"* column about the role of computers and multimedia in education in *Verbum Interactive 1.0, CD ROM Multimedia Magazine* involved the use of imported PostScript graphics, simulated textures, glows, embossing, bevels, and drop shadows (see Chapter 7, "Combining Photoshop and PostScript," and Chapter 8, "Special Effects," for the techniques). Photoshop was essential for creating and processing the thousands of images and animations needed for this ambitious project.

The interface for the *HiRez Audio* CD ROM demonstrates a way of meeting one of the primary challenges of interface design: having as many of the relevant options on-screen as possible so the user doesn't have to spend a lot of CD access time searching for them. A "quilting" technique (see "Carving, Embossing & Stamping" in Chapter 8) was used to make some of the buttons. Motion-blurred Noise was used for the "brushed metal" background.

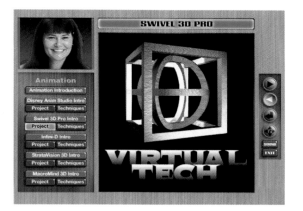

In this rough comp for the companion CD ROM for *Verbum's* **Multimedia Power Tools** book, the layout and buttons were generated in Adobe Illustrator (as were most of the other interfaces on these two pages). Since the highlighted edges and specular highlights were built of layers in the PostScript program, hundreds of text and color variations could be created quickly by importing the artwork into Photoshop with text already in place and color assigned. (See pages 201 through 203 for information about transferring layers between Illustrator and Photoshop.) The buttons were based on a technique developed by Tztom Toda, who originated his elements in FreeHand.

The virtual-reality-like interface for **Seemis**, a safety training program for offshore oil rig workers, was presented as an all-day Saturday TV session, with a TV programming guide that lets the student choose selections, a TV screen that enlarges to show the text and illustrations of the lessons, a changing drinking vessel (juice glass, milk glass, or Coke bottle) that empties to show progress through the syllabus, and a phone that rings to quiz the student on lessons learned. After the patterns and fabrics were created in Photoshop, the furniture and other elements were modeled in a 3D program. These were then brought back into Photoshop, where the lighting changes (for morning, afternoon, and evening) were added primarily with feathered selections and Levels adjustments. The Image, Effects, Distort command was used with rectangular selections to make the folds of the drapes.

CYBERBRIDGE

For the *CyberBridge logo* for a 3D Interactive entertainment company, **Jack Davis** designed the "C" and "B" letterforms in Adobe Illustrator and brought them into Adobe Dimensions separately. There he extruded each one and assigned a slightly rounded bevel. The two letters were rotated 45 degrees in opposite directions and positioned together, and the ball (a

Dimensions primitive, or preformed shape) was added. Since Dimensions does only a simplified smooth shading (as shown at the left), with no changes in shading across a flat plane, and since it has no colored light sources, these subtleties had to be added in Photoshop. To get the coloring he wanted, Davis created two versions of the logo, one gold and one blue. He positioned the two versions on two different layers, the gold above the blue. Then he loaded the transparency mask for the gold layer (Ctrl-Alt-T), and saved it as a layer mask (Select, Save Selection, Layer Mask). Now, with the

layer mask activated, he could use the Option-lasso to "cut away" parts of the gold logo by drawing selections and filling them with black. As the black area of the mask increased, it allowed more of the blue logo on the layer beneath to show. When he had the colors as he wanted them, Davis used Save A Copy to make a file with a single layer. In this new file he used a heavily feathered lasso to select the lower front corners of the letters and applied Image, Adjust, Hue/Saturation to change the colors enough to create the colored highlights.

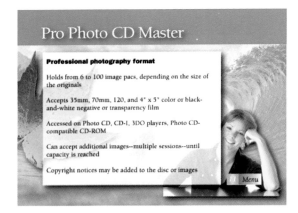

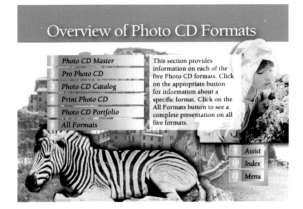

Janet Ashford and **John Odam** designed the interface screens for the CD portion of *The Official Photo CD Book*. For the screens shown here Ashford began with a Photoshop template file designed by Odam. It included a Background layer, a transparent layer with the title bar, one with a set of the "buttons" that could be interactive, and a Swatches palette that included the five colors that could be used for the title bars. Since the disc was being produced in Kodak Photo CD Portfolio format and might be displayed on a television, the template had been designed so that all the critical elements (buttons, title bar, and so on) were within an area small enough to show up on even the worst-case TV screen.

From the button layer Ashford selected and eliminated the buttons that would not be needed for that particular screen.

For each screen Ashford dragged and dropped photos from other Photoshop files to make a montage on the Background layer. Then she dragged and dropped silhouetted photos into separate layers above the Background. For each silhouette she created a drop shadow, linking the photo and shadow together so the shadow would stay with its object as she experimented with final placement (see "Dropping a Shadow" in Chapter 8).

Ashford set the type for the title, buttons, and information block in Adobe Illustrator, where it was easier to control spacing, size, wrap, and other type characteristics. She used her Photoshop screen template as a template in Illustrator also, so that the type she set would align with the buttons and title block. Then she imported the type as a layer in the Photoshop file and filled the title and button labels with white. She made a drop shadow for the title bar type.

Next she made a light area to hold the type for the information block. With the Background layer active, she selected a rectangular area around the type, made it into a separate layer above the background and below the type, used the Output slider in the Levels dialog box to reduce contrast (for the method, see "Putting Text over an Image" in Chapter 2), and applied a drop shadow.

Jack Davis modified a scan of a *Doré Woodcut* to achieve a stereoscopic 3D effect. (The techniques he used can also be applied to add depth to a photo.) He isolated four separate groups of background figures with the lasso and then applied the Gaussian Blur filter to each group. The filter was applied one, two, three, or four times, with the smallest (farthest back) figures being blurred the most. He also differentially lightened the figures with Image, Adjust, Levels.

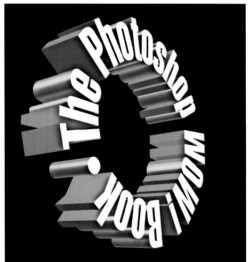

To make this *3D Logotype*, **Jack Davis** set type around a circle in Adobe Illustrator and imported the result into a 3D program, where he extruded it and established lighting and perspective. He saved the 3D type in EPS format and opened it in Photoshop. There he used Image, Adjust, Color Balance to turn it gold, exaggerating yellow in the highlights and magenta in the shadows. He dupli-

cated this file (Image, Duplicate) and applied the Photocopy filter from Gallery Effects Classic Art 2 to the duplicate. This filter exaggerates areas of contrast in the same way that a photocopy machine does, so that in this image with pure white faces on the type and relatively flat shading, it exaggerated the edge definition. The

original color-balanced version of the image was then layered on top of the filtered image in Multiply mode and with a slight reduction in Opacity, to arrive at an Art Deco airbrush effect.

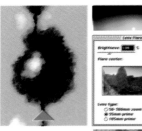 

Mars Canyon was created on the Macintosh by **Jack Davis** and **Michel Kripalani** for an animated fly-through for *The Journeyman Project,* the world's first photorealistic interactive adventure game on CD ROM. It began as a grayscale topographic view of the canyon created in Photoshop on the Macintosh and exported via CyberSave (a precursor of CyberMesh; see page 261). The arrow in the grayscale image indicates the camera viewpoint

used to produce the rendering above. Textures and bump maps were applied to the model in Electric Image. A sky image was wrapped on the inside of a cylinder that was built to enclose the canyon model, so the view of the sky changes during the flight around the environment. The Lens Flare filter was used to put the final touches on the scene. It was applied to frames in which the sun appears from behind some feature of the landscape during flight.

The Mine Transport was created for *The Journeyman Project* by **Phil Saunders, José Albañil, Eric Hook,** and **Jack Davis.** After the transport was modeled and rendered in a 3D program, the shading was added by hand in Photoshop. Shadows for most of the other environments for the game were also added in Photoshop to provide more control than could be accomplished at that time with a 3D program. A feathered lasso was used to select the shadow areas, and Image, Adjust, Levels (Output) was used to lower the contrast and darken the image. Details (such as the screen dump on the clipboard) were created separately and added to the scene.

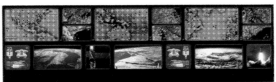

Phil Saunders, José Albañil, Michel Kripalani, Geno Andrews, and Jack Davis created the *NORAD Control Room* for *The Journeyman Project*. Davis combined 16 different images and a wall texture of "greeblies" into one large image that was exported to a 3D program and mapped onto the inside of the cylinder that enclosed the control room. The final animation of the scene, with walls, globe, and furniture, was rendered as a series of 36 images with the globe at a different degree of rotation in each image. A glow was added to each image (methods of making a glow are described on page 121 and pages 218 through 220), and each was composited with a Photoshop painting of unconscious workers and saved.

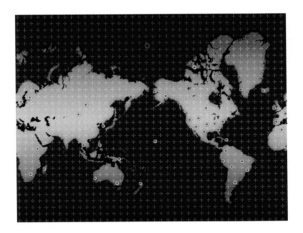

Jack Davis worked in Photoshop to create the images for a *Holographic Globe* that was animated as part of the underwater, futuristic NORAD Control Room. Shown here are three of the five textures used for the globe animation. The five elements were applied to transparent spheres of slightly different sizes to produce a layered effect in the final animation.

Appendix A: Image Collections

A list of addresses and phone numbers of the publishers of these images, most on CD-ROM, starts on page 278. Image sizes are for open RGB files (or CMYK as noted). Images are for both Windows and Mac platforms. Letter codes (explained below) refer to the rights conferred on the buyer of the disc.

Letter codes* *used in disc descriptions in Appendix A:*

A *Unlimited or nearly unlimited reproduction rights for print and digital publications other than electronic or printed image collections or other products (for instance, photo calendars, postcards, and posters) for which the primary value is in the images themselves*

B *Unlimited or nearly unlimited rights for print and digital publications other than image collections or other products for which the primary value is in the images themselves, with credit to the photographer/artist*

C *Some size, distribution, or usage limits on reproduction; may require credit to the photographer or special copyright notice*

D *For use on screen and in design presentations; other rights by negotiation*

MediaClips: Americana
100 photos of American landmarks by Roger Goldingay, along with original melodies in regional styles by Bruce Hanifan and 25 video clips; 900K; TIFF, BMP, PICT; C; Aris Entertainment

MediaClips: New York, NY
100 images of New York City landmarks photographed by Roger Goldingay, as well as original uptempo jazz compositions by Joe Gershen and 25 video clips; 900K; TIFF, BMP, PICT; C; Aris Entertainment

MultiMedia Discovery Series (4 discs)
400 images of undersea life, majestic places, rainforest, and views from space; along with 400 music clips and 75 videos; to 900K; TIFF, BMP, PICT; C; Aris Entertainment

MediaClips: Animal Kingdom
100 images of wild animals, along with audio clips of New Age music and 25 video clips; 900K; TIFF, BMP, PICT; C; Aris Entertainment

MediaClips: Space Odyssey
100 images of planets, deep space, and black holes, as well as audio clips of space music and 25 video clips; 900K; TIFF, BMP, PICT; C; Aris Entertainment

Marble & Granite (3 discs)
40 high-res scans of exotic marbles (21 MB); 120 multimedia backgrounds (2.7 MB), 225 buttons & mortises, 160 seamless tiles, grout bump maps; 8 metallic attributes; TIFF; A; Artbeats

Marbled Paper Textures (3 discs)
40 high-res scans of marbleized paper (most to 26 MB, with 2 spreads at 49 MB; TIFF); 120 backgrounds (2.2 MB, PICT), 225 buttons & mortises, 44 seamless tiles; 8 metallic attributes A; Artbeats

Wood & Paper (3 discs)
40 high-res wood & paper textures (to 26 MB, with 2 spreads at 49 MB; TIFF); 120 multimedia backgrounds (2.7 MB, PICT), 270 buttons & mortises, 50 seamless tiles; 8 metallic attributes; A; Artbeats

Designer Series Vol.], Paper & Fibers
25 paper and fiber background textures; to 25 MB; JPEG, TIFF, BMP; B; ColorBytes

Designer Series Vol. 2, Stone & Minerals
25 stone background textures; to 25 MB; JPEG, TIFF, BMP; B; ColorBytes

Sampler One
100 photos of business and industry, animals, and textures; to 22 MB; JPEG, TIFF, BMP; B; ColorBytes

Sampler Two
100 images of business and industry, animals, plants, scenic landscapes, and natural textures; to 22 MB; JPEG, TIFF, BMP; B; ColorBytes

Everyday Objects 1, 2, 3 (3 discs)
100 (per disc) "visual symbols" for saving, health services, movie making, and so on, on plain backgrounds; to 18 MB; Kodak Photo CD format; A; CMCD

Just Documents
100 "visual symbols" created with documents of various kinds on plain backgrounds; to 18 MB; Kodak Photo CD format; A; CMCD

Just Hands
100 "visual symbols" created with hands holding objects or making gestures, on plain backgrounds; to 18 MB; Kodak Photo CD format; A; CMCD

Just Tools
100 "visual symbols" created with household and office tools and equipment on plain backgrounds; to 18 MB; Kodak Photo CD format; A; CMCD

Metaphorically Speaking
100 images presenting a variety of "visual symbols"; to 18 MB; Kodak Photo CD format; A; CMCD

Folio 1, Print Pro CD (4 discs)
109 background and texture images, including abstracts, fabric, food, marble, masonry, metal, nature, novelties, paper, and wood; to 21.9 MB; also includes Peeping ROM (see below); TIFF; A; D'pix

Active Lifestyles
100 images of sports and activities; to 18 MB; Kodak Photo CD format with custom Kodak Color Management System profile; C; Digital Stock

Animals
100 images of birds, mammals, reptiles, amphibians, and butterflies and other insects; to 18 MB; Kodak Photo CD format with custom Kodak Color Management System profile; C; Digital Stock

Babies & Children
100 images of children to early teens, individually and in small groups, portraits and active shots; to 18 MB in Kodak Photo CD format; C; Digital Stock

Buildings & Structures
100 images of landmark buildings (ancient and modern), bridges, and cityscapes; to 18 MB; Kodak Photo CD format with custom Kodak Color Management System profile; C; Digital Stock

Business & Industry
100 images of factories, small businesses, offices, high-tech/laboratories, and money; to 18 MB; Kodak Photo CD format with custom Kodak Color Management System profile; C; Digital Stock

Flowers
100 images of flowers, from extremely close-up to vistas of flower fields; to 18 MB; Kodak Photo CD format with custom Kodak Color Management System profile; C; Digital Stock

Food
100 images by Joshua Ets-Hokin of food, beverages, and table settings; to 18 MB; Kodak Photo CD format with custom Kodak Color Management System profile; C; Digital Stock

Indigenous Peoples
100 photos from New Guinea, Bali, India, Thailand, Burma, Borneo, Ecuador, and Tanzania; to 18 MB; Kodak Photo CD format with custom Kodak Color Management System profile; C; Digital Stock

Landscapes
100 landscapes of western U. S. (including Hawaii), Mexico, New Zealand, and France; to 18 MB; Kodak Photo CD format with custom Kodak Color Management System profile; C; Digital Stock

Men, Women & Romance
100 images of individuals and couples; to 18 MB; Kodak Photo CD format with custom Kodak Color Management System profile; C; Digital Stock

Mountains & Waterfalls
100 mountains and waterfalls from western U. S., Canada, Switzerland, Austria, Mexico, Ecuador, and Tibet; to 18 MB; Kodak Photo CD format with custom Kodak Color Management System profile; C; Digital Stock

Oceans & Coasts
100 images with and without people; to 18 MB; Kodak Photo CD format with custom Kodak Color Management System profile; C; Digital Stock

Space & Spaceflight
100 images of earth, other planets, astronomical features, blast-offs, and space walks; to 18 MB; Kodak Photo CD format with custom Kodak Color Management System profile; C; Digital Stock

Sunsets, Skies & Weather
100 images, many with clouds or silhouetted trees; to 18 MB; Kodak Photo CD format with custom Kodak Color Management System profile; C; Digital Stock

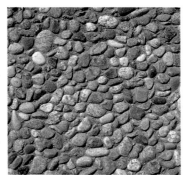

Textures & Backgrounds
100 images of natural and manmade textures; to 18 MB; Kodak Photo CD format with custom Kodak Color Management System profile; C; Digital Stock

Transportation
100 images of planes, trains, roads, traffic, cars, and boats; to 18 MB; Kodak Photo CD format with custom Kodak Color Management System profile; C; Digital Stock

Trees
100 images of trees, forests, fall foliage, winter scenes, and cactus, including some sunsets; to 18 MB; Kodak Photo CD format with custom Kodak Color Management System profile; C; Digital Stock

Undersea Life
100 images of fishes, octopus, coral, other invertebrates, kelp, sea mammals, and divers; to 18 MB; Kodak Photo CD format with custom Kodak Color Management System profile; C; Digital Stock

Undersea Textures
100 close-up images of corals and other undersea animals by Robert Yin; to 18 MB; Kodak Photo CD format, with custom Kodak Color Management System profile; C; Digital Stock

Western Scenics
100 images of scenery and wildlife in the western U.S. and Canada by Mike Sedam; to 18 MB; Kodak Photo CD format, with Kodak Color Management System profile; C; Digital Stock

Animals of the World
100 photos by Gene Warneke; mostly large mammals, plus an iguana, jellyfish, and others; Kodak Photo CD format; to 18 MB; A; Gazelle Technologies

Best of Nature's Way
100 photos by Mark Fey of mountains, meadows, coastline, waterfalls, and so on; Kodak Photo CD format; 18 MB; B; Gazelle Technologies

Best of People in Business
100 photos of people in the office, on job sites, at meetings, and in other business settings; Kodak Photo CD format; to 18 MB; A; Gazelle Technologies

Creative Backgrounds & Textures (2 discs)
200 images of natural and manmade textures, sunsets, skylines, bridges, deserts, and special effects; Kodak Photo CD format; 18 MB; A; Gazelle Technologies

Earth & Space Photos
100 images of the moon, shuttle launches, space and moon walks, and earth from space; Kodak Photo CD format; 18 MB; A; Gazelle Technologies

Essential Backgrounds & Textures
100 scenic backgrounds and photos of natural and manmade textures; Kodak Photo CD format; 18 MB; A; Gazelle Technologies

Medical Library Vol. 1
100 photos of doctors, nurses, patients, and pediatric subjects; Kodak Photo CD format; 18 MB; A; Gazelle Technologies

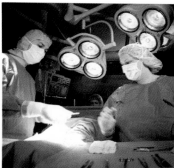

Medical Library Vol. 2
100 photos of surgery, instruments, and medical procedures; Kodak Photo CD format; 18 MB; A; Gazelle Technologies

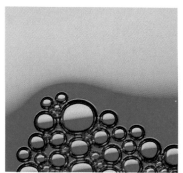

Professional Backgrounds
100 close-ups of synthetic and natural textures and special effects; Kodak Photo CD format; 18 MB; A; Gazelle Technologies

Professional Photography Collection
100 images of various subjects, including still lifes, architecture, and people; Kodak Photo CD format; 18 MB; A; Gazelle Technologies

Pixar One Twenty-Eight
128 seamlessly tiling digital photographic textures to be used as patterns; 512 x 512 pixels; TIFF; A; Pixar

Stock Options Vol. 1: Sports Equipment
77 photos of sport/game paraphernalia on white backgrounds with clipping paths as well as 61 Illustrator EPS graphics; to 17 MB; CMYK TIFF; A; Digital Media

Stock Options Vol. 2: Food & Grocery Items
81 photos of produce, breads, seafood, beverages, sweets, and nonfoods on white backgrounds, most with clipping paths; to 13 MB; CMYK TIFF; A; Digital Media

Stock Options Vol. 3: Toys, Models & Game Pieces
100 photos of dolls, animals, bikes, cars, trucks, trains, and game pieces on white backgrounds, most with clipping paths; to 10 MB; CMYK TIFF; A; Digital Media

Photogear Vol. 1: Backgrounds and Textures
30 photographic backgrounds and patterns; 21 MB; TIFF; A; Image Club Graphics

Photogear Vol. 2: Images of Business
100 Photos of business equipment and activities; 7.5 FMB; TIFF; A; Image Club Graphics

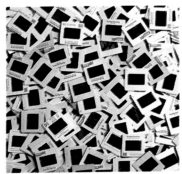

Photogear Vol. 3: Industrial Backgrounds
32 textures and collages; 21 MB; TIFF; A; Image Club Graphics

Photogear Vol. 4: Snackgrounds
32 images of crunchy, chewy, and sweet snack foods; 21 MB; TIFF; A; Image Club Graphics

Photogear Vol. 5: Mountainscapes
80 images of summits, cliffs, valleys, and other mountainous terrain; 7.5 MB; TIFF; A; Image Club Graphics

Photogear Vol. 6: Skyscapes
85 photos of clouds, sunsets, rainbows, and other dramatic skies; A; 7.6 MB; TIFF; Image Club Graphics

Photo Pro Vol. 2: People Doing Things
Over 110 images of people at work and at play; to 4.2 MB; TIFF; A; Wayzata Technology

Photo Pro Vol. 3: FotoBank
Over 125 images of autos, machinery, buildings, flags, gadgets, nature, patterns, backgrounds, people, and places by Bernie Sigg; to 3.6 MB; TIFF; A; Wayzata Technology

Backgrounds & Objects (2 discs)
120 backgrounds (many are collages of objects) (to 20 MB) and 226 miscellaneous objects with cast shadows on neutral backgrounds (to 10 MB); JPEG; C PhotoDisc

Backgrounds & Textures
111 studio stills and outdoor photos of natural and manmade textures; to 16 MB; JPEG; C; PhotoDisc

Business & Industry (2 discs)
408 images of business people, work scenes, plants, animals, and landscapes; to 10 MB; JPEG; C; PhotoDisc

Business & Occupations
336 images of people at work in a wide variety of medical, science, service, office, school, building site, and other settings; to 10 MB; JPEG; C; PhotoDisc

Food & Dining
336 food-oriented photos, from a classic hamburger to gourmet meals, stylized dishes, fresh ingredients, people shopping cooking, and dining; to 10 MB; JPEG; C; PhotoDisc

Holidays & Celebrations
336 images of the four seasons, religious and national (U.S.) holidays, and international festivals; 10 MB; JPEG; C; PhotoDisc

Italian Fine Art, Prints and Historical Photographs (2 discs)
236 images of paintings, antique maps, heraldic imagery, biological prints, illustrations, and historical photos; to 26 MB; JPEG; C; PhotoDisc

Nature, Wildlife & Environment
336 images of animals, plants, natural, and impacted environments from all continents; to 10 MB; JPEG; C; PhotoDisc

People & Lifestyles
409 images of families, teens, kids, and seniors in action; to 10 MB; JPEG; C; PhotoDisc

Retro Americana Collection
336 black-and-white images of business, industry, men, women, couples, children, teens, cityscapes, cars, and sports from the 1930s to the 1960s; to 8 MB; JPEG; C; PhotoDisc

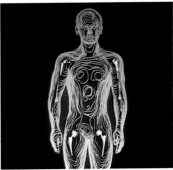

Science, Technology & Medicine
227 images of computers, health care settings, lab equipment, and people; to 10 MB; JPEG; C; PhotoDisc

Signature Series: Children of the World
100 images by Frederick Schussler of children, babies to teens, of many races and nationalities; to 28 MB; JPEG; C; PhotoDisc

Signature Series: Colors
100 images by Hans Wiesenhofer in bold, supersaturated colors or pastels; to 28 MB; JPEG; C; PhotoDisc

Signature Series: The Painted Table
100 still lifes of food, drink, florals, and table settings; to 28.5 MB; JPEG; C; PhotoDisc

Signature Series: Urban Perspectives
100 photos by Kent Knudson of day and nighttime city scenes, many with dramatic lighting; 28.5 MB; JPEG; C; PhotoDisc

Sports & Recreation
336 images of indoor and outdoor professional and amateur sports and recreational activities; to 10 MB; JPEG; C; PhotoDisc

World Commerce & Travel
352 images of people and business scenes in Europe, Asia, Africa, and the Americas; to 9.6 MB; JPEG; C; PhotoDisc

Backgrounds & Textures
100 images of natural and manmade environments, many suitable for overlaying type or graphics; to 18 MB; Kodak Photo CD format; A; PhotoSphere

Business & Commerce
100 images of business interactions, locations, and environments; to 18 MB; Kodak Photo CD format; A; PhotoSphere

Industry & Manufacturing
100 images of industrial activities, sites, environments, and equipment; to 18 MB; Kodak Photo CD format; A; PhotoSphere

Maps & Globes
100 maps of the world, hemispheres, continents, regions, and countries; to 18 MB; Kodak Photo CD format; A; PhotoSphere

People & Lifestyles
100 images of people of all ages in outdoor settings; often several views of same scene; 18 MB; Kodak Photo CD format; A; PhotoSphere

French Posters
Over 100 images of famous French posters by Toulouse-Lautrec and others; to 18 MB; Kodak Photo CD format; A; Planet Art

Van Gogh
Over 100 images of paintings by Vincent Van Gogh; to 18 MB; Kodak Photo CD format; A; Planet Art

Textures of Australia
100 photos of natural textures from the land down under; to 18 MB; JPEG; A; Gyro Interactive

Color Digital Photos, Vol. 5, Paramount
200 images of food, people, animals, birds, patterns, transportation, buildings, plants, water, sunsets, landscapes, and still lifes; 7 MB; JPEG; A; Seattle Support Group

Photographic Image Objects: Fashion Accessories
20 different vintage shoes, purses, and other accessories, each photographed in two views, with clipping path and alpha channel mask; 12 MB; TIFF; A; Classic PIO Partners

Photographic Image Objects: Kitchen Appliances
20 different vintage appliances, each photographed in two views, with clipping path and alpha channel mask; 12 MB; TIFF; A; Classic PIO Partners

Photographic Image Objects: Clocks
20 different vintage clocks, each photographed in two views, with clipping path and alpha channel mask; 12 MB; TIFF; A; Classic PIO Partners

Photo/Graphic Edges
More than 750 edge treatments (traditional darkroom looks to custom-designed artistic effects), to combine with grayscale or color photos; 3 x 3 to 8 x 10 inches at 400 dpi; also grains; TIFF; A; Digimation

KPT Power Photos
5 CD ROMs with 500 images of natural backgrounds and textures, food, urban textures and backgrounds, sky, water, landscapes, sports, and recreation, with various kinds of built-in masks; 18 MB; TIFF; A; HSC Software

KPT Power Photos II
5 CD ROMs with 375 images of kids' toys and backgrounds, hot rods, bugs and butterflies, nostalgia, and fall and winter holidays, with various kinds of masks; 18 MB; TIFF; A; HSC Software

Marine Life
100 close-up photos of fish, invertebrates, and marine mammals; to 18 MB; Kodak Photo CD format; A; Corel Corporation

Surfing
100 photos of waves, boards, and riders; to 18 MB; Kodak Photo CD format; A; Corel Corporation

Creative Crystals
100 colorful photos of crystals grown from chemicals at extremely low temperatures; to 18 MB; Kodak Photo CD format; A; Corel Corporation

Aviation Photography
100 photos of military aircraft from around the world, in the air and on the ground; to 18 MB; Kodak Photo CD format; A; Corel Corporation

Contact information for the photo discs listed in Appendix A. Don't miss the samples on the CD ROM disc that accompanies this book.

Aris Entertainment, Inc.
(now SoftKey International)
310 Washington Blvd., Suite 100
Marina del Rey, CA 90292
800-242-5588, 310-821-0234
310-821-6463 fax

Artbeats Software, Inc.
P.O. Box 709
Myrtle Creek, OR 97457
800-444-9392, 503-863-4429
503-863-4547 fax

CMCD
℅ PhotoDisc, Inc.
2013 Fourth Avenue, Suite 402
Seattle, WA 98121
800-664-2623, 206-441-9355
206-441-9379 fax

Classic PIO Partners
87 East Green Street, Suite 309
Pasadena, CA 91105
800-370-2746, 818-564-8106
818-564-8554 fax

ColorBytes, Inc.
830 Kipling Street, Suite #200
Denver, CO 80227
800-825-2656, 303-202-9200
303-202-5946 fax

Classic PIO Partners
87 East Green Street, Suite 309
Pasadena, CA 91105
800-370-2746, 818-564-8106
818-564-8554 fax

Corel Corporation
1600 Carling Avenue
Ottawa, Ontario, Canada K1Z 8R7
613-728-3733
613-761-9176 fax

Digital Knowledge Corp.
6271 Edgemont Boulevard, #B
Minneapolis, MN 53428
800-279-6099, 612-531-9811
612-531-9812 fax

Digital Media Corp.
28362 Via Nandina, Dept. C
Laguna Niguel, CA 92656
714-362-5103
714-643-2426 fax

Digital Stock Corp.
400 South Sierra Avenue, Suite 100
Solana Beach, CA 92075
800-545-4514, 619-794-4040
619-794-4041 fax

D'pix, Inc.
929 Harrison Avenue, Suite 205
Columbus, OH 43215
614-299-7192
614-294-0002 fax

Gazelle Technologies, Inc.
7434 Trade Street
San Diego, CA 92121
800-843-9497, 619-693-4030
619-536-2345 fax

Gyro Interactive
502 Albert Street
East Melbourne
Victoria 3002
Australia
+61-3-662-1027
+61-3-663-8805 fax

HSC Software
6303 Carpinteria Avenue
Carpinteria, CA 93013
805-566-6200
805-566-6385 fax

Image Club Graphics
10545 West Donges Court
Milwaukee, WI 53224-9967
800-661-9410, 403-262-8008
403-261-7013 fax

PhotoDisc, Inc.
2013 Fourth Avenue, Suite 402
Seattle, WA 98121
800-528-3472, 206-441-9355
206-441-9379 fax

PhotoSphere
250 H Street
Dept. 8110, Suite 413
Blaine, WA 98230
800-665-1496
800-757-5558 fax

Pixar
1001 West Cutting Boulevard
Richmond, CA 94804
800-888-9856, 510-236-4000
510-236-0388 fax

Planet Art
505 South Beverly Drive, #242
Beverly Hills, CA 90212
800-200-3405, 213-651-3405
213-651-5473 fax

Seattle Support Group
20420 84th Avenue South
Kent, WA 98032
800-995-9777, 206-395-1484
206-394-1487 fax

The Stock Solution
307 West 200 South, No. 3004
Salt Lake City, UT 84101
800-777-2076, 801-363-9700
801-363-9707 fax

Wayzata Technology, Inc.
21 Northeast Fourth Street
Grand Rapids, MN 55744
800-735-7321, 218-326-0597
218-326-0598 fax

Xaos Tools, Inc.
600 Townsend Street, Suite 270 East
San Francisco, CA 94103
800-289-9267, 415-487-7000
415-558-9886 fax

Appendix B
Software Information

Software of potential interest to readers of The Photoshop 3 Wow! Book

Adobe Systems, Inc.
P.O. Box 7900
Mountain View, CA 94039-7900
800-833-6687

Dimensions: Software for adding depth and perspective to type and line art

Gallery Effects (Vols. 1, 2, and 3): Plug-in filters of special effects that transform color, grayscale, and bitmapped images into sophisticated art

Illustrator: Design tool with powerful illustration and text-handling capabilities

PageMaker: Desktop publishing software that integrates text and graphics, allowing users to write, design, and produce professional-quality printed communications

Premiere: Digital video editing software

Alien Skin Software
2522 Clark Avenue
Raleigh, NC 27607
919-832-4124

The Black Box: A set of customizable plug-in filters that produce special effects

Andromeda Software Inc.
699 Hampshire Road, Suite 109
Westlake Village, CA 91361
805-379-4109

Series 1 Photography Filters: A set of plug-in filters that produce optical lens effects

Series 2 Three-D Filter: A plug-in filter that provides 3D surface mapping onto primitive objects

Series 3 Screens Filter: A plug-in filter that provides preset and customizable mezzotint treatments

Corel Corporation
1600 Carling Avenue
Ottawa, Ontario K1Z 8R7
Canada
613-728-8200
613-761-9176 fax

CorelDraw: Design and illustration program with text-handling and page layout capabilities

Macromedia, Inc.
600 Townsend Street
San Francisco, CA 94103
800-438-5080

FreeHand: Design and illustration tool for graphics professionals; combines easy-to-use interface with exceptional power

HSC Software
6303 Carpinteria Avenue
Carpinteria, CA 93013
805-566-6200
805-566-6385
kptsupport@aol.com

Kai's Power Tools: A set of plug-in filters for special effects designed by Kai Krause

KPT Convolver: A plug-in that makes it easier and faster to do sharpening and color correction, and also provides special effects treatments in a highly visual interactive interface

Quark, Inc.
1800 Grant Street
Denver, CO 80203
800-788-7835
303-343-2086 fax

QuarkXPress: Desktop publishing software. Integrates text and graphics, allowing users to write, design, and produce professional-quality printed communications.

Ray Dream, Inc.
1804 N. Shoreline Boulevard
Mountain View, CA 94043
800-846-0111

addDepth: A program for adding depth and perspective to line art and type

Ray Dream Designer: A program for creating 3D graphics. The software allows you to build 3D objects, assign surface textures to them, arrange them in a scene, light the scene and render the scene to produce photorealistic illustrations.

Symantec Corporation, Peter Norton Group
2500 Broadway
Suite 200
Santa Monica, CA 90404
800-441-7234

Norton Utilities: A set of applications for system maintenance

Appendix C
Publications

Books and other publications of potential interest to readers of The Photoshop 3 Wow! Book

Adobe Systems, Inc.
P.O. Box 7900
Mountain View, CA 94039-7900
800-833-6687

Adobe Technical Notes: Free by fax or mail (or find them on the Photoshop 3 Deluxe Edition CD ROM); on such Photoshop-related topics as The Lab Color Mode; Scanning Basics; Working with Type in Adobe Photoshop, Creating predictable Separations, Maximizing Performance, The Adobe Photoshop Raw File Format, Questions to Ask Your Printer, Adobe Photoshop Tips, Using Separation Tables, and many more.

Agfa Prepress Education Resources
P.O. Box 7917
Mt. Prospect, IL 60056
800-395-7007

An Introduction to Digital Color Prepress and *Digital Color Prepress Volume 2:* Short, colorful technical publications on digital color prepress; also available as 35mm slide shows

Peachpit Press
2414 Sixth Street
Berkeley, CA 94710
800-283-9444

Photoshop in Black and White by Jim Rich and Sandy Bozek: Coverage of tonal adjustment and other topics specific to achieving consistently good quality in reproducing black-and-white images

Four Colors/One Image (now *Photoshop in 4 Colors, Second Edition*) by Mattias Nyman: Coverage of scanning, calibration, separations, tonal value changes, image compression, screen angles, output resolution, and other topics as they relate to Photoshop

MIS Press
115 West 18th Street
New York, New York 10011
Contact Verbum: 619-944-9977

The Desktop Color Book by Michael Gosney and Linnea Dayton: An introduction to color, color models, desktop color software, and output options, with a gallery of artwork

Design Editorial Pty Ltd
11 School Road, Ferry Creek
Victoria, Australia 3786
61-3755-1149
fax: 61-3755-1155

Design Graphics: A bimonthly magazine with how-to's, case studies, hardware and software reviews, and interviews, all tailored to the needs of graphic design professionals. Subscription rates are the same in the United States and Australia.

Appendix D Artists and Photographers

ARTISTS

José Albañil 266, 267
Presto Studios, Inc.
P.O. Box 262535
San Diego, CA 92196-2535
619-689-4895
619-689-8397 fax
presto001@aol.com

Geno Andrews 267
Presto Studios, Inc.
P.O. Box 262535
San Diego, CA 92196-2535
619-689-4895, 310-454-8210

Mitch Anthony, 250
MADworks
415-494-3240
415-493-0270 fax
MADworks@aol.com

Janet Ashford 114, 264
327 Glenmont Drive
Solana Beach, 92075
619-481-7065
619-259-0993 fax
Umaintern@aol.com

Jim Belderes 77
Digital Design, Inc.
5845 Avenida Encinas, Suite 128
Carlsbad, CA 92008
619-931-2630
619-931-2632 fax
fotojim@aol.com

Jeff Brice 73
2416 NW 60th Street
Seattle, WA 98107
206-706-0406
cypsy@aol.com

Eric Chauvin 36
Industrial Light & Magic
415-258-2000

Jack Cliggett 122
College of Design Arts
Drexel University
Philadelphia, PA 19104
215-222-8511
cliggejj@duvm.drexel.edu

Nino Cocchiarella 171, 172, 211
Cocchiarella Design
201 NW 4th Street, Suite 103
Evansville, IN 47708
812-423-2500
812-467-0408 fax/modem

Rob Day 120
10 State Street
Newburyport, MA 01950
508-465-1386
508-462-9416 fax
73764,1136@compuserve.com

Ellie Dickson 113, 170
185 West End Avenue, #3L
New York, NY 10023
212-724-3598
212-724-7315 fax
ringding1@aol.com

Katrin Eismann 37, 90
PRAXIS.Digital Solutions
1233 North Courthouse Road, Suite 202
Arlington, VA 22201
703-524-3084
75720,1334@compuserve.com

Ty Ellingson 259
Industrial Light & Magic

Virginia Evans 120
10 State Street
Newburyport, MA 01950
508-465-1386
508-462-9416 fax
73764,1136@compuserve.com

Diane Fenster 71, 111
Computer Art and Design
140 Berendos Ave.
Pacifica, CA 94044
415-355-5007, 415-338-1409
415-338-6136 fax
fenster@sfsu.edu

Louis Fishauf 170, 208, 209
Reactor Art + Design Ltd.
51 Camden Street
Toronto, Ontario, Canada, M5V1V2
416-703-1913, ext. 241
416-362-6356 fax

Michael Gilmore 134, 184
CyberFlix
4 Market Square
Knoxville, TN 37902
615-546-1157
615-546-0866 fax
mjgilmore@aol.com

Jeff Girard 72
Victoria Street Graphic Design
1000 S. El Camino Real, Suite B
San Clemente, CA 92672
714-366-6730
714-366-6949 fax

Helen Golden 132
460 El Capitan Place
Palo Alto, CA 94306
415-494-3461, 415-608-3491
HSGolden@aol.com

Francois Guérin 139, 180, 182
33 Rue Alexandre Dumas
Paris 75011
France
43-73-36-62 phone/fax

Lance Hidy 135
10 State Street
Newburyport, MA 01950
508-465-1346
508-465-8632 fax

Eric Hook 266
Presto Studios, Inc.
P.O. Box 262535
San Diego, CA 92196-2535
619-689-4895
619-689-8397 fax
presto001@aol.com

Kory Jones 173, 244
Presto Studios, Inc.
2533 S. Highway 101, Suite 200
Cardiff, CA 92007
619-942-9926
619-942-9948 fax
KoryJones@aol.com

Peter Kaye 17
One on One Design
North Hollywood, CA

Stephen King 67, 210
980 Hermes Avenue
Encinitas, CA 92024
619-944-8914
king@imagitrek.gte.com

John Knoll 259
Industrial Light & Magic

Kai Krause 172
HSC Software
6303 Carpinteria Avenue
Carpinteria, CA 93013
805-566-6200
805-566-6385
kptsupport@aol.com

Michel Kripalani 266, 267
Presto Studios, Inc.
P.O. Box 262535
San Diego, CA 92196-2535
619-689-4895
619-689-8397 fax
presto001@aol.com

Bonny Lhotka 39
5658 Cascade Place
Boulder, CO 80303
303-494-5631
303-494-3472 fax
BonnyL5658@aol.com

Steve Lomas 260
CyberIsland Studios
2916 Commercial Avenue, #307
Anacortes, WA 98221-2998
SL@cyberisland.com

Steve Lyons 207
136 Scenic Road
Fairfax, CA 94930
415-459-7560

Jeff McCord 37, 243
Free-Lancelot
1932 First Avenue, Suite 820
Seattle, WA 98101
206-443-1965
206-443-1119 fax
freelancet@aol.com

Heidi Merscher 131
505-776-1333
hmerscher@aol.com

Bert Monroy 190, 204
11 Latham Lane
Berkeley, CA 94708
510-524-9412
510-524-2514 fax
waldus@aol.com

Victor Navone 256
Presto Studios, Inc.
P.O. Box 262535
San Diego, CA 92196-2535
619-689-4895
619-689-8397 fax
presto001@aol.com

Bill Niffenegger 209
c/o Random House Electronic Publishing
201 East 50th Street, 3rd Floor
New York, NY 10022

John Odam 198, 264
John Odam Design Associates
2163 Cordero Road
Del Mar, CA 92014
619-259-8230
619-259-8469 fax

Doug Peltonen 243
Color Service
509 Fairview Avenue North
Seattle, WA 98109
206-587-0278
206-625-9315 fax

Wayne Rankin 210
Rankin Bevers Design Pty Ltd
502 Albert Street
East Melbourne
Victoria 3002
Australia
61-3-662-1233
61-3-663-8805 fax

Richard Ransier 110
Classic PIO Partners
87 East Green Street, Suite 309
Pasadena, CA 91105
800-370-2746, 818-564-8106
818-564-8554 fax
cpio@ix.netcom.com

Eric Reinfeld 38
Digital Design
87 Seventh Avenue
Brooklyn, NY 11217
718-783-2313
718-783-2742 fax
Reinfeld@aol.com

Julia Robertson 110
Digital Design, Inc.
5845 Avenida Encinas, Suite 128
Carlsbad, CA 92008
619-931-2630
619-931-2632 fax

Phil Saunders 266, 267
Presto Studios, Inc.
P.O. Box 262535
San Diego, CA 92196-2535
619-689-4895

Max Seabaugh 196
MAX
302 23rd Avenue
San Francisco, CA 94121
415-750-1373
415-750-1369 fax

Mark Siprut 130, 171
School of Art, Design, and Art History
San Diego State University
San Diego, CA 92182
619-594-5446
siprut@aol.com

Russell Sparkman 111, 127, 242
2-100 Issha
Meito-ku, Nagoya
Japan 465
052-703-6305
052-703-6986
vfe04663@niftyserve.or.jp

Anna Stump 171
MBS Studios
744 G Street, Suite 205B
San Diego, CA 92101
astump@aol.com

Cher Threinen-Pendarvis 112, 178, 191
475 San Gorgonio Street
San Diego, CA 92106
619-226-6050
619-226-1762 fax
ctpendarvs@aol.com

Greg Uhler 254
Presto Studios, Inc.
P.O. Box 262535
San Diego, CA 92196-2535
619-689-4895
619-689-8397 fax
presto001@aol.com

Frank Vitale 260
Presto Studios, Inc.
P.O. Box 262535
San Diego, CA 92196-2535
619-689-4895
619-689-8397 fax
presto001@aol.com

Trici Venola 189
Trici Venola & Company
911 Marco Place
Venice, CA 90291
310-823-7308
310-823-5397 fax
triciv@aol.com

Colin Wood 209
Design Editorial Pty Ltd
11 School Road
Ferny Creek
Victoria 3786
Australia
61-3-755-1149
61-3-755-1155 fax
100241,2657@compuserve.com

Tommy Yune 59, 185, 190
Ursus Studios
P.O. Box 4858
Cerritos, CA 90703-4858
ursusstud@aol.com

PHOTOGRAPHERS

Tom Collicott 239

Ellen Grossnickle 92

Grant Heilman 132

Susan Heller 94

Douglas Kirkland 90

Mary Kristen 112

Craig McClain 14

Donal Philby 128

Roy Robinson 96

Index

More from Peachpit Press

A Blip in the Continuum

Robin Williams

In this full-color book, author Robin Williams and illustrator John Tollett celebrate the new wave of type design known as grunge typography. Famous and not-so-famous quotes about type and design are set in a range of grunge fonts, using rule-breaking layouts, with illustrations created in Fractal Design Painter. Companion disk contains 22 freeware and shareware grunge fonts. $22.95 *(96 pages, w/disk)*

Clip Art Crazy, Windows Edition

Chuck Green

Here's everything you need to incorporate sophisticated clip art into your desktop-created projects. *Clip Art Crazy* offers tips for finding and choosing clip art, along with a vast array of simple designs showing how to incorporate clip art into your documents and presentations. The CD-ROM includes almost 500 reproducible samples, culled from the archives of leading clip-art design firms. $34.95 *(384 pages w/CD-ROM)*

The Little Windows 95 Book

Kay Yarborough Nelson

Your guide to Windows 95. This easy, informative and entertaining volume spotlights the essentials so you can get to work quickly. Short, fully-illustrated chapters explore the Windows interface in detail, offering numerous tips and tricks. Each chapter includes a handy summary chart of keyboard shortcuts. $12.95 *(144 pages)*

The Official Photo CD Handbook: A Verbum Interactive Guide

Michael Gosney, et all.

With Photo CD, Kodak's breakthrough technology, you don't have to wait for tomorrow's electronic cameras to join the digital photography revolution. Learn how to use and store digital images and media files without spending a fortune. Two CDs include mutimedia presentations, valuable Photo CD utilities, and 68 MB of usable images, backgrounds and sounds. $39.95 *(384 pages, w/2 CD-ROMs)*

The PC Bible, 2nd Edition

Edited by Eric Knorr

The PC universe is expanding, and the second edition of *The PC Bible* has grown along with it. Sixteen industry experts collaborated on this definitive guide to PCs, now updated to include Windows 95 and Internet access. Whether you're a beginning or advanced PC user, you'll benefit from this book's clear, entertaining coverage of fonts, word processing, spreadsheets, graphics, desktop publishing, databases, communications, utilities, multimedia, games, and more. Winner of 1994 Computer Press Award for "Best Introductory How-to" book. $29.95 *(1,032 pages)*

Photoshop in Black and White, 2nd Edition

Jim Rich and Sandy Bozek

Updated to cover versions 2.5 and 3.0, this book explains how to adjust black-and-white images of any type for reproduction. Topics inlude image characteristics; adjusting highlights, shadows, and midtones; sharpening images; and converting from color to greyscale. Appendices cover scanning, resampling and calibration. $18 *(44 pages)*

Real World Scanning and Halftones

David Blatner and Steve Roth

Master the digital halftone process—from scanning images to tweaking them on your computer to imagesetting them. Learn about optical character recognition, gamma control, sharpening, PostScript halftones, Photo CD and image-manipulating applications like Photoshop and PhotoStyler. $24 *(296 pages)*

Windows 95: Visual QuickStart Guide

Steve Sagman

Windows 95, the long-awaited upgrade of Microsoft's operating system, offers an improved interface, faster performance, and numerous enhancements. This fast-paced, easy-to-read reference guide uses the same approach that's made other books in the Visual QuickStart series so popular: illustrations dominate, with text playing a supporting role. *Windows 95: Visual QuickStart Guide* provides a thorough tour of Windows 95, from introducing the basics, to managing your computer, to communicating online with Windows 95. $14.95 *(192 pages)*

Order Form

USA 800-283-9444 • 510-548-4393 • FAX 510-548-5991
CANADA 800-387-8028 • 416-447-1779 • FAX 800-456-0536 OR 416-443-0948

Qty	Title	Price	Total
	SUBTOTAL		
	ADD APPLICABLE SALES TAX*		
	SHIPPING		
	TOTAL		

Shipping is by UPS ground: $4 for first item, $1 each add'l.

*We are required to pay sales tax in all states with the exceptions of AK, DE, HI, MT, NH, NV, OK, OR, SC and WY. Please include appropriate sales tax if you live in any state not mentioned above.

Customer Information

NAME

COMPANY

STREET ADDRESS

CITY   STATE   ZIP

PHONE ( )   FAX ( )
[REQUIRED FOR CREDIT CARD ORDERS]

Payment Method

❑ CHECK ENCLOSED   ❑ VISA   ❑ MASTERCARD   ❑ AMEX

CREDIT CARD #   EXP. DATE

COMPANY PURCHASE ORDER #

Tell Us What You Think

PLEASE TELL US WHAT YOU THOUGHT OF THIS BOOK: TITLE:

WHAT OTHER BOOKS WOULD YOU LIKE US TO PUBLISH?